A
Lifetime's
Reading

A Lifetime's Reading

The World's 500 Greatest Books

Philip Ward

STEIN AND DAY/*Publishers*/New York

First published in the United States of America in 1983

Copyright© 1982 by Philip Ward and The Oleander Press
All rights reserved. Stein and Day, Incorporated

Printed in the United States of America

STEIN AND DAY/ *Publishers*
Scarborough House
Briarcliff Manor, N.Y. 10510

Library of Congress Cataloging in Publication Data

Ward, Philip.
  A lifetime's reading.

  Includes index.
  1. Bibliography—Best books.   2. Books and reading.
I. Title.
Z1035.W29   1983   011'.7   83-42976
ISBN 0-8128-2938-7

Acknowledgments

I owe my wife Audrey and my daughters Carolyn and Angela my usual infinite debt of gratitude for their love and forbearance over the long period of this book's gestation (indeed it began as long ago as 1949, when my mother gave me J. A. Hammerton's inspiring if sadly dated *Outline of Great Books*). If the present guide serves the next generation of readers, I shall feel that the labour that has gone towards its preparation and compilation has been well worth while.

———

# ✷ Introduction ✷

Like most professional librarians, I have at one time or another glanced across a library to see a man or woman of eighteen to twenty daunted – even bewildered – by the sheer richness of the literary treasures that are waiting to be enjoyed, the great minds to be understood, the poets' voices to be heard, the characters of fiction to be encountered. My heart has been touched by the magnitude of their choice. I long to offer them the plays of Euripides and the stories of Isaac Babel, the love songs of Dante and the wisdom of Mencius. But I know help must be given only when sought. A maturity that is bullied into life is not worth having.

So I have written this book – fruit of a lifetime's reading happily not quite yet over – in the hope that it will serve as a literary guide to readers looking forward to many thousands of hours of pleasure.

The Plan

The book is divided into fifty chapters, or 'years,' to give the reader who requires it a discipline according to which he can pace himself. Obviously the books *can* be read in any order, or at any speed, and most readers will make their own determination of how many great books they have the time and energy to read each year.

The books are all chosen for their ability to enhance a reader's life, not for their utility in the pursuit of hobbies, careers, or curricula.

A Lifetime's Reading stands parallel to the educational system, which sometimes seems incapable of teaching the intelligent reading of books, or even the intelligent reading of a page, or a paragraph. It is not merely knowledge we can gain from books but, if we go about it properly, perhaps some measure of wisdom. And that wisdom is not easily acquired elsewhere. Few of us have friends or neighbors who can impart to us in casual conversation the knowledge and the understanding that life has given them, but the philosopher Epicurus, or the poet Tu Fu, or any of the other hundreds of authors represented here are on call; the best of their writings are ours the moment we choose to take them.

Criteria for Selection

The orthodox Muslim, believing that *al-Qur'an* is the Word of God, consequently also believes in general that only the *Qur'an* need be read. If one does not possess the *Qur'an,* one need only obtain it. If one does already possess it, all other books are trifling.

Leibnitz once stated (though we need not believe his words literally) that his library contained only nine authors: Plato, Aristotle, Archimedes, Euclid, Plutarch, Sextus Empiricus, Pliny, Cicero, and Seneca.

Robert Southey's 'List of a Gentleman's Necessary Library' was not much more populous: the Bible, Shakespeare, Spenser's *Faerie Queene*, Sidney's *Arcadia*, the works of Sir Thomas Browne, the works of the Rev. Cyril Jackson, Walton's *Compleat Angler*, Clarendon, Milton, Chaucer, Jeremy Taylor, the sermons of Robert South, and the *Church History of Britain* by Thomas Fuller.

These somewhat exclusive criteria for the creation of a private library (and many similar that depended for their degree of success on the degree to which their compilers managed to free themselves from the shackles of religious and political prejudice, fashion, and native tongue) understandably fell short of the criteria worthy of an international body such as Unesco. In 1969, Unesco set about compiling a *Tentative List of Representative Works of World Literature*, published in 1972. It contained about 1,500 titles and claimed to provide 'an outline of what could become a minimum international index of the literary heritage of mankind.' The failure of this list was due to the outrageous imbalance by which almost every language spoken by a Unesco member state had to be represented by a book. There were fewer books in Chinese than in Dutch, or Polish, or Portuguese. No revision is planned.

So there is no shortage of pitfalls in the selection of *A Lifetime's Reading*.

I have preferred to assume that the reader will begin without a good grasp of any language other than English. A minority of books chosen were originally written in English; the majority are, of necessity, translations. I have tried to indicate only the best translations, though in some cases even the best translations are substandard (Schiller, Rilke, Heine, Chrétien de Troyes, Mallarmé, Beaumarchais, Epictetus, Terence) and in other cases I have preferred to cite a translation that is low-priced and currently available to a better translation that may be expensive or out of print. The correct titles of texts are given where known, as are the titles of translations – which may well of course be different.

Where both a hardback edition and a paperback are available, I have generally preferred the latter, and I have generally cited the latest edition I know if it is the best. For this reason, the dates shown may well not be those of the first impression, so bibliographers should be warned that this is not a professional book-selection tool but a reader's guide that should be used in conjunction with current national and author bibliographies.

Most chapters (that is, most years) have a bias towards a particular culture or language-area, so that for instance Year 9 has a bias towards Italy. It does not deal, however, with Italian literature exclusively. In Year 9 there is provision for reading the Chinese novel *Monkey*, the poems of Shakespeare,

Stendhal's novel *La Chartreuse de Parme,* and Weissbort's anthology *Postwar Russian Poetry.*

Similarly, a balance is sought between the literary genres, so that in any given year you will find at least one collection of poetry, one novel, one or more plays, and a significant prose work in philosophy, religion, history, or biography.

As if these checks and balances were not sufficiently constraining. I have also hoped to create within each year a wide chronological range, from antiquity to the present day.

But the most stringent condition placed on every potential candidate for inclusion has been that of intrinsic value, whether as regards beauty, wisdom, humor, humanity, or historic influence. Tedium has no place in literature, any more than in life, and you will find here neither the Euclid recommended as one of the best nine books by Leibnitz, nor the works of Cyril Jackson from Robert Southey's thirteen. I am not trying to impress anyone with ponderous tomes. An ounce of Lewis Carroll is in my opinion worth a ton of his contemporaries' sermons, just as a *haiku* by Matsuo Basho is worth all of the long didactic poems from the European baroque.

Availability

Not all of the books chosen in this book are in print, but enough of them are to give you a good start. You might begin by buying four or five of the books from Years 1–3 in new paperback editions. Penguin Books preponderate throughout *A Lifetime's Reading* because of their high standards in selecting, editing, and translating the world's classics. Out of print titles can usually be obtained in second-hand bookstores.

The more expensive books can usually be borrowed from your public library. If you take reading seriously, however, you will soon find there are many books you wish to own. A good private library, even if small at first, is an excellent investment, and its value to you and your family can only increase over the years. In addition to the five hundred basic books that I discuss in detail, you might consider purchasing background books (many of them recommended at the appropriate place in the text), still other books by the authors recommended, or even a basic reference library. This last might sound extravagant, but any person who is genuinely intent on educating himself in the course of his life should give it serious consideration.

A Basic Reference Library

Whatever your interests, a *general encyclopedia* is a requirement, and the rule is to buy the best that you can afford. The cheapest that is sufficiently large is the *World Book Encyclopedia,* though there are a number of worthy one-volume works that you can examine in your local public library.

General yearbooks for up-to-date information include the *World* and *Information Please* almanacs.

You may also want to own *specialized encyclopedias* in your particular fields, such as the *Home Medical Encyclopedia* (4 vols., World Book, 1980), or *Van Nostrand's Scientific Encyclopedia* (Van Nostrand Reinhold, 6th ed., 1983).

There are many chronologies available, such as the alphabetical *Everyman's Dictionary of Dates* and Bernard Grun's chronological *Timetables of History* (Simon and Schuster, 1975). The *Cambridge Ancient History, Cambridge Medieval History,* and *Cambridge Modern History* are all reliable works with contributions from authorities throughout the world.

You will find that a good modern atlas, such as the latest *Premier World Atlas* (Rand McNally) or the *Philip's International Atlas* (George Philip), is extremely useful. The *Atlas of American History* (Scribner's) is a fine work, and the *Columbia-Lippincott Gazetteer of the World* is irreplaceable.

For biographical information choose *Webster's Biographical Dictionary* and a recent *Who's Who in America.*

Always buy the best language dictionaries possible: pocket or compact dictionaries have a habit of omitting just those words you're likely to need. The most useful American English dictionary is Webster's *Third New International Dictionary* (3 vols., Encyclopedia Britannica, 1971). *The Oxford English Dictionary* is now available complete in only two volumes, with a magnifying-glass, at a fraction of the multi-volume price. The Cassell foreign-language dictionaries are dependable, but for Greek choose Liddell-Scott, for Arabic Hans Wehr, for Persian Steingass, for French Harrap, for Turkish Hony, for Chinese Mathews, and for Japanese one of the Vaccari series.

Stevenson's Book of Quotations (Dodd Mead, 10th ed., 1974) is the finest available in its field, though many are much cheaper.

Penguin has a wide range of low-priced subject dictionaries in fields such as psychology, architecture, decorative arts, and computers. Their four-volume *Companion to Literature* is uneven, and should be supplemented by the detailed *Oxford Companions* to literature. Other *Oxford Companions* are available to law, theater, and decorative art, for example.

If your special field is fine art, then the fundamental reference tool (if one discounts the old and very expensive Thieme-Becker) is Bénézit's *Dictionnaire des Peintres,* though the McGraw-Hill *Encyclopaedia of World Art* is better illustrated, with longer critical articles on fewer artists.

In the field of music, the latest edition of Grove's *Dictionary* is essential, as is Kobbé's *Complete Opera Book,* and the *Penguin Stereo Record Guide,* or *Recorded Classical Music* (Macmillan, 1982), which evaluates 12,000 works by 1,600 composers.

Among the guides to new books one must single out the *Times Literary*

Supplement and *The New York Times Book Review* in their very different ways.

If you are serious about building up your private library, you may want to join the Private Libraries Association, made up of like-minded people. In the U.S. and Canada write to William A. Klutts, 145 East Jackson, Box 287, Ripley, Tennessee 38063.

A Word of Caution

Even if I have devoted the major part of my life to reading, studying, and enjoying literature, I should not like the unwary reader to imagine that I set myself up as a kind of judge or assessor, whose word should be considered final. On the contrary, I am conscious of a bias toward the English language (which is the language I happen to know best) and toward the world-view generally considered normal in Western Europe in the second half of the twentieth century. A Hungarian would have written a different book: so would a Korean or a Congolese. So will a writer in a hundred years time.

But I have conscientiously tried to estimate the true value of the books that I have read, without prejudging them as to religion, politics, or morals. That is to say, I have chosen the literary, critical, and historical methods of evaluating books and their writers, believing that other criteria are irrelevant for my purpose.

Philip Ward
Cambridge 1983

'We should never cease to be *readers*; pure readers, reading not to learn, or for an ulterior motive, but for the joy of reading itself. We should know how to read and ardently desire to read and to receive, to nourish ourselves, as by delicious food, to grow in wisdom, organically, not to make use of what one reads socially, in polite society: to become human beings who understand the art of reading, that is to become capable of empathy.'

Charles Péguy

A
Lifetime's
Reading

Year 1

CHARLES LUTWIDGE DODGSON ('LEWIS CARROLL') (1832–1898)
   The Complete Works. (Modern Library, 1937; Nonesuch Library, 1939).

'Lewis Carroll', the eminent logician and mathematician, should be read entire. His *Symbolic Logic* and his *Game of Logic* are available in a single volume (Dover reprint of the 1896 edition), as are *Pillow Problems* and *A Tangled Tale.*

But the reason for Carroll's immortality is a book originally handwritten for a little girl called Alice Liddell and entitled *Alice's Adventures Under Ground* (1864). Later, Carroll added the Cheshire Cat, the Mad-Hatter's Tea Party, the Duchess, the Cook and the Baby, and *Alice's Adventures in Wonderland* was brought out to general rejoicing in 1865. Since the book has always had, and will always have, an appeal as great for adults as for children, the best edition will be *The Annotated Alice* edited by Martin Gardner (Penguin, 1970), which also sets out the authentic chess moves in *Through the Looking Glass and What Alice Found There* (1871), translated inimitably by C. H. Carruthers into Latin as *Aliciae per Speculum Transitus* (Macmillan and St. Martin's Press, 1966).

Martin Gardner has also enriched our understanding by his *Annotated Snark* (Penguin, 1967), which must be something approaching the last word on Carroll's nonsense poem 'The Hunting of the Snark'.

PLATO (*c.* 429–347 B.C.)
   Apology, Crito, Phaedo. Text of the law case and two dialogues in Oxford Classical Texts (5 vols., Oxford U.P., 1903–15) and with parallel translation in the Loeb Classical Library (12 vols., Heinemann and Harvard U.P., 1914 ff.). Translated as *The Last Days of Socrates* by Hugh Tredennick (Penguin, 1954).

Plato, some forty years younger than his teacher, the ugly, bald Socrates, divides the account of his teacher's trial into three speeches: the defence proper, the counter-proposal for the penalty after he had been found guilty, and the final address to the Court. The candour, dignity and nobility of the language and matter must be authentic, for Athenians would scarcely have tolerated misrepresentation of the facts in such a weighty case.

Crito deals with the attempt of an old man, Crito, to persuade Socrates to escape, and with his failure to do so, in dialogue form.

The *Phaedo* is a dialogue within a dialogue, in which the eye-witness Phaedo of Elis discusses the last day that Socrates spent in prison with a company of fellow-philosophers. Socrates was, in the opinion of Phaedo 'of all those whom we knew in our time, the bravest and also the wisest and most upright man'.

Before reading other works of Plato, such as the *Symposium,* the *Republic,* and the *Laws,* study the latest edition of A. E. Taylor's standard *Plato: the Man and his Work* (Methuen). The Classical Greek of Plato is so majestic and clear that it merits any amount of effort in the learning. Luckily there is an abundance of good grammars and dictionaries, such as Wilding's *Greek for Beginners* (2nd ed., Faber & Faber, 1959), and the latest edition of the Liddell and Scott *Greek Lexicon* (Oxford U.P.).

The Old Testament. Recommended versions are the Authorized Version (first published 1611), the Revised Version (first published 1881), the Jerusalem Bible (first published 1966), and the New English Bible (first published 1970).

Of the Authorized Version, which was based on Tyndale's (first published in 1525-6) and Coverdale's slightly amended version of Tyndale's, G. M. Trevelyan has written: 'For every Englishman who had read Sidney or Spenser, or who had seen Shakespeare acted at the Globe, there were hundreds who had read or heard the Bible with close attention as the words of God. The effect of the continual domestic study of the book upon the national character, imagination and intelligence for nearly three centuries to come, was greater than that of any literary movement in our annals, or any religious movement since the coming of St. Augustine'.

In addition to the Old Testament and the Talmud, the Dead Sea Scrolls tell us much of the life and thought of the early Jews. See G. Vermes' *The Dead Sea Scrolls in English* (Penguin, 1962) and A. Powell Davies' *The Meaning of the Dead Sea Scrolls* (New American Library, 1956). .

There is a wide range of study aids to the acquisition of Hebrew, including Harold Levy's *Hebrew for All* (Vallentine, Mitchell, 1970), and R. K. Harrison's *Teach Yourself Hebrew* (English Universities Press, 1955). Robert Graves and R. Patai have compiled a memorable selection of *Hebrew Myths* (Cassell, 1964).

VÁCLAV HAVEL (b. 1936).

Zahradní Slavnost. Translated by Vera Blackwell as *The Garden Party* (Cape, 1969). *Vyrozumění.* Translated by Vera Blackwell as *The Memorandum* (Cape, 1967).

Czech drama, recently revived by the dissidents Havel and Kohout, first achieved world fame with the over-rated plays of Karel Čapek (1890–1938), whose *R.U.R.* (1920) originated the word 'robot' since in common use. Čapek's *Makropoulos Case* (1922) had the distinction of being turned into an opera by Janáček.

Havel is a more considerable writer altogether. Until 1968 he was involved with the ABC and Balustrade theatres in Prague, but he subsequently turned to full-time writing, and it was in 1968 that his third play, *Ztížená možnost soustředění* ('The Increased Difficulty of Concentration'), was staged at the Balustrade.

In *The Memorandum,* a profound satire on all aspects of bureaucracy, a new and impossibly difficult language, 'Ptydepe', is introduced into the office with the alleged function of improving communications by standardization. Kafka and Ionesco are recalled, but there is something profoundly up-to-date in the zany mania for mechanization and uniformity which Havel cleverly exposes.

The Epic of Gilgamesh.

An English version with an introduction by N. K. Sandars (Penguin, 1960).

Antedating Homeric epic poetry by at least fifteen hundred years, the various poems which together make up the poem of the legendary demigod and king of Uruk (or Warka) in Babylonia are as secular in nature as the *Odyssey.* 'Gilgamesh' (the name itself means 'hero') travels with his companion Enkidu to subdue the guardian of the cedar forest. The goddess of love (Ishtar is the Babylonian Aphrodite and Venus) offers herself in marriage to Gilgamesh, but he disdains her and, with Enkidu, destroys the divine bull sent to punish them. In revenge, the gods kill Enkidu, though his ghost later returns to Earth to tell Gilgamesh secrets of the other world. Now Gilgamesh's journey takes him to Utnapishtim, survivor of a Babylonian Flood, to learn the secrets of immortality. The magic plant of immortality is stolen from Gilgamesh by a snake.

Originally from Sumeria, the epic was augmented in the Akkadian of Babylonia on twelve tablets discovered in the library of King Ashurbanipal (669–630 B.C.). The text has been edited by R. Campbell Thompson, and translated by S. N. Kramer and E. A. Speiser in *Ancient Near Eastern Texts* (2nd ed., Princeton U.P., 1955), and Eva Strommenger's *The Art of Mesopotamia* (Thames & Hudson, 1964) for the archaeological and artistic background. Explore your national museum for Assyrian material, such as the palace friezes in the British Museum.

PUBLIUS CORNELIUS TACITUS (*c.* 55–*c.* 120 A.D.).

> *Annales.* And *Historiae.* The *Annals,* with a facing translation by J. Jackson, are in the Loeb Classical Library (3 vols., Heinemann and Harvard U.P., 1931) and have been translated by Michael Grant (Penguin, reprinted with revisions, 1959). The *Histories,* with a facing translation by C. H. Moore, are in the Loeb Classical Library (2 vols., 1925–31) and been translated by Kenneth Wellesley (Penguin, 1964).

About the year 80, Tacitus published his *Dialogus de oratoribus,* which enquired about the causes of the decline in Roman oratory, and assessed its future prospects. In 98, he made available essays on his father-in-law (the *Agricola,* which has much to say concerning Britain), and on the Germani tribespeople (the *Germania*), ruefully respected as an untamed, uncorrupted adversary of the decadent Romans. For Tacitus had observed the terrible last years of Domitian (see also the anecdotes compiled by Suetonius), and it was this experience more than any other that was to influence the historian in his future writings. Tacitus himself filled high office, becoming governor of 'Asia' (to be understood as Western Anatolia, in modern Turkey) in 112 for a period of just under two years. He was a famed orator, and history was regarded by the Romans as a branch of oratory – a polite expression for persuasive prose or, in the wrong hands, even for propaganda. Tacitus, like all the Roman historians, felt obliged to express moral opinions, and he prefers to see his characters – and to imagine their speeches – in black and white, so that future leaders shall be guided towards private virtue and the public good. His *Annals* (published about 117) and *Histories* (published about 106–7) cover the period from 14 to 96, but neither work survives in its entirety.

ONDRA LYSOHORSKY (b. 1905).

> *Selected Poems,* selected and introduced by Ewald Osers (Cape, 1971).

Lysohorsky was born at Frydek, in the industrial Ostrava region of modern Czechoslovakia which was, at the time of his birth, in the Austro-Hungarian Empire. His native language is Lachian, and he has also written in German, but he has always been under considerable political pressure to write in Czech or Slovak, and it was as recently as 1958 that the first part of his collected poems appeared in Lachian, no further parts being permitted to appear, in the erroneous belief that Lysohorsky's aim was Lachian separatism. In fact, Czech readers have no difficulty in understanding Lachian, to judge by the large sales of his first books: *Spiwajuco piaść* ('The Singing Fist', Prague, 1934), *Hłos hrudy* ('The Voice of the Native Soil', Prague, 1935), and *Wybrane wérše* ('Selected Verses', Olomouc, 1936).

Lysohorsky is the major writer in Lachian, and the excellent translations of his selected poems by Osers, McKinley, Levitin and Auden and Lydia Pasternak Slater deserve the widest possible audience.

ERNST HANS GOMBRICH (b. 1909).
The Story of Art. First published 1950. (Phaidon Press. Latest edition). E. H. Gombrich, Director of the Warburg Institute of the University of London, runs an organisation enviably at home equally with art, literature, thought and society. *The Story of Art* is a faultless exposition of the essentials of (mainly Western) art history by a Viennese whose grasp of psychology and music, classical scholarship and modern experimentation, is surely unrivalled.

Professor Gombrich has also written a seminal book on *Art and Illusion* (Phaidon Press, 1960) and several other works, concentrating mainly on the Italian Renaissance.

The Story of Art admits that 'painting is unduly favoured as compared to sculpture and architecture'. The reader could supplement it with Herbert Read's well-illustrated *The Art of Sculpture* (2nd ed., Faber and Faber, 1961) and *World Architecture: an Illustrated History* (Paul Hamlyn, 1969) or the latest edition of Sir Banister Fletcher's standard *History of Architecture on the Comparative Method* (Athlone Press).

Poem into Poem: World Poetry in Modern Verse Translation, introduced and edited by George Steiner (Penguin, 1970).

'With several interesting exceptions such as Dylan Thomas, who knew no other language, and Wallace Stevens, whose uses of English were deliberately permeable to the insinuations of Latin, French and Italian', writes George Steiner, 'there is scarcely an important English or American poet since the Victorians who has not been a translator as well'.

Starting with a Gladstone version from Horace and ending with a George MacBeth version from Ponge, George Steiner's selection contains translations from twenty-two languages. The debate over modes and methods of translating poetry is restated and exemplified by the diverse styles in the anthology, the watershed being Ezra Pound's *Homage to Sextus Propertius;* it is thus helpful to read as many as possible of *The Translations of Ezra Pound* (Faber & Faber, 1971) and the *Imitations* by Robert Lowell (Faber & Faber, 1966). George Steiner's other books have constantly been preoccupied with the possibilities and problems of translation: see in particular the closely-argued *After Babel* (Oxford U.P., 1976).

The important translation journal *Delos* has unfortunately ceased, but there is a current magazine, *Modern Poetry in Translation,* of which your local public library will be able to provide details.

A much longer and more expensive anthology of the same type as Steiner's is *The Oxford Book of Verse in English Translation* (Oxford U.P., 1980), edited by Charles Tomlinson. It does not, however, confront any more problems or offer any more solutions than the cheaply-priced and pocketable Steiner.

PÏERRE ABÉLARD (1079–1143) and HÉLOÏSE (1101–1164).
   Letters. And the *Historia Calamitatum* of Abélard. Translated from the Latin by Betty Radice (Penguin, 1974).

Abélard was the greatest French logician and scholastic philosopher of the twelfth century, but his literary immortality is due to his correspondence with his mistress Héloïse, a lady of great learning who married Abélard secretly. Abélard then prevailed upon her to wear a postulant's habit and her uncle Fulbert, thinking that Abélard was trying to avoid his responsibilities, sent his servants into Abélard's room at night to castrate him. Abélard then became a monk, in the Abbey of St. Denis and Heloïse rose to become prioress and eventually abbess of the Convent of the Paraclete which Abélard had founded.

Abélard's autobiographical 'Story of my Sorrows' recounts his life from the period in St. Denis (from 1119) to some time after 1132. Though his young students found him an inspiring, questioning teacher specialising in *disputatio* (question and answer) rather than in the traditional *lectio* (lecture and commentary), Abélard found himself surrounded by enemies, and at one time even thought of seeking refuge with the Muslims. Finally condemned by the Church after open conflict with St. Bernard of Clairvaux, Abélard spent his last months under the protection of Peter the Venerable, whose correspondence with Heloïse is also extant. The best edition of the *Historia* and *Letters* I-VII appears in *Mediaeval Studies* of the Pontifical Institute of Mediaeval Studies, Toronto, vols. XII, XV, XVII, XVIII (1950, 1953, 1955 and 1956).

There is a valueless romantic paraphrase of the correspondence by F. N. Du Bois which distorted understanding of the *Letters* until 1945, when the Temple Classics edition finally went out of print. The Radice version is sound, with a useful introduction. Helen Waddell's novel *Peter Abelard* (Constable, 1933), it must be emphasised, *is* only a novel.

Year 2

The New Testament. Recommended versions are the Authorized Version (first published 1611), the Revised Version (first published 1881), the New English Bible (in its 2nd ed., first published 1970), and the Jerusalem Bible (first published 1966).

Of the Authorized Version, which was based on Tyndale's (first published in 1525–6) and Coverdale's slightly amended version of Tyndale's, G. M. Trevelyan has written: 'For every Englishman who had read Sidney or Spenser, or who had seen Shakespeare acted at the Globe, there were hundreds who had read or heard the Bible with close attention as the words of God. The effect of the continual domestic study of the book upon the national character, imagination and intelligence for nearly three centuries to come, was greater than that of any literary movement in our annals, or any religious movement since the coming of St. Augustine'.

The plain prose of the New English Bible will appeal to those who simply wish to read the Bible stories. The Jerusalem Bible is set out more clearly, and is generally an excellent instrument for New Testament study.

However, those who are impelled to listen to the original Greek cadences of the compilers of the New Testament will want *The Interlinear Greek-English New Testament* (Samuel Bagster, 1877; constantly reprinted), which prints the Greek text of Nestlé interlinear with a literal translation by Alfred Marshall and the Authorized Version in the margins. A useful grammar is D. F. Hudson's *Teach Yourself New Testament Greek* (English Universities Press, 1960).

Devote two months to the New Testament and ancillary readings and listen to J. S. Bach's *St. Matthew Passion* in the version of Münchinger (4 discs, Decca SET 288–91) or of Klemperer (4 discs, HMV SLS 827).

GAIUS SUETONIUS TRANQUILLUS (*c.* 69 – after 121 A.D.).
   De vita Caesarum. First published 1470. Text with a facing English translation by J. C. Rolfe in the Loeb Classical Library (2 vols., Heinemann

and Harvard U.P., 1914–20). Translated as *The Twelve Caesars* by Robert
Graves (Penguin, 1957).

Suetonius is a disreputable character of whom little is known. His father was a
colonel and Suetonius himself trained (and practised briefly) as a lawyer before
taking a post in the administration as chief secretary to the Emperor Hadrian,
who dismissed him for behaving indiscreetly with the Empress Sabina.
Suetonius wrote many books, including *The Lives of Famous Prostitutes,* but his
only extant work is the gossipy *De vita Caesarum.* The Julius Caesar who wrote
De bello Gallico and *De bello civile* is unrecognisable from the racy, ambitious
Caesar whom Suetonius reduces to human proportions with his inveterate sense
of humour. If there are so many scandals in *The Twelve Caesars,* it is perhaps
merely a reflection of the truth; there is no doubt that few Roman historians cite
conflicting evidence without bias, as Suetonius often does. His anecdotes enliven
what other historians make pompous: the story of those great years from 85 B.C.,
when Julius Caesar was 15, to the death of the degenerate Domitian in 96
A.D.

'MURASAKI SHIKIBU' (*c.* 978–1030).

> *Genji monogatari.* Translated by Arthur Waley as *The Tale of Genji* (New ed.,
> Allen & Unwin and Houghton Mifflin, 1952).

The greatest Japanese novel, and one of the longest, was written by a lady of the
court of the Empress Akiko whose name is lost: she is known only by her pen-
name.

The great saga tells the history of the court of a certain Prince Genji and his
amorous adventures in the first forty-four chapters, and the story of his putative
son in the final ten chapters, which may be by a different hand, or may simply
reflect a change in Lady Murasaki's prose style.

High society in the Fujiwara period can be observed in the fictional narrative,
though the coarseness and spite of the men and women is transmuted into subtle
alliances and tiffs. The background is elaborated in Ivan Morris' *The World of the
Shining Prince: Court Life in Ancient Japan* (Oxford U.P., 1964). Murasaki's own
diary, in a stilted translation by Annie S. Omori and Kochi Doi, can be found in
Diaries of Court Ladies of Old Japan (Houghton Mifflin, 1920; 2nd ed., Maruzen,
Tokyo, 1935).

This is a good point to study *Japanese Painting* (Skira, Geneva, 1961) by
Akiyama Terukazu, starting from the early 12th-century hand scroll depicting
scenes from the *Genji monogatari.*

WILLIAM SHAKESPEARE (1564–1616).
> *Tragedies*. First published 1623. Individual plays are available in reliable Arden editions (Methuen), New Shakespeare editions (Cambridge U.P.) and New Penguin Shakespeare editions (Penguin).

A recommended order to read the tragedies is chronological, beginning with *Romeo and Juliet* (1594–5 – like most dates, conjectural), *Hamlet* (1600–2), *All's Well That Ends Well* (1602), *Troilus and Cressida* (1602), *Othello* (1604–5), *Measure for Measure* (1604), *King Lear* (possibly Shakespeare's greatest achievement, 1605–6), *Macbeth* (1605–6), *Antony and Cleopatra* (1607), *Coriolanus* (1608), *Timon of Athens* (1608), and *Pericles, Prince of Tyre* (1608).

If you are unable to see plays performed easily, it is worth buying or borrowing records of the plays, and also listening to broadcasts as they occur.

Prokofiev's music for the ballet *Romeo and Juliet* is available in two versions equally fine: Previn's (3 discs, HMV SLS 864) and Maazel's (3 discs, Decca SXL 6620/2). The Fonteyn-Nureyev film of the ballet is as definitive in the West as the Ulanova was in its day in the U.S.S.R.

Verdi's operas *Macbeth* and *Othello* are experiences very different from the plays, but equally haunting. *Macbeth* has been recorded by Abbado (3 discs, DGG 2709 062), and Serafin's *Otello* (3 discs, RCA SER 5646-8) is outstanding for Tito Gobbi's Iago.

VINCENT VAN GOGH (1853–1890).
> *Complete Letters*. 3 vols. (Thames & Hudson, 1958; new ed., New York Graphic Society, 1978, distributed by Little, Brown).

A missionary among the Belgian miners after an early disappointment in love and a time as a schoolmaster in England, Van Gogh studied painting in the Hague and then in Antwerp. His brother introduced him to the Impressionists in Paris, where Vincent quickly established himself as a leader of the School, with Gauguin and Cézanne.

Always physically weak, the act of painting would bring on epileptic seizures. He eventually went to an asylum at Auvers-sur-Oise, where he shot himself. His letters, like the autobiography of Cellini, reveal an extraordinary originality and individuality. Nobody has ever painted with a palette as audacious as Van Gogh's. See the *Paintings, Drawings and Prints* (Phaidon Press, 1974) edited by Brian Petrie.

There is an abridged selection of the *Letters* made by Mark W. Roskill in Fontana Books (Collins, 1963).

For comparison and contrast, see *Gauguin* (Thames & Hudson, 1974), by Daniel Wildenstein and Raymond Cogniat.

ALEXEI MAXIMOVICH PESHKOV (MAXIM GORKI) (1868–1936).
   Na Dne. The Lower Depths and other plays. Translated by Alexander Bakshy
   and Paul S. Nathan. (Yale U.P., 1959).

Gorki's *Lower Depths* (1902) appeared in the same year as that in which his
election to the Russian Academy of Sciences and Letters was forbidden because
of the outspoken socialist ideas in his short stories.

   The play was greeted as another political statement, and in 1905 he was
imprisoned as a revolutionary, a sentence commuted to exile after protests by
Western writers. In 1913 he returned to the Soviet Union to support the
Bolsheviks, and organised the immense project of translating the greatest world
classics into Russian: the series 'Vsemirnaya Literatura' ('World Literature'). It
was during this period that he wrote the autobiographical trilogy *Detstvo* (1913),
V lyudyakh (1918) and *Moi universitety* (1923), translated for Penguin by Ronald
Wilks as *My Childhood* (1969), *My Apprenticeship* (1974) and *My Universities*
(1979).

   The final volume is ironically titled, for Gorki enjoyed only five months of
formal schooling, and his 'universities' were docks, a shoemaker's shop, a
baker's shop, and other poor establishments on the banks of the Volga where he
scraped a precarious living. Exiled again by the Bolsheviks in 1921, he finally
returned to the Soviet Union in 1931, where he was greeted as the father of
Socialist Realism (in fact his earliest stories were Romantic) and has since
become canonised as a servant of the proletariat. It is true that his style is often
slovenly, but the intensity of his vision in the novels *Mat'* (*Mother,* 1907) and *Delo
Artamonovikh* (*The Artamonov Business,* 1925) marks Gorki as a writer of high
talent. *The Lower Depths* inspired Eugene O'Neill's great play *The Iceman Cometh*
(1946).

SAMUEL TAYLOR COLERIDGE (1772–1834).
   The Portable Coleridge. (Viking and Penguin, 1961).

Coleridge's criticism is among the most suggestive in English, and the *Biographia
Literaria* of 1817 is amply represented here.

   But Coleridge is loved first and foremost as a poet. His *Rime of the Ancient
Mariner,* which first appeared in the *Lyrical Ballads* he wrote with Wordsworth
(1798), is available in a separate edition with the haunting illustration of Gustave
Doré (Arno Press, 1979). I. A. Richards' *Portable Coleridge* also includes most of
the shorter poems, and the *Kubla Khan* (1816) which Coleridge composed in his
sleep in 1797 while living at a lonely West Country farmhouse. He had set down a
fragment of fewer than three hundred lines when he was interrupted by 'a person
from Porlock' and his train of thought was never reconstructed. However, a

model of literary detection by John Livingston Lowes, *The Road to Xanadu* (Constable, 1966), has unearthed from Coleridge's notebooks of 1795–8 the processes by which the images in the fragment were transmuted from sources in Coleridge's life and reading.

A more comprehensive but comparable example of the art of literary detection, applying to the whole life and writings of an author who deliberately laid false trails, is *The Quest for Corvo* (Penguin, 1944) by A. J. A. Symons. A fictional treatment of a part of 'Baron Corvo's' life can be found in Pamela Hansford Johnson's *The Unspeakable Skipton* (Penguin, 1968).

LIN YUTANG (*b.* 1895).
   The Importance of Living. (Heinemann, 1938).

One of those rare books which enchants while it enlightens, *The Importance of Living* is written lightly yet with extraordinary insight. Lin is particularly wise on 'Our Animal Heritage', in which he draws analogies between human nature, and the beings created by Wu Ch'eng-en in his great 16th-century novel *Hsi-yu chi* ('Monkey'). In the chapter 'Who can best enjoy life?', several types are discussed: Chuang Tzu, Mencius, Lao Tzu, the author of *The Golden Mean,* and T'ao Ch'ien, also called T'ao Yüan-ming. Sections are devoted to the enjoyment of loafing, the home, living, nature, travel and culture.

A final appeal is made to 'talk reason' (*chiangli*) as the controlling factor in logical arguments. Common sense and arrival at a consensus are Chinese habits of mind that may be encouraged or discouraged in any given period, but are always there to be drawn to the surface if occasion arises.

AESCHYLUS (525–456 B.C.).
   Oresteia. Text with a translation by Herbert Weir Smyth in the Loeb Classical Library (2 vols., Heinemann and Harvard U.P., 1922–6). Translated by Richmond Lattimore (Washington Square, 1967).

The *Oresteia,* a trilogy comprising *Agamemnon, Choephori,* ('The Libation-Bearers') and *Eumenides* ('The Furies'), is the only surviving complete trilogy on the House of Atreus and the vengeance of Orestes.

The Persians, produced in 472, formed part of a tetralogy of seemingly unrelated plays. The *Seven against Thebes,* produced in 467, formed part of a tetralogy dealing with the royal house of Thebes. *The Suppliant Women,* produced about 465, is the first play in a tetralogy on the legend of Danaus. *Prometheus Bound,* produced late in the life of Aeschylus, is probably the central play in a trilogy on the legend of Prometheus.

It is the *Oresteia,* however, dating to 458, which brings us closest to the Greek concept of tragedy. We are reminded that the Trojan war was won by the Greeks as a result of Agamemnon's sacrifice of Iphigeneia: the human tragedy reflecting national conflict and ultimately divine conflict must be resolved, and its resolution occurs amid unsurpassed poetry and rivalry. Compare with the *Oresteia* the Oedipus trilogy of Sophocles, and those plays by Euripides which employ Oresteian subjects (the two Iphigeneia plays, *Helen, Orestes* and *The Trojan Women*) but bring the conflict down from divine majesty to the human arena.

Year 3

SAMUEL LANGHORNE CLEMENS ('MARK TWAIN') (1835–1910).
The Adventures of Tom Sawyer. First published 1876. *The Adventures of Huckleberry Finn.* First published 1885. Many editions available, some (such as in Everyman's Library, Dent and Dutton 1944) containing both novels in one volume.

'Mark Twain' is a slang phrase used on the river to mean 'two fathoms deep' and indeed Clemens wrote his best work on and around the Mississippi, his *Life on the Mississippi* first appearing in 1883 (New American Library, 1961; World's Classics edition from Oxford U.P., 1962).

His masterpiece is *Huck Finn,* with the steadily maturing relationship between Nigger Jim and the boy Huckleberry, who narrates the story. Their adventures down the river, and the picaresque characters they meet, including the fraudulent 'Duke of Bridgewater' and the temperance faker and actor calling himself 'Louis XVII of France'. Tom Sawyer reappears towards the end of the adventure.

Together, Mark Twain's novels form a memorable picture of nineteenth-century life in the southern States, where slavery was still considered a God-ordained custom, despite the success in 1851–2 of Harriet Beecher Stowe's powerful fictional tract against slavery, *Uncle Tom's Cabin.*

Buddhist Scriptures, selected and translated by Edward Conze. (Penguin, 1959).

The literature of Buddhism is vast, and only the greatest classics are recommended for those who prefer not to become practising Buddhists. The utility of Conze's selection is that it concentrates on the central tradition, and principally on texts written down between 100 and 400 A.D., or from 600 to 900 years after the Buddha's demise. The oral traditions were first written down to safeguard their survival at a time of decline in faith, and the different schools of Buddhism wrote down their traditions in their own way. The Buddhist way of life, known generally as 'the Middle Way' because of its avoidance of extremes, is still evolving. Other anthologies offer different texts and Conze himself has produced another: *Buddhist Texts Through the Ages* (Faber & Faber for Bruno Cassicer, 1954), a companion to Conze's *Buddhism: its Essence and Development* (2nd ed., Faber & Faber for Bruno Cassirer, 1953).

The best textbook for the general reader is still Christmas Humphreys' *Buddhism* (Penguin, 1951), but see also Edward J. Thomas' *The Life of Buddha as Legend and History* (Kegan Paul, 1927). Hallade's *Gandhara Style and the Evolution of Buddhist Art* (Thames & Hudson, 1968) is an excellent introduction to the sculpture by Greeks or under Greek influence in 'Gandhara', an area in the east of present-day Afghanistan and in the north-west of present-day Pakistan. Many museums have intriguing examples of this composite style.

FYODOR MIKHAILOVICH DOSTOEVSKY (1821–1881).
> *Brat'ya Karamazovy*. First published 1879–80. Translated as *The Brothers Karamazov* by David Magarshack (2 vols., Penguin, 1958).

Probably the greatest Russian novel ever written, *The Brothers Karamazov* was the complex, feverish masterpiece of Dostoevsky, completed about three months before his death.

From Schiller's play *Die Räuber,* and from the true experiences of a fellow-prisoner in Siberia serving twenty years for parricide, Dostoevsky derived the central idea for the plot of his last novel. The background was the turbulent Russia at the end of the 1870s, and the driving force was Dostoevsky's belief in the Orthodox Church as a redeemer of the nation in the face of anarchy. 'Combine all the four main characters', he wrote to the editor of *The Moscow Herald,* in which the novel was being serialized, 'and you will get a picture, reduced it may be to a thousandth degree, of our contemporary educated Russia: that is why I regard my task as so important'. His loathing and fear of the socialists in the last years of his life strikes the reader as ironic in view of our knowledge that it was as a member of a socialist group, led by Petrashevsky that he was arrested in 1849 and taken to execution – a sentence countermanded at the last minute.

His translator Magarshack has written a valuable biography: *Dostoevsky: a Life* (Secker & Warburg, 1962).

RAMÓN GÓMEZ DE LA SERNA (1888–1963).
A selection of 1,800 *Greguerías* has been translated by Philip Ward (The Oleander Press, Cambridge, 1982). *Greguerías. Selección, 1910–1960.* (6th ed., Espasa-Calpe, Madrid, 1960).

A *greguería* is defined by Ramón as 'humour + metaphor' and was chosen because – among other reasons – it is used by farmers to describe the squealing of piglets chasing their sow. The *Total de greguerías* (2nd ed.) published by Aguilar in 1962 contained 1591 pages, so that a selection such as the one recommended above is advised.

The wit of Ramón's original *greguerías* can be judged from the following examples: 'There are so many people gathered in front of the monkeys' cage that they must be giving lectures'. 'The pauper's worst moment is when even his buttons abandon him'. 'The scarecrow looks like a shot spy'. 'Some married couples sleep back to back so that neither will steal the other's dreams'. 'Pearl necklace – a rosary of sin'. 'Six is the number that is going to have a baby'. 'A pencil writes only the shadow of words'.

Apart from the unique gnomic humour of the *greguerías*, Ramón is perhaps at his best in *Automoribundia* (Editorial Sudamericana, 1948), in which he tells the story of his life with hilarious good humour and originality.

WILLIAM TREVOR (b. 1928).
The Love Department. (Penguin, 1970). And *The Children of Dynmouth* (Penguin, 1980).

William Trevor was born in Mitchelstown, County Cork, but now lives in Devon with his wife and two sons. Having removed himself from his native Ireland, he can write about its imagined people with the same clarity of distance that he commands over his London and provincial characters. His short stories are considerable works of art, but it is probably in his novels that he reaches the highest peak of his achievement so far. Though the two novels above are masterpieces, the rest of Trevor's output is remarkably even, beginning with *The Old Boys* (Penguin, 1966) and *The Boarding House* (Penguin, 1968). He is adroit in adapting stories as plays for radio and television: they lose very little, since much of his shrewd characterisation of the weak and eccentric depends on idiosyncratic dialogue.

The trilogy of stories called 'Matilda's England' shows how a stubborn mania for nostalgia can be understood with compassion by author and reader. The humanity necessary in ordinary dealings is William Trevor's constant preoccupation, behind the smugness he finds in suburbia and the egotism in masters and fathers.

TERESA DE JESÚS, *St.* (1515–1582).
  Vida. First published 1588, edited by Fray Luis de León. Translated in
  the *Complete Works* (3 vols., edited by E. Allison Peers, Sheed & Ward,
  1963), and as *The Life of Saint Teresa* (Penguin, 1957).

Where all the sermons of the sixteenth century are as dead as Jacob Marley, the
simple, pure and spontaneous autobiography of the illustrious Carmelite
reformer is as fascinating as it was to her own contemporaries, such as the equally
illustrious poet and reformer St. John of the Cross.

Teresa, born into the Spanish nobility at or near the Castilian city of Avila, was
inflamed by reading the romances of chivalry that were to turn the brain of Don
Quixote, and the lives of saints, to the point of running away from home with her
brother Rodrigo at the age of seven to convert the infidel and achieve brisk
martyrdom. She became a Carmelite at 19, but was disenchanted with the
immoral and blatantly unholy lives of the nuns and set out, with John of the
Cross, to reform existing convents and to found new Discalced (Barefoot)
Carmelite convents, mainly in Castile and Andalusia.

It was in 1562 that she founded her first convent (in Ávila) and during the next
three years she set down the story of her life at the request of her spiritual director,
Francisco de Soto y Salazar. She writes pungently and frankly, as she speaks, with
no idea of punctuation and little of grammar. The best recent edition of her works
is in the 'Biblioteca de Autores Cristianos' (3 vols., 1951–9). E. Allison Peers has
written a sensitive portrait: *Mother of Carmel* (S.C.M. Press, 1945).

LUCIUS APULEIUS (*c.* 125– *c.* 180 A.D.).
  Metamorphoses. Text with an English translation of 1566 by W. Adlington
  revised by S. Gaselee in the Loeb Classical Library (Heinemann & Harvard
  U.P., 1915). Translated as *The Transformations of Lucius, otherwise known as
  The Golden Ass,* by Robert Graves (Penguin, 1950).

A comic adventure novel in Latin, based on an extant Greek original but much
amplified. Apuleius, born at Madauros or Madaura in present-day Algeria,
settled at Carthage but travelled a good deal in Roman Africa giving lectures
which he collected as the *Florida.* Accused of sorcery, Apuleius composed an
Apologia for the court of Sabratha (in modern Libya) and was acquitted. He was
in fact very interested in magic, and intercalated a number of magical episodes in
his Golden Ass. This, the best novel surviving from Roman Africa, tells the story
of Lucius, a Greek who visits Thessaly hoping to learn something of the
province's notorious magical practices. While staying in the home of a certain
Milo, he sees his host's wife turn herself into an owl by the rubbing of ointment

on her skin. He bribes the maid to obtain some of the ointment, but she gives him the wrong one, and he turns into an ass. The fun waxes ever more fast and furious, and the reader of the magnificent Graves translation will be transported into the ancient world as if by Apuleian magic. Some scholars see the whole book as an allegory, including the celebrated story of Cupid and Psyche and the hero/author's initiation into the oriental mysteries of Isis and Osiris.

See the studies by Sir E. A. Budge: *Egyptian Magic* and *Egyptian Religion* (both University Books, New York, 1968).

EMILY DICKINSON (1830–1886).
    Complete Poems. Edited by Thomas H. Johnson (Little, Brown, 1960).

The editor of the three-volume critical variorum edition of Emily Dickinson has selected one form of each poem. There is a selection, *Final Harvest* (Little, Brown, 1962), containing only 575 of the total 1775 poems. Emily Dickinson's *Letters* (World Publishing Co. and Gollancz, 1951) is a selection by Mabel Loomis Todd. Thomas H. Johnson has arranged 1,049 letters written by Emily from the age of 11 in *The Letters* (3 vols., Harvard U.P., 1958).

Emily is a genius whose work should be savoured as it was written, in privacy. At the age of twenty-three she wrote 'I do not go from home', and by the time she was 30 she had become a recluse, spending many years without setting foot beyond her front door, and publishing none of her poems by her own consent during her lifetime – indeed only three or four appeared. She was, however, no misanthrope or embittered spinster: 'I find ecstasy in living', she wrote. 'The mere sense of living is joy enough'. Elsewhere: 'To live is so startling, it leaves but little room for other occupations'.

No reader of Emily can be so insensitive as to leave this extraordinary woman (who could be relentlessly sarcastic on occasion) and her poetry without a sense of exhilaration. She experimented audaciously with rhyme and assonance, being as far ahead of her poetic generation as was her contemporary Gerard Manley Hopkins.

FLAVIUS ARRIANUS (ARRIAN). (*c.* 100–180 A.D.)
    Anabasis. Text (and the *Indica*) with a translation by E. I. Robson in the Loeb Classical Library (2 vols., Heinemann & Harvard U.P., 1929–33). Translated by Aubrey de Sélincourt (Penguin, 1958).

Arrian, a Greek born in Nicomedia, Bithynia, was a student of the philosopher Epictetus and luckily for us kept notes of the pagan's teachings in eight books of

Dissertations, half of which are extant. He also produced an abridged edition, known as the *Encheiridion,* or 'Manual' which was, oddly enough, used as a guide by Christian monks in the Middle Ages.

Arrian was one of a group of highly articulate writers who contributed to the renaissance of Greek letters under the Emperor Hadrian: others included the satirist Lucian, the Greek historian of Rome Appian, the medical writer Galen, and the distinguished travel writer Pausanias.

Arrian took the title of his history of Alexander the Great, *Anabasis,* from the work of Xenophon. But Xenophon's *March Up-Country* was a parochial affair indeed compared with Alexander's extraordinary adventures during the twelve years and eight months of his reign (356–323 B.C.). Arrian used the first-hand accounts of Ptolemy and Aristobulus, just as Diodorus and Quintus Curtius did: his narrative is never pompous, but plain and straightforward. For documents of the period, see Sir Ernest Barker's *From Alexander to Constantine* (Oxford U.P., 1956). Freya Stark has followed *Alexander's Path* (John Murray, 1958).

Sir ARTHUR CONAN DOYLE (1859–1930).
   The Penguin Complete Sherlock Holmes (Penguin, 1981).

The first story that Conan Doyle ever published was *A Study in Scarlet* (1887) and, despite trying his hand at adventure-novels, and historical romances, it is as the creator of Sherlock Holmes that he is still best known. The inspiration for the character was an eminent Edinburgh surgeon, Dr Joseph Bell (1837–1911). Sherlock's brother Mycroft, his enemy Moriarty, and his chronicler and confidant, Dr Watson, remain in the memory as long as Holmes himself, whose enormous success spawned a host of imitators and rivals, among them Agatha Christie's Hercule Poirot and Maurice Leblanc's debonair gentleman-thief Arsène Lupin (see *Arsène Lupin contre Herlock Sholmes,* 1908).

Year 4

The Penguin Book of French Verse (Penguin, 1975).

This rich anthology began life as four volumes, divided chronologically and edited by Brian Woledge (to the 15th century), Geoffrey Brereton (16th–18th centuries), and Anthony Hartley (19th century and 20th century).

Selections from *La vie de Saint Alexis* of the 11th century and from *La Chanson de Roland* begin the work, and poems by René Guy Cadou and Yves Bonnefoy bring it to an end.

The tried and proven Penguin methods of setting plain prose renderings at the foot of the page with the original French, and chronological arrangement, with the poet's name at the head of each page, contrast all too clearly with those of William Alwyn's *Anthology of Twentieth Century French Poetry* (Chatto & Windus, 1969), which prints no texts, uses an alphabetical arrangement by author's surnames, and offers no page-heading clues to authorship throughout. Alwyn's principles of selection and the versions themselves are good, but the techniques of presentation serve only to tantalise the reader.

There are numerous records available of French poets and actors reading verse: your nearest Institut Culturel Français will be glad to help with a current list. Meanwhile it is worth exploring the rich field of French songs, less celebrated than German *Lieder* but equally enchanting, such as the *Chants d'Auvergne* of Marie-Joseph Canteloube sung by Victoria de los Angeles (HMV ASD 2826), and the 16th-century *chansons* of Clement Jannequin sung by the Paris Polyphonic Ensemble (Telefunken AW 6.41877).

Talmud.

The so-called Babylonian Talmud, as opposed to the lesser or Palestinian Talmud, was virtually complete by the mid 8th-century A.D., but the only complete MS. codex to survive Christian persecution is a 14th-century codex. The first full printed edition was that of Daniel Bomberg (Venice, 1520–3). There is an English translation in *The Soncino Talmud,* ed. by I. Epstein (35 vols., 1935–52).

The Talmud is a huge encyclopaedia of laws both Levitical and ceremonial (the Hallakhah) and of parables, tales and anecdotes (the Haggadah). Selections have been made by Polano (*The Talmud,* Warne, 1877 and constantly reprinted); by Cohen (*Everyman's Talmud,* Schocken, 1978); and by Galai (*The Essential Talmud,* 1978), among others.

Points of departure might be a consideration of *Judaism* by Epstein (Penguin, 1970), the contributions of eminent Jews to Western civilization as described in *The Legacy of Israel* (Oxford U.P., 1927), and the history and antiquities of the city of Jerusalem in a book such as Michel Join-Lambert's *Jerusalem* (Putnam's & Elek, 1958).

GUSTAVE FLAUBERT (1821–1880).
  L'Éducation Sentimentale. First published 1869. Translated by Robert Baldick as *Sentimental Education* (Penguin, 1964).

Flaubert met the 'Maria' of the autobiographical fragment *Mémoires d'un fou* when he was sixteen, and wrote the beginnings of the tale the following year, but it was first published much later in the *Oeuvres de jeunesse inédites.*

'Maria' (a Madame Schlésinger), reappears in his great novel *L'Éducation Sentimentale* (a *roman à clef*) as 'Madame Arnoux', while Flaubert himself is 'Frédéric Moreau', Maxime du Camps is the ambitious 'Deslauriers' and Maurice Schlésinger is the reckless, dreaming yet avaricious businessman 'Jacques Arnoux'. Flaubert himself considered that the novel was doomed to popular failure because it destroys illusions, ironically reversing the 'sentimental' in favour of the realistic, and the Naturalistic novelist Huysmans called it the Bible of his school. The young man's romantic attachment to an older woman, never consummated, strikes a particularly deep note in contemporary readers because we realise that Flaubert was describing, with impressive objectivity, his own story and his own profound regrets.

SYLVIA PLATH (1932–1963).
  Poems. *The Bell Jar* (Faber & Faber, 1966).

During her lifetime, the Boston-born poetess published the collection of poems *The Colossus and other Poems* (Heinemann, 1960) and the novel *The Bell Jar* (as by 'Victoria Lucas', (Heinemann, 1963). Subsequent collections of her verse are *Ariel* (Faber & Faber, 1965), *Crossing the Water* and *Winter Trees* (both Faber & Faber, 1971), and there are short stories, prose writings and a diary in *Johnny Panic and the Bible of Dreams* (Faber & Faber, 1977).

Her *Letters Home* (edited by her mother Aurelia Schober Plath, Faber & Faber,

1976) begin as she goes to Smith College on a scholarship, makes her first suicide attempt, and meets her future husband, the British poet Ted Hughes, for the first time in Cambridge, Mass. How Sylvia Plath came to commit suicide at the tragically early age of thirty can be examined in A. Alvarez's *The Savage God* (Weidenfeld & Nicolson, 1971), a consideration of writers at the end of their tether.

PIERRE-AUGUSTIN CARON DE BEAUMARCHAIS (1732–1799).
   Le Barbier de Séville. First published 1775. *Le Mariage de Figaro*. First published 1778, but not produced until 1784. Translated together by John Wood (Penguin, 1964).
Beaumarchais's 'Barber', the witty and resourceful Figaro, offered a more sophisticated view of the servant or valet as comic hero in the tradition running from Roman comedy to the *commedia dell' arte*. In the *Marriage*, however, a more serious note is struck by anti-aristocratic dialogue and situations. A third play, *La Mère Coupable* (1792), shows Figaro as a pompous moralizer in highly artificial and melodramatic situations.

   Gioacchino Rossini fully exploited the comedy in his opera *Il Barbiere di Siviglia* (3 discs, HMV SLS 853), and Mozart in his *Le Nozze di Figaro* (either 4 discs, Philips 6707 014, conducted by Colin Davis, or 3 discs, Decca GOS 585–7, conducted by Erich Kleiber).

PUBLIUS OVIDIUS NASO (OVID) (43 B.C. – 17 A.D.).
   Metamorphoses. Text with an English translation by F. J. Miller in the Loeb Classical Library (2 vols., Heinemann & Harvard U.P., 1921). Modern verse translation by Rolfe Humphries (Indiana U.P., 1955) and modern prose translation by Mary M. Innes (Penguin, 1955).

In classical antiquity, Virgil overshadowed Ovid in popularity, but the 12th and 13th centuries have been called the 'aetas Ovidiana' and throughout the whole of the Middle Ages, Ovid overshadowed Virgil. His influences is felt everywhere, from the *Roman de la Rose* and the Spanish *Libro de Alexandre* to the German Minnesänger and Chaucer. Chrétien de Troyes translated parts of the *Metamorphoses*, and Ovid was honoured by Dante (who places him with Homer, Horace and Lucan) and by Boccaccio, who retells several Ovidian stories in his *Amorosa Visione*. Shakespeare knew and used Golding's translation of the *Metamorphoses*.

   To understand the world of medieval writers one must digest the world-view of Ovid, who taught that human history was a story of decline: from a Golden Age of harmony and peace, to a Silver Age of seasons, instead of eternal spring, to a

Bronze Age when men practised warfare – but heroically, without wickedness or treachery, to the Iron Age of Ovid's own time, when 'all manner of crimes broke out; modesty, truth and loyalty fled'.

JEAN DE LA FONTAINE (1621–1695).
> *Fables choisies mises en vers.* First published in 1668 (six books), 1678 (five books), and 1694 (a twelfth book). The text is complete, with notes by José Lupin, in the Livre de Poche (1964), and there is a reliable edition in Garnier (1966). A bilingual selection with translations by Elizur Wright has the great advantage of illustrations by Gustave Doré (Jupiter, 1975) in large format, but the best translations are undoubtedly those by Marianne Moore (Viking, 1954).

Earlier fabulists such as 'Aesop', Phaedrus, Horace, and the Oriental collector of the *Panchatantra* are overshadowed by the universal appeal, the ingenious free verse, and the inveterate good humour of the Frenchman La Fontaine.

Human failings and foibles are criticised gently, and the Epicurean wit of La Fontaine is at odds with the solemn morality of his time. 'The Wolf turned Shepherd', 'The Mule boasting of his Genealogy', 'The Ass dressed in the Lion's Skin' and 'The Astrologer who Stumbled into a Well' are vivid anecdotes that bear constant rereading.

PLUTARCH (*c.* 46– *c.* 127).
> Parallel Lives. Texts with an English translation by B. Perrin in the Loeb Classical Library (11 vols., Heinemann & Harvard U.P., 1914–26). Translations in Penguin are Rex Warner's *Fall of the Roman Republic* (1958), and Ian Scott-Kilvert's *Makers of Rome* (1964), *Rise and Fall of Athens* (1960), and *The Age of Alexander* (1973).

Plutarch's *Lives* were first printed in Latin in 1517, and they were early translated into French (by Amyot) and into English (by Sir Thomas North). Their influence has been significant, for Shakespeare relied on the *Lives* for his view of ancient Rome, and many biographers have followed Plutarch's method.

Plutarch was a Greek from Boeotia, who was given an official position by the Roman Emperor Hadrian but spent most of his time writing and teaching at his school in Chaeronea. He was a Platonist, and wrote numerous dialogues and essays on literary and philosophical subjects collected in the *Moralia* (15 vols., Loeb Classical Library, 1927–76, for text and translation). But his chief glory is the series of *Lives,* usually pairing a Greek with a Roman in the same field, such as generalship or historiography, and drawing particular attention to the character of his subjects, rather than to any objective statement of a career.

The comparison of Greek and Roman culture made by Plutarch has always been a fruitful source of discussion. He saw eleven emperors rule in his lifetime, and was as diligent in his literary research as he was lucky in his connections.

Sir CECIL MAURICE BOWRA.
　　Primitive Song. (Weidenfeld & Nicolson, 1962).

Most of the poetry that one reads will have been written for the page, but there is a far greater mass of songs which were originally composed simply for performance, whether for enjoyment, or in competitions like the *mushaira* of India or the *eisteddfod* of Wales.

The best way of appreciating such performances is by listening to gramophone records, but it is also useful to read collections and to explore the background to the songs in a book such as that by Maurice Bowra, with examples drawn from every continent, and in journals such as *Alcheringa* devoted to ethnopoetics.

Enjoy too the pleasure of 'primitive' art in books on the bark paintings of Australian aborigines or the magnificent masks of African tribes. Franz Boas' *Primitive Art* (Dover Publications, New York and Constable, 1955) is a useful starting-point before one specialises on a given area, such as Oceania, one aspect of which is well-served by Terence Barrow's *Art and Life in Polynesia* (Pall Mall Press, 1972). The pejorative label 'primitive' is absurd in the context of rock paintings and rock carvings. See Paolo Graziosi's superbly-illustrated *Palaeolithic Art* (Faber & Faber, 1960) for a general survey, and then concentrate on a given area, such as Lascaux in France (Annette Laming's *Lascaux,* Penguin, 1959) or Val Camonica in Italy (Emmanuel Anati's *Camonica Valley,* Knopf, 1961).

CHARLES DICKENS (1812–1870).
　　The Pickwick Papers. First published 1837. Oxford Illustrated Dickens series.
　　(Oxford U.P., 1948).

Apart from the amusing but lightweight *Sketches by Boz* (first published 1836; Oxford U.P., 1957), *The Posthumous Papers of the Pickwick Club* can be considered Dickens' first important work, and thus it plays an important part in understanding the evolution of Dickens, whose fourteen major novels constitute the central tradition of English fiction. The serious student of Dickens will acquire the complete Oxford Illustrated Dickens, but at much less expense one can acquire all the major novels in the Penguin English Library.

Though it would be disproportionate to recommend allocating a further 13 months to the other thirteen major novels at this point, they are listed here in their order of composition, and hence in the order in which they should be read if time allows, or if you prefer a Dickens novel to the suggested book in any given month.

The Adventures of Oliver Twist, 1837–8.

The Life and Adventures of Nicholas Nickleby, 1838–9.

The Old Curiosity Shop, 1840–1.

Barnaby Rudge, 1841.

The Life and Adventures of Martin Chuzzlewit, 1843–4.

Dealings with the Firm of Dombey and Son, 1846–8.

The Personal History of David Copperfield, 1849–50.

Bleak House, 1852–3.

Hard Times for These Times, 1854.

Little Dorrit, 1855–7.

A Tale of Two Cities, 1859.

Great Expectations, 1861.

Our Mutual Friend, 1864–6.

And at Christmas spend an evening with *A Christmas Carol,* written in 1843 and available in Oxford's edition of *Christmas Stories* (1956) and in vol. 1 of the Penguin *Christmas Books.*

See Norman and Jeanne Mackenzie's *Dickens: a Life* (Oxford U.P., 1979).

Year 5

GUSTAVE FLAUBERT (1821–1880).
  Madame Bovary. First published 1857. Translated by G. Hopkins for the World's Classics (Oxford U.P., 1959) and by Alan Russell (Penguin, 1970).

As slow a writer as Balzac was rapid, Flaubert took nearly six years to compose *Madame Bovary,* possibly the greatest of all French novels. Bovary herself is a frustrated Romantic, who finds no fulfilment in her marriage to a country doctor, and hardly any more in affairs with a local landowner and lawyer's clerk. Flaubert identified himself with his heroine in order to realize her personality to its utmost, and his portrait of her life and provincial manners were vivid enough for a court case to be brought against him and the Editor of *La Revue de Paris* in which the novel was serialised. Enid Starkie has studied the genesis of *Madame Bovary* in *Flaubert: the Making of the Master* (Penguin, 1971).

For a complete contrast, Flaubert went to Tunisia in 1857 to collect material and absorb the atmosphere of ruined Carthage for his historical novel *Salammbô* (1862; translated by J. C. Chartres, Dent and Dutton, 1956). *Salammbô* is by comparison with *Madame Bovary* a failure.

Another North African journey by a Frenchman produced some of Eugène Delacroix's most radiant paintings. Delacroix (1798–1863) visited Morocco and Algeria in 1832 – see 'The Jewish Wedding' in the Louvre and 'The Sultan of Morocco' in Toulouse – and returned to Moroccan themes again as late as the 1850s. See Delacroix's *Journal* abridged (Phaidon Press, 1980) and Lee Johnson's *Delacroix* (W.W. Norton, 1963).

ARISTOPHANES (*c.* 448–*c.* 388 B.C.).
  Plays. Texts of the surviving plays with an English translation by B. B. Rogers in the Loeb Classical Library (2 vols., Heinemann & Harvard U.P., 1924) for those who wish a bilingual, expurgated edition. The best translator so far is Dudley Fitts: *Four Comedies* (Harcourt Brace, 1959), including *Lysistrata, The Frogs, The Birds,* and *Ladies' Day*). The complete

11 comedies appear in 3 Penguin volumes of unequal merit (1964, 1973 and 1978).

The Frogs and *The Thesmophorians* are attacks on Euripides, whom the conservative Aristophanes hated for his radical views on the Greek gods. The lost *Babylonians* and the extant *Knights* of 424 B.C. attacked fhe demagogue Kleon. *The Acharnians,* the *Peace,* and the *Lysistrata* are all anti-war plays. *The Wasps* satirizes the Athenian system of trial by mass paid juries.

The most interesting of the eleven comedies is *The Clouds,* which attacks the popular sophists of the time through the person of Socrates, a most unjust caricature, since Socrates detested the superficial sophists who taught rich young men for money as much as did Aristophanes himself. When Socrates later declared, at his trial, that his most dangerous enemies were not those in court, he meant that Aristophanes had scurrilously portrayed Socrates as an idle speculator on things above the earth and beneath it, and a perverter of right and wrong. *The Clouds* is beautifully written, with subtle barbs against metaphysical trickery: it was too profound for the audience, who preferred vulgar farce, and it won neither first nor second prize at the Great Dionysia of 423.

ALBERT CAMUS (1913–1960).
   L'Étranger. First published 1942. *La Peste.* First published 1947. *La Chute.* First published 1956. *L'Étranger* and *La Peste* translated by Stuart Gilbert (Penguin, 1961 and 1960). *La Chute* translated by Justin O'Brien (Penguin, 1963). Camus's *Collected Fiction* (Hamish Hamilton) appeared in 1961.

Camus, born in Algeria, lived there until 1940 and then wrote in the daily *Combat* for the French Resistance. His published works include notebooks, plays, short stories, and the celebrated essays of *Le Mythe de Sisyphe* (1942; translated by Justin O'Brien as *The Myth of Sisyphus,* Hamish Hamilton and Knopf, 1955) and *L'Homme Revolté* (1951; translated by Anthony Bower as *The Rebel,* Knopf, and 1954, and Penguin, 1969).

The Stranger exemplifies the stoicism, bordering both existentialism and fatalism, which Camus advocated. An ordinary man commits a senseless murder, for which he is condemned.

The Plague on one level describes a city infected with plague, but can also be read as an allegory of Europe under Hitler's occupation.

The Fall, Camus's third great novel, shows a marked ideological change. Beneath the superficial irony and blasphemy, Camus is now pleading for recognition of our sinful nature and the hope of Grace.

Camus's philosophical fiction leads on to the precocious study of Colin Wilson, *The Outsider,* (Pan, 1970) and its sequel *Beyond the Outsider* (Pan,

1966).

TEODOR JOSEF KONRAD KORZENIOWSKI (JOSEPH CONRAD)
(1857–1924). *The Secret Agent.* First published 1907. (Doubleday, 1953; Penguin, 1963). *Under Western Eyes.* First published 1911. (Doubleday, 1963; Penguin, 1957).

F. R. Leavis claimed in *The Great Tradition* (which stressed the significance of George Eliot, Henry James and Conrad), that *The Secret Agent* is 'one of Conrad's two supreme masterpieces, one of the two unquestionable classics of the first order that he added to the English novel'.

From the age of 17 to the age of 37, the Polish-born Conrad worked at sea, gaining in 1884 a Board of Trade Certificate as a Master Mariner. He then became a naturalised British subject, and the success of his first novel, *Almayer's Folly,* in 1895 encouraged him to devote himself to writing. The sea provides the background to most of his fiction, such as *The Nigger of the 'Narcissus'* and *Lord Jim;* but it is in the political novels that he achieves full stature. *The Secret Agent* portrays nihilists and anarchists in London and *Under Western Eyes* is concerned with Russian politics and psychology in the year 1911, and in particular with the revolutionary mind.

For the factual background, read Christopher Hill's *Lenin and the Russian Revolution* (English U.P., 1947) and Leon Trotsky's *The Age of Permanent Revolution,* edited by Trotsky's definitive biographer Isaac Deutscher (Dell, 1964). For the anarchist point of view, read Peter Kropotkin's *Memoirs of a Revolutionist* and *Revolutionary Pamphlets* (both Dover Publications, New York; Constable, 1970).

FRANÇOIS DE MONTCORBIER ('VILLON') (1431– after 1462).
Poems. Edited by R. Guiette (1964). Translated by Galway Kinnell (bilingual; Houghton Mifflin, 1978) and by Peter Dale (Macmillan, 1973).

Villon was brought up in Paris by Guillaume de Villon, a chaplain who remained his patron. He graduated as Master of Arts in 1452 but fell among thieves and in 1455 killed a priest, then next year took part in the robbery of 500 gold pieces from the Collège de Navarre. He now wrote the *Lais* or *Petit Testament,* facetiously bequeathing his worthless belongings to friends, enemies and false mistress. He then wandered around France for five years until he was imprisoned in 1461 by the Bishop of Orléans. Released by order of Louis XI, Villon now composed the *(Grand) Testament,* a great poem of 2,000 or so lines which develops the 'legacy' theme but also interpolates the great ballads (some written earlier) by which he is remembered, such as the 'Ballade des dames du temps jadis'. Again twice arrested in 1462, he was sentenced to death, and wrote the mocking 'Ballade des pendus' before his sentence was quashed and he vanished into exile.

The violence of his life and the direct appeal of his brilliant poetry make Villon an irresistible figure.

SSU-MA CH'IEN (145– *c.* 86 B.C.).
    Shih Chi. Partially translated by Burton Watson as *Records of the Grand Historian of China* (2 vols., Columbia U.P., 1961).

The *Shih Chi* has been revered as a literary classic by Chinese, Japanese and Korean scholars for two thousand years. Shortly after Emperor Wu acceded in 141 B.C., he appointed Ssu-ma T'an to be Grand Historian, a position which then carried with it the tasks of astrologer and augur. But the Court historian began to collect materials for a history of China and, on his deathbed, charged his son Ssu-ma Ch'ien to write the work. The Emperor did appoint Ssu-ma Ch'ien as his father's successor in the post, and the work was compiled, over the next twenty years, despite his having to travel with the Emperor on many tours of inspection, and despite castration and a three-year imprisonment when the Emperor was displeased with his historian's defence of a defeated general.

Court historians were known at least a thousand years before the time of Ssu-ma Ch'ien, but their histories have been lost in the many wars and disturbances since, notably during the notorious 'burning of the books' under the Ch'in.

Burton Watson's masterly translation accounts for that section (fifty per cent of the Tokyo edition of 1934) covering the Han dynasty. Ssu-ma Ch'ien is a vivid biographer and historian. He divides his book into 'Basic Annals' (on the imperial court); 'Tables of Events' (chronologies of the imperial families and lists of officials); the 'Records' of aspects of government such as administration, court ceremony, finance; the 'Noble Families' (accounts of the history of the families of the leading feudal princes and the 'Biographies' of other celebrities, such as poets, philosophers, and great merchants. Archaeological and documentary evidence has proved the authenticity of most of Ssu-ma Ch'ien's narrative.

For Han archaeology, read *Princes of Jade* (Nelson, 1973) by Edmund Capon and William MacQuitty.

REINER KUNZE (b. 1933).
    Poems, Stories and *Die Wunderbaren Jahre.* First published 1976. Translated by Ewald Osers as *The Lovely Years* (Sidgwick & Jackson, 1978) and by Joachim Neugroschel (Braziller, 1977).

The quiet voice of protest against totalitarianism. Irony and the fable are the weapons of the mild-mannered East German poet whose work was banned in his own country but found immediate success in West Germany with his poems *Sensible Wege* (1969) and *Zimmerlautstärke* (1972) and the stories in *Der Löwe Leopold* (1971).

His satirical poem 'Die Bringer Beethovens' ('The Bringers of Beethoven') deals with a certain man, M., who preferred not to listen to Beethoven's Symphony No. 5 when the authorities ask him to, urge him to, and force him to.

Die Wunderbaren Jahre is an oblique prose work about adolescents at school, at home, and on holiday which appeared in West Germany in 1976. Kunze was instantly expelled from the East German Writers' Union, and was finally compelled to emigrate to West Germany in April 1977.

An anthology of Kunze's poetry was translated by Ewald Osers under the title *With the Volume Turned Down* (London Magazine Editions, 1973).

JEAN BAPTISTE POQUELIN ('MOLIERE') (1622–1673).
   Selected Plays. *The Misanthrope and other Plays* (including translations of *Le Misanthrope, Le Sicilien, Le Tartuffe, Le Médecin malgré lui* and *Le Malade Imaginaire* by John Wood). (Penguin, 1959). And *The Miser and other Plays* (including translations of *L'Avare, Le Bourgeois Gentilhomme, Les Fourberies de Scapin, L'Amour Médecin* and *Dom Juan* by John Wood). (Penguin, 1962).

Molière, after a Jesuit education in Clermont, founded a theatrical company in Paris with the Béjarts and others, and toured France as an actor with the company from 1645 to 1658. His first important comedy of manners, *Les Précieuses Ridicules,* was produced in 1659, and from then on he wrote numerous plays, chiefly comedies ridiculing a foible of society or human nature. Before his day, the farces of intrigue had been based on the stock characters of the Italian *commedia dell' arte.* Now, with careful writing to replace the earlier improvisation and consistent characterisation of familiar social types, comedy took on a darker tinge, and attacks were made on Molière for challenging hypocrisy in *Tartuffe,* while his treatment of the Don Juan theme vanished from the boards completely after a fortnight's run. *Le Bourgeois Gentilhomme* (1670) is the favourite with modern audiences, for it shows a social climber in all his absurdity but does not suggest that he is evil or even at all reprehensible, merely a lasting figure of fun, or perhaps even to be pitied . . .

The 'Livre de Poche' edition of Molière's *Théâtre complet* is in four volumes, with notes. There is no complete English translation. The further enjoyment of Molière is suggested for Year 25.

BORIS PASTERNAK (1890–1960).
   Doctor Zhivago. First published in Italian (Feltrinelli, 1957). Translated
   from the Russian (first published 1959) by Max Hayward and Manya Harari
   (Collins, 1969).

Pasternak's literary work can be divided roughly into two periods: the first of lyric
and epic poetry, predominantly the years from 1917 to 1932; and the second of
silence during the age of official Socialist Realism, when Pasternak made the
finest Russian translations from Shakespeare, until 1953. Though his work was
banned, he was awarded the Nobel Prize in 1958 (the year after *Doctor Zhivago*
had appeared in the West), but was forced to decline it as a result of mounting
political pressure.
   Doctor Zhivago includes a panoramic view of Russian history during the first
thirty years of the twentieth century, a classic love story, and philosophical and
religious observations on questions of life, morals, and power which inevitably
drew attention to the inadequacies of Marxism as a way of life, and to the bloody
events during and after the Russian Revolution that led to the emasculation
under Stalinism of intellectual and artistic activity. Pasternak's great novel, in the
full tradition of Tolstoy and Dostoevsky, concludes with a celebration of
individual integrity and the primacy of human love over ideology.

———

FRANCOIS-MARIE AROUET ('VOLTAIRE') (1694–1778).
   Candide. First published 1759. Translated by John Butt (Penguin, 1970).
   Zadig and *L'Ingénu.* First published 1747 and 1767. Translated by John
   Butt (Penguin, 1946). *Select Letters.* Translated and edited by Theodore
   Besterman (Nelson, 1963).

Voltaire was a universal genius: satirist, wit, dramatist, poet, novelist, historian,
philosopher, critic, and one of the most stylish letter-writers ever published.
   As a historian, he is best known for the solid *Le Siècle de Louis XIV* (1751). *The
Philosophy of History* (1765) is a major collection of thoughtful essays. His plays,
verse and criticism are generally undervalued today, but there is no shortage of
admirers of his philosophical short stories.
   Candide satirizes what Voltaire considered to be the irrational optimism of
Leibnitz in the person of Dr Pangloss, whose perennial view is that "everything is
for the best in this best of all possible worlds".
   Zadig, first published as *Memnon,* deals with a youth who practises all the
virtues but still meets with misfortune. An angel finally explains that some good
comes out of all evil, and that everything is predestined. Voltaire snipes at clerical
practices and Roman Catholic church dogma in *Zadig* and also in *L'Ingénu,*
about a youth, born in Canada of French parents, who spends twenty years

among the Huron Indians and, arriving in France, finds much to wonder at in Roman Catholic tenets and much to attack in the bureaucracy of Louis XV.

Voltaire's twelve thousand letters have been published in more than 100 volumes edited by Besterman, whose selection can be relied upon for enduring interest.

GAIUS PLINIUS CAECILIUS SECUNDUS (PLINY) (*c.* 62–*c.* 113 A.D.).

Letters. Texts of the surviving correspondence by the Younger Pliny with an English translation by Betty Radice in the Loeb Classical Library (2 vols., Heinemann & Harvard U.P., 1969) for those who wish a bilingual edition. A. N. Sherwin-White has edited *Fifty Letters of Pliny* (2nd ed., Oxford U.P., 1969) and written a historical and social commentary entitled *The Letters of Pliny* (Oxford U.P., 1966). Mrs Radice has also translated *The Letters of the Younger Pliny* (Penguin, 1963).

Pliny the Elder, uncle to the letter-writer we know as the Younger Pliny, was a naturalist whose love of noting facts at second-hand (he claimed to have recorded 20,000 in his *Natural History* from 473 authors) was perverted by the credulity of medieval writers to a variety of superstitious dogmas.

Pliny the Younger was helped in his government career by his uncle, and befriended both Tacitus and Suetonius. His *Letters* were written for publication, the first 247 appearing in print during his own lifetime. Posterity views the letters with equal appreciation, for they combine readability with important information on the manners and life of the 2nd century A.D. Among the many anecdotes is a description of the early Christians.

Pliny the Elder died while helping victims of the great Vesuvian eruption of A.D. 79 which buried Pompeii and Herculaneum. Look now at a book on these ancient cities such as Brion's *Pompeii and Herculaneum* (Elek, 1960), and then at a more general work such as Sir Mortimer Wheeler's *Roman Art and Architecture* (Thames & Hudson, 1964).

Year 6

The Poem Itself, edited, and with an introduction, by Stanley Burnshaw. (Holt, Rinehart & Winston, 1960; Penguin, 1964).

Forty-five poets in French, Italian, Spanish, Portuguese and German are represented in this anthology of over 150 poems. Each poem has a literal line-by-line translation ideal for novices, a word-by-word commentary on its text, notes on the poet, and aids to pronunciation. An appendix gives the same treatment to a Russian poem by Blok. All of the poets except Hölderlin (b. 1770), Belli (b. 1791) and Leopardi (b. 1798) were born in the 19th and 20th centuries, and most are well-known to an English-speaking audience.

Burnshaw's method seems to be the most satisfactory yet devised (though he admits that accompanying records would add even more to the reader's enjoyment) for recapturing the excitement of the poet's own hand and voice in flow. *The Poem Itself* is an ideal bedside book all the year round.

MAX FRISCH (b. 1911).
Andorra. First published 1961. Translated by Michael Bullock (Methuen, 1962). And *Stiller.* First published 1954. Translated by Michael Bullock as *I'm not Stiller* (Penguin, 1961).

Frisch, who practised as an architect in Zürich, was involved in local and international politics, acting – in the phrase of Günter Grass – as a productive irritant within his native environment. His controversial statements in unpopular causes can be read alongside his plays and fiction in the Suhrkamp collected edition of his works without incongruity.

The play *Andorra,* influenced by Brecht, attacks anti-Semitism, prejudice and complacency in society. The novel *Stiller* is divided into two unequal parts: the notebooks in prison of the sculptor Anatol Ludwig Stiller, and a brief postscript by the Public Prosecutor. The constantly-slipping identity of Stiller and his complex relationship with his wife form some of the problems in this absorbing study, which merits comparison with the best of Thomas Mann.

Frisch has written many more plays and novels, constantly developing in new directions: perhaps the most interesting later novels are *Homo Faber* (1957; translated by Michael Bullock, Penguin, 1959) and *Mein Name sei Gantenbein* (1964; translated by Michael Bullock as *A Wilderness of Mirrors*, Methuen, 1965).

La Chanson de Roland. Probably composed in its 'Oxford' version in the late 11th or early 12th century. Edited by J. Bédier (1947). Translations by D. L. Sayers (Penguin, 1957), P. Terry (Bobbs – Merrill, 1965) and by D. D. R. Owen (Allen & Unwin, 1972).

The so-called 'Oxford' version of *The Song of Roland* (possibly set down by Turoldus, whose name occurs in the last line) is an epic poem based on some historical events. Thus, Charlemagne did invade Spain in 778 at the invitation of two Muslim princes, occupied Pamplona, but was unable to take Saragossa. He then withdrew, sacking Pamplona and taking one of the formerly allied princes with him as hostage. Ambushed in a mountain pass north of Roncesvalles, the rearguard of Charlemagne's army was massacred, the hero Roland among them.

These events were celebrated in numerous songs, not only in Old French, but also in Latin, Provençal, Basque and German. By common consent the 'Oxford' version in Old French is the finest celebration. The friendship of Oliver and Roland, demonstrating the medieval ideal of *sapientia* combined with *fortitudo,* is only one of the stirring elements in the vigorous narrative: others include the exaltation of Christendom over Islam, the enmity of Roland and his stepfather Ganelon, and the magnanimity of Charlemagne as a conqueror and lord.

FRIEDRICH DÜRRENMATT (b. 1921).
  Der Besuch der alten Dame (1956; translated as *The Visit* by P. Bowles, Cape, 1962). And *Die Physiker* (1962; translated as *The Physicists* by J. Kirkup, Samuel French, 1963).

The Swiss playwright and novelist Dürrenmatt turned to writing only when his expressionist paintings failed to achieve success in Berne in the early 1940s, and he is also passionately concerned with criticism, philosophy and astronomy.

The Visit is a typical, if not outstanding, example of Dürrenmatt's social criticism. An old lady with virtually unlimited wealth comes back to a small town to avenge herself on the man who dishonoured her. *The Physicists* is another tragi-comedy, in which three men are found in a lunatic asylum, claiming to be

Newton, Einstein and a spokesman for King Solomon. The philosophical seriousness of the theme of scientists' social responsibilities is intentionally deflated by absurdist techniques.

Dürrenmatt has also written paradoxical detective stories: *Der Richter und sein Henker* (1950; translated as *The Judge and his Hangman* by C. Brooks, Penguin, 1960); and *Das Versprechen* (1950; translated as *The Pledge* by R. and C. Winston (Cape and Knopf, 1959).

ÉMILE ZOLA (1840–1902).
> *Thérèse Raquin.* First published 1867. Translated by L. W. Tancock (Penguin, 1962). *L'Assommoir.* First published 1877. Translated by L. W. Tancock (Penguin, 1970). *Germinal.* First published 1885. Translated by L. W. Tancock (Penguin, 1969).

Thérèse Raquin, Zola's first major novel, deals with a married woman and her lover, the shadowy Laurent, who determine to murder Camille Raquin in order to live together openly. But Camille's paralysed old mother gradually becomes aware of what has happened, and a dreadful climax illustrates Zola's tenets, on the parallel between Naturalistic novelist and natural scientist: both, he insists, explore the physical and nervous processes of their objects of study without passing a judgement on them.

L'Assommoir and *Germinal* form parts of the 20-volume Rougon-Macquart series: 'l'histoire naturelle et sociale d'une famille sous le Second Empire' which attempts to reveal the recurrence of inherited characteristics over five generations. In *L'Assommoir,* Gervaise Macquart comes to Paris with her lover Lantier and their two children. Lantier deserts her, but she marries Coupeau and starts a laundry on borrowed money. For a while all goes well, but then Coupeau has an accident, and spends most of his time (and the housekeeping money) in the drinking-shop of the title. In *Germinal,* Gervaise's son Étienne loses his job in Lille and finally obtains employment in the coal-mines. Étienne forms a friendship with the Russian nihilist Suvarin and together they incite the miners to strike for bearable living conditions. Zola spares his reader none of the wretchedness he saw and heard about in the Paris and industrial North in his day: the result is stark, convincing, and ultimately compassionate, despite the author's well-known pseudo-scientific theories.

If you can find a copy of Zola's *L'Oeuvre* (1886; translated by Thomas Walton as *The Masterpiece,* Dufour, 1960), and read it as though you were Zola's friend, the great painter Paul Cézanne, you will be able to see why Cézanne was mortally offended and never again exchanged a letter with the novelist. This is a good time to explore the art of Cézanne in monographs such as Marcel Brion's *Cézanne* (Thames & Hudson, 1974) and his life in such works as Henri Perruchot's *La vie de Cézanne* (1956; translated by H. Hore as *Cézanne,* Perpetua, 1961).

EDGAR ALLAN POE (1809–1849).
Complete Stories and Poems (Doubleday, 1966). Among the many anthologies of selected works is the *Selected Writings* (Penguin, 1970).

Though his poems are often derivative (from Byron, Thomas Moore and their contemporaries), Poe's assimilation of various tendencies including the Tennysonian, and his mastery of a variety of verse forms and such genres as the melodramatic and the poem of suspense or even horror led to a cult of Poe which strongly influenced Baudelaire, Mallarmé, Swinburne and Hart Crane.

His stories have remained deservedly popular, and some have achieved classic status, including 'William Wilson' and 'The Fall of the House of Usher' (1839), 'The Murders in the Rue Morgue' (1841), and 'The Cask of Amontillado' (1846). Taken all in all, much of his writing is however occasional, and readers of the *Complete Works* edited by J. A. Harrison (17 vols., 1902) will find many *longueurs.*

HONORÉ BALZAC (1799–1850).
La Comédie Humaine. 92 novels collectively so called. First published 1829–1848. There is a modern edition by P. Citron (7 vols., 1966–7). Numerous translations.

Perhaps the most successful of all Balzac's huge output are those novels forming the group known as the 'Studies in Manners', which includes *Eugénie Grandet* (1833; translated by M. A. Crawford, Penguin, 1969), tracing the rise of a small vine-grower to a position of wealth and power; *Père Goriot* (1834; translated by Henry Reed, New American Library, 1962), showing 'civilized' Paris as an urban 'jungle' of the type that the American novelist Upton Sinclair was to attack in the shape of Chicago in his own *The Jungle* (1906); and the diptych 'Poor Relations': *La Cousine Bette* (1846; translated by M. A. Crawford, Penguin, 1965) and *Le Cousin Pons* (1848; translated by H. J. Hunt, Penguin, 1968).

Balzac's obsession with the authenticity of his fictions is said to have led him to interrupt a friend talking about problems at home with "Revenons à la realité. Avec qui marierons-nous Eugénie Grandet?". He worked up to fourteen hours a day on his novels, but still found time for a number of love-affairs, notably with Corntesse Éveline Hanska, whom he married shortly before his death. André Maurois' biography *Prometheus* (Harper, 1966) reads like another Balzac novel. *Louis Lambert* (1832), an autobiographical novel of a boy prodigy, is the central volume of a psychological trilogy including *La Peau de Chagrin* (1831; translated by H. J. Hunt as *The Wild Ass's Skin,* Penguin, 1977) and the Swedenborgian romance *Séraphita* (1835).

Devote two months to an exploration of Balzac's fiction.

ALEXANDER NIKOLAYEVICH OSTROVSKY (1823–1886).
  Groza. First published (in a magazine) 1860. Edited by N. Henley (Bradda, 1964). Translated by Andrew MacAndrew as *The Thunderstorm* in the anthology *19th Century Russian Drama* (Bantam, 1963).

Groza, first performed in Moscow in 1859, is one of Ostrovsky's greatest plays, with *Les* (1871; translated by C. V. Winslow and G. R. Noyes as *The Forest,* 1926) and the early *Svoi Lyudi Sochtemsya* (1850; translated by G. R. Noyes as *It's a Family Affair,* 1917).

David Magarshack has translated *Easy money and two other plays: Even a Wise Man Stumbles, and Wolves and Sheep* (1944; reprinted by the Greenwood Press).

Ostrovsky is a satirist and social critic in his earlier plays. *Groza* deals with life in a provincial town on the Volga, with its vindictiveness and narrow-mindedness. A wild, poetic girl called Katya falls in love with a man not her husband, and suffers the consequences: even now the part of Katya is eagerly sought on the Russian stage. The play gave Leoš Janáček the plot for his opera *Katya Kabanova,* sung in Czech on Supraphon (2 discs, SUAST 50781–2).

Incidentally, Ostrovsky's great fairy-tale *Snegurochka* (The Snow Maiden), first published in 1873, was used by Rimsky-Korsakov in his opera of the same title, sung in Russian on Decca (4 discs, GOS 642/5).

GILBERT KEITH CHESTERTON (1874–1936).
  The Father Brown Stories. (Cassell, 1949).

A Roman Catholic controversialist who sided with his friend Hilaire Belloc against the radical socialism of Shaw and H. G. Wells, Chesterton was an exuberant wit, inclining to paradox, a short-story writer, and a novelist of outstanding gifts (*The Napoleon of Notting Hill,* 1904; and *The Man who was Thursday,* 1908).

His most popular writings today, now that the Johnsonian force of his personality has been to some extent forgotten, are the detective stories solved by the unpretentious, wise and penetrating cleric Father Brown, a small dumpy figure whom people are apt to ignore. Chesterton intended to ridicule the analytical and scientific methods of the Sherlock Holmes school of detection by showing that crime is related to sin, and a priest's intuition is more necessary in discovering a sinner than is a policeman's experience in discovering a criminal.

Year 7

The Penguin Book of Latin Verse, introduced and edited by Frederick Brittain. (Penguin, 1962).

'No language', stated C. R. L. Fletcher, 'has had so long or so useful a history as Latin. It was able to adapt itself to all the needs of European thought for seventeen centuries and even to take, by the pens of the hymn-writers from Saint Ambrose onwards, a new life when everything else that was Roman was decaying'.

Brittain's anthology, with its admirable prose translations at the foot of the page, takes a controversial position by devoting 263 of its 363 pages to writers after Prudentius (348– c. 410), including Notker, Stephen Langton, Petrarch, Castiglione, Sir Thomas More, Ronsard, Donne, Vaughan, Baudelaire and Swinburne. If Catullus, Virgil and Horace still seem to dominate the collection, at least Brittain has proved his case for the continuity and ubiquity of Latin to our own day.

NAGAI KAFU (1879–1959).
    Kafu the Scribbler: the Life and Writings (by) Edward Seidensticker. (Stanford U.P., 1965).

Part 1 is an account of Kafu's life and Part 2 a selection from Kafu's writings in new translations, also by Seidensticker.

Kafu's two loves were the French Naturalism of Zola (whom he translated into Japanese) and the Edo culture that was disappearing as he was writing novels to celebrate the street life, the arts, and the teahouses and courtesans of the rapidly-changing capital.

Prose-poems rather than novels in the Western style, Kafu's works, such as *The River Sumida* (1909), evoke the world of Tokyo which was uncomprehendingly destroyed in the Meiji era. Kafu saw the future at first hand when spending the years from 1903 to 1908 in the U.S.A., and on his return he spent many years describing the nostalgia of those about to be overtaken by events.

TITUS MACCIUS PLAUTUS (*c.* 254–184 B.C.).
   Comedies, Texts of the surviving plays with an English translation by
   Paul Nixon in the Loeb Classical Library (5 vols., Heinemann & Harvard
   U.P., 1916–1938) for those who wish a bilingual edition. Translations
   include the uneven *Complete Roman Drama* (2 vols., Random House, 1942)
   edited by George E. Duckworth, which also contains Terence's comedies
   and Seneca's tragedies; *Six Plays* translated by Lionel Casson (Doubleday,
   1963); and *The Rope and other Plays* and *The Pot of Gold and other Plays*
   translated by E. F. Watling (Penguin, 1964–5).

Plautus learnt his stage-craft as an actor, and was not afraid to repeat plots,
devices and even speeches from the Greek New Comedy or from his own earlier
output. He is believed to have written over 100 plays; 21 survive, including some
in fragmentary form. Though not an innovator, Plautus can be read today for an
insight into the kind of production that one might have witnessed in the Roman
theatres throughout Italy and the Empire. *Casina* is the only one of the *Six Plays*
in the Casson version above not also represented in the Watling version.
Watling's extra plays are *Captivi, Miles gloriosus,* and *Mostellaria.*

JUAN RUIZ, *Archpriest of Hita* (*c.* 1283–*c.* 1350).
   Libro de Buen Amor. First published 1790 in expurgated form. Cheapest
   reliable edition is that by J. Joset in Clásicos Castellanos (2 vols., 1974).
   Translated by E. K. Kane as *The Book of Good Love* (University of North
   Carolina Press, 1969).

The only major Spanish literary work of the 14th century, the 'Book of Good
Love' is an extraordinary long poem deriving from the Scriptures, civil and canon
law, the stories of Don Juan Manuel, Ovid, a 12th-century Latin comedy entitled
Pamphilus, the *Carmina Burana,* Goliardic verse, and the catechism, among
other sources no less diverse. Irony, parody and coarse laughter are never far
from the surface (we do not even know if the author was in fact an 'archpriest' at
all), and the most amusing sections concern the doings of a notorious old
procuress called Trotaconventos, and her attempts to obtain mistresses for the
author. If the phrase 'medieval literature' sounds ominously dull and ponderous,
the playful Juan Ruiz will quickly convince the reader of the opposite.

MARCUS TULLIUS CICERO (106–43 B.C.).
Selected Works. Translated with an introduction by Michael Grant.
(Penguin, 1965).

The Loeb Classical Library has published 28 volumes of the works of Cicero with facing English translation, and the specialist will require all or most of these. The general reader, however, will be satisfied with the above selection, which contains *Against Verres* I, twenty-three letters, the second Philippic against Antony (who later demanded the 'head of the man who had openly inveighed against me in the Senate'), *On Duties* III, and *On Old Age*. For background reading, there is F. R. Cowell's *Cicero and the Roman Republic* (Penguin, 1956).

Other notable volumes of selections are *Selected Political Speeches* (Penguin, 1969), translated by Michael Grant; and *Nine Orations and the Dream of Scipio* (New American Library, 1967), translated by Palmer Bovie.

CHARLES SINGER.
A Short History of Scientific Ideas to 1900. (Oxford U.P., 1962).

The general reader may go through life with only the haziest notion about the development of science, the slow progress of scientific method, and its enemies in dogma and superstition. Singer's is one of dozens of highly readable surveys in this field, but it is still probably the best.

Creative writing in the field includes Bertolt Brecht's *Leben des Galilei* (written in 1938 but not published until 1955; translated by Eric Bentley in *The Life of Galileo in Seven Plays,* Grove Press, 1961); the poetry of the Czech scientist Miroslav Holub; the long Epicurean poem *De rerum natura* of Lucretius; and the corpus of literature centred on the astrologer/astronomer Johann Faust or Faustus.

To offset Singer's Western bias (and your own), set aside some time to read the introductory volume to Joseph Needham's monumental *Science and Civilisation in China* (Cambridge U.P., 1954) and Debiprasad Chattopadhyaya's *Science and Society in Ancient India* (K. P. Bagchi, 286 B. B. Ganguly Street, Calcutta 700 012). If you prefer studying technology to studying science, read T. K. Derry and T. I. Williams' *A Short History of Technology* (Oxford U.P., 1970).

EMILY JANE BRONTË (1818–1848).
Wuthering Heights. First published 1847. Current editions include Everyman's Library (with a selection of poems, Dent and Dutton, 1964); World's Classics (with Charlotte Brontë's memoir of Emily and Anne, Oxford, U.P., 1901); and David Daiches' edition (Penguin, 1970).

This haunting masterpiece is only technically Emily's first book for, as Mary Visick proves in *The Genesis of 'Wuthering Heights'* (2nd ed. Oxford U.P., 1965), the well-rounded characters of the novel appeared nebulously in the 'Gondal Poems', a manuscript which Charlotte accidentally discovered in 1845. C. W. Hatfield has edited Emily's *Complete Poems* (Columbia U.P., 1941).

Wuthering Heights is a remarkable first novel which springs from the dour people and countryside around Haworth and the moors where Emily spent her life. For another glimpse of the writer, read Charlotte Brontë's novel *Shirley* (1949), whose heroine was based on Emily.

PUBLIUS VERGILIUS MARO (VIRGIL) (70–19 B.C.).
> *Aeneid.* Text with an English translation in the *Works* of Virgil translated by H. R. Fairclough in the Loeb Classical Library (2 vols., Heinemann & Harvard U.P., 1935) for those who wish a bilingual edition. The best verse translation of recent years is that by Rolfe Humphries (Scribner's, 1950); also to be recommended are the versions by W. F. Jackson Knight (Penguin, 1956) and by P. Dickinson (New American Library, 1965).

Virgil's epic poem on the glory of Rome from its (spurious) origin at the fall of Troy to the time of the first Roman Emperor, Augustus, was a conscious attempt to endow his city with a poem to equal the *Iliad* of Homer. Towards the end of his life, however, he felt sure that he had failed, and gave orders that on his death the MS. should be destroyed. Augustus countermanded the provisions of the will, and the *Aeneid* has stood ever since as a model of the grand style, an explicit model for the *Commedia* of Dante, for Chaucer, Spenser, Ariosto and Tasso.

Five German Tragedies, translated with an introduction by F. J. Lamport (Penguin, 1969).

Five plays suggestively collected together in chronological order of their completion and (incidentally) of their authors' date of birth.

Emilia Galotti (1772) is a psychological tragedy by Gotthold Ephraim Lessing (1729–1781) set in a minor 18th-century Italian court. *Egmont* (1787) was begun in the *Sturm und Drang* period of Goethe (1749–1832) but not completed until 1787, nearly twenty years later. Like his earlier *Götz von Berlichingen, Egmont* has little by way of plot but shows the downfall of a great man as a result of treachery and despotism. *Maria Stuart* (1800) is the most significant play by Friedrich Schiller (1759–1805), showing Elizabeth I's confrontation with the Catholic Mary Stuart (which never in historical truth took place). *Penthesilea* (1808) by Heinrich von Kleist (1777–1811) and *Medea* (1820) by Franz Grillparzer

(1791–1872) are tragedies based on themes from classical antiquity. Kleist was to commit suicide, and his violent, morbid nature is memorably exemplified in *Penthesilea,* a clash between the heroine as wholly feminine and Achilles the hero as wholly masculine. *Medea* is the last play in Grillparzer's *Golden Fleece* trilogy: it is less about the daughter of the King of Colchis than about the Fleece itself, which symbolizes guilt, victory, and revenge, ambition and wilfulness. Together, these five plays provide an excellent survey of classical German drama.

This is an appropriate time to listen to the symphonies of Beethoven. There is an eight-disc set of all nine conducted by Herbert von Karajan (DGG 2740 172), but if you are buying them singly, choose Kleiber's Fifth (DGG 2530 516) and Klemperer's Sixth (HMV ASD 2565).

EDWARD GIBBON (1737–1794).
The History of the Decline and Fall of the Roman Empire. First published in 6 vols., 1776–88. Cheapest complete edition is in Everyman's Library, edited by Oliphant Smeaton (6 vols., Dent and Dutton, 1954). One-volume edition abridged by D. M. Low (Chatto & Windus, 1960).

Gibbon tells us that it was in 1764, amid the ruins of the Capitol in Rome, that he first conceived the idea of his life-work which was to take more than twenty years of continuous effort and finally spanned the centuries from the death of Marcus Aurelius in 180 B.C. to the fall of Constantinople in 1453.

No single scholar today can absorb what is now known on all aspects of the Roman Empire, but not even Livy and Mommsen have left behind such a lasting memorial in Roman studies. Superseded in almost all details by later research and excavation, Gibbon's *Decline and Fall* nevertheless remains a masterly synthesis which can be read with profit for its insights and its style. Gibbon's *Autobiography,* edited by Lord Sheffield in the World's Classics (Oxford U.P., 1907), shows him as a truly dedicated cosmopolitan, at home equally in France, Italy and Switzerland and master of classical and Romance languages, with an enthusiasm for science, military and political matters such that he felt able to become an M.P. (1774–8) and to take part in Shelburne's government (1779–82).

Year 8

BENEDETTO CROCE (1866–1952).
Philosophy, poetry, history: an anthology, translated by Cecil Sprigge (Oxford U.P., 1966).

These 1210 pages give an insight into the mind of the greatest of all Italian philosophers, who was as influential in aesthetics and historiography as in the study of literature. A Liberal Minister of Education (1920–1), he retired from public life when Mussolini came to power, but helped to form a new government after World War II.

His major work is the four-volume *Filosofia dello spirito* (1902–12), translated by D. Ainslie as *Aesthetic* (best ed., 1922), *Logic* (1917), *Philosophy of the Practical* (1913) and *Theory and History of Historiography* (1921).

Croce's view that all art is essentially intuitive led to the gradual fall of 19th-century critical theories and the establishment of new theories still influential today: see for example his *La Critica Letteraria* (1894), *Poesia e Non Poesia* (1923), *Poesia Popolare e Poesia d'Arte* (1933), *Poesia Antica e Poesia Moderna* (1940), and *La Letteratura della Nuova Italia* (6 vols., 1914–40).

CARLO GOLDONI (1707–1793).
Three Comedies: Mine Hostess (La Locandiera), The Boors (I Rusteghi) and *The Fan (Il Ventaglio).* Translated respectively by C. Bax, I. M. Rawson and E. & H. Farjeon (Oxford U.P., 1961).

Goldoni, Italy's immortal comic playwright, began to reform the stock improvisatory *commedia dell'arte* in 1738 with *Momolo cortesan,* introducing realistic situations, starting to abolish the masks, and providing dialogue suitable to each character. To the end of his life he was affected by the *commedia dell'arte* tradition, but never fell victim to its coarseness and repetitiveness.

He wrote in Venetian dialect, Italian, and French, and has left us with many dozens of plays as good as those listed above. The Penguin *Four Comedies* of

1968 (translated by F. H. Davies) again includes his acknowledged masterpiece *La Locandiera* (as *Mirandolina*), with *The Venetian Twins, The Artful Widow,* and *The Superior Residence.* Translations from Heinemann Educational Publishers include *It Happened in Venice, The Fan, The Liar,* and *The Servant of Two Masters,* the last a fitting epitaph to the *commedia dell' arte,* exploiting its stock characters with brilliant invention.

The standard edition is *Tutte le Opere di Carlo Goldoni,* edited by G. Ortolani (14 volumes, 1935–56). Goldoni's *Mémoires,* written·in French, are an invaluable source for life and letters, actors and acting, in 18th-century Venice and Paris. They were translated into English by J. Black (1877) but deserve a fresh version today.

Listen to the finest eighteenth-century Italian music, by Antonio Vivaldi, such as *La Stravaganza* (violin concerti, 2 Argo discs, ZRG 800-1) and *L'Estro Armonico* (concerti, 2 Argo discs, ZRG 733-4), and look at such important eighteenth-century Venetian artists as Giambattista Tiepolo (1696-1770), Francesco Guardi (1712-93) and Antonio Canal, called Canaletto (1697-1768).

Modern Arab Poets, 1950-1975, translated and edited by Issa J. Boullata. (Heinemann Educational Books, 1976).

Boullata's compilation has English translations only. For those who can read Arabic, M. M. Badawi has selected an *Anthology of Modern Arabic Verse* (Dar an-Nahar, Beirut, with Oxford U.P., 1969), and there is a useful bilingual *Anthology of Modern Arabic Poetry* translated and edited by M. A. Khouri and H. Algar (University of California Press, 1974).

Boullata publishes no poets from the Arabian Peninsula or the Maghrib; the countries represented are Iraq (as-Sayyab, al-Mala'ika, al-Bayyati, and al-Haydari), Lebanon (Hawi, al-Hajj, and al-Khal), Syria (Qabbani, Abu Dib, al-Maghut, and 'Adonis'), Egypt (as-Sabur and Hijazi), Sudan (al-Fayturi and 'Abd ar-Rahman), and Palestine (Darwish, al-Qasim, Tuqan, Jabra, Sayigh, al-Jayyusi, and Suyyagh).

Egyptian music of the modern period is best represented by the immortal Umm Kulthum, a singer whose every record was deservedly popular.

DINO BUZZATI (1906-1972).
   Il deserto dei Tartari. First published 1945. Translated by S. C. Hood as *The Tartar Steppe* (Secker & Warburg, 1952).

Buzzati, whose work has been compared for its atmosphere of unease and menace to that of Franz Kafka, has written here a fictional equivalent of Kavafis' poem 'Waiting for the Barbarians' and Beckett's play *Waiting for Godot:* waiting as the major preoccupation of one's life.

Giovanni Drogo is sent to the Bastiani Fortress, on the edge of the Tartar Steppe, and he waits for the enemy to attack. Nothing is fantastic or exaggerated: Buzzati's daily life on the staff of the *Corriere della Sera* in Milan since 1928 had given him sufficient contact with the fogs and damp of Lombard winters to diminish his sense of fantasy. On the contrary, he writes as though he (and the reader) is Drogo, and that we are all victims of a brutal, inexplicable but very practical joke.

Sessanta Racconti (Mondadori, 1958) collects most of his finest stories, often laconic or ironic, and it is as a short-story writer that most readers remember him. Now explore the films of Antonioni and Fellini.

GIORGIO VASARI (1511–1574).
　　Le Vite de' più Eccellenti Pittori, Scultori e Architettori. First published 1550; definitive edition 1568. Edited by C. L. Ragghianti, 1942–9. Translated by A. B. Hinds (4 volumes) in Everyman's Library (Dent and Dutton, 1963) unillustrated but complete. Translated in part by G. Bull unillustrated (Penguin, 1966) and illustrated (Allen Lane, 1978; Viking Press, 1979).

The first modern history of art takes the biographies of 161 Italian painters, sculptors and architects up to the year 1567. Vasari, himself a respected artist, travelled throughout the length and breadth of Italy to collect oral testimony, written documents and manuscripts, and to see paintings which he then described at first hand.

His methods were imitated by art historians of the 17th to 19th centuries, and in our own day refined by the great connoisseur Bernard Berenson, whose *Italian Painters of the Renaissance* (Phaidon Press, 1952) is only the most general of his many significant contributions. Reading Berenson's books, with those of Gombrich, Wölfflin, Saxl, Panofsky, Wittkower, and Kenneth Clark, is part of any preparation for visits to such great Italian galleries as the Uffizi and Pitti in Florence, the Vatican Museums and the Villa Borghese in Rome, the Pinacoteca of Siena, the Brera and Poldi-Pezzoli in Milan, and the great museums and galleries of Venice, Perugia and Turin.

CATULLUS (*c.* 84 – *c.* 54 B.C.).
　　Poems. Text with an English translation by F. W. Cornish in the Loeb Classical Library (Heinemann and Harvard U.P., 1913) for those who wish a bilingual edition. Of the many English versions, the two best are Frank O. Copley's *Complete Poetry of Catullus* (University of Michigan Press,

1957) and Peter Whigham's *Poems of Catullus* (Penguin, 1966).

Gaius Valerius Catullus is a brilliant, sophisticated and original poet who strikes each new generation afresh with the force of his genius. Catullus infected Latin poetry with gaiety, informality, and idiosyncrasy. He is mocking, ironic and often malicious, but never dull. The Loeb edition, with a pedestrian, literal translation, also prints the poetry of Tibullus with a translation by J. P. Postgate, and the glorious anonymous hymn to Spring and young love known as the *Pervigilium Veneris* (3rd century A.D.), which is to Roman poetry what Botticelli's *Primavera* is to Italian painting.

LUIGI PIRANDELLO (1867–1936).
   Il fu Mattia Pascal. First published 1904. Translated by William Weaver as *The Late Mattia Pascal* (Doubleday, 1964). And *Sei personaggi in cerca d'autore.* First published 1921. Translated by Frederick May as *Six Characters in Search of an Author* (Heinemann Educational, 1954).

Pirandello's lovely wife Antonietta went mad after their parents were ruined and had to be committed to an asylum in 1918, twenty-four years after their marriage. The tragedy of his personal life was written out between 1900 and 1918 in the form of short stories on the impossibility of communication between two people, and of detecting the difference between truth and illusion, sanity and madness. In later years he converted 28 of those stories into plays, and wrote a further 15 plays which established him as the most serious Italian playwright of the century. *Sei personaggi* is a radical view of human egotism and insensibility to suffering expressed in the form of a series of confrontations, each of which overturns our previous assumptions.
   A volume of plays available in Penguin (1962) contains *Cosí è (se vi pare)*, translated by Frederick May as *Right you are! (if you think so)*; *Tutto per bene*, translated by Henry Reed as *All for the best*; and *Enrico Quarto*, translated by Frederick May as *Henry IV*.
   Possibly Pirandello's greatest novel, *Il fu Mattia Pascal*, poses the dominant questions of his life in semi-autobiographical form, but with as little attention to form as in the novels of Pío Baroja. The hero wanders from his Sicilian home until he is thought dead, then assumes a new name and identity, until that too is insupportable. . .

CHARLES DARWIN (1809–1882).
   On the Origin of Species by Means of Natural Selection. First published 1859. A facsimile of the first edition has been published by Harvard U.P.

(1975), but it is the sixth edition of 1882 which is crucial, embodying all Darwin's final additions and revisions. It is this sixth ed. which Sir Arthur Keith follows in Everyman's Library (Dent and Dutton, 1972). Also available in Penguin, 1970.

Sceptics from Lucretius to Lamarck had long guessed that the theological dogma of the immutability of species was erroneous. Darwin mentions that among his predecessors who had speculated on an evolutionary theory of creation were St Hilaire, Dean Herbert, Patrick Matthew, Herbert Spencer and T. H. Huxley. Charles Darwin's own grandfather Erasmus was also of their number, as was the profoundly influential geologist Charles Lyell, whose *Principles of Geology* (Volume 1, 1830; volume 2, 1833) can be considered a neglected companion-piece no less important than Darwin's *Origin of Species*.

Darwin recognized that constant change is the principle underlying the natural world, revolutionizing our methods of thinking about ourselves and the universe we inhabit. Darwin's demonstration of the theory of natural selection provoked widespread anger and hatred among the pillars of the Establishment.

The tenacity with which the anti-evolutionists held fast their fundamentalist dogma can be illustrated by the celebrated 'Monkey Trial' of 1925 in which the biology teacher J. T. Scopes was prosecuted by the State of Tennessee. See *Monkey Trial: the State of Tennessee vs. John Thomas Scopes*, edited by S. N. Grebstein (Houghton Mifflin, 1960).

DANTE ALIGHIERI (1265–1321).
   La Vita Nuova. Completed about 1292. Editions by Barbi (Florence, 1932), Casini (1946) and others. Translations by Barbara Reynolds (superseding the 1964 version by Anderson, Penguin, 1969) and M. Musa (Indiana U.P., 1962).

Luigi Pietrobono has stated that 'The New Life' is the 'story, invariably vivid and moving, of the love for Beatrice which, despite the infidelities of Dante, finally captures the poet's entire being'. For Barbara Reynolds, it is 'a treatise by a poet, written for poets, on the art of poetry'. Between these two extreme positions, the common reader may choose a middle way, enjoying the 31 poems, mainly sonnets, as a celebration of Dante's love for a real girl, Beatrice Portinari, whom he first met in 1274, and using them as a textbook for the allegorical and symbolic treatment of human love in poetry.

La vita nuova, as an ideal preparation for the detailed reading of Dante's *Commedia*, should be read in conjunction with the unfinished *De vulgari eloquentia* (1303–5; translated by Sally Purcell as *Literature in the Vernacular*, Carcanet New Press, 1981), which is another extensive treatise on the poet's craft, urging the choice of a standard Italian vernacular as a vehicle instead of the more respectable Latin. *A Translation of the Latin Works* (Dent, 1904) by A. G. Ferrers Howell and P. H. Wicksteed in the Temple Classics series has been reprinted by the Greenwood Press. Its contents include not only *De vulgari eloquentia,* but also the *De monarchia* (about 1311–13, which argued for strong rule by the emperor), the epistles, eclogues and the *Quaestio de aqua et terra.*

HENRI BEYLE ('STENDHAL') (1783–1842).
> *Le Rouge et le Noir.* First published 1830. Translated by Lloyd C. Parks (New American Library, 1970), and rather better by M. R. B. Shaw (Penguin, 1969).

Stendhal's first major novel could not have been more topical, appearing only five months after the 'glorious days' of 1830 and the abdication of Charles IX.

Le Rouge et le Noir won great popular acclaim on its publication, of course, but we read it today as a novel of manners and character, and not for its author's Liberal, Bonapartist views. Simply told, the novel reveals a panorama of early 19th-century life in France through the tale of Julien Sorel, an ambitious but low-born hero, and through his relations with Mme. de Rênal, wife of a small-town mayor.

For an insight into the complex mind of Stendhal, read his *Private Diaries* (Gollancz, 1955), translated and edited by Robert Sage.

Year 9

DANTE ALIGHIERI (1265–1321).
> *La Commedia.* First printed 1472. (First described as 'Divina' in 1555). The best edition is that of the Società Dantesca Italiana (1921, reprinted 1960), and the most accessible of the many translations that by D. L. Sayers and Barbara Reynolds (3 vols., Penguin, 1949–1962).

Three months should be devoted to the three parts of Dante's *Commedia,* using a standard annotated text such as those of C. Grabher, M. Porena, or Scartazzini-Vandelli, together with a modern translation such as the Sayers-Reynolds (in verse) cited above or the J. D. Sinclair (in prose, with facing text, 2 vols., Oxford U.P., 1939–47).

Dante's Tuscan became the norm from which modern Italian evolved, and his poem – deriving its theology from Paul and its epic drive from Dante's avowed mentor Virgil – is the central jewel in the crown of Italian literature.

While reading the great poem use the three major accompanying sets of illustrations: *The Drawings by Sandro Botticelli for Dante's Divine Comedy* (Thames & Hudson, 1976), with introduction by Kenneth Clark and translations by the American poet John Ciardi; *Blake's Illustrations to the Divine Comedy,* with a commentary by A. S. Roe (Princeton U.P., 1953); and *The Doré Illustrations for Dante's Divine Comedy,* with captions from Longfellow's translation (Dover, 1976).

WU CH'ENG-EN (*c.* 1510–1582).
> *Hsi-yu chi.* Translated in part as *Monkey* by Arthur Waley (Penguin, 1973).

One of the greatest of all Chinese novels, *Monkey* (also known as *The Journey to the West*) can be viewed on two distinct levels: as a children's adventure story, full of tricks, magic and folklore; and as a moral fable, with satire against greed, officious bureaucrats, and a message of serenity through the practice of Buddhism. All the verse is omitted in the Waley abridgment.

The hero is the historical pilgrim Hsüan Tsang, who sought the Buddhist sutras in India in the 7th century. Wu Ch'eng-en's novel, however, gives the pilgrim, called here Tripitaka, three companions: the magic-working Monkey, the gluttonous Pigsy, and the rather shadowy figure of Sandy. In order to reach India safely, the band of four surmount many extraordinary obstacles.

BENVENUTO CELLINI (1500–1571).
> *Vita*. First published 1728. Translated by John Addington Symonds, and introduced by John Pope-Hennessy (Phaidon Press, 1949) with a certain emasculation of the text. More reliably translated by G. Bull as *The Autobiography of Benvenuto Cellini* (Penguin, 1956).

One of the leading goldsmiths and sculptors of his day, Cellini is also the greatest autobiographer of his day, having dictated his memoirs to an apprentice in his Florentine workshop beginning in 1558. For the years of his tumultous and eventful life after 1562, the sources are Cellini's *Ricordi* (private memoranda), his petitions to the Medicean princes and to the Soprasindachi of Florence, and a handful of official documents in which his name occurs.

The author's genius, egotism, and careless bravado are admirably caught too in the opera *Benvenuto Cellini* by Berlioz (4 records, Philips 6707 019). Cellini's *Treatises on Goldsmithing and Sculpture* have been translated by C. R. Ashbee (1928; Dover and Constable, 1968).

Cellini's contemporaries in Italy included the Bolognese Annibale Carracci, the Lombard Caravaggio, the Mannerist Parmigianino, and the Venetian Tintoretto. See John Shearman's *Mannerism* (Penguin, 1967).

WILLIAM SHAKESPEARE (1564–1616).
> Poems.

It is useful to read the lyric poetry of Shakespeare as a whole, for even the functional songs within the plays can stand on their own. Apart from these, the homosexual *Sonnets* (rearranged and altered in the edition entitled *Poems* of 1646 to imply that they were addressed to a woman) are the best-known of Shakespeare's lyrics.

The *Sonnets* appear with *A Lover's Complaint* in the Penguin Shakespeare of 1938, though note that the latter may be spurious.

Other poems are *Venus and Adonis* and *The Rape of Lucrece* (published respectively in 1593 and 1594 and dedicated to Henry Wriothesley, Earl of Southampton) and possibly some of the lyrics in *The Passionate Pilgrim*, an unauthorized anthology of poems by various authors, first published in 1599, and attributed on the title-page to William Shakespeare. *Venus and Adonis* and *The Rape of Lucrece* are edited together by Ridley in the New Temple Shakespeare (Dent). *The Complete Sonnets, Song and Poems* are edited by Oscar J. Campbell (Schocken, 1965).

This is the best moment to read a reliable biography, such as F. E. Halliday's *The Life of Shakespeare* (Penguin, 1964).

ITALO CALVINO (*b.* 1923).
> *I nostri antenati*. A trilogy consisting of *Il visconte dimezzato* (first published 1952), *Il barone rampante* (first published 1957), and *Il cavaliere inesistente* (first published 1959). Translated by Archibald Colquhoun as *The Non-Existent Knight & The Cloven Viscount* (Harcourt Brace, 1977) and *The Baron in the Trees* (Harcourt Brace, 1977).

Calvino is one of the most entertaining prose stylists of the century, with a fantastic imagination at times reminiscent of Piranesi and at others of Magnasco.

He first came to critical attention with the neo-realist stories of World War II in *Il sentiero dei nidi di ragno* (1947; translated by Archibald Colquhoun as *The Path to the Nest of Spiders,* 1956; reprinted by Ecco Press, 1976). His collection of fairy-tales and folk-tales *Fiabe italiane* (1956) has been translated as *Italian Folk-Tales* (Dent, 1975).

Calvino experimented, not altogether successfully, with science-fiction fables in *Cosmicomics* (1968) and *Ti con zero* (1969), both translated by William Weaver (Harcourt Brace, 1976). His irony, metaphysical playfulness, and powerful invention are more recently embodied in *Le città invisibili* (translated by William Weaver as *Invisible Cities,* Secker & Warburg and Harcourt Brace, 1975) and *Il castello dei destini incrociati* (translated by William Weaver as *The Castle of Crossed Destinies,* Secker & Warburg and Harcourt Brace, 1979).

HENRI BEYLE ('STENDHAL') (1783–1842).
> *La Chartreuse de Parme*. First published 1839. Translated by Lowell Blair (Bantam, 1960), and by M. R. B. Shaw (Penguin, 1958).

Nine years after the bitterness of *Le Rouge et le Noir,* Stendhal wrote *La Chartreuse de Parme* in seven weeks, and spoilt the end by curtailing it too hastily at the insistence of his publisher.

What remains is an adventure story of the highest quality set in a small Italian court between 1815 and 1830, tracing the career of Fabrizio del Dongo with Napoleon's armies in France and thereafter as a cleric and preacher. The most successful character is the lovely, passionate Duchessa Sanseverina, but there are numerous cameos deriving from Stendhal's understanding of the Italian character and familiarity with Italian landscapes.

Explore the historical background to the novel in Georges Lefebvre's *Napoleon* (2 vols., Routledge and Columbia U.P., 1969) and the political controversies in Pieter Geyl's *Napoleon: For and Against* (Penguin, 1965).

GIACOMO LEOPARDI (1798–1837).
> *Canti.* First published 1836. Annotated edition by Giuseppe de Robertis (Florence, 1954). Translated (with Italian text) by J. H. Whitfield (Naples, 1962), and by Geoffrey Bickersteth (*Poems,* Russell, Tampa, Fl., 1973).

Combining the descriptive powers of Wordsworth, the atmosphere of longing of Keats, and the lyrical expressiveness of Shelley, the hunchbacked Leopardi was the finest Italian poet of the 19th century, rejecting the empty rhetoric of Vincenzo Monti and the Baroque tradition so powerful in 18th-century Italy.

Though repeatedly stated to be a pessimist – even a nihilist – Leopardi found at last a humanism to transcend his despair. *Tutte le Opere* (5 vols., 1940) edited by F. Flora is worth obtaining for the complete *Zibaldone* ('Notebooks' kept from 1817 to 1832) and the 24 short dialogues and essays collected as *Operette morali.* In English there are two volumes of selections from Leopardi: the bilingual *Poems and Prose,* edited by Angel Flores (Indiana U.P., 1966), and *Selected Prose and Poetry* (Oxford U.P., 1966) edited by Iris Origo and John Heath-Stubbs.

Post-War Russian Poetry, edited with an introduction by Daniel Weissbort (Penguin, 1974).

The peculiar tensions of post-war life in the Soviet Union are hardly visible in official magazines such as *Soviet Literature.* Weissbort's anthology is naturally idiosyncratic (including such minor figures as Kazakova and Vanshenkin), but most of the major writers are here: the full list is Akhmatova, Pasternak, Zabolotsky, Martynov, Tvardovsky, Slutsky, Soloukhin, Okudzhava, Vinokurov, Daniel, Vanshenkin, Iskander, Gorbovsky, Plisetsky, Kazakova, Rozhdestvensky, Yevtushenko, Voznesensky, Matveyeva, Sosnora, Gorbanyevskaya, Kushner, Akhmadulina, Morits and Brodsky.

Most of these poets have fuller English selections available, and Pasternak is even better known as a novelist.

For a comparison of Weissbort's selection with the officially-approved Soviet poems of the present time, see *Soviet Literature,* no. 6, 1980, devoted to 'An Anthology of Soviet Poetry, 1960-1980'.

Year 10

Medieval Literature in Translation, edited by Charles W. Jones (Longmans Green, 1950).

A thoughtful selection of translations divided into ten sections: the Christian tradition, Irish literature, Old English literature, Romanesque literature, Arthurian literature, Teutonic literature, Romance literature, Dante, Late Latin literature and Drama.

It is important to realise that modern nation-states did not exist in the Middle Ages, and that clerks (those who could read and write) generally corresponded and wrote in Latin. It is only with Dante that the vernacular begins to earn respect, and as recently as the Romantic Revival that nations sought an epic to establish their identity: the *Chanson de Roland,* the *Cantar de Mio Cid,* the Icelandic sagas, and so on.

Background books include *European Literature and the Latin Middle Ages,* by Ernst Robert Curtius (Pantheon, 1953) and *Literary Language and its Public in Late Latin Antiquity and in the Middle Ages,* by Erich Auerbach (Routledge & Kegan Paul, 1965).

MIGUEL DE CERVANTES (1547–1616).
  El ingenioso hidalgo Don Quixote de la Mancha (Part 1, 1605; part 2, 1615). Translated as *The Adventures of Don Quixote* by J. M. Cohen (Penguin, 1950).

'Children handle it, youngsters devour it, adults understand it, and old people praise it. In short, it is universally so thumbed, devoured, studied and familiar that people have only to see a hungry nag to call it "Rocinante" '. Thus spoke Cervantes of his immortal novel, with the lean Knight and his stout esquire Sancho Panza. Quixote is not merely a figure of fun, but becomes by the end of part 2 a tragic philosopher, full of both pathos and dignity.

Walter Starkie's version of the *Quixote* (New American Library, 1964) is accurate as well as readable; he has also translated some of Cervantes' *Novelas ejemplares* as *The Deceitful Marriage and other Exemplary Novels* (New American Library, 1964). J. M. Cohen has translated two of the exemplary novels ('Rinconete y Cortadillo' and 'El casamiento engañoso') with the anonymous 16th-century novel *Lazarillo de Tormes* as *Blind Man's Boy* (New English Library, 1962). There is a classic account of Quixote's route in Azorín's *La ruta de Don Quijote* (first published in 1905), edited with introduction, notes and critical study by H. Ramsden (Manchester U.P., 1966).

WILLIAM SHAKESPEARE (1564–1616).
   The historical plays, first collected in 1623 ('First Folio') with all the other canonical plays except 'Pericles'.

Shakespeare wrote imaginative dramatic biographies of a number of English kings: Henry VI (*c.* 1590–1), Richard III (*c.* 1592), Richard II (*c.* 1595), John (*c.* 1596), Henry IV (*c.* 1597–8), Henry V (*c.* 1599), and Henry VIII (with Fletcher? *c.* 1612–3).
   Henry VI was probably his earliest play, and has serious flaws, like *King John* and the collaborative *Henry VIII*. If you prefer to read the major English histories in their true historical perspective, rather than in their order of composition, then the sequence is *Richard II, Henry IV, Henry V* and *Richard III*. There are many trustworthy editions, including the Arden, the New Shakespeare from Cambridge University Press, and the New Temple, but the cheapest and most easily portable single-volume texts which can confidently be recommended are those published by Penguin.

PABLO NERUDA (1904–1973).
   Canto General. First published complete (Mexico City) in 1950. Partially translated (mainly by Anthony Kerrigan) in the *Selected Poems* of Neruda edited by Nathaniel Tarn (Cape, 1970).

Of the Chilean poet's vast *Obras Completas,* perhaps the most enduring achievement is the *Canto General.* Neruda was a lifelong communist and an ally of Allende in his shortlived government. It is worth learning Spanish for Cervantes and Gabriel García Márquez, but Neruda is a more universal figure than either in his radical view of the task of Latin American artists and intellectuals. After *Canto General,* read the poems in *Estravagario* (Cape, 1972), a bilingual edition with excellent translations by Alastair Reid, and the autobiographical *Confieso que he Vivido,* translated as *Memoirs* by H. St. Martin (Penguin, 1978).

THOMAS MANN (1875–1955).
Buddenbrooks. First published 1901. Translated by H. T. Lowe-Porter
(Penguin, 1957).

Subtitled 'the decline of a family', *Buddenbrooks* was Mann's first novel,
appearing when he was 26. The family concerned is not unlike Mann's own
mercantile family of Lübeck, North Germany, but Mann's dominant theme is
not the family itself, as it was in Galsworthy's Forsyte Saga, but the alienation of
the artist in society and the contrast of emotionalism and intellectualism. Adolf
Hitler burned and banned *Buddenbrooks:* contrast the novel's aesthetic
liberalism with the stifling frenzied ideology of Hitler's *Mein Kampf.* Other
threads that could be drawn out in connection with this novel are a study of the
Hanseatic towns, a comparison with Mann's shorter novels such as *Death in
Venice, Tristan,* and *Tonio Kröger,* and similarities between Mann's exile in the
U.S.A. and Switzerland and the exile of other German writers under Hitler, such
as Hermann Hesse, Stefan Zweig and Franz Werfel.

This is a good time to listen to the nine symphonies of Gustav Mahler
(1860–1911). The best complete set available is currently that of Solti (16 discs,
Decca 7BB 173–187 and CSP 7), but the Third is best conducted by Horenstein
(2 discs, Unicorn RHS 302–3); the Fourth by Szell (CBS Classics 61056), the
Fifth by Barbirolli (2 discs, with the 5 Rückert Lieder, HMV SLS 785), and the
Ninth by Haitink (2 discs, Philips 6700 021).

Fray GABRIEL TÉLLEZ ('TIRSO DE MOLINA') (1583–1648).
El burlador de Sevilla y convidado de piedra. First published 1630 in its
present form. The best current edition is by B. de los Ríos in Tirso's
Obras dramáticas completas (3 vols., 1947–58) but there are good texts
in Clásicos Castellanos and Colección Austral. There is no good translation
into English: the best available is Robert O'Brien's *The Rogue of Seville*
in *Spanish Drama* edited by Ángel Flores (Bantam, 1962).

Tirso's play was written against the unprincipled young noblemen of his day, in
which a young seducer (also guilty of treachery, murder, defilement of the
sacrament of marriage, *lèse-majesté,* and violation of the laws of hospitality) is
drawn down to Hell by a 'stone guest', the taunted statue of the father of one of
Juan's victims.

The theme was taken up by Molière, Goldoni, Byron, Pushkin, Montherlant,
and by Mozart in his great opera *Don Giovanni* (on 3 records, HMV SLS 5083).
Antonio de Zamora's version leaves the protagonist's fate in the balance, while
the Romantic playwright José Zorrilla (in *Don Juan Tenorio,* 1844) allows Juan to
be redeemed by the love of a chaste woman.

A near contemporary of Tirso is Diego Velázquez (1599–1660), whose art can be studied in the writings of José López-Rey available from Faber & Faber (1963 and 1968) and from Studio Vista (1980).

Songs of the Provençal Troubadours.

Provence in the twelfth century was a major centre of poetry, stimulated by late Latin lyrics, folksongs of the countryside, and the repertory of the professional *jongleurs*. Noblemen created songs on the three principal themes of love, war and honour: at least two thousand five hundred such songs have survived until the present day, some with instrumental scores. The love songs were addressed by courtiers to married women, but the genre soon spread to the betrothed. Masters such as Guiraut de Bornelh, Arnaut Daniel, Bernart de Ventadorn, and Bertrand de Born paved the way for French lyric poets up to the fourteenth and fifteenth centuries, including Guillaume de Machaut.

Bilingual editions of the troubadours, greatly to be preferred to mere translations, include *Lyrics of the Troubadours and Trouvères: an Anthology and a History,* translated and introduced by Frederick Goldin (Anchor, 1973); and *Anthology of Troubadour Lyric Poetry,* edited by Alan R. Press (Edinburgh U.P., 1971). *Anthology of the Provençal Troubadours,* edited by Thomas Goddard Bergin (2 vols., Yale U.P., 1973) contains texts, notes and vocabulary, but is much more expensive than Goldin or Press.

Listen to the album 'The Art of Courtly Love' (from Machaut to Dufay) by the Early Music Consort of London, directed by David Munrow (3 records, HMV SLS 863).

CAMILO JOSÉ CELA (b. 1916).
  Viaje a la Alcarria. First published 1948. Translated as *Journey to the Alcarria* by F. M. López-Morillas (University of Wisconsin Press, 1964).

A deceptively plain manner conceals one of the most remarkable travel books by a great novelist, whose *La familia de Pascual Duarte* (1942) helped to spread the vogue for *tremendismo* in the Spanish novel.

Cela called his book 'ancient' in the sense of the classical travel book – offering the truth, simplicity and straightforward descriptions of the new and strange that one finds in the *Travels* of Marco Polo. And Cela's Alcarria is indeed not on the wellworn tourist route: it is the area enclosed by Guadalajara, Brihuega, Cifuentes and Córcoles, northwest of Madrid. The average traveller would pass through it without a second glance. But Cela's poetic vision allows him to record the essential and accidental with a master's touch surpassing that of Stevenson in

Travels with a Donkey. You might also enjoy Cela's other travel books: *Del Miño al Bidasoa* (1952), *Primer viaje andaluz* (1959), and *Viaje al Pirineo de Lérida* (1965), and his later *Madrid* (1966) and *Barcelona* (1970).

P'U SUNG-LING (1640–1715).
> *Liao-chai chih-i*. First published in 1766. Partially translated by H. A. Giles as *Strange Stories from a Chinese Studio* (Dover, 1966).

An enormously popular collection of tales (431 in the original; 164 in Giles) which combines moral sayings with fantasies of devils, ghosts and magic. P'u Sung-ling's style is succinct, allusive an witty. There is nothing comparable to the *Liao-chai* in English: perhaps its closest relation is the *Alf layla wa layla* (or *Arabian Nights*). P'u Sung-ling may also be the author, according to Hu Shih, of the pseudonymous *Hsing-shih yin-yüan chuan,* a story of a shrewish wife somewhat akin to Alfredo Panzini's *Santippe* (1914), a satire on the wife of Socrates.

P'u was a contemporary of the brothers Wang Kai, Wang Shih and Wang Nieh who were responsible for preparing the illustrations for the painting manual most widely used in China – the *Chieh Tzu Yüan Hua Chuan* (1679–1701) translated and edited by Mai-mai Sze as *The Mustard Seed Garden Manual of Painting* (Princeton U.P., 1977).

ANTONIO MACHADO (1875–1939).
> *Juan de Mairena: epigrams, maxims, memoranda, and memoirs of an apocryphal professor, with an appendix of poems from 'The Apocryphal Songbooks'*. First published 1936. Translated by Ben Belitt (University of California Press, 1963).

Mairena, and his teacher Abel Martín, are two of the thirteen 'doubles' invented by Machado to explore a variety of viewpoints and attitudes, philosophies and modes of feeling. Machado is even better known as a poet. His *Poesías completas* (Espasa-Calpe, 1940) and the supplementary *Prosas y poesías olvidadas* (1964) are often dark to the point of despair, but the happy period of the sequence 'Campos de Castilla', with its eager borrowings from Spanish ballads, gave Machado's work an extra dimension. There are no complete translations of Machado's poetry into English.

Year 11

LOPE FÉLIX DE VEGA CARPIO (1562–1635).
> *Obras escogidas* (3rd ed., 3 vols., Aguilar, Madrid, 1958). (The first and third
> volumes contain a selection of the 500 plays by Lope de Vega, while the
> second is devoted to selected poems, prose, and the novels *La Arcadia,
> Pastores de Belén, Novelas a Marcia Leonarda,* and *La Dorotea*). *Five Plays*
> translated by Jill Booty (Hill and Wang, 1961).

It is virtually impossible to propose a truly representative array of Lope's works, for his plays are as varied and exciting as his life. But Jill Booty, the best translator of Lope so far, has chosen wisely: *Peribáñez* (1610?), *Fuentovejuna* (1613?), *El Perro del Hortelano* (entitled here 'The Dog in the Manger'), *El Caballero de Olmedo* ('The Knight from Olmedo'), and *El Castigo sin Venganza* ('Justice without Vengeance', 1631).

The phrase 'Es de Lope' ('it is by Lope') is still used to commend a prodigy of perfection, and indeed the extraordinary quality of his stagecraft and verbal genius contrasts notably with those of Lope de Rueda, the leading Spanish playwright at the time of the Phoenix's birth. Lope de Vega took part in the ill-fated Spanish Armada, was involved in numerous seductions and abductions, and was eventually ordained as a priest. Himself a fitting hero for one of his own 'capa y espada' productions, Lope de Vega is considered the Spanish Shakespeare.

See Heinz Gerstinger's *Lope de Vega and Spanish Drama* (Ungar, 1974).

WANG CH'UNG (27–*c.* 97 A.D.).
> *Lun-Heng*. Philosophical and Miscellaneous Essays. Translated by August
> Forke (2nd ed., 2 vols., Paragon Book Gallery, New York, 1962).

We do not possess the entire body of the *Lun-Heng,* which originally consisted of more than a hundred essays or chapters. Only 84 survive in Chinese, and of these Forke has translated 44. In his introduction to a modern Chinese edition, Yu Chun Hsi defends the Han sceptic against those traditionally scandalised by any kind of attack on Mencius, Confucius, and other canonical writers and compilers. 'People of the Han period', he remarks, 'were fond of fictions and fallacies. Wang Ch'ung pointed out whatever was wrong; in all his arguments he used a strict and thorough method, and paid special attention to meanings. Rejecting erroneous notions he came near the truth. Nor was he afraid of disagreeing with the worthies of old. Thus he furthered the laws of the State, and opened the eyes and ears of the scholars. People reading his books felt a chill at first, but then they repudiated all falsehood and became just and good. They were set right, and discarded all crooked doctrines'.

Characteristic of Wang Ch'ung's approach is his refutation of the objective reality of ghosts. 'When people are sick', he writes, 'they are inclined to melancholy and easily frightened. In this state of mind they see ghosts appear'

JUAN DE YEPES, *later* JUAN DE SAN MATIA *and* JUAN DE LA CRUZ (St. John of the Cross) (1542–1591).
Poesías completas de San Juan de la Cruz, edited by Dámaso Alonso (Aguilar, Madrid, 1963). The 1963 edition has all the poems and a commentary. English translations include those by Edgar Allison Peers (*The Complete Works,* Burns, Oates & Washbourne, 1934) and by K. Kavanaugh and O. Rodríguez (*The Collected Works,* Doubleday, 1963).

Born at Fontiveros, in Castile, Juan lost his father at the age of five, and had to work in a Medina del Campo hospital until he came under the protection of a wealthy merchant, who financed his studies at a Jesuit school. Juan entered the Carmelite Order in 1563, and nine years later became Teresa de Ávila's spiritual director. He remained active in reform of the Carmelites until he was imprisoned by unreformed monks in 1577, and spent nearly nine months in a single cell, with only an hour each day outside, and a compulsory weekly interrogation, during which he was continually humiliated.

During this period of enforced isolation he wrote the poems that have made his name immortal in the literature of mysticism: the 'Llama de amor viva', the 'Cántico espiritual', and the 'Noche oscura', to give them their familiar titles. All three have been translated by Roy Campbell in his selection *Poems* (Penguin, 1960). They are concerned with the path to perfect union with God, and Juan saw that he was fortunate in his suffering, which made solitude and contemplation necessary. Frequent references to carnal love make the poems immediately attractive to secular readers.

El Greco, as Domenikos Theotokopoulos was known in Spain (in fact he was a Cretan, not a Greek), was a contemporary of San Juan in Toledo, and was equally inspired in his art. El Greco's paintings – some of the city of Toledo itself and many of its inhabitants – can be studied best in *El Greco y Toledo* (Espasa-Calpe,

Madrid, 1956) by Gregorio Marañón; and in English there is Ludwig Goldscheider's *El Greco* (latest edition, Phaidon Press).

WILLIAM SHAKESPEARE (1564–1616).
The Comedies, first collected in 1623 ('First Folio') with all the other canonical plays except *Pericles*.

There is no clear-cut division of Shakespeare's plays into 'comedies', 'tragedies' and so on. But it would be reasonable to consider the following plays in some sort as 'comedies' in roughly chronological order, to show the dramatist's development: *The Comedy of Errors* (1593– like all other dates, an approximation to the year of composition), *The Taming of the Shrew* (1594), *Love's Labour's Lost* (1594), *A Midsummer Night's Dream* (1595), *The Two Gentlemen of Verona* (1595), *The Merchant of Venice* (1596), *Much Ado About Nothing* (1599), *The Merry Wives of Windsor* (1600), *As You Like It* (1600), *Twelfth Night* (1601), *All's Well That Ends Well* (1602), and *The Tempest* (1611). There are many trustworthy editions of individual plays, including the Arden, the New Shakespeare from Cambridge U.P., and the New Temple, but the cheapest and most easily portable single-volume texts which can confidently be recommended are those published by Penguin.
A truly magnificent adaptation by Benjamin Britten has brought *A Midsummer Night's Dream* to the opera house and the record turntable (3 discs, Decca SET 338/40). Berlioz transformed *Much Ado About Nothing* into *Béatrice et Bénédict* (some dialogue omitted 2 discs, Oiseau-Lyre SOL 256/7). There are three excellent current versions of Verdi's *Falstaff,* based on *The Merry Wives of Windsor:* perhaps the finest is Karajan's (3 discs, HMV SLS 5037).

GABRIEL GARCÍA MÁRQUEZ (b. 1928).
Cien años de soledad. First published 1967. Translated by Gregory Rabassa as *One Hundred Years of Solitude* (Pan, 1978).

Unlike any other novel in its mixture of comedy, fantasy, magic, exoticism, obsessive repetition, and simple wonder at the world of South America: its jungles, lust and fatalism through the laconic eyes of a twentieth-century sophisticate, *Cien años de soledad* is set in an imaginary town of Macondo that was hacked from the jungle and will revert ultimately, when all is said and done, to the jungle. Macondo is based on the author's home town, Aracataca.
'Many years later', the book begins, 'as he faced the firing squad, Colonel Aureliano Buendía was to remember that distant afternoon when his father took him to discover ice'. Macondo, two years' march from the northern coast of Colombia, was founded by José Arcadio Buendía. His friend Melquíades

possesses a Sanskrit MS about the future of his family; this MS, translated into Castilian, is this novel and Melquíades is found to be the narrator. Incest, incessant rain, drought, plague, imperialism and civil wars march through Macondo during seven generations of the Buendía family. The parallel opening of Cervantes in the *Quijote's* introduction, the Biblical analogies, the playful yet bitter reflection of the traditional Latin American conflict between *civilización* and *barbarie:* everything blends to make Garcıa Márquez's masterpiece quite unforgettable.

The magic realism exemplified in *Cien años de soledad* recurs in other novels and long stories, each as compelling in its own way, such as *La Hojarasca* (1955; translated by Rabassa as *Leaf Storm,* Pan, 1979), *El Coronel no tiene quien le escriba* (1961; translated by J. S. Bernstein as *No one writes to the Colonel,* Pan, 1979) and *El otoño del patriarca* (1975; translated by Rabassa as *The Autumn of the Patriarch,* Pan, 1978).

The other great Colombian novelist is J. E. Rivera, whose *La Vorágine* (1924) has been translated by E. K. James as *The Vortex* (Putnam, 1935).

HERODOTUS (*c.* 484–*c.* 424 B.C.).
> *Historiae.* Greek text first printed in Venice by Aldus Manutius in 1502. (For the significance of this printer see Martin Lowry's *The World of Aldus Manutius,* Basil Blackwell, 1979). Text with a facing English translation by A. D. Godley in the Loeb Classical Library (4 vols., Heinemann and Harvard U.P., 1920–4). Translations by Harry Carter in World's Classics (Oxford U.P., 1962), G. Rawlinson (2 vols., Modern Library and Everyman's Library), and A. de Sélincourt (Penguin, 1954).

Called 'the Father of History' because of his systematic collection of materials and his critical attitude to sources (relative to that of his predecessors), Herodotus took for his theme the invasion of Greece by the Persians between 490 and 479 B.C. Two-thirds of the work are devoted to the history of the Greeks and Persians prior to the invasion, and there is also a condensed history of Egypt. His weaknesses include a tendency to fail to see underlying causes beneath superficial events, occasionally to mix the fabulous with the real, and to miss the interpretation of military strategy.

The strengths of Herodotus include a capacity of epic description, an unusual lack of racial or religious prejudice, boundless curiosity in nature and his fellow-men, and an ability to organize material in such a way as continuously to maintain the reader's interest to the final full stop.

To offset the natural bias of a writer born in Halicarnassus who migrated first to Samos and then to Athens, read *The Legacy of Persia,* edited by A. J. Arberry (Oxford U.P., 1953), R. Ghirshman's *Iran from the Earliest Times to the Islamic*

Conquest (Penguin, 1954), and A. T. Olmstead's *History of the Persian Empire* (University of Chicago Press, 1959).

The Penguin Book of Spanish Verse, introduced and edited by J. M. Cohen (Penguin, 1956).

I used this anthology when it was first published, and even though I now possess the complete works of many of the poets included – so important do they seem – it remains one of my most treasured possessions.

A first-rate selection of texts in authoritative readings is accompanied in usual Penguin-style by plain prose translations which do not seek to emulate the beauty of the original but simply to form a bridge towards is appreciation. This method has worked triumphantly with each succeeding Penguin Book of Verse and there is presumably no better method of becoming acquainted with a national school of poetry.

The Spanish anthology opens with an extract from the *Cantar de Mio Cid* and concludes with the Mexican poet Alí Chumacero.

Later, however, it was rightly decided to publish a separate *Penguin Book of Latin-American Verse,* edited by E. Caracciolo-Trejo (1971), which is best read much later, for it both presupposes the indigenous Spanish poetic tradition and extends it, technically, geographically and chronologically (there was a virtual vacuum of excellent new poetry in Franco's Spain).

Panchatantra. Translated by Arthur W. Ryder (University of Chicago Press and Cambridge U.P., 1925) and by Franklin Edgerton (Allen & Unwin, 1965).

The ancient Indian fables collected as *Panchatantra* (Sanskrit for 'the Five Books') have exerted an influence greater than that of any other secular collection over the centuries. The 'Five Books' deal with the five categories of worldly wisdom and the art of practical government: both the winning and the losing of friends, war and peace, the loss of one's property, and the perils of acting too hastily. But of course the 'morals' (and one uses the word with a certain sense of irony in many fables) are of much wider significance: most readers will find the stories enchanting for children as well as thought-provoking for themselves. The *Panchatantra* crossed to Europe as early as the eleventh century, but in its present form it cannot be older than the late fourth century B.C., since it contains quotations from the *Arthashastra* of Kautilya, who may have been Prime Minister to the King of Bihar around that time.

A. B. Keith's *History of Sanskrit Literature* (Oxford U.P., 1928) gives a great deal of background information, too, on the genetically-related *Hitopadesa.*

A wonderful version of some of these tales and fables is the so-called *Marzubannama* ('Tales of Marzuban'), compiled in Persian about 1220 by Sa'd al-Warawini of Azerbaijan, and translated by Reuben Levy (Indiana U.P., 1959).

This would be an appropriate moment to study the art and architecture of India at least in outline, using perhaps *The Art of India* by Stella Kramrisch (2nd ed., Phaidon Press, 1955), or the latest edition of Vincent A. Smith's *A History of Fine Art in India and Ceylon* (Oxford U.P.).

JORGE LUIS BORGES (b. 1899).

> *Obras completas* (Latest edition, Emecé Editores, Buenos Aires). Translations of Borges' stories overlap: *Fictions,* translated by Anthony Kerrigan (Calder, 1965); *Labyrinths,* translated by D. A. Yates and J. E. Irby (Penguin, 1970); *The Aleph and other stories* (with an important autobiographical essay) translated by N. T. di Giovanni (Čape, 1971), and more are appearing all the time.

In his essays, his poems, and above all in his strange stories, Borges is the myth-maker of the twentieth century. His central preoccupations are the problems of time, identity, paradox, and the cyclical nature of knowledge and history. His literary problems are stated with brevity, and possible resolutions are achieved with economy and grace. 'Funes el Memorioso' concerns the tragedy of a man unable to forget anything he had ever seen, thought, read, heard, felt or smelt. 'La Biblioteca de Babel' is an infinite-seeming library containing every possible book. In 'Pierre Menard, autor del Quijote', a French writer composes the fragmentary *Quixote* not in imitation of the novel of Cervantes, but in re-creation. In one aside, Borges has asked whether the universe might not be a page of a book. . .

Borges collaborated in making a number of anthologies with the novelist Adolfo Bioy Casares (b. 1914), and it is interesting to compare Bioy's creative work with that of Borges. Bioy is best known for *La Invención de Morel* (1940; translated as *The Invention of Morel* by Ruth Simms, University of Texas Press, Austin, 1964).

Borges is also attracted to the figure of the Argentine *gaucho* in literature. Compare his *gaucho* tales to *Don Segundo Sombra* (1926) by Ricardo Güiraldes (1886–1927), which has been translated by Harriet de Onis (New American Library, 1966).

LUCIUS ANNAEUS SENECA (*c.* 4 B.C.–65 A.D.).

Epistulae Morales ad Lucilium. Text with a translation by R. M. Gummere in the Loeb Classical Library (3 vols., Heinemann and Harvard U.P., 1917–25). Translated by Robin Campbell as *Letters from a Stoic* (Penguin, 1969).

Seneca was an indifferent playwright (his tragedies are pale shadows of the Greek originals we possess on the same themes, such as *Medea, Oedipus,* and *Agamemnon*) and a satirist of modest attainment (the *Apocolocyntosis* deals with the 'Pumpkinification' or deification of Claudius).

His significance lies in his personality, and in his philosophical writings: the moral essays, and the moral letters which are the progenitor of the whole genre of brief essays we have from Bacon to Lamb and the leader-writers in *The Times*. They were obviously polished for publication from the outset – no replies from Lucilius are known – and date from the last few years of his life, when he had retired from the public arena as adviser to Nero (whose tutor he had been) and eventually unofficial chief minister. Nero was warned against Seneca, whose Stoic ideals seemed at variance with his great wealth and alleged immorality, so Seneca was finally persuaded to commit suicide on a charge of conspiracy with Piso, as were many others. Tacitus tells the story in his *Annals* (XV, 60–64).

Claudio Monteverdi wrote one of the earliest of all operas on the hatred that Nero's mistress Poppaea bore towards Seneca, calling it *L'Incoronazione di Poppea* (5 discs, Telefunken HD 635247).

Year 12

GIL VICENTE (*c.* 1465–*c.* 1536).
Quem tem farelos? (1508). And *Auto da Índia* (1509). And *Farsa do Velho da Horta* and *Auto dos Físicos* (both 1512). No translations of these plays are in print; the bilingual *Four Plays* edited and translated by A. F. Bell (1920; available from Kraus Reprint) are *Auto da Alma, Exhortação da Guerra, Farsa dos Almocreves,* and *Tragicomedia pastoril da Serra da Estrella.*

Possibly the greatest European dramatist before Shakespeare, Vicente wrote in both Portuguese and Spanish, the language of the Lisbon court in his time.

But he is equally master of a dozen other dialects and vocabularies, such as those of gypsies and Jews, doctors and priests. The companion comedies *Quem tem farelos?* and *Auto da Índia* satirize the disastrous effect of riches and power derived from the East on the morals and work habits of the Portuguese back in the old country.

The two 1512 plays are both comic triumphs, the one ridiculing an old man looking for a mistress, and the other on a priestly buffoon who falls ill with love and is treated by a succession of outrageous doctors. He is finally given up for dead into the hands of a priest-confessor, who confesses that he too has suffered from unrequited love for many years. . .

Vicente is a song-writer of great charm and his characters emerge from their medieval stereotypes with verve and sharp delineation.

Perhaps the most important painter that Portugal has produced, Nuno Gonçalves, flourished between 1450 and 1472, a little earlier than Vicente. Doubtless influenced by the Flemish masters, Gonçalves can be studied in Reynaldo dos Santos' *Nuno Gonçalves* (Phaidon Press and Garden City Books, 1955). To complement this work, see R. Chester Smith's *Art of Portugal, 1500–1800* (Weidenfeld & Nicolson, 1968).

TANIZAKI JUNICHIRO (1886-1965).

Sasameyuki (1943-8). Translated by Edward Seidensticker as *The Makioka Sisters* (Tokyo, 1957).

Sasameyuki ('Light Snow' in Japanese) is a great Proustian novel concerned with an Osaka family, and their quest for a husband for one of the sisters. Yukiko, the sister in question, is a classical Japanese symbol of beauty: we see the daily life of herself and her sisters in every detail, and the gradual encroachment of a brutal world on their peace and harmony in the latter years of the 'Thirties. A *roman fleuve* in which apparently insignificant detail is piled upon detail, *The Makioka Sisters* brings western literary techniques to a dissolving Japanese society with unique sensibility.

Tade kuu mushi (1928; translated by Edward Seidensticker as *Some Prefer Nettles*, Penguin, 1970) is a *roman à clef* in which Kaname (Tanizaki) has grown bored with his wife Misako (Tanizaki's own wife), who has a lover (in real life the poet Sato Haruo, 1892-1964). Kaname is attracted by his father's mistress Ohisa, but carries on an affair with the Eurasian prostitute Louise. Husband and wife, victims of *ennui* (the young Tanizaki had been influenced by Wilde, Poe and Baudelaire), cannot summon up the energy to separate.

Compare Tanizaki's fiction with that of the novelist Mishima Yukio (1925-70), and for the background see Richard Storry's *History of Modern Japan* (Penguin, 1969).

LUÍS VAZ DE CAMÕES (1524-1580).

Os Lusíadas. First published 1572. Edited by Frank Pierce (Oxford U.P., 1973). Translated as *The Lusiads* by William C. Atkinson (Penguin, 1952), and by Leonard Bacon (Hispanic Society, 1950).

The young Camões, born into Portugal's lesser nobility, early discovered that his grandfather had married into the family da Gama, and Camões had been born in the year of Vasco da Gama's death. Furthermore, his father, Simão Vaz de Camões, went to the East as ship's captain, and was wrecked off Goa.

Luís was educated at Coimbra University, where he received a good classical grounding, and made up his mind to emulate the *Aeneid* of Virgil by evoking the glories of Portuguese travel and exploration. In 1546, leaving Lisbon after an unhappy love affair, he became a common soldier in the defence of Ceuta, on the northern coast of Africa. Serving a prison sentence in 1552, after having wounded a court official in Lisbon, he was pardoned to serve the King in the East.

The *Lusiads* is consequently no artifice written by a poet to pass idle hours in an ivory tower, but the vigorous narrative of a man of action steeped in the Latin and Italian poets (Ariosto as well as Petrarch), and tells the story of the Portuguese overseas empire to its apogee in 1548, the year of João de Castro's death.

Foreign readers needing a fully-annotated *Lusíadas* can be recommended the latest edition of the epic poem by Emanuel Paulo Ramos (Porto Editora, Oporto): the annotations cover nearly two hundred pages. An important adjunct to the reading of Camões is Boxer's *Portuguese Seaborne Empire* (Hutchinson, 1969).

KONSTANTIN PAUSTOVSKY (1892–1968).
  Povest' o Zhizni (1946–1964) *(The Story of a Life*, translated by Manya Harari and Michael Duncan, Pantheon and Harvill Press, 1964 ff.).

Paustovsky made his name as a writer of short stories and a novelist, but his last years were spent on a magnificent autobiography which delineates life in the Soviet Union during the first half of the twentieth century (he travelled very widely) in all its endless variety. Paustovsky's integrity and popularity enabled him to sign dissident protests and manifestos without harming his status as head of the Gorki Literature Institute in Moscow.

His personality is as magnanimous as his prose is elegant. He loved literature and the unknown folk with whom he mixed on his journeys. 'But most of all', he wrote, 'I am indebted to life itself in all its simplicity and significance. I was happy enough to witness and take part in it'.

Selected Stories (Progress Publishers, Moscow, 1970) admirably complements the multi-volume *Story of a Life.*

JOSÉ MARÍA EÇA DE QUEIRÓZ (1843–1900).
  O Crime de Padre Amaro. First published 1875. And *O Primo Basílio.*
  First published 1878. And *Os Maias.* First published 1888. Translated into English as *The Sin of Father Amaro* (Reinhardt, 1962), *Dragon's Teeth* 1889; reprinted by Greenwood Press, 1970). and *The Maias* (Reinhardt, 1965).

This majestic trilogy of social protest novels was written while Eça de Queiróz was serving in the Portuguese consular service.

Eça de Queiróz spent his creative life in trying to awaken the Portuguese middle classes from what he considered their intellectual and spiritual torpor. The first, set in Leiria, attacks the corrupt clergy, the second dissects the morals of a middle-class family in Lisbon, and the third observes with bitter irony the antics of high society in metropolitan Portugal.

Eça is the greatest novelist that Portugal has produced, and ranks with Balzac and Flaubert, rather than with Zola, as a realist increasing in maturity with each successive novel. See *Eça de Queiróz* by J. G. Simões (Lisbon, 1964).

The so-called 'Generation of 1870' dedicated to reform, which included Eça among its members, was led by Antero de Quental (1842-92), a socialist with communist leanings whose *Sonetos completos* (1886; translated by S. Griswold Morley as *Sonnets and Poems*, 1922; reprinted by Greenwood Press, 1977) form a passionate 'autobiography of thought. . . memoirs of a conscience', a considerable achievement towards expressing the ineffable and understanding the incomprehensible.

SURYAKANT TRIPATHI NIRALA (1898-1961).
A Season on the Earth: Selected Poems. Translated by David Rubin (Columbia U.P., 1977).

Nirala's poetry in Hindi can be divided into two phases: the Romantic phase corresponding to the literary style called *Chayavad,* influenced by English Romanticism and devoted to aspects of Nature; and the later *Pragativad* style, roughly analogous to Soviet socialist realism of the period from about 1933. His best historical poem is *Chatrapati Sivaji ka patra* ('A Letter of King Sivaji', 1922).

As a novelist, Nirala can be compared with his older contemporary Premchand, depicting the lives of the Indian masses in such works as *Kulli bhat* (1939) and *Billesur bakriha* (1941).

One should at this point also try to read as much as possible of the other supreme Hindi poet of the century, Sumitranandan Pant, who like Nirala turned from *Chayavad* poetry to *Pragativad.* Pant was influenced by Marxism and by Aurobindo in such works as *Svarnkiran* ('A Golden Ray', 1946) and *Svarndhuli* ('Golden Dust', 1948). His most ambitious poem is the epic *Lokayatan* ('The House of the People', 1964), in a form dictated by the *Mahabharata* but with a content inspired by modern Indian problems seen from the neo-humanist viewpoint.

ALVES REDOL (b. 1911).
A barca dos sete lemes. First published 1959. Translated by L. L. Barrett as *The Man with Seven Names* (Knopf, 1964).

A neo-realist Portuguese novel of great length and detail, in which a poor man, Alcides, is changed by circumstances into a murderer. Its theme is similar to that of *La familia de Pascual Duarte* (1942), by the Spaniard Camilo José Cela.

with a series of novels and stories on the plight of the poor both in particular and in general, indicating that a change of heart in the rulers was needed before there could be any change of heart in the lower classes.

Alves Redol spent some time in Angola: this is a good moment to investigate the story of Portuguese colonies in Africa – Guinea-Bissau, Angola and Mozambique – in a book such as *Portuguese Africa* by Duffy (Harvard U.P., 1959).

Classical Literary Criticism. Aristotle: *On the art of poetry;* Horace: *On the art of poetry;* 'Longinus': *On the sublime.* Translated by T. S. Dorsch (Penguin, 1965).

Plays in Western languages are generally written, and always have been written, in accordance with, or in revolt against, the tradition laid down by Aristotle in his *Peri Poietikes.* The last four chapters deal with epic poetry, and Aristotle concludes that in all respects the tragic art is superior to the epic. Aristotle's essay is often considered a mere reply to Plato's disparagement of poets on the grounds that they compose their works under the influence not of wisdom but of mere inspiration, but this charge is baseless, since Aristotle puts forward many original ideas of his own.

Horace's *Epistula ad Pisones,* designated by Quintilian as the *Ars Poetica,* is one of three extant aesthetic statements by Horace. It deals largely with drama, so to find Horace's views on poetry we turn to Epistles II, 1 and 2. The first is the Epistle to Augustus, which attacks those who pay lip-service to ancient literature but condemn their contemporaries; scorns those spectators who prefer stage spectacle to good writing and acting; and urges the Emperor to patronise forms of literature other than the dramatic. The second is principally autobiographical, but also satirizes the shallower poets of his time, who throw off poetic effusions without revising and polishing them first. 'The best words should be in the best order' is a memorable dictum.

Peri Hypsous ('On the Sublime') is a Greek prose epistle of the 1st century A.D. addressed to a certain Terentianus, and the authorship is unknown, though traditionally attributed to Longinus or a pseudo-Longinus. 'Sublimity', in this unfinished work, has a meaning different from that understood today, but can be defined as that distinction and excellence of expression by which certain authors (and he names Homer and Plato, among others) have gained immortal fame.

The translations of Aristotle's *Poetics and Rhetoric* in Everyman's Library (Dent and Dutton, 1953) are inferior, but the book also contains T. A. Moxon's version from Demetrius' *On Style.*

In the Loeb Classical Library, Demetrius and 'Longinus' are found in a volume headed by Aristotle's *Poetics* (Heinemann and Harvard U.P., revised edition, 1932), while Horace's *Satires, Epistles, and Ars Poetica* are in another volume, in the Latin series of course, translated by H. R. Fairclough (new ed., Heinemann and Harvard U.P., 1929).

For the background, see J. W. H. Atkins' *Literary Criticism in Antiquity* (Methuen, 1952). For Plato's literary criticism, see principally his *Republic, Phaedrus, Philebus* and *Protagoras.*

FERNANDO PESSOA (1888-1935).
Obras completas. First published (incomplete, despite the title) in 8 volumes by Edições Ática of Lisbon, 1942-56. The best of the several selections in English translation is by Peter Rickard, with facing Portuguese text, in *Selected Poems* (Edinburgh U.P., 1971).

Growing up in an English-language milieu in South Africa, with a Portuguese mother, Pessoa wrote all his early poems in the style of Shakespeare, in English.

The work for which he will be remembered was written by himself, under his own name, and under three heteronyms, each of which represented a complete autonomous poetic life and work in the Pirandellian sense of divided but whole identities.

The original Pessoa wrote poetry that questions the efficacy of poetry. His three alternative selves have no doubt. The relatively short-lived 'Alberto Caeiro' wrote rural, sensual and intellectual verse as a result of inspiration. 'Alvaro de Campos', a naval engineer purportedly educated in Glasgow, wrote by impulse, in generous Whitmanesque proportions. 'Ricardo Reis', a pagan whose work is classical, formal, and traditional, is a pessimist who has come to terms with tragic destiny.

Taken all in all, the body of work produced by all four poets in the body of Fernando Pessoa can be considered the most solid achievement by a Portuguese poet since the death of Camões.

FRANÇOIS RABELAIS (*c.* 1494-1553).
The Histories of Gargantua and Pantagruel. First published 1532-64. Translated and with an introduction by J. M. Cohen (Penguin, 1955).

The medieval French of Rabelais is a riotous word-feast matching the exuberance of the matter: his five books known collectively as *Gargantua and Pantagruel* are uneven in inspiration, but the satire against the Papacy and monasticism is always potent and amusing. Cohen's translation of the novel is the best available, but his introduction is inadequate and the keen Rabelaisian should consult M. Screech's *Rabelais* (Duckworth, 1980). The original, in five volumes, has been edited by Pierre Michel for the 'Livre de Poche' series, published by Gallimard with the Librairie Générale Française. Michel includes also the 'Oeuvres diverses', with an important letter to Erasmus.

Gustave Doré's suitably grotesque illustrations have been reprinted (Dover and Constable, 1979) separately from the text.

Year 13

The Penguin Book of German Verse, introduced and edited by Leonard Forster
(Reprinted with revisions, Penguin, 1959).

Conforming to the normal pattern of national anthologies in 'The Penguin
Poets', Forster's careful selection prints original texts from the *Hildebrandslied* to
Friedrich Georg Jünger, with plain prose translations at the foot of the page.

Even those who do not particularly enjoy learning languages, or who find
German unsympathetic, will find that they already know and enjoy some songs
of Goethe, Schiller, Klopstock, Heine, Mörike and Eichendorff set to music by
Schubert, Beethoven, Schumann, Brahms and Hugo Wolf.

The joy of such anthologies, however, lies chiefly in the discovery of
unexpected or anonymous treasures, the flashes of genius or perception found
among otherwise minor or forgotten writers to whom no single collection of
translations has been devoted. Lenz, Novalis, Storm and Morgenstern are
personalities to be cherished, and the exploration of the masterworks of medieval
German can begin here too. There are numerous records of poets and actors
reading German poetry: a short list of those currently available can be sought at
your nearest Goethe-Institut.

JOHANN WOLFGANG VON GOETHE (1749–1832).
    Faust. First published in 1808 (Part I) and 1832 (Part II). There are
    numerous German editions, and a number of more or less passable English
    translations, among them Bayard Taylor's for World's Classics (Oxford
    U.P., 1932) and Philip Wayne's (2 vols., Penguin, 1959). The abridged trans-
    lation by Louis MacNeice is not recommended.

Faust is the masterpiece of a great spirit, whose *Conversations with Eckermann*
can also provide a good deal of delight and intellectual stimulation.

    Faust was a lifelong preoccupation of Goethe, and the drama was published in
fragments intermittently: it was not until after his death that the whole of Part II

appeared as Volume I of the *Nachgelassene Werke*. The themes of intellectual and spiritual questing, of hunger for experience, cause Faust to lose patience with the pedantic scholar Wagner and to summon the Earth Spirit. Finally, Mephistopheles appears and the drama can begin.

The endless quest for knowledge and experience can lead men to temptation, and even to crime, but they derive from a divine spark which can also lead to ultimate salvation.

The 16th-century original of Goethe's Faust-figure was a historical person of whom lurid tales and a terrible end were told, in Johann Spiess' *Historia von D. Joh. Fausten* (1587). Christopher Marlowe transmuted the 'penny-dreadful' of Spiess into his *Tragicall history of Dr. Faustus* (written 1588–9, first performed 1592 and printed 1604), and the legend of Faust's pact with the devil was perpetuated in Lessing's fragments of a Faust play (1759 and 1784), which first reversed the damning indictment of the traditional-story, and expounded Faust's worthiness as a fearless seeker after knowledge.

Gounod's opera *Faust* (1859) is performed on 3 discs (HMV SLS 816) by Gedda, Christoff and de los Angeles. Boito's opera *Mefistofele* (1868) is performed on 3 discs (Decca GOS 591-3) by del Monaco, Siepi and Tebaldi.

This is an appropriate time, too, to become familiar with the symphonies of Mozart (1756–91), whose brief life span is overshadowed by that of Goethe. The boy prodigy is one of the few universal geniuses whose excellence is appreciated by virtually everyone who enjoys music.

HAROLD PINTER (b. 1930).

> *The Caretaker.* (2nd ed., Methuen, 1967). And *The Room* and *The Dumb Waiter.* (Methuen, 1966).

Harold Pinter burst on to the theatrical scene in 1960 with *The Caretaker,* a brilliant tragi-comedy for three male actors set in a room with a leaky roof.

Pinter removes the metaphysical element from Beckett's *Waiting for Godot* (in which the two main characters are tramps) and endows his own central character, a Welsh tramp battening on to anyone who will listen, with a speech-pattern alternating between the pathetic and the prosaic.

The Room and *The Dumb Waiter* (written in 1957) similarly take apparently normal encounters and expand their significance into the extraordinary, the disturbing, the menacing.

Pinter's stagecraft has matured through long experience as an actor and director (he directed his own *The Hothouse,* a halting early work first staged in 1980), but much of his recent work has repeated facets of such successes as *The Caretaker,* and *The Collection* first produced in 1962.

JOHANN JAKOB CHRISTOFFEL VON GRIMMELSHAUSEN (*c.*1625–
1676). *Der Abenteuerliche Simplicissimus teutsch.* First published under a
pseudonym in 1669 (and not 1668 as printed). Translated as *Simplicius
Simplicissimus* by H. Weissenborn and L. Macdonald (Calder, 1964).

The finest German novel of the 17th century, *Simplicissimus* is an absorbing
adventure novel of the picaresque genre, the first Robinson Crusoe story in
German, an ironic commentary on human failings and foibles set against the
Thirty Years' War, and finally a mature and good-humoured statement of the
vanity of earthly goods and aspirations by a convert to Roman Catholicism who
demonstrates experience of life and a deep knowledge of literature.

A boy, reared on the farm of his putative father, flees when the farm is raided by
troops during the Thirty Years' War, and is given the name 'Simplicius' in
recognition of his innocence by a hermit who protects the fugitive and teaches
him the elements of religion. When the hermit dies, Simplicius goes to Hanau,
where he is carried off by Croatian soldiers, from whom he manages to escape.
He then joins the imperial troops and becomes an intrepid soldier, but falls into
Swedish captivity and enjoys a number of love affairs, one of which ends with
forced marriage. He leaves for Cologne, and then for Paris, where he has more
love affairs. After many further adventures, he becomes a hermit, but in a later
book VI, or *Continuatio,* he is wrecked on an island in the South Atlantic.

The other Simplician writings of Grimmelshausen include *Die Landstörtzerin
Courasche* (1670; translated by Walter Wallich as *Mother Courage,* Folio Society,
1965), *Der seltzame Springinsfeld* (1670), and *Das wunderbarliche Vogelnest*
(1672). They all attempt, more or less unsuccessfully, to expand themes and
characters from the main work, which was enjoying immense popularity, as it has
done ever since. Bertolt Brecht took the character and situation of *Mutter
Courage* (though little else) from Grimmelshausen. For an absorbing study of
Simplicissimus in the context of the Spanish picaresque novel undoubtedly
familiar to Grimmelshausen, see A. A. Parker's *Literature and the Delinquent*
(Edinburgh U.P., 1967).

The best editions of *Simplicissimus* and the *Simplicianische Romane* are in the
'Neudrucke Deutsche Literaturwerke des XVI. und XVII. Jahrhunderts' (Halle),
vols. 302/9 (1939) and 246/8 (1923), 249/52 (1928), 288/91 (1931), 310/14
(1939).

WANG WEI (*c.* 699– *c.* 761).
Wang Yu-ch'eng Chi Chien-chu. Published in 1736 and available in numerous reprints. *Poems.* Translated selections by G. W. Robinson (Penguin,
1973).

The great T'ang dynasty poet, composer and painter Wang Wei was a practising Buddhist whose *Lines* in his last years show both his art and his preoccupations:

> With age I am growing too lazy to write verses
> And now old age is my only company.
> In a past life I was mistakenly a poet.
> In a former existence I must have been a painter.
> Unable to throw off my remnant habits,
> I find the world has come to know me for them.
> My name and style: these they have right.
> But this heart of mine they still do not know.

Rather more than a quarter of Wang's poems appear in the Robinson translations: others can be found in the numerous anthologies of Chinese verse. An excellent companion is *The Art of Chinese Poetry* by James J. Y. Liu (University of Chicago Press and Routledge & Kegan Paul, 1962), and the surviving art of the great T'ang dynasty can be studied in Leigh Ashton and Basil Gray's *Chinese Art* (Faber & Faber, 1935), pp. 109–163, for example, and Mario Prodan's *The Art of the T'ang Potter* (Thames & Hudson, 1960).

BERTOLT BRECHT (1898–1956).
> *Der gute Mensch von Sezuan.* First published 1953 (though written 1938–40). And *Der kaukasische Kreidekreis.* First published 1949 (though written 1944–5). Both translated by Eric Bentley and M. Apelman in *Parables for the Theatre* (University of Minnesota Press and Oxford U.P., 1948).

One set in modern China, and the other set first in Soviet Georgia and subsequently in feudal Georgia, these plays are both accurately described as 'parables', and indeed Brecht is an epic satirist never far from the morality play, though his great gifts as a poet are constantly breaking through his Marxist ideological straitjacket.

The music to these two plays was by Paul Dessau, but Brecht's best-remembered musical collaborator was Kurt Weill, with whom he wrote *Die Dreigroschenoper* (first performed 1928; available on 2 CBS records, CBS 77268), *Happy End* (first performed 1929; available on 1 CBS record, CBS 73463), and *Aufstieg und Fall der Stadt Mahagonny* (first performed 1930, available on 3 CBS records, CBS 77341).

The best introduction to the complex world of Brecht is Martin Esslin's *Brecht: a Choice of Evils* (Eyre Methuen, 1965).

TITUS LUCRETIUS CARUS (*c.* 99–*c.* 55 B.C.).
   De rerum natura. Text with an English translation by W. H. D. Rouse in
   Loeb Classical Library (Heinemann and Harvard U.P., 1928). Translated by
   Rolfe Humphries as *The Way Things Are* (Indiana U.P., 1970).

The teachings of Epicurus (341–271 B.C.) have not come down to us entire, but
can found partially preserved in Book X of the *Vitae philosophorum* of Diogenes
Laertius (translated by R. D. Hicks for the Loeb Classical Library, 2 vols., 1925)
and interpreted – sometimes inaccurately – in the great poem *De rerum natura,*
often rendered 'On the nature of things'.
   Epicureanism, broadly speaking the systematisation of common sense, was
introduced into Rome about 175 B.C. Opposed first by the authoritarians and
then by the Christian Church, it never became numerically significant, but has
lived on in various guises as scepticism, rationalism and humanism. Men, writes
Lucretius, must be delivered from the bondage of religion (illustrated by the tale
of Iphjgeneia), and from fears of death and hell. Only the evidence of our senses
is to be believed. The atomic theory, which Epicurus had borrowed from
Democritus, is expounded. The soul and the world are both mortal, but the
universe is infinite. Book VI, accounting for geological and meteorological
phenomena, and concluding with a theory of disease, appears to be unfinished,
and like Book V appears never to have been revised, possibly due to the
premature death of the poet.
   Milton imitated Lucretius in several passages of *Paradise Lost,* and Dryden
translated parts of the first five books. Cicero attacked the alleged selfish
indifference and withdrawal from active life of the Epicureans (compare the
Taoists in China with the Confucianists) in his *Tusculanae disputationes* i.21 and
ii. 3.

VICTOR HUGO (1802–1885).
   Notre Dame de Paris. First published 1831. Translated by W. J. Cobb (New
   American Library, 1965). And *Hernani.* First published 1830. Translated
   in *Three Plays,* by H. A. Gaubert (Washington Square; 1964).

French Romanticism reached its apogee in this novel and this play, both
historical in setting.
   The Hunchback of Notre Dame, as the novel is usually known in English
translation, traces the adventures of the gipsy dancer Esmeralda in 15th-century
Paris, overshadowed by the great cathedral of Our Lady.
   Esmeralda is coveted by the cathedral's archdeacon, Claude Frollo, and
worshipped by the grotesque bell-ringer, Quasimodo. The midnight attack of the

gipsies and beggars on the Cathedral, where Esmeralda is being shielded by Quasimodo, ranks as one of the more exciting moments in a narrative spilling over with colour and invention.

Hernani's first two performances at the Comédie-Française marked the victory of the Romantics (led by Théophile Gautier and Petrus Borel) over the traditionalists. Subject, treatment and versification: all were opposed to the conventions of classical literature already exemplified by Hugo's *Odes* and Vigny's *Poèmes* of 1822. The victory was soon complete, and Romantic opera seized its opportunity. Verdi's *Ernani* adapted Hugo's *Hernani,* just as his *Rigoletto* (3 discs, HMV SLS 5018) adapted Hugo's *Le Roi s'amuse* (1832). The third of the *Three Plays* translated by Gaubert is *Ruy Blas* (1838), set in the heavily-romanticized Spain of *Hernani.* See André Maurois' *Victor Hugo* (Cape, 1956).

East German Poetry: an Anthology, edited by Michael Hamburger (Carcanet Press, 1972).

The tensions arising from a divided Germany have affected East German writers more than West Germans.

Tension is at the heart of most great poetry (language 'at the end of its tether' is the most compelling, memorable language), and the writers who have contributed most to post-war German poetry are those of the D.D.R., with 'protest' writers of the West such as Grass and ironists such as Enzensberger. The names in Hamburger's excellent bilingual anthology include those of Brecht, Huchel, Bobrowski, Kunert, Kunze, Biermann and Volker Braun. All of these poets are worthy of further exploration.

For the political background, see *The German Democratic Republic* edited by Lyman H. Legters (Westview Press, 5500 Central Avenue, Boulder, Colo. 80301, 1977).

ALBERT SCHWEITZER (1875-1965).
Aus meiner Kindheit und Jugendheit. First published 1924. And *Aus meinem Leben und Denken.* First published 1932. *Out of My Life and Thought* translated by C. T. Campion (New American Library, 1953). *Zwischen Wasser and Urwald* and *Mitteilungen aus Lambaréné* translated by C. T. Campion as *On the Edge of the Primeval Forest* and *More from the Primeval Forest* for Fontana Books (Collins, 1970).

Schweitzer, born in Alsace, trained as a pastor and a New Testament scholar in Strasbourg before qualifying as a physician and reaching eminence as an interpreter and editor of the organ works of J. S. Bach. Listen to Karl Richter's interpretation of a selection of Bach's organ works on DGG SLPM 138907.

In 1913, Schweitzer founded his tropical hospital in Lambaréné (Gabon), and broadened his Christianity by the study of Schopenhauer and Indian philosophy. He became respected, too, for his wide-ranging views on political idealism. "We must substitute the power of understanding the truth that is really truth", he said in 1947, "for propaganda; a noble kind of patriotism which aims at ends that are worthy of the whole of mankind, for the patriotism current today; a humanity with a common civilization, for idolized nationalisms, a restored faith in the civilized state, for a society which lacks true idealism. . . a faith in the possibility of progress, for a mentality stripped of all spirituality. These are our tasks". Schweitzer was awarded the Nobel Peace Prize in 1952.

Year 14

LEO NIKOLAYEVICH TOLSTOY (1828–1910).
Anna Karenin. First published complete 1878. Translations include those by David Magarshack (New American Library, 1961), Rosemary Edmonds (Penguin, 1954), and Constance Garnett (Heinemann, 1911).

It is a pity that Tolstoy is known in the West only for his great novels *Voina i mir* (*War and Peace*) and *Anna Karenin,* for in terms of bulk the short stories far outdistance the novels in Tolstoy's creative life: there are forty-five volumes of diaries and correspondence in his published works in addition to excellent plays.

Anna Karenin tells the extraordinary love story of Anna and Vronsky. Vronsky, with his debonair style, attractive uniforms, and gambling debts, seems to recall the younger Tolstoy, just as Levin, the restless sceptic, mirrors the older Tolstoy. But despite his autobiographical portraits, the novelist achieves a remarkable detachment from his creatures, making of Anna a heroine even more realistic, if that were possible, than Flaubert's Emma Bovary.

Since Tolstoy was probably the most influential writer of his age, it is worth reading a biography such as *Tolstoy Remembered* (Atheneum, 1962) by his eldest son Sergei; a critical work, such as George Steiner's *Tolstoy or Dostoevsky?* (Knopf, 1959, and Penguin, 1967); and some essays by the social thinker, such as *What Then Must We Do?* in World's Classics (Oxford U.P., 1925).

PAUL ANCEL (PAUL CELAN) (1920–1970).
Ausgewählte Gedichte (und) *Zwei Reden* (Suhrkamp Verlag, Frankfurt, 1968). *Poems: a Bilingual Edition,* selected, translated and introduced by Michael Hamburger (Carcanet New Press, 1980).

Born in a part of what was the Austro-Hungarian Empire, later annexed by Romania and subsequently became part of the U.S.S.R., Celan began to write in German and continued to do so, though he spent only one year in a German-speaking country (Austria). In 1942, Celan's Jewish parents were killed in a concentration camp, and Celan himself was sent to a forced-labour camp. From 1948 he lived in Paris with his wife, the graphic artist Gisèle Celan-Lestrange, but committed suicide in the Seine.

A recurring theme, naturally enough, is the death of the Jews at Nazi hands, and the wider problem of man's inhumanity to man. If Adorno wondered how it was possible to write poems after Auschwitz, it was Celan who provided the complex reply in his neo-surrealistic, dark, sardonic and eventually (in 'Tenebrae') blasphemous work. He attempted to forge a new poetic language which could not be mistaken for the German used and debased by Nazis. Celan always feared that he was writing in and for a vacuum, calling to a god (perhaps) who is not there, his poems mere messages in bottles which might or might not be picked up. We must ensure that the bottles of this great tragic poet are picked up, and the messages both deciphered and learnt.

The Presocratic Philosophers: a critical history with a selection of texts, by G. S. Kirk and J. E. Raven (Cambridge U.P., 1957).

To understand Plato and the systems against which he reacted in several of the Socratic dialogues, it is desirable to understand something of the prehistory of philosophy, as it were, from Thales in the early sixth century B.C. to the Atomists in the late fifth century. Two hundred years of intellectual ferment are explained by Kirk and Raven, with Greek texts and English translations. The early scientists and philosophers, studied in their own words, include Anaximander, Xenophanes and Heraclitus and Zeno of Elea of the Italian Schools, and the post-Parmenidean Empedocles, Anaxagoras, Leucippus and Democritus.

This is a good moment to extend one's knowledge of classical Greek in the fields of science and thought, and to explore how far the following definitions cover the Greek words in question: *dike* (right, justice); *adikia* (wrong, injustice); *hubris* (arrogance, pride); *logos* (word, reason, 'law' in Heraclitus, 'The Word of God' capitalised in Biblical translation); *nous* (mind, thought, intellect); *Ouranos* (like *Kronos* an ancient deity, but now meaning 'heaven' or 'sky').

Biographical material on early Greek philosophers can be found in the *Lives of Eminent Philosophers* by Diogenes Laertius in the Loeb Classical Library (text, and translation by R. D. Hicks, 2 vols., Heinemann and Harvard U.P., 1935). It should be used with caution, however, and the information verified in Kirk and Raven. Zeno can be studied further in *Zeno's Paradoxes,* edited by Wesley C. Salmon (Bobbs-Merrill, 1970), and Parmenides in *The Route of Parmenides,* by A. Mourelatos (Yale U.P., 1970).

FRIEDRICH VON SCHILLER (1759–1805).
  Don Carlos, Infant von Spanien: ein dramatisches Gedicht. First full
  publication 1787. Translated by Charles E. Passage (Ungar, 1959).

Schiller's immense verse tragedy (curtailed from 6,282 lines in its original form to
the 5,370 lines of the 1805 recension) is more familiar outside German-speaking
countries in the operatic version by Giuseppe Verdi (*Don Carlo,* conducted by
Giulini on HMV SLS 956 and by Solti on Decca SET 305-8, both on 4 discs).
  In his *Briefe über Don Carlos* (1788), Schiller ably defended the shortcomings
of his splendid drama, with its vigorous and impassioned blank verse. Lack of
unity is admitted to be a weakness, for in the course of the writing, Don Carlos,
King Philip II of Spain, and the Marquis of Posa in turn stir the imagination as the
principal protagonist. Intricate personal and political alliances stem from the
Inquisition's fear of subversion in the Netherlands and at home, and from the
love of Don Carlos for his stepmother Elisabeth de Valois (now married to his
father the King), to whom he was originally betrothed for love and who is now
sacrificed on the altar of politics. The Marquis of Posa stirs the libertarian views of
Carlos, Infante of Spain, and Princess Eboli – repudiated by the Infante whom
she loves – is moved to vengeance against the Queen.
  Throughout his writings, and especially in the essay *Über Anmut und Würde*
(1793), Schiller attempts to show that man is intended not merely to perform
isolated moral acts, but to become a completely moral being, a 'beautiful soul' in
whom duty and inclination coincide without conflict, as in the St Joan of the early
acts of his romantic tragedy in verse, *Die Jungfrau von Orleans* (1801; translated
with *Maria Stuart* by Charles E. Passage, Ungar, 1960). Compare Bernard Shaw's
play *St Joan* (1924) and Brecht's Communist parody of Schiller's *Jungfrau, Die
heilige Johanna de Schlachthöfe* (1932; translated as *St Joan of the Stockyards* in
Seven Plays, edited by Eric Bentley, Grove Press, 1961).

SHIH NAI-AN (1296–1370).
  Shui hu chuan. Probably first published in the 14th century, though the
  earliest editions extant are from the 16th century.

Shih was a novelist who is thought to have taken part in an unsuccessful rebellion
against the Mongols of the Yüan dynasty, and was forced to live in hiding until
the Ming came to power. He probably found an account of the Sung rebellion of
Sung Chiang and his Thirty-Six, who had become legendary popular heroes
against an unpopular government. Shih then seems to have written his novel on
the basis of the historical and embroidered events, and the *Shui hu chuan* then
became in its turn an inspiration for rebellion against subsequent regimes, and
indeed has never lost its fascination for generation after generation of Chinese

readers. All novels were considered degenerate in China, where painting and poetry were the arts *par excellence* of the ruling classes. The novelist assumes that the popular outlaw, familiar in most cultures, will be sustained by the enemies of the ruling classes in every age, and the style is vigorously colloquial.

'The available English translations, although in some cases conscientiously done', writes Yi-tse Mei Feuerwerker (*Approaches to the Oriental Classics,* ed. by W. Th. de Bary, Columbia U.P., 1959), 'are not only inadequate, but actually falsify the spirit of the book'. These versions include Pearl S. Buck's *All Men are Brothers* (2 vols., Methuen, 1957), and J. H. Jackson's *Water Margin* (2 vols., Commercial Press of Hong Kong, 1963).

It is time that a Chinese scholar and narrator of genius translated afresh the complete *Shui hu chuan.* The best version of a part that we have so far is an excerpt by Sidney Shapiro appearing in the monthly *Chinese Literature* (December 1959, pp. 3–61, corresponding to chapters 6–9 of the Pearl Buck travesty).

HUGO VON HOFMANNSTHAL (1874–1929).

> *Gesammelte Werke.* 15 vols. First published from 1964 ff. Three good anthologies in the Bollingen Series have made the best of Hofmannsthal available to the English-reading world: *Selected Prose* (including fiction and travel notes), translated by Mary Hottinger and Tania and James Stern Princeton U.P. and Routledge, 1952); *Poems and Verse Plays* (1961) and *Selected Plays and Libretti,* both edited by Michael Hamburger (1963).

Achieving miraculous poems at a precocious age, Hofmannsthal suddenly saw the disunity and incoherence behind what he had considered unity and coherence and found bitterness in the collapse of the old order in central Europe. He turned to *Elektra* (1903) and the classical Greek stage for inspiration, but gained more success with his medieval-morality style in *Jedermann* ('Everyman', 1911). As an Austrian, he was deeply proud of his nation's culture, in particular as regards music, and helped to found the Salzburg Festival in 1920.

His inspired libretti for the operas of Richard Strauss (see their *Correspondence,* Collins, 1961) are the most distinguished writing for the operatic stage yet produced. Elisabeth Schwarzkopf's definitive Marschallin in Strauss' *Der Rosenkavalier* can be heard on HMV SLS 810 (4 discs), and Lisa della Casa's Arabella in Strauss' *Arabella* on Decca GOS 571–3 (3 discs).

The satirical artist George Grosz drew the types and personalities of the Weimar Republic: see for example Uwe M. Scheede's *George Grosz: his Life and Work* (Universe, 1979) or Beth Lewis' *George Grosz: Art and Politics in the Weimar Republic* (University of Wisconsin Press, 1971).

KARL MARX (1818–1883).
Das Kapital. First published 1867–1894. Translated by D. Fernbach as
Capital (2 vols., Penguin, 1976–8).

Subtitled 'a critique of political economy', and apparently devoted to an analysis
of capital, its circulation, the concept of surplus-value, and capitalist production,
Marx's influential book, translated first into Russian and then into French,
eventually appeared under the editorship of Engels in English in 1887, four years
after the author's death.

Marx had spent much of the quarter-century preceding the publication of his
first volume in the Reading Room of the British Museum. He suffered from
political complications, financial hardship, and especially carbuncles. His
'critique' ended by becoming a devastating attack on capitalism using documents
from British official sources, and Marx wrote to Engels, 'I hope the bourgeoisie
will remember my carbuncles all the rest of their lives'.

Directions that a reader could take from *Das Kapital* include study of the first
Communist Manifesto, originally printed in London by the German J. E.
Burghard (1848) as *Manifest der Kommunistischen Partei* by Marx and Friedrich
Engels, and first published in English in the *Red Republican* of 1850. The
authorized English translation of Samuel Moore (1888), was edited by Engels
himself. One might also examine Marxist views on literature and art, such as
Mao's speeches at the Yenan Forum, Ernst Fischer's *The Necessity of Art*
(Penguin, 1963), and the significant corpus of criticism by György Lukács, such
as *The Historical Novel* (Penguin, 1969).

Shaking the Pumpkin: traditional poetry of the Indian North Americas, edited with
    commentaries by Jerome Rothenberg (Doubleday, 1972).

If you enjoyed Maurice Bowra's *Primitive Song,* this is a feast of versions, more or
less reinvented for a 'literary' North American public, from the Indians of North
(and Central) America. The success is not always complete, as Rothenberg
confesses: 'To the reader who imagines that a book like this can really hold the
spirit-of-a-people, etc. the editor testifies that in instance after instance the best
remains untold or its powers reserved for those who 'have ears to hear', etc. But
the rest of us have to begin somewhere'.

The Seneca Indians' sacred curing songs entitled 'Shaking the Pumpkin' are
included, as is a section of the pre-Conquest Maya play *Rabinal Achí,* which has
appeared in Spanish in full (Mexico City, 1955). Rothenberg is not only a poet in
his own right, but was editor of the important but defunct magazine of
ethnopoetics *Alcheringa,* founded in 1970, and of the anthology *Technicians of the
Sacred: a range of poetries from Africa, America, Asia and Oceania* (Doubleday,

1969).

Alternatively, Natalie Curtis' *The Indians' Book* (Dover and Constable, 1968) can be thoroughly recommended in that it includes musical notation with many of its songs and legends translated from North American Indian tongues, and is profusely illustrated with drawings and photographs.

JOHANN WOLFGANG VON GOETHE (1749–1832).
Aus meinem Leben: Dichtung und Wahrheit. First published 1811–1833. No translation is recommended. There is a version by R. O. Moon: *Autobiography: Poetry and Truth from my Own Life* (Public Affairs Press, 1949) and another by J. Oxenford: *Autobiography* (2 vols., University of Chicago Press, 1975).

One of the most absorbing autobiographies ever written, *Dichtung and Wahrheit* covers the 26 years from 1749 to 1775. In the latter year, Goethe was invited by the Duke Karl August to visit him as a guest in Weimar. Goethe remained in Weimar to the end of his life, and did compose a few more writings of an autobiographical nature, such as the *Italienische Reise* (excellently translated by W. H. Auden and E. Mayer as *Italian Journey 1786–1788,* Penguin, 1970); the *Sankt-Rochus-Fest zu Bingen* (in the second volume of *Über Kunst und Altertum,* 1817); and the *Tag- und Jahreshefte* covering his literary work and his life up to 1822, published in vols. 31–2 of the *Ausgabe letzter Hand,* 1830.

The Italian journey was undertaken impulsively, using the pseudonym Möller. Goethe slipped away from Carlsbad, where members of the Duke's court were taking the waters. He was finding life in Weimar, outwardly pleasant, increasingly restrictive. He had outgrown the period of *Die Leiden des jungen Werthers* (1774), the novel which had achieved fame throughout Europe and had caused its young author to be invited to Weimar. He had outgrown Herder, his friends, and the superficial attractions of the Court circles. The *Faust* was still to come: that, too, can be considered in certain particulars and in the overall conception a work of autobiography. As Goethe said: 'Alle meine Werke sind Bruchstücke einer grossen Konfession' ('All my works are fragments of a great autobiography').

Explore now some of the wealth of Haydn's symphonies, and such operas as *La Vera Costanza* (1779; 3 discs, Philips 6703 077) and *La Fedeltà Premiata* (1781; 4 discs, Philips 6707 028).

PAUL KLEE (1879–1940).
Das bildnerische Denken. First published 1956. Translated by Ralph
Manheim as *The Thinking Eye* (Lund Humphries, 1961). And *Unendliche
Naturgeschichte.* First published 1970. Translated by Heinz Norden as *The
Nature of Nature* (Lund Humphries, 1973).

These two beautiful illustrated notebooks of the great Swiss artist demonstrate
how good a teacher he must have been at the Bauhaus, and how discipline and
patient investigation of colours and the excitement of 'taking a line for a walk' can
be coupled with poetic and graphic originality of the highest order. Klee emerges
not only as the inveterate experimenter, but also as a warm human being with
immense charm. An oil entitled 'Harmony from rectangles in red, yellow, blue,
white and black' can be transformed a few pages later in a rectangular-box pattern
entitled 'Castle of a chivalric order': verbal felicity combines with his abundant
pictorial energy. The microscopic scale of many of Klee's drawings lends itself
easily to book reproduction.

Klee's collected poetry first appeared as *Gedichte* (Die Arche, Zürich, 1960).
English translations of *Some Poems* by Anselm Hollo were published by the
Scorpion Press (1962) and other versions by Harriett Watts appear in *Three
Painter-Poets: Arp, Schwitters, Klee* (Penguin, 1974), a happy collective.

Another view of the age in modern art can be taken from Wassily Kandinsky's
Über das Geistige in der Kunst, translated as *Concerning the Spiritual in Art*
(Wittenborn, 1947).

Klee's *Pedagogical Sketchbook* (Faber & Faber, 1968) gives another insight into
his teachings at the Bauhaus, on which also see Walter Gropius' *The New
Architecture and the Bauhaus* (Faber & Faber, 1965).

Year 15

FRANZ KAFKA (1883–1924).
Gesammelte Werke. First published in this edition 1950–8. *Die Verwandlung* (1912; translated with other stories as *Metamorphosis* by Willa and Edwin Muir, Penguin, 1961). *Beschreibung eines Kampfes* (1931; translated by the Muirs with other stories as *Description of a Struggle and other stories,* Penguin, 1979). *Hochzeitsvorbereitungen auf dem Lande* (1953; translated in *Wedding Preparations in the Country and other stories,* Penguin, 1978).

Kafka, a Jew born in Prague who wrote in German, was dominated by his father and was emotionally incapable of lasting relationships with a woman, or indeed of sympathising closely with Zionism.

He felt imprisoned by the insurance company in which he was obliged by his father to work until tuberculosis ended his working life.

Kafka's expertise in the short story, or rather fable, of dread, metamorphosis, and uncertainty, has been extraordinarily influential. Borges, Beckett, and hundreds of lesser writers have been impressed by the curt simplicity of his style at odds with the nameless menace and even hopelessness of the situations in which his characters find themselves, puppets of an unknown but presumably malign destiny.

Though his stories are supreme, a cult has also arisen around his novels, his *Diaries* (edited by Max Brod, Penguin, 1964), and the *Letters* to his confidantes, Felice Bauer (in German, *Briefe an Felice,* edited by E. Heller and J. Born, 1967; translated as *Letters to Felice* by J. Stern and E. Duckworth, Schocken, 1973), to whom he was twice briefly engaged, and Milena Jesenska-Pollak (1952; translated as *Letters to Milena* by T. and J. Stern, Schocken, 1962; Corgi, 1967).

Kafka instructed his literary executor, Max Brod, to destroy the manuscripts of *Der Prozess* (1925; translated as *The Trial* by the Muirs, Penguin, 1953), *Das Schloss* (1926; translated as *The Castle* by the Muirs, Penguin, 1957), and the fragmentary *Der Verschollene* (published as *Amerika* in 1927; translated by Willa and Edwin Muir as *Amerika,* Schocken, 1962; Penguin, 1970). Brod's refusal to carry out his duties may be morally indefensible, but the overriding literary argument is equally irrefutable, for it is in the demonstrably high quality of the novels, flawed as they are by Kafka's lack of interest in character as opposed to situation, that the writer's judgement of his own genius is vindicated against the obsessive materialism of his father.

SU TUNG-P'O (1036–1101).
   Selections from a Sung Dynasty Poet. Translated by Burton Watson (Columbia U.P., 1965).

While England was being conquered by the Normans, Su Shih (also known as Su Tung-P'o), who had passed the highest state examination as a prodigy in 1057, was entering on a wide-ranging political career.

It is not sufficient to read the 83 poems in Burton Watson's versions (taken from a corpus several hundred times that size): one should also read Lin Yutang's excellent biography, *The Gay Genius* (Heinemann, 1948). There one will discover that Su was a great painter, who brought to perfection that impressionist style known as 'scholar painting'. He was an engineer, whose dyke on the Upper Yangtze long commanded admiration. As Governor of Hangchow he founded the first public hospital in China, and landscaped the East Lake which is now the leading recreation area for the modern industrial city of Wuchang, across the Yangtze. As an administrator he was an inveterate critic of abuses, reminding the Court that the Emperor held his mandate not only from the people, but also on their behalf – *for* the people. He was occasionally punished by banishment, degradation, and even imprisonment for his reports and for his satirical poems, but he survived through four reigns of the northern Sung, a fact which argues for the respect, if grudging, in which he was always held.

But it is as a poet that we love 'the gay genius', whose inspiration while tipsy reminds us of the case of the Persian poet, Hafiz – and a number of others in our own time, such as Dylan Thomas.

HERMANN HESSE (1877–1962).
   Das Glasperlenspiel. First published 1943. Translated by Richard and Clara Winston as *The Glass Bead Game (Magister Ludi)* (Penguin, 1972).

The self-entranced younger generation of the 1950s and 1960s made a cult-figure of the German writer Hesse who became a naturalised Swiss in 1923. The generation was attracted by his interest in Indian mysticism (*Siddhartha,* 1922; translated by H. Rosner, Peter Owen, 1970), by his stories of artist-dreamers (*Peter Camenzind,* 1904; translated by W. J. Strachan, Penguin, 1974) and his understanding of Jungian depth psychology (*Demian,* 1919; translated by W. J. Strachan, Panther, 1969).

But his masterpiece, for which he received the Nobel Prize for Literature in 1946, was the Utopian *Das Glasperlenspiel,* one of the few intellectual novels of the century. Hesse postulates a province called 'Castalia' (in Greek myth, the Castalian Spring on Mount Parnassus is sacred to Apollo and the Muses), where the highest political office belongs to the sage Master of the Glass Bead Game, who personifies the serenity and aesthetic appreciation resulting from a life devoted to the refinement of the mind and soul. Hesse poses the eternal question of the scholar in the ivory tower, and his suitability for political and religious power. Human passions and desires, including sex, food and drink, and even close family ties, are repudiated for a life of pure intellect. As a fiction, Hesse's book is both stimulating and disturbing: as a parable, it will lead each reader to work out his own response to the challenges it will provoke.

A companion volume could be Johan Huizinga's *Homo Ludens: a study of the play element in culture* (Granada, 1970), which defines the importance of games in Western culture seen from the broadest viewpoint, such as theatricality by prosecutors in law-courts to secure a conviction. With oral practice dominating grammar-learning in the modern language courses, and with end-of-term shows taking up syllabus-time, are we perhaps not exaggerating the usefulness in play today, just as we exaggerated the usefulness of work in the 19th-century environment parodied by Dickens in his novel *Hard Times*?

Is not the notion of Utopia bound to be illusory, with perspectives of the Desirable changing from generation to generation, nation to nation, and, even within an individual's own development, from day to day?

Hesse is the author of three of Strauss' *Four Last Songs* sung to perfection by Elisabeth Schwarzkopf on HMV ASD 2888.

SIGMUND FREUD (1856–1939).
> *Die Traumdeutung.* First published 1900. Translated as *The Interpretation of Dreams* by James Strachey (Allen and Unwin, 1955).

Terms coined by Freud, or made famous by him, such as the 'Oedipus Complex', the 'libido', and the 'subconscious', as well as the erotic nature of dreams: all these cardinal features of Freudian theory are crystallised in *Die Traumdeutung,* complete in all essentials by early 1896 but not published until four years later. 'The interpretation of dreams is in fact the royal road to a knowledge of the unconscious (later redefined 'subconscious'); it is the securest foundation of psychoanalysis and the field in which every worker must acquire his convictions and seek his training', wrote Freud in the third of *Five Lectures on Psychoanalysis* in the U.S.A. and available in *Two Short Accounts of Psycho-analysis*, translated and edited by James Strachey (Penguin, 1962).

Freud taught that day-dreams express open and conscious wish-fulfilment, while night dreams express the repressed desires of the subconscious, censored during the day by the conscious mind.

It is important to recognise the line of Freud's scientific development from neurological studies in Paris under Charcot (from 1885), in Nancy (1889) and with his old family friend Josef Breuer. The opposition to Freud's theories can best be studied in Ernest Jones' great biography *Sigmund Freud: His Life and Work* (3 vols., Hogarth Press, 1954–57).

As supplementary reading to David Stafford-Clark's *What Freud Really Said* (Penguin, 1967), study E. A. Bennet's *What Jung Really Said* (Macdonald, 1966) and Frieda Fordham's *Introduction to Jung's Psychology* (Penguin, 1953), as well as Alfred Adler's *Practice and Theory of Individual Psychology* (Routledge, 1929) and J. A. C. Brown's *Freud and the post-Freudians* (Penguin, 1969).

FERNANDO DE ROJAS (*c.* 1465–1541).
> *La Comedia de Calisto y Melibea.* First published anonymously in 1499, and since popularly known as *La Celestina.* Translated as *The Spanish Bawd* by J. M. Cohen (Penguin, 1964) and as *Celestina* by Lesley B. Simpson (University of California Press, 1955).

In the form of a play (but clearly more for the ease of group reading than for staged performance), the *Celestina* can be considered a novel, and is certainly the greatest work of 15th-century Spain. The author, of whom little is known beyond the fact that he was born in a village near Toledo of Jewish parents, who had been forcibly converted to Christianity. Rojas himself fled, and later became Mayor of Talavera, where he died.

The superior (shorter) sixteen-act version comes to a quick and effective climax, whereas the 21-act version merely introduces a *miles gloriosus,* one Centurio, whose presence is valueless except for comic relief. The plot of both versions concerns the love of the nobly-born youth Calisto for Melibea, the lovely daughter of the Jew Pleberio. She rejects Calisto, so his servant Sempronio advises making use of the old go-between Celestina. It is as this point of *loco amor* that we are reminded of the 14th-century classic *Libro de Buen Amor* by Juan Ruiz, an analogy splendidly worked out by María Rosa Lida de Malkiel in her study *Dos Obras Maestras Españolas* (Editorial Universitaria de Buenos Aires, Viamonte 640, B.A., 1966). See too the fine critical work *La Celestina* (Espasa-Calpe, Buenos Aires, 1947) by Marcelino Menéndez y Pelayo.

HANS MAGNUS ENZENSBERGER (b. 1929).

Gedichte. Die Entstehung eines Gedichts (Suhrkamp Verlag, Frankfurt/ Main, 1962). A largely different selection, translated by Michael Hamburger, Jerome Rothenberg, and the author, published as *Poems* (Penguin, 1968).

A truly international poet in the international poetic arena of the mid-20th century, Enzensberger writes in German, lives in Norway, and is so fluent in English that he prefers to be his own translator.

He originally rose to fame with a bitter indictment of the German bourgeoisie (who had allowed Nazis to come to power and then to prosper), 'Verteidigung der Wölfe gegen die Lämmer', or 'A Defence of the Wolves against the Lambs'. Similar poems include 'Portrait of a House Detective' and 'Middle Class Blues'.

One of his most interesting experiments is the 'Summer Poem' of 1964, which is a 'cut-up' not in the deliberately arbitrary sense of a William Burroughs cut-up, but a reflection of the distorted, broken and interrupted speech overheard today in airports, on telephones, in the street, and on television. He has recently completed an ambitious long poem, *The Sinking of the 'Titanic'* (translated by the author, Carcanet New Press, 1981), which sees the drowning of Western civilization in the ship that sank.

Enzensberger maintains the tradition of the poem as utensil which Brecht made feasible.

HERMAN MELVILLE (1819–1891).

Moby Dick, or The White Whale. First published 1851. Numerous editions available, including those in Modern Library (1944), World's Classics (Oxford U.P., 1947), and Harper & Row (1966).

Until 1830, Melville lived in comfort and security. But then his illusions were shattered as his father went bankrupt, and later died insane from overwork and nervous exhaustion. Melville tried several careers, including farmhand and bank clerk, but in 1839 he signed on as a cabin boy, and again found illusions of a healthy outdoor life swept away by the vice and cruelty on board ship. In 1841 he signed on the whaler *Acushnet* which made for the Pacific, but deserted in the Marquesas Islands and, once away on an Australian whaler, mutinied with the crew and was imprisoned in Tahiti. After numerous other exploits savouring more of fiction that of fact, Melville devoted himself to writing, enjoying the acquaintance in 1850 of Nathaniel Hawthorne, on whom he published an essay in the same year: 'Hawthorne and his Mosses'. They became close friends in the year that Hawthorne published his best novel, *The Scarlet Letter*, but while

Hawthorne enjoyed widespread recognition, even Melville's family and friends repudiated *Moby Dick* as too complex and demanding. Melville died unrecognized, and *Billy Budd* appeared posthumously (listen to Britten's opera based on the story, 3 discs, Decca SET 379–81).

Moby Dick is not only a novel of the whaling industry, but an allegorical view of humanity seen as a crew on the ship *Pequod,* its monomaniac Captain Ahab and each of the varied crew together representing all the kinds of human personality. The first mate Starbuck is slow and prudent; the second mate Stubb is easy-going; the third mate Flask is unimaginative and views whaling as just another job. Melville's prose is often tortuous and archaic, and his dialogue often oddly out of keeping with expectations. Thus Melville makes Ahab say to Stubb in Chapter 29: 'Am I a cannon-ball, that thou wouldst wad me that fashion? But go thy ways; I had forgot. Below to thy nightly grave; where such as ye sleep between shrouds, to use ye to the filling one at last. Down, dog and kennel!'

If one can come to terms with such verbosity and rhetoric, one will find a powerful allegory of the loneliness of man, his unending quest for the known and the unknown, and his unalterable fate in death.

GERHART HAUPTMANN (1862–1946).
   Five Plays. Translated by Theodore H. Lustig (Bantam, 1961).

Influenced by his early upbringing as a science student, by years studying art in Breslau and Rome, by the lectures of the Darwinian Ernst Haeckel at the University of Jena, by Ibsen, and by the naturalist and realist French writers such as Zola and Flaubert, the young Hauptmann produced in Berlin *Vor Sonnenaufgang* (1889; translated by L. Bloomfield as *Before Dawn,* 1909), a play which reflected on stage the real Silesian peasant dialect and a determinist view of alcoholic degeneracy. Conflict within a family provokes the catastrophe of his second play, *Das Friedensfest* (1890), but Hauptmann's greatest play is probably *Die Weber* (1892), the first of the *Five Plays* above. The 'hero' is a whole Silesian village, made desperate by the misery of the Industrial Revolution.

The other plays of Hauptmann which deserve to be read today include *Rose Bernd* and *Fuhrmann Henschel* (both naturalistic tragedies), the dream-play *Hanneles Himmelfahrt,* and the 'thieves' comedy' *Der Biberpelz* ('The Beaver Coat') of 1893.

Hauptmann, who had won the Nobel Prize in 1912, gave tacit approval to the Nazi regime, and was rewarded with a 17-volume collected edition in 1942, now superseded by the Centenar Ausgabe of the *Sämtliche Werke* (11 vols., 1962–73), which appeared at the time when he was reworking Iphigeneia plays, and one-acters on Agamemnon and Electra. Note the contrast to Gluck's treatment of the Iphigeneia subjects in *Iphigénie en Aulide* (1774; 2 discs RCA ARL 2 1104) and

Iphigénie en Tauride (1779; 2 discs Cetra Opera Live L054). Gluck's greatest opera is the *Orfeo ed Euridice* (1762; 3 discs RCA SER 5539–41).

JOHANN WOLFGANG VON GOETHE (1749–1832).
    Poems. There are numerous editions in German. For the English reader with modest German there is a bilingual edition of 100 poems, *Goethe the Lyrist* (2nd ed., University of North Carolina Press, 1958) and texts with plain prose versions by David Luke in Goethe's *Selected Verse* (Penguin, 1964). The *Roman Elegies* are available in separate translations (Chatto & Windus, 1977).

Throughout his very active and varied life, Goethe produced lyric poetry of the very highest order. He began with the immortal 'Heidenröslein', 'Willkommen und Abschied' and 'Mailied' during his ten-month love affair with Friederike Brion (1770–1). In Frankfurt he composed the powerful 'Prometheus' (1774) in free rhythms – it has been set to music by Schubert and again by Wolf, and such masterpieces of titanism as 'An Schwager Kronos' ('To the Coachman Time') and 'Wanderers Sturmlied' ('Stormsong of the Wanderer').
    The more placid Weimar, influenced by Charlotte von Stein, inspired such perfect lyrics as 'An den Mond' and 'Wanderers Nachtlied', as well as the tragic intensity of 'Erlkönig' and 'Nur wer die Sehnsucht kennt'.
    Momentous changes appear in the *West-östlicher Divan* (1819), deriving its origin from the great Persian poet Hafiz (1320–89), whom he read in translation in 1814. In September and October 1814 Goethe was the guest of J. J. von Willemer, and fell in love with Willemer's young bride Marianne, his third wife. They corresponded to the end of Goethe's life, and some of Marianne's own lyrics were incorporated by Goethe in that part of the *Divan* called the 'Buch Suleika'.

JEAN JACQUES ROUSSEAU (1712–1778).
    Les Confessions. First published posthumously in 1781 (Books I–VI) and 1788 (Books VII–XII). Several translations are available, the best being that by J. M. Cohen (*Confessions*, Penguin, 1953).

As Lytton Strachey justly observed in his *Landmarks in French Literature* (1912): 'It is very easy to draw a cutting comparison between Rousseau's preaching and his practice, as it stands revealed in the *Confessions* – the lover of independence who never earned his own living, the apostle of equality who was a snob, and the educationist who left his children in the Foundling Asylum'.

But what distinguishes Rousseau's autobiography from so many others (though not from Montaigne's, which Rousseau characteristically denigrated) is that Rousseau is very keen to show his own weaknesses and failures and his inability to make durable friendships both directly, and indirectly by the testiness of his observations. He was certainly not such a success with the ladies as he would imply, and he often behaved childishly, meanly, and neurotically. Yet the very display of his failings and the pre-Byronic egotism of his writings were to exercise enormous influence on writers both autobiographical and fictional in the subsequent two hundred years.

If you are temperamentally impatient with Rousseau's foibles, try *Du Contrat Social* (1762; translated by G. D. H. Cole as *The Social Contract,* Dent and Dutton, 1950), or *Émile* (1762; translated by Barbara Foxley as *Émile; or Education,* Dent and Dutton, 1930). The former is a treatise on political rights which helped pave the way for the French Revolution. The latter is a philosophical romance on new methods of education for a boy, Émile (the first four books) and for a girl, Sophie (the fifth). Advocating teaching by processes of observation rather than by textbook and rote-learning, Rousseau anticipated the pedagogical methods of both Froebel and Pestalozzi.

Year 16

The Penguin Book of Greek Verse, edited by Constantine A. Trypanis, with plain
   prose translations of each poem (Penguin, 1971).

A miraculously successful anthology, which manages to give an impressive
representation from each and every period of Greek literature, from Homer to
Odysseus Elytis.

   The six parts are 'Ancient Greece', 'The Hellenistic World', 'The Period of
Transition' (from the 4th to the 6th centuries A.D.), 'The Byzantine Empire',
'Under Frankish and Turkish Rule', and 'Modern Greece' (from liberation in
1828).

   Three other anthologies might be mentioned: *The Oxford Book of Greek Verse*
(O.U.P., 1930), its complement *The Oxford Book of Greek Verse in Translation*
(O.U.P., 1938), and C. A. Trypanis' *Medieval and Modern Greek Poetry* (O.U.P.,
1951).

   A useful companion to all of these is Professor Trypanis' *Greek Poetry from
Homer to Seferis* (Faber & Faber, 1981).

   Parallel exploration of Greek art and architecture contemporary with each
period would be rewarding. Among the numerous authorities to be
recommended are the latest edition of Gisela M. A. Richter's *A Handbook of
Greek Art* (Phaidon Press) and David Talbot Rice's *The Appreciation of Byzantine
Art* (Oxford U.P., 1974).

Great Sanskrit Plays in new English transcreations by P. Lal (New Directions,
   1957).

A good introduction sets six major Indian plays in their literary and historical
context.

   The Dream of Vasavadatta attributed to Bhasa (*c.* 400 B.C.?) is a love story
taken from an incident in the *Ramayana* epic. *Shakuntala* by Kalidasa (*c.* 400
A.D.) tells how King Dushanta falls in love with Shakuntala, who falls under a
curse that she shall be forgotten by the King until he sees again the ring he gave

her. There are equally unsatisfactory versions by M. Monier-Williams and A. W. Ryder, the latter in Everyman's Library. *The Little Clay Cart* by Shudraka (*c.* 400 A.D.) is also available in better translations by R. P. Oliver (University of Illinois Press, 1938) and by J. A. B. van Buitenen (see below). *Ratnavali,* attributed to Harsha (606–647 A.D.), dramatises episodes from the legends of King Udayana and his Queen Vasavadatta, other parts of which had already been treated by Bhasa (see above). *The Later Story of Rama* by Bhavabhuti (8th century A.D.) is a dramatic sequel to the *Ramayana* of Valmiki, and enjoys a reputation as one of the few experimental works in later Sanskrit. *The Signet Ring of Rakshasa* by Visakhadatta is better rendered by J. A. B. van Buitenen in *Two Plays of Ancient India,* Columbia U.P., 1968).

This is an appropriate moment to study *Indian Painting* (Macmillan, 1978) by Douglas Barrett and Basil Gray, and Heinrich Zimmer's *Myths and Symbols in Indian Art and Civilization* (Harper & Row, 1962).

PAUSANIAS (*c.* 120–180).
> *Hellados Periegeseos* ('Description of Greece'). Text with a translation in 4 volumes, and a companion volume, in the Loeb Classical Library (Heinemann and Harvard U.P., 1955). Translated by Peter Levi as *Guide to Greece* (2 vols., Penguin, 1971).

Pausanias (himself a Lydian) travelled widely in southern and central Greece, to judge from his writings, but little in the north or the islands. Much of what he wrote of, and in particular the religious cults of provincial and rural Greece, will not interest the modern traveller except as a first-hand view of the superstitious fears of educated sightseers in the 2nd century A.D. As a writer he is tediously fond of lists of names, but in the sensitive hands of the Roman Catholic priest and poet Peter Levi, the annotated Penguin translation serves the original supremely well, and anyone using the Loeb companion, with its plans, photographs, and full index, will find his understanding of Greek topography greatly broadened and deepened.

Pausanias alone is inadequate preparation for travels in Greece. Your local bookseller or librarian will assist in recommending up-to-date titles, but any short-list will include the latest editions of the *Blue Guide to Greece* (Benn) and the *Companion Guide to the Greek Islands* by Ernle Bradford (Collins).

'HOMER' (Exact identity, and thus dating, not known),
> *Odysseia.* Written between the 12th and the 7th centuries B.C., probably in the 9th. Text and translation, as *The Odyssey,* by A. T. Murray in the Loeb

Classical Library (2 vols., Heinemann and Harvard U.P., 1919). Translations, each good in its own way, by Robert Fitzgerald in Anchor Books (Doubleday, 1963); by E. V. Rieu (Penguin, 1945); and by Richmond Lattimore (Harper & Row, 1967).

Matthew Arnold's *On Translating Homer* (1861) defined the problems in translating from the dactylic hexameters of Homeric Greek into English as those of achieving a rapid flow, plainness, nobility, simplicity, and directness in both idea and language. He argued that one can only render the great epic poems in dactylic hexameters like the original, in blank verse, or in iambic pentameters, and criticised each translation made up to that time.

'Homer', thought to be a woman by Samuel Butler (*The Authoress of the Odyssey,* 1897; University of Chicago Press, 1967), was more likely a man, who lived on the coast of Asia Minor, and forged out of the most disparate source materials the original epics, the *Odyssey* and the *Iliad,* by which all subsequent long epic poems have been judged. The *Odyssey* recounts the wanderings of Odysseus (Ulixes in Latin, later Ulysses) and the final homecoming to Ithaca and the faithful Penelope. It is the first adventure novel in the West. Nikos Kazantzakis, in *The Odyssey: a Modern Sequel* (1938; translated by the Author and Kimon Friar, Simon & Schuster, 1962), has taken the story further.

It is worth learning Greek solely for Homer, though one would not start Greek literature with the epics, but with the easier Attic works of Sophocles (say the *Aias,* 'Ajax') and of Plato (say the *Apologia* of Socrates). Background reading to intersperse with the taxing language of the *Odyssey* might well include Moses I. Finley's remarkable evocation, *The World of Odysseus* (Penguin, 1962), the topographical basis of the epic in Ernle Bradford's *Ulysses Found* (Sphere, 1967), and the literary succession in W. B. Stanford's *The Ulysses Theme: a Study in the Adaptability of a Traditional Hero* (2nd ed., Barnes & Noble, 1964).

The most illuminating author on Homer may be G. S. Kirk (*The Songs of Homer,* Cambridge U.P., 1962; *Homer and the Epic,* C.U.P., 1965; and *Homer and the Oral Tradition,* C.U.P., 1976).

DAVID HERBERT LAWRENCE (1885–1930).
Sons and Lovers. First published 1913 (Penguin, 1948).

The best introduction to the diverse literary output of D. H. Lawrence (who also painted, was a poet of some stature, and wrote entertaining travel sketches and essays) is the overtly autobiographical *Sons and Lovers.* Lawrence was born in Eastwood, Nottinghamshire, to a coarse, uneducated miner who had worked at Brinsley Colliery since the age of seven. With the inspiration and devotion of his mother, Lawrence won a scholarship to Nottingham High School, became a pupil-teacher in Eastwood, and attended Nottingham University to obtain a teaching certificate.

In *Sons and Lovers,* Paul Morel is a sensitive, artistic boy protected by Mrs. Morel from his hard-drinking father. As Paul grows up, his loving relationship with his mother changes imperceptibly as first Miriam, and then Clara, come into his life. *Sons and Lovers* describes all these relationships, and hints at undercurrents.

Further reading in Lawrence might take the course of the *Complete Short Stories* (3 vols., Viking and Heinemann, 1955–61), the *Collected Letters,* (Viking and Heinemann, 1962), or a sequence of the novels in chronological order, including *The White Peacock, The Rainbow, Women in Love,* and *Kangaroo.*

See F. R. Leavis' *D. H. Lawrence, Novelist* (Chatto & Windus, 1955; Knopf, 1956) and Harry T. Moore's *The Life and Works of D. H. Lawrence* (Allen & Unwin and Twayne, 1951).

ARISTOTLE (384–322 B.C.).
> *Politica.* Edited by W. D. Ross for Oxford Classical Texts (Oxford U.P., 1957). Translated as *Politics* by J. A. Sinclair (Penguin, 1962).

One of the most durable virtues of the *Politics* of Aristotle is that it not only takes into account Plato's *Republic* and *Laws* (criticizing them where Aristotle feels they are wrong, but it condenses and expresses the long tradition of Greek theory and practice in their self-conscious attempts to form the perfect city-state. Ironically, the careers of Aristotle's Macedonian patrons – we realise with hindsight – wrote the death-warrant for the type of Greek community that he regarded as the highest of which human endeavour was capable.

We can no longer agree with him that slavery is an indispensable basis for any civilization, nor do all of us concur that commerce degrades the individual and destroys the community's morality. But we must read what he has to say, for his moral rectitude stands – with certain definite exceptions – for the ideal of modern rulers and model electors. If each of us has the obligation to vote for a system of government through its known candidates, then much of this obligation is owed to a mental and moral world-attitude crystallised by Aristotle in the fourth century B.C. When we speak of our political ancestors and think of Pitt, Burke, Gladstone, Disraeli or Lloyd George, it is truer to go farther back, to Aristotle and to Plato, for the source of our political preconceptions and opinions.

PLATO (*c.* 429–347 B.C.).
> *Politeia.* Edited by J. Burnet for Oxford Classical Texts (Plato Vol. IV, Oxford U.P., 1905). Translated by H. D. P. Lee as *The Republic* (Penguin, 1955).

The conventional anglicised title 'Republic' is misleading, *politeia* meaning originally 'state', 'society' or 'constitution', that is much the same significance as the Latin *respublica*.

The subjects dealt with are however much wider still: morals (parts I and V), politics and society (parts II, IV and VI), education (parts III and VIII), philosophy (parts VII and X), and religion (part XI). In general, the Greeks believed 'that the law of the state is the source of all standards of human life, and that the virtue of the individual is the same as the virtue of the citizen' (as Werner Jaeger wrote in *Paideia* (vol. 2, Oxford U.P., 1971). The larger a political or industrial or social or commercial entity becomes, the less affection and loyalty is felt towards it by each individual within it.

Every reader discovers his own *Republic*. A. E. Taylor, in his *Plato* (7th ed., Methuen, 1966), makes no adverse criticism. R. H. S. Crossman, however, in *Plato Today* (2nd ed., Allen & Unwin, 1959), considers Plato a reactionary encouraging in practice 'the dictatorship of the virtuous Right', a position arguable from the actual situation in which Plato found himself. Karl Popper, in his thoughtful *The Open Society and its Enemies* (4th ed., Routledge, 1962), takes Plato to be Utopian, preparing a 'blueprint of the society at which we aim' and then to be ruthless in trying to achieve that society. For Popper, anyone like Plato who aims to reduce politics to an exact science is mistaken.

Nobody should deprive himself of the exciting challenge of discussing Plato's great dialogue, *Politeia*.

Shih Ching ('The Book of Songs'). Compiled between 1000 and 700 B.C. Translated with text and transcriptions by B. Karlgren (*The Book of Odes*, Museum of Far Eastern Antiquities, Stockholm, 1950); Arthur Waley (*The Book of Songs*, 2nd ed., Allen & Unwin, 1954); and James Legge (*The She King, or The Book of Poetry*, in vol. IV of *The Chinese Classics*, several reprints).

Ssu-ma Ch'ien records that there were originally over 3,000 songs, drawn from all parts of China, but Confucius reduced this vast collection to a basic anthology of about 300. This is debatable, to say the least, but since Confucius refers to '300 poems', the collection must have been in something like its present form by 550 B.C.

By the end of the 3rd century B.C. the *Shih Ching* had become one of the *Wu Ching* or 'Five Classics', the others being the *I Ching* ('Book of Changes'), the *Shu Ching* ('Book of History'), the *Li Chi* ('Book of Propriety') and the *Ch'un Ch'iu* ('Spring and Autumn Annals').

The *Shih Ching* is divided into three parts, according to the type of musical accompaniment: *sung* (including the Chou and Shang ceremonial dances, often on the virtues of ancestors, preparations for war, and the work of the peasant's year); *ya* (the later secular court poems, from the Western Chou and early Eastern Chou periods, often influenced by folk poetry and dealing with fighting between noble families, unfair taxes and oppression, and the work of peasants and farmers); and *feng,* the bulk of the work, including love songs, wedding songs, and work songs.

Most Chinese poets felt the appeal of at least some of the *Shih Ching;* T'ao Ch'ien (365–427) was particularly closely connected with the straightforward, domestic verse of the Book of Songs. Ezra Pound is the most important modern poet to have rendered the *Shih Ching:* see his *Confucian Odes: the classic anthology defined by Confucius* (New Directions, 1959).

OSIP EMILIEVICH MANDELSTAM (1891–1938).
   Sobraniye sochinenii, edited by Gleb Struve and Boris Filippov (2 vols., 2nd ed., Inter-Language Literary Associates, New York, 1967). *Selected Poems,* translated by Clarence Brown and W. S. Merwin (Penguin, 1977).

Mandelstam's tormented life reached a worldwide public with the great biographies written by his widow Nadezhda, *Hope against Hope* (Penguin, 1975) and *Hope Abandoned* (Penguin, 1976), both translated by Max Hayward.

His poems are much better known, though even now he is a 'non-person' in the Soviet Union, having been persecuted from November 1933, when 'The Stalin Epigram' beginning "Our lives no longer feel ground under them" was written. He was first arrested in 1934 and sent to Cherdyn, then spent the years 1935–7 in Voronezh. In 1938 he was arrested again, shortly after release, and died in captivity.

Mandelstam stands for the survival of poetry in an age of cruelty and terror. He had been a member of Gumilev's Acmeist group from 1910 to the outbreak of World War I, and after Gumilev had been executed by firing squad in 1921 Mandelstam and all other former associates of Gumilev came under suspicion. Mandelstam's muse was silent from 1925 to 1930, the year in which his protector Nikolai Bukharin had sent him and Nadezhda off to Armenia, ostensibly to study sovietization there, but in fact just to keep them out of harm's reach. The *Journey to Armenia* has been translated by Sidney Monas, and published, with a critical essay by Henry Gifford, by George F. Ritchie, 665 Pine Street, No. 503, San Francisco, California 94108 (1979).

Year 17

XENOPHON (*c.* 429–*c.* 354 B.C.)
Kurou Paideia. Text with a translation (as *Cyropaedia*) by W. Miller in Loeb
Classical Library (2 vols., Heinemann and Harvard U.P., 1914). Translated
as *The Education of Cyrus* by H. G. Dakyns and revised by F. M. Stawell in
Everyman's Library (Dent and Dutton, 1914).

Xenophon, unusually long-lived for a Greek general in the fourth century B.C.,
wrote a great deal in his retirement. The best-known of his writings are the
Hellenica, a history of his times explicitly following from the last book of
Thucydides, that is from 411 B.C., to the inconclusive Battle of Mantinea in 362;
the adventures of the Ten Thousand on their way back from Persia to Greece
after the death of Cyrus as told in the *Anabasis;* and the three works in which his
mentor Socrates is the central figure: the *Memorabilia,* the *Apologia* for Socrates
which adds to the portrait presented by Plato, and the *Symposium.*

However, his most interesting and complex work, invariably underrated, is the
so-called *Cyropaedia,* which has been consistently misunderstood.

To appreciate it, one must set Xenophon in his context as a brave and efficient
general who had led many of his men back safely from Persia, only to learn with
horror that his fellow-Athenians had put to death the wise sceptic Socrates,
whom he had loved, and had come to hold the knightly class to whom Xenophon
belonged in contempt and hatred. In disgust, Xenophon and the returning troops
joined the conquest of the East. His *Education of Cyrus* is a political fiction, in
which the ideal ruler (Cyrus, known personally to Xenophon) undergoes the
education of a Spartan youth. The teacher of Tigranes is not a Persian, but
Socrates. The ideal constitution is not that of Persian but of Sparta. The simple
food and dress of the Persians is also clearly Spartan. As well as the intriguing
Socratic dialogues – in some of which we catch the authentic tones of the
Athenian's voice – there is the charming love story of Panthea and Abradatas.
The *Cyropaedia,* then, succeeds on several levels and is worth reading for its
military tactics, its romance, its biographical and historical information (if read
with caution), and its picture of the education of the ideal Spartan in a city-state
governed by an ideal constitutional monarchy.

Xenophon is available complete in the Oxford Classical Texts (5 vols., Oxford U.P., 1901–21). Translations that have so far appeared in Penguin are by Rex Warner (*Anabasis,* rendered 'The Persian Expedition', 1949; *Hellenica,* rendered 'History of My Times', 1966) and by H. Tredennick (*Memorabilia* and *Symposium,* 1970).

ROBERT BURNS (1759–1796).
> *Poems and Songs.* Edited by James Kinsley. Oxford Standard Authors (Oxford U.P., 1971). The Oxford English Texts set (Oxford U.P., 1968) is in three vols.

The Alloway-born poet was the son of a cottar, who took pains that the boy should read widely but could not prevent the wenching and drinking which were to shorten Rabbie's life. Working as a farm-labourer at Mossgiel with his brother Gilbert from 1784–88, he composed some of his best poems, among them the satires 'Holy Willie's Prayer' (against a church elder of Mauchline) and 'Death and Dr. Hornbook' (against an apothecary). In 1786 he published the *Poems, Chiefly in the Scottish Dialect* which made his name, and he was soon a welcome guest in Edinburgh literary circles. With the £500 he received from the second, Edinburgh, edition of his poems, Burns was able to buy a small farm and to marry Jean Armour, one of his many mistresses. Burns took pains to collect traditional songs of the Lowlands, and adapted many with his own genius for evoking the field, the wood, and the human and animal creatures around him. A true poet for the people, Burns also composed erotic verse for *The Merry Muses of Caledonia* (Panther, 1970).

Since Burns wrote in dialect, he is best appreciated on records, and must be accompanied by a glossary.

The reason that the shorter Kinsley edition is recommended above lies in the fact that the minor verse of Burns derives from the English Augustans and has consequently little value.

Burns has always been highly valued overseas. The Dane Jeppe Aakjaer (1886–1930), the son of a poor farmer, began by writing bad socialist novels, but finally evolved into a fine dialect poet, under the influence of Burns.

EURIPIDES (*c.* 480–406 B.C.).
> Tragedies. Text with translations by A. S. Way in Loeb Classical Library (4 vols., Heinemann and Harvard U.P., 1912–23). Several good translations are available (though none is wholly recommendable), including five volumes (Euripides I–V) of *The Complete Greek Tragedies,* edited by David Grene and Richmond Lattimore (University of Chicago Press, 1959).

Euripides composed about 92 plays, mostly tragedies with very few satyr plays (one has been translated in R. L. Green's *Two Satyr Plays,* Penguin, 1957), but won only four victories in his lifetime, because his work was considered too sensational or intellectual by the conservative audiences of his time. Subsequently his work was so greatly prized, however, that nineteen of his plays are extant, and we have fragments of many more, indicating greater popularity in later generations than either Aeschylus or Sophocles enjoyed. His earliest dated work is the *Alcestis,* in a tetralogy placed second in 438 B.C. A great Kirsten Flagstad recording of Gluck's *Alceste,* on the same theme, can be heard on 3 discs (Decca GOS 574–6).

The innovations of Euripides include the separation of chorus from action, using the prologue as an explanation to introduce the action, advancing dramatic treatment of female psychology to the very limit, and making language correspond to the colloquial styles of his own day – a device shocking to audiences accustomed to the rhetoric of Aeschylus. In the *Helena* (412 B.C.) and the *Ion* (411), Euripides anticipates the melodrama of the New Comedy.

Admirers of Euripides will ruefully enjoy the *Acharnians* and *Frogs* of Aristophanes, who pilloried the misunderstood tragedian to the delight of the crowds, and will benefit from T. B. L. Webster's *Tragedies of Euripides* (Methuen and Barnes & Noble, 1967). At least two months should be devoted to Euripides, ending with his last masterpiece, *The Bacchae,* dating to 405, the same year as the *Iphigeneia in Aulis.*

An excellent background book is P. Vellacott's *Ironic Drama* (Cambridge U.P., 1975).

LEONARDO DA VINCI (1452–1519).

Notebooks. Arranged, rendered into English and introduced by Edward MacCurdy (2 vols., New ed., Cape, 1978).

An indispensable treasury of original insights, jokes, inventions, and observations by one of the most remarkable men the world has ever known.

MacCurdy's careful editing classifies some five thousand pages of the original MS. into some fifty headings, naturally omitting such irrelevancies as pages of Latin declensions and conjugations.

An alternative compilation is Jean Paul Richter's *The Literary Works of Leonardo da Vinci* (3rd ed., 2 vols., Phaidon Press, 1970) and the useful *Commentary* by Carlo Pedretti on Richter's edition (2 vols., Phaidon Press, 1977) with a supplement of newly-transcribed and translated texts, and a selection from the recently-discovered Madrid MSS.

One will need a full edition of the *Paintings and Drawings* of Leonardo, such as that by Ludwig Goldscheider (latest ed., Phaidon Press). The *Drawings* are available separately (Cape, 1973), as are the *Paintings* (Weidenfeld and Nicolson, 1969).

Among the general monographs on Leonardo's achievement, one must single out that by Sir Kenneth Clark (Penguin, 1968).

EPICURUS (341–270 B.C.).
Writings. As quoted in the *Vitae philosophorum ('Lives and opinions of the eminent philosophers')* of Diogenes Laertius, with a translation by R. D. Hicks in Loeb Classical Library (2 vols., Heinemann and Harvard U.P., 1925, Book X).

Diogenes Laertius cites the 'Letter to Herodotus', on physics; the 'Letter to Pythocles', on astronomy; the 'Letter to Metrodorus', on ethics and our chief source (other than the *De rerum natura* of Lucretius, q.v.) for the teachings of Epicurus; forty *Kuriai Doxai* ('Sovereign Maxims'); and Epicurus' Will. A further eighty maxims were found in a Vatican MS. in 1888.

The powerful schools of Plato and Aristotle neglected the Epicurean texts, so that nearly all the 300 works he is believed to have written are no longer extant. Further, his teachings were maligned as immoral and hedonistic, whereas in fact Epicurus taught the renunciation of worldly ambition and desires, freedom from fear of death and of gods.

The teaching of his school was neatly summarised by Diogenes of Oenoanda: "Aphobon ho theos. Anaistheton ho thanatos. To agathon eukteton. To deinon euekkartereton", rendered by Gilbert Murray 'Nothing to fear in God. Nothing to feel in Death. Good can be attained. Evil can be endured'.

Assessments of the thought of Epicurus include N. W. de Witt's *Epicurus and his Philosophy* (University of Minnesota Press, 1954), Benjamin Farrington's *The Faith of Epicurus* (Weidenfeld and Nicolson, 1959), and J. M. Rist's *Epicurus* (2nd ed., Cambridge U.P., 1977).

Epicurus appears in two of the *Imaginary Conversations* (1824–53) by Walter Savage Landor.

HEINRICH VON KLEIST (1777–1811).
Erzählungen. First published collection in 2 vols., 1810–1811.

Kleist, born into an old military family, served in the Foot Guards in his youth, but resigned his commission in 1799, undergoing the so-called 'Kant Crisis' in 1801 when his reading of Kant's *Kritik der reinen Vernunft* ('Critique of Pure Reason', 1781) persuaded him of the futility of acquiring knowledge by intellectual means alone, and induced him to write to his fiancée that his "only and highest goal" had been extinguished.

Nevertheless, Kleist wrote a number of plays (none performed during his lifetime) of exceptional worth, in particular *Prinz Friedrich von Homburg,* written in 1810 and published in 1821 (translated by Charles E. Passage, Liberal Arts-Merrill, 1956).

Today he is highly regarded for his *Novellen,* or short stories. *The Marquise of O- and other stories* (translated by Martin Greenberg, New American Library, 1962) contains in addition to the title story, 'Michael Kohlhaas', 'The Beggarwoman of Locarno', 'The Engagement in Santo Domingo', 'The Foundling', 'The Earthquake in Chile', 'St. Cecilia', and 'The Duel'. Of these stories, the finest is the tragic 'Michael Kohlhaas', concerned with the discrepancy between justice in theory and practice and drawn from actual events culminating in the execution of the historical Kohlhase in 1540.

Kleist died at his own hand on the shore of the Wannsee, after having shot Henriette Vogel at her own request to cut short her sufferings (probably from terminal cancer). See Robert E. Helbling's *Heinrich von Kleist: the Major Works* (New Directions, 1975) and John M. Ellis' *Heinrich von Kleist* (University of North Carolina Press, 1979).

This is an appropriate time to concentrate on the symphonies and songs of Franz Schubert (1797–1828). The best available set of the symphonies is that by the Berlin Philharmonic under Karl Boehm (5 discs, DGG 2740 127).

'HOMER' (Exact identity, and thus dating, not known).
    Ilias. Written between the 12th and the 7th centuries B.C., probably in the 9th. Text and translation, as *The Iliad,* by A. T. Murray in the Loeb Classical Library (2 vols., Heinemann and Harvard U.P., 1924–5). Translations, each good in its own way, by Robert Graves (as *The Anger of Achilles,* New English Library, 1962); by E. V. Rieu (Penguin, 1953); and by Richmond Lattimore (University of Chicago Press, 1951). Book XVI has been translated as *The Patrocleia* in verse by Christopher Logue (University of Michigan Press, 1963) and is a good example of structural translation.

The *Iliad* is a major epic poem in dactylic hexameters which narrates forty days' events in the war of the Greeks against Troy. It is more unified than the Odyssey, but inevitably much more static and rhetorical.

Troy and the Trojans by Carl W. Blegen (Praeger and Thames & Hudson, 1963) is a succinct statement of recent work on Troy, but this is a good moment to study the excavations at Troy and elsewhere by the extraordinary Heinrich Schliemann. Schliemann's books have been reprinted entire, but those without a special interest in antiquarian archaeology would benefit from Leo Deuel's *Memoirs of Heinrich Schliemann: a documentary portrait* (Hutchinson, 1978). Greek gods, heroes and other mythic figures can be studied in Robert Graves' *Greek Myths* (2 vols., Penguin, 1955), and two other excellent background books convey the feeling of the mental and physical environment of the early Greeks: H. D. F. Kitto's *The Greeks* (Penguin, 1951), and *The Greek World,* edited by Hugh Lloyd-Jones (Penguin, 1965).

CHIKAMATSU MONZAEMON (1653–1725).
Major Plays. Translated by Donald Keene (Columbia U.P., 1961).

A strange phenomenon – that puppet plays could rank above stage plays both in popular favour and in critical esteem. But it is true that, except for the years 1688 to 1703, when Chikamatsu was collaborating with the *kabuki* actor Sawamura Tojuro, his best writing was all for the *joruri* (puppet theatre) of Japan. From 1703 to the end of the 18th century the *joruri* theatre was more highly esteemed than the *kabuki.* His first definite signed work is the *Yotsugi Soga* ('The Soga Heir') of 1683, anticipating in its contrast between battlefield and brothel the incongruity characteristic of later *joruri* productions.

For the chanter Takemoto Gidayu, Chikamatsu wrote the play *Sonezaki Shinju* ('Love Suicides at Sonezaki') of 1703, a success resting on the topicality of the tragic theme, the beauty of the writing, and the impressive chanting of Gidayu. A similar plot occurs in the famous *Shinju ten no Amijima* ('Love Suicides at Amijima') of 1721, well translated by Donald H. Shively in *The Love Suicide at Amijima* (Harvard U.P., 1953).

Chikamatsu also wrote plays based on history and legend, the best being *Kokusenya Kassen* ('The Battles of Coxinga') of 1715, which has been performed by *kabuki* actors, as well as by *joruri* companies.

A good background book is *Japanese Theatre* (Tuttle, Tokyo, 1974) by Faubion Bowers.

SOPHOCLES (*c.* 496–*c.* 406 B.C.).
Tragedies. Text with translations by Francis Storr in Loeb Classical Library (2 vols., Heinemann and Harvard U.P., 1912). Several good translations are available (though none is wholly recommendable), including two volumes (Sophocles I and II) of *The Complete Greek Tragedies,* edited by David Grene and Richmond Lattimore (Washington Square, 1961–7).

The probable order of composition (with very approximate dates of first performance of the extant Sophoclean plays – there is also a surviving satyr play in R. L. Green's *Two Satyr Plays,* Penguin, 1957) – is as follows: *Ajax,* 445 B.C., *Antigone,* 441, *Oedipus Rex,* 430, *Women of Trachis,* 413, *Electra,* 410, *Philoctetes,* 409, and *Oedipus at Colonus,* posthumously in 401.

Sophocles wrote about 120 plays, and won victories with eighteen tetralogies (comprising a trilogy of tragedies with a comedy or 'satyr play' for light relief), his first victory – over Aeschylus – being in 468.

Among the great dramatic innovations of Sophocles was the introduction of the third actor; the idea that men play a larger part in life (and hence in drama) than do gods; the introduction of stage scenery; and the augmenting of the chorus from twelve players to fifteen. Sophocles instructs the audience by endowing most of his characters with high motives for their actions, reproaching Euripides (in Aristotle's account) for portraying people as they are instead of how they ought to be.

His great heroines, who have influenced numerous later playwrights, are the types of feminine courage: Antigone, contrasted with the time-serving bureaucrat Creon, in one reading; and Electra, contrasted with the hesitant Orestes and the tragic regicide and adulteress Clytemnestra. Sophocles invents nothing and imagines very little: the art of his drama lies in the moral questions which are resolved or left in the disturbed minds of his audience.

The most useful companion to Sophocles is R. P. Winnington-Ingram's *Sophocles: an Interpretation* (Cambridge U.P., 1980).

Year 18

It is suggested that Year 18 should be devoted mainly to the literature, civilization and topography of either Turkey or Iran, depending on interests and circumstances. Four months are devoted to literary works classic and modern of each culture, so that if, for instance, one concentrates on Turkey, the language and history can be studied in the four months allocated to Persian literature, and *vice versa*.

SOMADEVA BHATTA (11th century A.D.).
> *Kathasaritsagara*. Translated by C. H. Tawney with the subtitle 'Ocean of the Streams of Story' and reprinted, under the editorship of N. M. Penzer (10 vols., C. J. Sawyer, 1924–8).

The Indian equivalent of the *Arabian Nights* was the lost *Brhatkatha* ('Great Narrative') by Gunadhya, who made his compilation before the 6th century A.D. in the Paisaci form of Prakrit. The frame-narrative deals with the life and adventures of King Udayana.

Two recensions have survived in part: the Nepali and the Kashmiri. The Kashmiri recension is known in two versions: Somadeva's, and the *Brhatkathamanjari* (*c.* 1037) compiled by Ksemendra. Somadeva's Sanskrit version retells some 350 fairy-tales, anecdotes, and adventure stories in plain but adequate verse. The book, like its Arabian equivalent, can be considered a useful source for Indian social and religious life in Somadeva's time, and for many later poets and dramatists.

Jacob Samuel Speyer's *Studies about the Kathasaritsagara* (J. Müller, Amsterdam, 1908) is a valuable background book.

NAZIM HIKMET (1902–1963).
> *Seçilmiş Şiirler* ('Selected Poems'). First published in Sofia, 1954. Different compilations, all translated by Taner Baybars, are *Selected Poems* (Cape, 1967), *Moscow Symphony and other Poems* (Rapp & Whiting, 1970), and

The Day Before Tomorrow (Carcanet Press, 1972).

Hikmet was born in Thessaloniki (then a Turkish town) and educated in a naval school at Heybeliada, on the Sea of Marmara. In 1921 he reached the Soviet Union, where he studied French, physics and chemistry. An ardent Marxist, Hikmet spent periods in prison for his political ideals and in 1938 was sentenced to 35 years' imprisonment for allegedly inciting Army and Navy cadets to spread Communism among the Turkish armed forces. Released in 1915 under a general amnesty, Hikmet again sought refuge in the Soviet Union, where he died.

Much of his poetry is standard Marxist rhetoric familiar from the worst patches of Mayakovsky, Pablo Neruda and many more of lesser talent. But his best poems, which found their way round Anatolia by word of mouth, among the peasants, revolutionised Turkish poetry by introducing intimate lyrics based on robust optimism in free verse of constantly fluctuating rhythms. He also wrote plays and novels, but his influence – throughout the Soviet Union as well as in Turkey and Eastern Europe – has been through his poems, which reach out from prison to the higher reaches of the human spirit with indomitable humour and colloquial power in such lines as those of 'Pierre Loti' (against imperialism) and 'Advice to our Children' (against village quranic schoolteachers).

MUSHARRIF AD-DIN b. MUSLIH SA'DI (*c.* 1208–*c.* 1292).
  Gulistan. Translated by Edward Rehatsek (Allen and Unwin, 1964), and by
  E. B. Eastwick (Octagon Press, 1974).

Born and dying in Shiraz, Sa'di spent many years travelling in the Middle East, including the pilgrimage to Mecca. He returned to his native city in 1256, and in the following year presented the ruler with the didactic poem *Bustan* ('The Rose Garden') which is generally regarded as the apogee of classical Persian prose and verse by the 'philosopher of common sense' teaching not the superficial etiquette of court life, but the wisdom of the mystic who governs himself by the strictest code yet regards his fellow-creatures with tolerance and understanding. The *Gulistan* inspired the graceful *Baharistan* ('Spring Orchard') of Nur ad-Din Abd ar-Rahman Jami (1414–1492), and the *ghazals* of Sa'di likewise inspired those of Jami as well as those of Hafiz (q.v.).

Shiraz, with Isfahan, is the most lovely of Persian cities: its women and its gardens are equally highly regarded for their beauty. An indispensable guide to the latter is Donald N. Wilber's *Persian Gardens and Garden Pavilions* (Tuttle, 1962). For the cultural background, see A. J. Arberry's *Shiraz* (Luzac, 1960).

MEHMET b. SÜLEYMAN FUZULI (*c.* 1490–*c.* 1556).
Leyla ve Mecnun. Written 1535–6. Edited by N. H. Onan as *Leyla ile Mecnun* (Istanbul, 1955). Freely translated by Sofi Huri as *Leyla and Mejnun* (Allen & Unwin, 1970).

The poet Mehmet adopted the pseudonym 'Fuzuli' (meaning both 'presumptuous' and 'virtuous') because he was certain that nobody else would assume it. Despite his humble position (for many years an attendant on the shrine of 'Ali at Najaf, in present-day Iraq), Fuzuli mastered the Azeri dialect of Turkish, Arabic, and Persian sufficiently well to compose a *divan* in all three tongues. The Turkish *divan* is a mystical compendium of surprising unity in which the poet despairs of reaching in life the essence of the divine reality, yet feels that the attempt must still be made.

But his chief claim to fame is the finest Turkish narrative poem on the sad loves of Leyla and Mejnun, which achieves depth by allegorizing the story as a quest for spiritual love.

Ilyas b. Yusuf Nizami of Ganja (now Kirovabad in Soviet Azerbaijan) wrote a Persian example of the *Leyla o Majnun* genre in 1188, and it is Nizami's version which is now most highly praised by Persian scholars. Originally of Arab descent, the story tells of the young bedu Qais and his tragic love for Laila, who is married to another while Qais wanders the desert mad (*Majnun*). There are unfortunately no good translations of Nizami in English: J. Atkinson's has been outdated by V. Dastgirdi's edition (Tehran, 1954), while R. Gelpke's prose version (made with E. Mattin and G. Hill (Faber & Faber for Cassirer, 1966) is faithless and woefully incomplete. There is a good critical edition by A. A. Aleskerzade and F. Babaeva (Akademiya Nauk SSSR. Institut Narodov Azii, Moscow, 1965).

A companion to Nizami might be Basil Gray's *Persian Painting* (Skira and World Publishing Co., 1961). Regrettably there is no comparable work on Turkish painting, but two brief illustrated monographs can be confidently recommended: Richard Ettinghausen's *Turkish Miniatures from the 13th to the 18th Century* (Collins with Unesco, 1965), and G. M. Meredith-Owens' *Turkish Miniatures* (British Museum, 1963).

Both Iran and Turkey are well covered by representative masterpieces in *Islamic Architecture and its Decoration* (latest ed., Faber & Faber), by Derek Hill and Oleg Grabar. *Turkish Art and Architecture,* by Aslanapa (Faber & Faber, 1971) and *The Art and Architecture of Turkey* edited by E. Akurgal (Oxford U.P., 1980) are also recommended.

EVLIYA b. DERVIŞ MUHAMMAD ('EVLIYA CELEBI') (*c.* 1611–*c.* 1684).
Tarihi seyyah ('Chronicle of a Traveller'), better known as the *Seyahatname* ('Book of Travels'). First published in 10 vols., 1896–1936. The first two

vols., translated by J. von Hammer-Purgstall as *Narrative of Travels in Europe, Asia and Africa* (1846–50), have been reprinted by Johnson Reprint Corporation, 111 Fifth Avenue, New York, N.Y. 10003.

The whole of Evliya's great travel book has never been translated in full into any Western language, despite the fact that it is the major work by a perennially interesting Turk who observed life in the Middle East and Eastern Europe (as far of Vienna), starting in 1631–7, while in his twenties. He accompanied his uncle the Grand Vizier Melek Ahmet Pasha to Sofia and the other European cities, and took part in the Polish Campaign. The early volumes describe Istanbul, Bursa, and other cities of Asia Minor, the Cretan campaign, and journeys to Baghdad, Hungary and Czechoslovakia. The later volumes deal with Syria, Arabia, Sudan, Ethiopia, and Egypt.

He rarely quotes sources for his second-hand observations, and some of them are wildly fantastic or exaggerated, but his first-hand notes are reliable enough, ranging from languages and customs to geography, architecture and striking landscapes.

Evliya's great book deserves to be translated in full.

JALAL AD-DIN RUMI (1207–1273).
   Mathnawi. Text (3 vols.) and translation by R. A. Nicholson (3 vols., Luzac 1977). And *Fihi ma fihi* ('It Contains what it Contains') translated by A. J. Arberry (Murray, 1961).

The prose Persian *Discourses* is a parallel companion to the great Persian poem *Mathnawi* with its 26,000-odd couplets in the *ramal musaddas* metre. This is the heart of Sufism, that aspect of Islam (though rejected by orthodox Muslims) which is founded in mysticism and spirituality.

Jalal ad-Din had arrived in Konya, in central Anatolia, with his father Baha ad-Din Valad of Balkh, through the town of Nishapur, where the great poet and mystic Farid ad-Din 'Attar had presented the twelve-year-old boy with a copy of his *Asrar-nama* ('Book of Secrets'), through Baghdad, and through Mecca to accomplish the pilgrimage.

Baha ad-Din was invited to become an honoured teacher and spiritual leader in th Salijuq capital of Konya (the Iconium of St Paul), which had been wrested by the Muslims from Byzantine rule in about 1070 and had since resisted capture by the Christian crusaders. After his father's death in 1230, Jalal ad-Din was instructed in Sufi mysticism by Burhan ad-Din Muhaqqiq, himself a refugee from Tartar-held Balkh. Rumi then encountered the wild Shams ad-Din, his recovery, and his final disappearance occasioned not only the extraordinarily exalted verses of the *Mathnawi*, poured out in torrents by Rumi, but also the whirling dance by which the dervishes of Rumi's mystic sect are now best known to the general public. On this latter feature, see Ira Friedlander's *The Whirling Dervishes* (Wildwood House, 1975). On the Saljuqs and their arts, there is a readable account by Tamara Talbot Rice: *The Seljuks in Asia Minor* (Thames & Hudson, 1961).

OLIVER GOLDSMITH (1729–1774).
> *The Vicar of Wakefield*. First published 1766. *She Stoops to Conquer*. First published 1773. *The Deserted Village*. First published 1770. Combined edition in Collins New Classics (Collins, 1953).

Earning a precarious and varied living in London after a carefree youth in Ireland, Goldsmith changed his luck when he met Samuel Johnson in 1761. The following year Johnson managed to sell the manuscript of Goldsmith's novel *The Vicar of Wakefield,* saving its author from arrest for debt. Living as a hack writer, Goldsmith found some success with his play *The Good-natur'd Man.* His second comedy *She Stoops to Conquer* was an instant success and is still enjoyed on the boards today, making up in high spirits what is lacking in the stodgier parts of his fiction (Mark Twain caustically noted that any reading list was a good one if it omitted *The Vicar of Wakefield*).

The Goldsmith country in the heart of Ireland, north-east of Athlone, is not so different today from its appearance in Goldsmith's age. Oliver was born at Pallas; Ardagh is the scene of *She Stoops to Conquer* (subtitled 'The Mistakes of a Night' and allegedly autobiographical); while 'Auburn' of *The Deserted Village* lies on the banks of the river Inny. This narrative poem stresses the advantages of agriculture over industry and trade, lamenting the society in which 'wealth accumulates and men decay'. Goldsmith's eulogy of village life was answered by George Crabbe's sombre poem *The Village* (1783), in which rural peasantry is glimpsed in its true state of squalor. Crabbe's best poem is *The Borough* (1810), which Benjamin Britten transmuted into the opera *Peter Grimes* (3 discs, Decca SXL 2150-2).

SADEQ HEDAYAT (1903–1951).
> *Bufe kur.* First published in Bombay, 1937. Translated by D. P. Costello as *The Blind Owl* (Calder, 1957).

Born of an old aristocratic family in Tehran, with high court officials among its members, Sadeq Hedayat was destined by his family for a similar position, but after leaving the French School in Tehran he completed his education in Belgium and France, where he became fascinated by Western literature, and began to write.

On returning to Iran, he rejected high positions which demanded a great deal of time and took minor posts which allowed him ample time for writing, and formed the *Rab'e.*Group with his friends Farzad, Minovi and Alavi, to spread the new Western ideas and methods of expression in Iran. Among Sadeq's contributions are the introduction of psychoanalytic theories by example, the use of slang (exaggerated in the work of his disciple Sadeq Chubak), and a view of the circularity of time and being drawn partly from Sufi mysticism and partly from the West. Sadeq naturalised existentialism into Iran. He tried to commit suicide on two occasions while studying in Paris, and succeeded while on a visit there in his late forties. See M. C. Hillman's *Hedayat's 'The Blind Owl'* (University of Texas Press, 1978).

Bufe kur is mentioned above, since it has been translated into English, and is thought by some admirers to be his masterpiece. Others, however, prefer the stories set in the lower depths of society. Translations are also needed of the prose writings of Jamalzadeh and Bozorg Alavi.

To understand the land of Hedayat's birth, of the monarchy, and of conditions that led to the rise of Ayatollah Khomeini, read Peter Avery's *Modern Iran* (latest edition, Benn) in the 'Nations of the Modern World' series.

YAHYA KEMAL BAYATLI (1884–1958).
Selected Poems. Translated by S. Behlül Toygar (Istanbul, 1965).

The *Divan* or collected works of Bayatlı was not published in his lifetime, though he was esteemed as one of the greatest Turkish writers of modern times, with a characteristically cosmopolitan career in both life and literature. Born in Skopje, Yugoslavia, he continued his education in Thessaloniki (Northern Greece), joining the Young Turks in exile in Paris in the year 1902. From 1908 he edited a literary journal in Istanbul and between 1915 and 1923 he taught history and literature at Istanbul University. A political career in Turkey was interrupted by periods as Ambassador to Poland, Spain and Pakistan.

His work is classical in both metre and Ottoman nationalist style, in total contrast to the secular post-Atatürk secular patriotism of his contemporaries. Bayatlı resists the westernisation of Turkish culture with dignity and restraint. His poetry is small in extent and circumscribed in range, but as perfect in its richness and harmony. it is reminiscent of Turkish miniatures.

This is a good moment to learn the origins of modern Turkey and the contributions of Atatürk from a standard history such as Geoffrey Lewis' *Turkey* (latest edition) in Benn's 'Nations of the Modern World' series.

MOHAMMED SHAMSUDDIN HAFIZ (1327-1390).

Divan. Edited by Khanlari (1959). Translated complete into French verse by A. Guy (Paris, 1927), complete into English by Clarke and Bistavi (*Divan,* Octagon Press, 1974) and partially by Gertrude Bell (*Poems from the Divan of Hafiz,* 1897); and by A. J. Arberry (*Fifty Poems of Hafiz,* Cambridge U.P., 1947).

'There is as much sense in Hafiz as in Horace', remarked Conan Doyle's detective Sherlock Holmes (in 'A Case of Identity'), 'and as much knowledge of the world'. The Fitzgerald who immortalized himself with his versions from the quatrains of Omar Khayyam believed that 'Hafez is the most Persian of the Persians', and indeed he is read today with as much delight as ever.

The surviving work of Hafiz consists chiefly of some six hundred lyrics or *ghazals,* whose form he brought to the zenith of perfection. His themes are wine, love (thought once to be mystical but now more generally believed to be literal), and panegyrics of his ruler, in particular Shah Shoja, from 1358 until Hafiz was banished from 1368–74 by the Shah, himself an aspiring poet influenced by the priesthood against the freethinking Hafiz.

Hafiz avoids the flowery artificiality of most writers of panegyrics, harmonising a fervent love of the earthly woman (Dordane, during his years of exile) with a feeling of unity with the cosmos. Though probably not a mystic himself, Hafiz employs the startling imagery of the Sufi for poetic purposes. Most of his poems defy translation, and will always remain the exclusive property of those who can read Persian.

Try to obtain tapes or records of the lyrics of Hafiz. For background reading, use A. J. Arberry's *The Legacy of Persia* (Oxford U.P., 1953).

Year 19

Anthology of Islamic Literature, from the rise of Islam to modern times, edited
by James Kritzeck (Penguin, 1964).

Reynold A. Nicholson's *A Literary History of the Arabs* (first published 1907, and
available since 1969 in paperback from Cambridge U.P.) contains many
excellent quotations, but readers will have been seeking an anthology
representative not so much of the Arabs and their language, but of Muslims as a
whole, writing in a dozen languages such as Arabic, Persian, Turkish and Urdu.
Kritzeck's work does not help with Urdu, and ends about the year 1800 A.D., but
there are generous extracts from most of the major writers to enable the reader to
select authors for further exploration.

This is a good moment to learn something about the course of Arab history,
the best introduction being the *History of the Arabs* (latest edition, Macmillan), by
Philip Hitti, of which the author has also made his own abridgment. There is a
brilliant study of Europe during and after the Muslim Conquests by Henri
Pirenne: *Mohammed and Charlemagne* (Allen & Unwin, 1939).

Explore 'Music in the World of Islam' (6 discs, Tangent TBX 601) and the book
Music and Musical Instruments in the World of Islam (Music Research, 36
Packington St., London N1, 1976) by Jean Jenkins and Poul Rovsing Olsen.

JEAN-PAUL SARTRE (1905–1980).
La Nausée. First published 1938. Translated as *Nausea* by Robert Baldick
(Penguin, 1965).

Equally at home in the novel and short story, the play, the extended literary essay,
and the philosophical statement, Sartre has passed through numerous phases of
more or less violent revolutionary activity and involvement with existentialism,
whose history he has helped to form and then to change.

Sartre views man as an automaton without external meaning in a chaotic
universe until and unless he takes the step to exist as himself, as an individual. In
La Nausée, the semi-autobiographical anti-hero Antoine Roquentin finds

himself trapped in the viscosity of existence. The recognition of his own existence is a point of crisis in a man's life to which he must somehow relate. *Le Mur* (1939) is a collection of short stories dealing with aspects of the same philosophical problem, which is the crux of his metaphysical book *L'Être et le Néant* (1943; translated by H. E. Barnes as *Being and Nothingness,* Methuen, 1969).

In 1945 Sartre founded the significant intellectual journal *Les Temps Modernes,* and continued to play an important part in post-war French intellectual life. In 1964 he rejected the Nobel Prize for Literature, partly because he considered it to be for Western or pro-Western writers, and partly because 'a writer must refuse to allow himself to be transformed into an institution, even if it takes place in the most honourable form'. In 1964 he published the opening volume of his autobiography, *Les Mots* (translated as *Words,* Penguin, 1969), a wry, obliquely revealing account of his early fascination with language.

Among his more successful plays are *Les Mouches* (1942; translated by Stuart Gilbert as *The Flies,* Knopf, 1946), restaging the Electra myth in German-occupied France, and *Les Séquestrés d'Altona* (1959; translated by Sylvia and George Leeson as *Loser Wins,* Knopf, 1961).

Al-Qur'an ('The Koran'). First set down in writing *c.* 610–632 A.D. No version but the original in Arabic is regarded as authentic or even suitable for use by Muslims.

English translations vary from the pseudo-Biblical style of Rodwell (1861 but reissued in Everyman's Library, Dent and Dutton, 1953); the Muslim convert Marmaduke Pickthall (New American Library, 1953); and A. J. Arberry (*The Koran Interpreted* in World's Classics, Oxford U.P., 1964); to the plain modern style of N. J. Dawood (Penguin, 1956).

For Muslims, *al-Qur'an* is the infallible Word of Allah, spoken by Him in the first person singular, first personal plural, and occasionally the third person singular (except in some passage spoken by His Prophet Muhammad, and others spoken by the Angel 'Jibra'il', or Gabriel), and preserved in Heaven on a tablet.

Muslims believe that Muhammad is not divine, as Christians believe Jesus to be, but one in a line of Prophets, among whom another is Musa (Moses) and another 'Isa (Jesus). Absolute submission (*Islam*) to the Will of Allah demands worship of Him alone, and emphasises divine mercy and forgiveness. Allah will forgive all once He is acknowledged as the Only God. 'Allahu akbar. La ilahu ill' Allah. Muhammadun rasul Allah' ('God is Great. There is no god but Allah, and Muhammad is His Prophet'). The traditional arrangement of *al-Qur'an* followed in Pickthall and Arberry is abandoned by Dawood on the grounds that there is no authority for it, and it lacks both continuity and coherence.

No reading in solitude can equal the supreme effect of following the Arabic text while it is being intoned by an eminent imam on the records now available. One learns not only the masterpiece of classical Arabic prose, but also the doctrines by which so many hundreds of millions have lived.

For background reading, see W. Montgomery Watt's *Muhammad at Mecca* (1953) and *Muhammad at Medina* (1956), and Ishaq's *Sirat Rasul Allah* translated by A. Guillaume as *The Life of Muhammad* (1955), all published by Oxford U.P. A magnificently-illustrated companion is *The Quranic Art of Calligraphy and Illumination* by Martin Lings (World of Islam Festival Trust, 1976).

PUBLIUS TERENTIUS AFER (TERENCE) (*c.* 195–159 B.C.).
　　Comedies. Texts of the six plays with an English translation by John Sargeaunt in the Loeb Classical Library (2 vols., Heinemann and Harvard U.P., 1912) for those who wish a bilingual edition. Translations include *The Brothers and other Plays* and *Phormio and other Plays* translated by Betty Radice (Penguin, 1965–7), and those in the uneven *Complete Roman Drama* (2 vols., Random House, 1942), edited by George E. Duckworth.

Born a slave in Carthage but set free by Terentius Lucanus, a Roman senator, Terence wrote for the artistocracy of Rome, taking his themes from the Greek New Comedy and greatly surpassing Plautus in his handling of plot and character. The regard in which his plays have always been held can be judged from the fact that all have survived from antiquity.

Indeed, so few Greek comedies have come down to us that it is only through the distorting mirror of the *fabula palliata* (a Roman play in Greek dress) that we can glimpse the world of Menander in a more rounded way.

Because the farcical element is underplayed, and Terentian humour is less broad than is Plautine, Terence has often been thought dull by comparison, but his influence has been felt from the adaptations by Hrotswitha, abbess of the Benedictine convent of Gandersheim, to the more sophisticated inventions of Congreve, Steele, and Sheridan.

Al Mu'allaqat as-Sab', translated as *The Seven Odes, the first chapter in Arabic Literature*, by A. J. Arberry (Allen & Unwin, 1957).

One of the most bitterly-contested controversies in the history of Arabic literature is the dating of the 'Seven Suspended Ones', poems so-called because they had allegedly been (in Gibbon's words) 'inscribed in letters of gold, and suspended in the temple of Mecca'. The problem was adumbrated in 1872 by Ahlwardt, and pursued by the great blind Egyptian scholar Taha Husain in *Fi 'sh-*

sh'ir al-jahili ('On Pre-Islamic Poetry', 1925), revised as *Fi'l-adab al-jahili* ('On Pre-Islamic Literature', 1927) and by D. S. Margoliouth of Oxford in the *Journal of the Royal Asiatic Society* (1925). We cannot be sure of the authenticity of the *Mu'allaqat* as pre-Islamic poetry of the sixth century A.D., but there can be no disagreement on their high intrinsic quality. The seven poets are Imr al-Qais, Tarafa, Zuhair, Labid, 'Antar, 'Amr and al-Harith, and their subject-matter ranges from the deserted dwelling-places of Imr al-Qais (a topos he did not create, as Arabs normally claim, but took over from one Ibn Khidham or Ibn Humam) to the arrogant claims of the Black Knight, 'Antar or 'Antara, addressing his beloved 'Abla, in terms which moved Rimsky-Korsakov to dedicate Opus 9 to him as 'The Antar Symphony'.

Arberry's detailed introduction includes specimens of the work of other translators from the 'Seven Odes'. His *Arabic Poetry: a Primer for Students* (Cambridge U.P., 1965) is also to be recommended.

Sir RICHARD FRANCIS BURTON (1821–1890).
  Personal Narrative of a Pilgrimage to El-Medinah and Meccah. First published
    in 3 vols., 1855–6 (Reprinted, 2 vols., Dover and Constable, 1965).

'Our notions of Mecca must be drawn from the Arabians', observed Gibbon. 'As no unbeliever is permitted to enter the city, our travellers are silent'. But in fact a number of infidels have managed to escape detection and make the pilgrimage, none to greater literary effect than Richard Burton.

Burton was a genius who mastered twenty-nine languages (forty if we include dialects), travelled and wrote without ceasing, and spent time as a soldier and later as a diplomat. As a translator he is often brilliant: his *Alf Layla wa Layla* (rendered as 'The Arabian Nights' Entertainments') remains the finest and most readable version in a western language. Among his valuable travel books are *The Gold-Mines of Midian* (first published 1878; corrected and reset, The Oleander Press, 1979) and *The Land of Midian Revisited* (1879; The Oleander Press, 1982), *A Mission to Gelele, King of Dahome* (1864), and *Abeokuta and the Camaroons Mountains* (1863).

For an up-to-date view of the *Hajj,* or Muslim pilgrimage, see the spectacular *Pilgrimage to Mecca* (Macdonald and Jane's, 1978) by Mohamed Amin, or the less expensive *Mecca; the Muslim Pilgrimage* (Paddington Press, 1979) by Ezzedine Guellouz, with photographs by Abdelaziz Frikha.

PROCOPIUS (*c.*498- *c.*560).
  Works. Text with an English translation by H. B. Dewing and G. Downey in
    the Loeb Classical Library (8 vols., Heinemann and Harvard U.P.,
    1914–40). The *History of the Wars of Justinian* is illuminatingly annotated in

abridged form by P. N. Ure in his *Justinian and his Age* (Penguin, 1951), and the *Anekdota* have been translated with an introduction by G. A. Williamson as 'The Secret History' (Penguin, 1960).

Modelling himself on Herodotus and Thucydides, the Byzantine historian Procopius is widely recognised as the first major historian after Polybius.

Of his three works, by far the longest and most useful is the *Discourses about the Wars,* generally known as the *History of the Wars of Justinian* and published in 554. The first two of its eight books deals with the Persian Wars fought in Mesopotamia, another two with the Vandal Wars fought in North Africa, and three with the Gothic Wars fought in Italy. The eighth book takes events on all fronts from 552 to 554.

Peri Ktismaton ('On the Buildings' *–sc.* of Justinian) also appeared in 554. It describes in eulogistic manner how Justinian and his Empress Theodora enriched their capital, Constantinople, with beautiful new buildings: the language of Procopius is tarnished with sycophancy.

He took his revenge in the *Anekdota* ('Unpublished'), a secret chronicle showing the other side of the picture, in which Justinian and the ex-prostitute Theodora are shown up in their 'true' colours, often exaggerated for effect. It was written after Theodora's death, and obviously Procopius assumed that the tyrannical Justinian, much older than Procopius and vulnerable like all Byzantine emperors to unexpected assassination attempts on all sides, would predecease his faithful historian. As we know, however, Procopius died about five years before his Emperor and was cheated of popular acclaim for his two-faced writings. We may reprove him for either the eulogy or the bitter attack, but he would have faced certain death if the latter had been published, and we should have lost a valuable record of Byzantine history if the former had not been published. On balance, therefore, we must exonerate both sycophant and libeller.

'ALI AHMAD IBN HAZM (994–1064).
Tawq al-hamama ('The Dove's Necklace'). Translated by A. J. Arberry as *The Ring of the Dove: a treatise on the Art and Practice of Arab Love* (Luzac, 1953).

Although ibn Hazm was best known to his contemporaries as a philosopher and exegete of *al-Qur'an* (q.v.), a legal scholar, historian, and student of comparative religion, we know the Cordova-born poet for his *Tawq al-hamama,* a comprehensive, subtle and often elegant insight into the types of love common in eleventh-century Arab Andalusia.

Ibn Hazm lived at the very end of Umayyad power and splendour in Cordova, and saw the sacking of Cordova by the Berbers in 1013, after which he fled his native city, which was to be demoted from its capital status to the rank of one among warring independent principalities whose weakness was to culminate in the Reconquest of Spain and the Fall of Granada in 1492.

The *Tawq al-hamama* is one of that genre known to Arabs as *adab*. Specifically, this might be translated into French as 'belles-lettres' and more generally it can signify 'culture', but the kind of prose-poetry compound it exemplifies can be seen in a Western work such as Dante's *La Vita Nuova,* in which a prose commentary is illuminated by a poem, or in an Eastern work such as Basho's *Narrow Road to the Deep North,* in which a given setting can act as a catalyst for a meditation or variation on the theme.

GIUSEPPE GIOACHINO BELLI (1791–1863).
   I Sonetti. First published 1886–89. Edited by Bruno Cagli (5 vols., Newton Compton, Rome, 1980). *The Roman Sonnets* are translated by Harold Norse (Perivale Press, 13830 Erwin St., Van Nuys, California 91401, 1974).

The dilemma of the dialect poet is displayed by the Roman Belli, many of whose two thousand sonnets would be widely celebrated had they been written in standard Italian. A founder member and secretary of the Accademia Tiberina from 1813 until his resignation in 1828, Belli was constantly in financial difficulties after the death of his father (of the plague) in 1802 and that of his mother five years later.

Belli's wife died in 1837 and he was compelled to find copying and other clerical work to keep himself alive. His clandestine dialect poems were appreciated by only an intimate few, among them Gogol and Sainte-Beuve, and he died without seeing any of them published.

Averse to the Establishment, with its elitist classicism, its rigid forms (which his sonnets parody even while apparently following), and its aristocratic bias, Belli was influenced by French and Italian writers of the Enlightenment, among them Voltaire, Volney, Rousseau, Giannone, Carli and Filangieri. He sought a tradition that would reflect the life of the people in their own language, and found models in the *Meo Patacca* of Giuseppe Berneri, and in the comedies of Molière. His *Sonetti* ridicule the corrupt and powerful in Roman society (sonnet 1431) and describe the misery and injustice oppressing the poor (sonnet 1677). Church ceremonies have become empty, and those who go to Mass are ignorant yet fanatical. Laziness leads to beatification, only fools tell the truth (by mistake), and the rule is not progress but regress. In a memorable line of sonnet 1060, Belli observes that the "canchero sta in ne la radice" (the canker lies in the root). Good humour mingles with wild Goyaesque cruelty that cackles at misfortune and disfigurement.

MUHAMMAD BIN 'ABDULLAH IBN BATTUTA (1304–1369).

Tuhfat an-nuzzar fi ghara 'ib al-amsar wa 'aja 'ib al-asfar ('A Gift for those interested in the curiosities of cities and the wonders on the routes') commonly known as the *Rihla* ('Journey'). Edited and translated into French by C. Defrémery and B. R. Sanguinetti (4 vols., 1853–8). Selections translated into English by H. A. R. Gibb (Routledge & Kegan Paul, 1929) as *Travels in Asia and Africa*, 1325–1354). Fully translated in 4 vols. by H. A. R. Gibb (Vols. 1–3, Hakluyt Society, 1958, 1961 and 1971) and by C. F. Beckingham (Vol. 4, in preparation 1981).

Ibn Battuta began his travels by the usual pilgrimage to Mecca (in his case by a roundabout route that included Jerusalem and Damascus), which he accomplished late in 1326, having set out from his native Morocco the previous year. He then travelled in the rest of Arabia, Mesopotamia, Azerbaijan, and spent three years in Mecca. He sailed down the Red Sea to Yemen and Aden, following the East African coast as far as Kilwa and returning through Oman and the Gulf. Doubt has been cast on the veracity of his tales of Constantinople and China, but he certainly travelled across Afghanistan to India, spending seven years as a judge in the service of the Sultan of Delhi. He made yet another pilgrimage from Baghdad in 1347, and then visited Tunisia and Sardinia, Spain and Mali. He returned to Fez in 1353 and spent the rest of his life as a judge in Morocco. While in Fez he dictated his memoirs to Muhammad ibn Juzayy, who certainly incorporated some notes and comments of his own, as well as poetic effusions and elegant prose.

Ibn Battuta's *Rihla* is an excellent first-hand narrative of life in the (predominantly Muslim) world of the second quarter of the fourteenth century, from which one can elicit numerous conclusions about the decline of order and control in government and administration. The author's accuracy is nearly always beyond praise, and where it may be questioned there is often a simple explanation of his error or misunderstanding.

For background reading on Ibn Battuta's native country, see the many books by Rom Landau, such as *Morocco* (Elek, 1967).

One of the influences of Ibn Battuta was the Valencia-born Abu 'l-Husain Muhammad b. Ahmad ibn Jubayr (1145–1217), whose own *Rihla* includes Andalusia, North Africa, Egypt, Sudan, the Arabian Peninsula (and in particular the holy cities of Mecca and Medina), Iraq, Syria with present-day Lebanon, Sicily and Eastern Spain. Ibn Jubayr's *Travels* have been translated by R. J. C. Broadhurst (Cape, 1952).

Year 20

JEAN-NICOLAS-ARTHUR RIMBAUD (1854–1891).
Oeuvres. First collected edition 1898. Complete edition by Jules Mouquet
and Roland de Renéville 1946. Several good modern editions are available,
the cheapest being the 'Livre de Poche' *Poésies Complètes* (Hachette, 1963).
A bilingual selection entitled *Rimbaud* is introduced and edited by Oliver
Bernard (Penguin, 1962).

A precocious adolescent, his poetic theories virtually formed for life, Rimbaud
was a boorish and arrogant youth of genius who ran away from home several
times, read voraciously in his local public library at Charleville (northern France)
and was influenced by Baudelaire, the semi-mystical writer Pierre-Simon
Ballanche, and various occultists.

In his view the poet is a man apart, a *voyant* who must go beyond good and evil
to express the inexpressible, if necessary by inducing states of delirium. At the
age of 21 Rimbaud may already (though this is not certain) have abandoned
literature for a life of adventure and action, at first in Germany, Italy, Indonesia,
Cyprus and Aden, and later – for most of his life – in Africa.

During Rimbaud's long absence, his homosexual lover Paul Verlaine
published an important essay on him in *Les Poètes Maudits* (1884), a critical work
intended to advance the reputation of Corbière, Desbordes-Valmore, Villiers de
L'Isle-Adam, Mallarmé, Rimbaud, and 'Pauvre Lelian' (an anagram). Two years
later, Rimbaud's *Les Illuminations* were published by Verlaine, but we now
realise that the correct text comprises only the prose poems and two poems in *vers
libre,* and is thus much shorter than Verlaine's first edition. For Rimbaud
criticism, see Fowlie's *Rimbaud* (University of Chicago Press, 1968) and for his
biography see Starkie's *Arthur Rimbaud* (Faber & Faber, 1973).

Benjamin Britten's settings from *Les Illuminations,* originally written for
soprano, have been recorded by Heather Harper on HMV SXLP 30194, and by
Peter Pears on Decca SXL 6449.

Alf Layla wa Layla ('A Thousand and One Nights'). There are several variant editions in Arabic. The best translation in English is that by Richard Burton (16 vols., 1885–8; Heritage Press, 6 vols. in 3, 1956).

The *Alf Layla wa Layla* is merely a borrowed work in Arabic, though authentic Arabic tales, often in authentic Cairo slang, were added during the Mamluk period.

Originally the *Hazar Afsana* ('Thousand Stories') was a Persian work of the Sassanian period (3rd to 7th centuries A.D.) with many Indian elements treated in a Persian spirit. The Persian King Shahriyar, despising women for their infidelity, took a new wife each night and arranged for her execution the following day. The ingenious and beautiful Shahrazad (in French, Schéhérazade) kept the king so entranced, however, that he begged her to continue her tale the following night, and eventually fell in love with her and took no more new wives.

The collection was translated into Arabic no later than the tenth century, and there received its definitive form, though there was no standard text until the fifteenth century. It is despised for its colloquialisms by Arab purists, but its amusing and imaginative mixture of humour and fantasy are the basis of our modern pantomime (Aladdin, Ali Baba, and Sindbad all derive from the so-called 'Arabian Nights').

The fascinating personality of Shahrazad and her clever tales have been invoked in Rimsky-Korsakov's symphonic suite *Schéhérazade* (Haitink's version is on Philips 6500 410) and in Ravel's song cycle of the same title (sung by Janet Baker on HMV ASD 2444, with the *Nuits d'été* of Berlioz).

PEDRO CALDERÓN DE LA BARCA (1600–1681).
La Vida es Sueño. First published 1636. Edited by A. E. Sloman (Manchester U.P., 1961). Translated by Edward and Elizabeth Huberman as 'Life is a Dream' in Ángel Flores' anthology *Spanish Drama* (Bantam, 1962); and by William E. Colford (Barron's, 1958).

Calderón wrote far fewer plays than did his contemporary and rival Lope de Vega (q.v.), and spent more care on their construction and more elaboration on their language, but he can be said to lack something of the wilder lyrical fantasy that we enjoy in Lope. He is more serious, didactic, even more doctrinal: it is easier to point the moral in a Calderón play than in a *comedia* by Lope. This disadvantage in secular drama becomes a positive asset in the allegorical *autos sacramentales* – those largely Golden Age one-act plays performed at the feast of Corpus Christi on moveable carts (*carros*) which were easily converted into stages and then dismantled to be pulled by oxen to the next performance.

La Vida es Sueño is the title of not only one of the most celebrated of Spanish philosophical plays, on the problems of illusion and reality, life and death, virtue and sin, but also of one of the (unrelated) *autos sacramentales* of Calderón. The two have been edited together by G. M. Bertini (1949) and the latter can also be found in volume 1 of the two 'Clásicos Castellanos' volumes of Calderón's *Autos Sacramentales* edited by Á. Valbuena Prat (1957).

Excellent accounts of Calderonian drama have been produced by A. E.Sloman (*The Dramatic Craftsmanship of Calderón*, Dolphin Book Co., 1955) and by A. A. Parker (*The Allegorical Drama of Calderón*, Dolphin Book Co., 1968).

Hadith ('Narrative') or Traditions of Islam.

In the third century *Hijriah*, corresponding to the ninth century A.D., a need was felt to systematise the thousands of traditions which had grown up around the life, work and sayings of the Prophet Muhammad, the criterion of authenticity being the *isnad*, or chain of transmission, some sources being more reliable than others. Six major collections of traditions arose from the search for authentic *ahadith*, and of these the most reliable is considered to be the *Sahih* of al-Bukhari (810–870), and the second most dependable the *Sahih* of Muslim, who died in 875.

In his *Orient under the Caliphs*, von Kremer states: 'The life of the Prophet, his discourses and utterances, his action, his silent approval and even his passive conduct, constituted next to the Qur'an the second most important source of law for the young Muslim empire'. Islamic booksellers will be able to provide you with modern Arabic editions of al-Bukhari (though Muslim is not so commonly found), and there are good accounts of the traditions in A. Guillaume's *The Traditions of Islam* (Oxford U.P., 1924; reprinted by Aris & Phillips, 1980); Muhammad Zubayr Siddiqi's *Hadith Literature* (Calcutta University, 1961); and the bilingual *Manual of Hadith* by Maulana Muhammad 'Ali (Curzon Press, 1978).

I know of no complete English translation of Bukhari's *Sahih*, but there is a complete French *Recueil Authentique* (4 vols., 1903–14) translated by O. Houdas, and a useful selection by G. -H. Bousquet in *L'Authentique Tradition Musulmane* (Bernard Grasset, 61 rue des Saints-Pères, Paris VIe, 1964).

DANIEL DEFOE (*c.* 1660–1731).
   The Life and Strange Surprizing Adventures of Robinson Crusoe, of York, Mariner. First published 1719. The *Further Adventures* appeared in 1719 and *Serious Reflections* in 1720. Several good modern editions are available, including that by Angus Ross (Penguin, 1965).

A novel of its time in its moralising and philosophising, *Robinson Crusoe* has also been the model for two quite distinct genres: the 'back to nature' school epitomised by Rousseau in his *Émile* (1762), and the science fiction industry exemplified in one generation by H. G. Wells and in another by Ray Bradbury and Robert Heinlein, where a future, devastated Earth (or a hitherto unknown planet, perhaps) corresponds to the desert island of Defoe.

The book became instantly and perennially popular, so that it bred its own minor classics, such as Wyss's *Der Schweizerische Robinson* (4 vols., 1812–27), translated back into English as *The Swiss Family Robinson*.

Defoe was a hack writer and prolific pamphleteer who immediately cashed in on the celebrity of his first novel with a string of clever but often mechanical successors: *Captain Singleton, Moll Flanders, A Journal of the Plague Year* (often thought to be factual, but Defoe was only an infant when Plague broke out in 1665), *Colonel Jack,* and *Roxana.* Often mercenary and opportunistic in money and political matters, Defoe nevertheless suffered for his outspoken opinions in dozens of pamphlets and magazine articles, and is one of the most interesting Englishmen of the eighteenth century. Compare his satirical pamphlet *Shortest Way with the Dissenters* (1702) against ecclesiastical intolerance, with Dean Swift's satire *A Modest Proposal for preventing the Children of Poor People from being a Burden to their Parents or the Country* (1729) – his method being to provide poor children as food for the rich.

Explore the music of Defoe's contemporary, Henry Purcell (1658–95).

'ABD AR-RAHMAN BIN MUHAMMAD IBN KHALDUN (1332–1406).
Kitab al-'Ibar ('Book of Instructive Examples'). Written in 1375–8. The *Muqaddimah* ('Prolegomena') to the work has been translated by Franz Rosenthal (3 vols., Routledge and Pantheon, 1958; abridged edition in 1 vol., 1967) and there is a selection from the *Muqaddimah* translated as *An Arab Philosophy of History* by Charles Issawi in the 'Wisdom of the East' series (John Murray and Grove Press, 1950).

The *Kitab al-'Ibar* is a careful dynastic history of North Africa prefaced with a deeply-meditated introduction which has become a classic in its own right. As Toynbee writes in *A Study of History* (volume 3), 'in his chosen field of intellectual activity (Ibn Khaldun) appears to have been inspired by no predecessors, and to have found no kindred souls among his contemporaries, and to have kindled no answering spark of inspiration in any successors; and yet... he has conceived and formulated a philosophy of history which is undoubtedly the greatest work of its kind that has ever yet been created by any mind in any time or place'.

Born in Tunis of an aristocratic family from Muslim Spain, he received a good education and filled several important administrative and diplomatic posts, including that of ambassador from the Sultan of Granada to Pedro el Cruel of Castile in 1364. His life was full of incidents, both humiliating and exalting, but reached a climax when he spent four years from 1375 at the Castle of Ibn Salama near Oran (present-day Algeria) to write *Kitab al-'Ibar*. He then spent more time studying and lecturing in Tunis, before undertaking the pilgrimage to Mecca in 1382. He spent some years as Chief Justice in the service of the Sultan of Egypt, negotiating on his behalf in 1400 with Timur-i-Leng ('Tamerlane'), who was threatening Damascus with his Tartar hordes. He returned to Cairo as Chief Justice, a post he still occupied when death overtook him.

His view of history is cyclical in the main, propounding the concept of a sequence of urban dynasties interrupted at decadence by a new wave of nomads or invaders from outside. The exception is that nomads wholly inspired with a common ideology (such as Islam) can survive much longer, even absorbing fresh waves of nomads not collectively inspired.

FRIEDRICH WILHELM NIETZSCHE (1844–1900).
Also sprach Zarathustra. First complete edition 1892. Many current editions. Translated by R. J. Hollingdale as *Thus Spoke Zarathustra* (Penguin, 1961).

Nietzsche did not evolve a large-scale, coherent philosophical system: the threads of his many works must be drawn together by the reader. Perhaps the most characteristic of them, and the most important for a view of the dominant themes of his life's work, is *Also sprach Zarathustra*. Zarathustra is not the 6th-century Persian who founded the Magian religion, the prophet of Ormazd (the wise spirit) who struggles against Ahriman (the evil spirit): he is the *alter ego* of Nietzsche himself.

The book outlines the doctrines of the *Übermensch* or Superman, eternal recurrence, and the Will to Power. Nietzsche scorns the Christian virtues of selflessness, suffering and charity, and stresses the importance of living in the present and not for a spurious afterworld. He was enraged at the prevailing prejudice, ignorance and self-deception, and he professed disgust with imperial Germany and bourgeois ideals and sentiments. Men must strive to overcome their weaknesses and sublimate their will to power in some aspect of creativity. Some will become their own finest creations – and Nietzsche gives the examples of Julius Caesar and Goethe.

The prophetic, often poetic, tone of *Also sprach Zarathustra* caused some anxiety among his supporters, and indeed Nietzsche did become certifiably insane, though many of his writings were perverted by his sister Elisabeth Förster-Nietzsche, a rabid anti-Semite and German nationalist. Richard Strauss' symphonic poem *Also sprach Zarathustra* (conducted by Herbert von Karajan) is recorded on DGG 2530 402.

Nietzsche's early friendship – and later frenzied enmity – with Richard Wagner looms larger in the writer's life than in the composer's. But their points of contact would lead a sympathetic reader to Wagner's *Ring des Nibelungen* conducted by Solti (on 19 Decca discs D 1000 D 19), ideally heard over four consecutive evenings.

ABU MUHAMMAD AL-QASIM AL-HARIRI (1054–1122).
Maqamat. Critical edition by S. de Sacy (Paris, 1849–1853). Translated by Thomas Chenery and F. Steingass as *The Assemblies* (Royal Asiatic Society, 1867–98).

A miracle of Arabic rhymed prose, al-Hariri's *Maqamat* is a collection of fifty episodes telling the confidence tricks and adventures of the fictitious Abu Zayd of Saruj (in present-day Iraq, like Basra, al-Hariri's birthplace).

The author was a rich, influential government official in the service of the Saljuq Sultan Malikshah and his celebrated vizier, Nizam al-Mulk.

Familiar with the *Maqamat* of al-Hamadhani (968–1008), who was known as 'Badi' az-Zaman' ('Wonder of the Age'), al-Hariri elaborated the genre in several ways, by style, diction, cunning and content. Amusing stories of trickery and robbery are told with a huge zest for the immense vocabulary of classical Arabic and its propensity for complex rhyme and alliteration.

In one disreputable story, a brilliant sermon in Samarqand's Friday Mosque is delivered by Abu Zayd, disguised as a learned *imam,* who at night drinks forbidden wine with the narrator, al-Harith bin Hammam. Another story set in Tiflis shows Abu Zayd as a palsied beggar who tricks the people into giving him alms and reveals his identity to al-Harith only when safe beyond the city walls. Each *maqama* in al-Hariri is isolated from the rest: there is no novelistic continuity.

See also al- Hamadhani's *Maqamat* in the translation by W. J. Prendergast (Luzac, 1915).

Since portrayal of the human being is forbidden to orthodox Muslims, the principal graphic art of the Muslims has always been in the fields of calligraphy and illumination. An excellent introduction is *Islamic Calligraphy* (Thames & Hudson, 1978) by Yasin Hamid Safadi. A more comprehensive work on Islamic art is Titus Burckhardt's *Art of Islam: Language and Meaning* (World of Islam Festival Trust, 1976), with magnificent illustrations.

TAKEDA KIYOSADA, known as TAKEDA IZUMO (*c.* 1690–*c.* 1749).
Kanadehon chushingura. Written 1748 in collaboration with Miyoshi

Shoraku and Namiki Senryu. The best available translation is *Chushingura* by Donald Keene (Columbia U.P., 1971).

Takeda took over the mantle of Chikamatsu (q.v.) as playwright to the Takemoto puppet-threatre company, writing 33 *joruri* (puppet plays), two thirds of them in collaboration.

Stage portrayal of contemporary events being banned in Japan at the time, Takeda and his colleagues adapted their play to another period, but its relevance was never in doubt and it has continued to be popular.

A lord is provoked to kill a court official and is subsequently ordered to commit suicide. His retainers band together to avenge his death. The play is interspersed with love scenes, thus combining the two most popular plots of the puppet stage. The *joruri* plays were often imported into the *kabuki* repertory, and both versions have since been given in abridged versions, or even in extracts of single scenes, due to the great length of the original scripts.

MARCUS ANNAEUS LUCANUS (LUCAN) (39–65 A.D.).
De bello civili (*Concerning the Civil War*). With an English translation by J. D. Duff in the Loeb Classical Library (Heinemann and Harvard U.P., 1928) for those who wish a bilingual edition. Translated by Robert Graves as *Pharsalia: Dramatic Episodes of the Civil Wars* (Penguin, 1956).

Marcus Annaeus Lucanus was a nephew of Seneca the Younger (Nero's tutor and the most celebrated writer of his day) and enjoyed the tuition of the Stoic L. Annaeus Cornutus and the friendship of the satirist Persius. With the example of Virgil before him, Lucan started work on an epic poem, and the first three books of his *De bello civili* were circulated in 62–3 A.D.

Nero, who believed himself to be the greatest poet and musician in his Empire, grew jealous of Lucan, and forbade him to publish or recite his work. It is believed that Lucan's suicide was due to his involvement with Piso's conspiracy against Nero, but whatever the reason, it cut short the composition of the *Pharsalia,* as his epic on the struggle between Pompey and Caesar is generally known. Book X was left unfinished, and there are grounds for believing that another two books were projected, to take the story up to the death of Caesar.

Lucan's literary quality is far inferior to that of Virgil: his major virtues are a hysterical vitality (compared by Graves to that other eccentric, Rudyard Kipling), vividness of epigram, and a command of the Latin language second to none (with its obverse fault, verbosity).

Read the *Julius Caesar* before, and *Antony and Cleopatra* of Shakespeare after, the *Pharsalia*.

Year 21

JOSEPH, *Freiherr von* EICHENDORFF (1788–1857).
Aus dem Leben eines Taugenichts. First published 1826. Translated as
Memoirs of a Good-for-Nothing by R. Taylor (Calder, 1968).

A Silesian nobleman, Eichendorff studied law in German universities and
became a well-respected government official in the Prussian state (1816–44). As
a Romantic poet, however, he attracted Schumann (whose Eichendorff
Liederkreis Op. 39 contrasts with the Heine *Liederkreis* Op. 24, both sung by
Robert Tear on Argo ZRG 718), and Richard Strauss, as well as Mendelssohn.

Eichendorff's long Romantic novel *Ahnung und Gegenwart* (1815) may be
flawed, but his much shorter *Aus dem Leben eines Taugenichts* (whose hero is
never named) is a paradigm of Romantic art. The *Novelle* shows a world of perfect
harmony in which men may uproot a vegetable garden in favour of flowers, and
live light-heartedly despite being sent away from home for idling. Sentimentality
is avoided by the telling use of irony on the part of the internal narrator and of the
writer himself.

A conservative in politics and a Roman Catholic, Eichendorff wrote a number
of works on the history of German literature from the religious viewpoint in the
1840s and 1850s. His ideals and qualities are considered old-fashioned today,
and he is little read, but there is no doubting his originality and skill.

Eichendorff's contemporary Carl Maria von Weber (1786–1826) was
instrumental in establishing German Romantic opera with *Der Freischütz* (3 discs
conducted by Carlos Kleiber, DGG 2720 071), *Euryanthe* (4 discs conducted by
Marek Janowski, HMV SLS 983), and *Oberon* (2 discs conducted by Rafael
Kubelik, DGG 2726 052). Note Hindemith's remarkable 'Symphonic Variations
on a Theme by Carl Maria von Weber' (conducted, with Janáček's 'Sinfonietta',
by Claudio Abbado on Decca SXL 6398).

ABU 'UTHMAN AMR BIN BAHR, *called* AL-JAHIZ ('The Goggle-Eyed')
(*c.* 780–*c.* 868). *The Life and Works of Jahiz:* translations of selected
texts, by Charles Pellat. Translated from the French by D. M. Hawke
(Routledge & Kegan Paul, 1969).

Born in Basra, the grandson of an East African slave, al-Jahiz spent most of his
life in Baghdad, where he became the first truly great Arab prose writer of *adab,*
or secular literature, proving that Arabic is rich not only in theological and
philosophical thought, which had already been shown, but that it is capable of
subtle satire, irony in controversy, and clever characterisation of human types.
His *Kitab al-Bukhala'* has been translated in full into French as *Le Livre des
Avares* (1951) and his *Kitab at-Taj fi Akhlaq al-Muluk* as *Le Livre de la Couronne,
sur les règles de conduite des rois* (1954) by Charles Pellat, whose background
book *Le Milieu Basrien et la formation de Gahiz* (1953) is fundamental.

Al-Jahiz aims principally to educate the reader by a disjointed series of
entertaining anecdotes, propagating the Mu'tazilite views within Islam,
generous Arab culture against the mean Persian 'middle' class (in *The Book of
Misers*), and good humour against the blossoming intolerance of social groups
against each other. The *Kitab al-Hayawan* ('Book of Animals') is a major though
desparate collection of essays on animals which succeeds in glorifying Islam,
offering contemporary views of the miracles of creation (not confined to animal
life), and in continually retaining the reader's interest. Al-Jahiz seems to write as
he spoke, but his works, and particularly the *Kitab al-Bayan* ('Book of
Eloquence') are held up as major examples of early *adab.*

PO CHÜ-I (772–846).
   Poems. *Chinese Poems,* translated by Arthur Waley (Allen & Unwin, 1946).
   And *The Life and Times of Po Chü-I* by Arthur Waley (Allen & Unwin,
   1949; Macmillan, New York, 1950).

'The fact that I have translated ten times more poems by Po Chü-I than by any
other writer does not mean that I think him ten times as good as any of the rest,
but merely that I find him by far the most translatable of the major Chinese
poets', writes Arthur Waley.

Many of Po Chü-I's poems were specially translated for the biography, and
bear out in their dignified simplicity the claim made for them by Waley. Apart
from his courageous admonitions in verse addressed to the throne and to
powerful officials, the most significant of his poems (some 2,800 of which
survive) are occasional poems written for friends or for his own amusement. He
is not a profound philosophical poet, but addresses the passing moment,
catching people and landscapes with a vivid touch.

Among the many background books aiding the reader's enjoyment of Po Chü-I one might take up *The Art of Chinese Poetry* by James J. Y. Liu (Routledge & Kegan Paul and University of Chicago Press, 1962). *Poetry and Experience* (Penguin, 1965) by Archibald MacLeish is a sensitive and civilized investigation of several aspects of poetry in both Chinese and western styles, taking examples from the *Shih Chi,* Tu Fu and Li Po as well as from Emily Dickinson, W. B. Yeats, Rimbaud and Keats.

Compare *Chinese Landscape Painting* (Harper, Row, 1971) by Sherman E. Lee with Kenneth Clark's view of the subject in western eyes: *Landscape into Art* (Harper, Row, 1978).

ABU HAMID MUHAMMAD AL-GHAZZALI (1059–1111).

Al-Munqidh min ad-Dalal ('The Deliverer from Error'). Translated in *The Faith and Practice of al-Ghazali* (Allen & Unwin, 1953) by W. Montgomery Watt.

Al-Munqidh is the personal spiritual statement by the Persian-born Arab al-Ghazzali. He started to teach at the Nizamiyya College in Baghdad when his outstanding gifts were recognised by Nizam al-Mulk, but while there suffered a mental breakdown and a crisis of faith. He left Baghdad in 1095 to travel in the Muslim world, seeing Jerusalem just before it was taken by the Crusaders, making the pilgrimage to Mecca, and seeing such important cities as Damascus and Alexandria.

From this period he rejected orthodox Islam (*Kalam*) and dialectic philosophy *(Falsafa),* and adopted a moderate Sufi position. *Ihya' 'Ulum ad-Din* ('The Revitalizing of Religious Sciences') is a compendium of his system, abridged in Persian as *Kimiya-ye Sa'adat,* the book by which he is still best known in Iran. His doctrine is simply that religion must be rooted in spirutual experience and meditation, and not in casuistry and complex manmade systems. This view is expounded in *Tahafut al-Falasifah* ('Incoherence of the Philosophers', translated by Sabid Ahmad Kamali, and published by Mohammad Ashraf, 8 McLeod Road, Lahore, Pakistan, 1958), which provoked the reply *Tahafut at-Tahafut* ('Incoherence of the Incoherence', translated by Simon van den Bergh, Luzac, 1954) from Averroes (Ibn Rushd, 1126–98).

See W. Montgomery Watt's *Muslim Intellectual: a Study of al-Ghazali* (Edinburgh U.P., 1963), and A. J. Arberry's *Revelation and Reason in Islam* (Allen & Unwin and Macmillan, New York, 1957).

SINUHE (*c.* 2000 B.C.).

The Story of Sinuhe. Edited by A. H. Gardiner in *Hieratische Papyrus aus d.*

königl. Museen zu Berlin, vol. 5, 1909. Complete hieroglyphic text with interlinear transliteration and translation, plus basic grammatical commentary, by Ronald Bullock (2nd ed., Probsthain, 41 Great Russell Street, London WC1B 3PH, 1978).

How does anyone interested in the world of Egyptian literature and hieroglyphics obtain a true insight into the Pharaonic age? According to Ronald Bullock one spends two years working through every exercise in A. H. Gardiner's *Egyptian Grammar* (3rd ed., Oxford U.P., 1957). Confronted with the problem of finding absorbing texts for part-time evening students of Egyptology, Bullock found that they regarded *The Book of the Dead* as surpassingly dull. Of the other options, 'The *Eloquent Peasant* is a prize bore; *The Shipwrecked Sailor* is a pale shadow of *Sindbad*; *The Man Who Was Tired of Life* is a suicidal psychotic. Then I thought of *Sinuhe.* Here there were two fairly reliable texts (the B and R) with Ramessid variants; the scribe had not only used a wide vocabulary but had also utilised every established grammatical rule of Middle Egyptian. The story itself is a rattling good yarn, well illustrating what it must have been like to live in Ancient Egypt'.

The Bullock edition is an ideal instrument for learning hieroglyphics on your own. Sinuhe was a high administrative official who fled from the service of Queen Nofru after an unsuccessful palace revolt, wandered across the desert, and sought refuge with a Syrian chieftain, whose daughter he married. Always nostalgic for Egypt, Sinuhe finally travelled home and established himself there once more.

Lange and Hirmer's *Egypt* (4th ed., Phaidon Press, 1968) is an excellent pictorial record to accompany a solid history such as Gardiner's *Egypt of the Pharaohs* (Oxford U.P., 1964) or a wide-ranging portrait such as William A. Ward's *The Spirit of Ancient Egypt* (Khayats, 90–94 rue Bliss, Beirut, 1965).

Examine the Egyptian antiquities in the nearest national museum or Egyptological Museum, such as the British Museum, the Louvre, or the Metropolitan Museum of Art, New York.

A comparison between the monumental art of Egypt and Sumer is provided in *The Beginnings of Architecture* (Oxford U.P., 1964) by Siegfried Giedion. This is volume 2 of *The Eternal Present*; the first volume, *The Beginnings of Art* (Oxford U.P., 1962), is equally valuable for its insights into prehistoric art.

YEVGENI IVANOVICH ZAMYATIN (1884–1937).

My. Written 1920. First published in Russian (in the U.S.A.) 1924. Translated by Bernard Guilbert Guerney as *We* (Penguin, 1972).

'Real literature', according to Zamyatin,'can be created only by madmen, hermits, heretics, dreamers, rebels, and sceptics, not by diligent and trustworthy functionaries'. In a moving letter to Stalin, translated with *The Dragon and other Stories* by Mirra Ginsburg (Penguin, 1975), Zamyatin begged to be allowed to go into exile rather than submit to writing nothing, or publicly repudiating his views. After Gorki's intercession, Stalin allowed Zamyatin to leave Russia in 1931 and to settle in Paris, where he died, an honoured novelist and short-story writer, in 1937.

Zamyatin's *We* is a nightmare of life in the distant future, when human beings are known by numbers and they live in the One State ruled by the so-called Benefactor. Written in 1920, the novel was translated by Gregory Zilboorg (Dutton, 1924). The resemblance of the One State to the Soviet Union has caused perpetual banning of the book there, and most Russians still only know the novel by hearsay. Its influence on Aldous Huxley's *Brave New World* (1932) and George Orwell's *1984* (1949) is marked, and appropriately so, for Zamyatin knew England well, having spent most of 1916 and 1917 in Newcastle-upon-Tyne to supervise the construction of ten icebreakers for the Tsarist government, having read the anti-Utopian novels of H. G. Wells, and having written a short novel, *The Islanders* (1918) to satirise the self-satisfied English. He acquired English characteristics such as clipped speech and a certain reserve, and translated not only Wells but Sheridan.

Zamyatin's intriguing, even eccentric, essays have been translated by Mirra Ginsburg in *A Soviet Heretic* (University of Chicago Press, 1970).

Related reading might concentrate on Zamyatin's most interesting disciple, Konstantin Fedin, whose best novel is *Brat'ya* (*The Brothers*, 1928). See also the great Soviet silent film *Battleship Potemkin* (1925) directed by Sergei Eisenstein, dealing with events of the 1905–7 Revolution.

HENRY BROOKS ADAMS (1838–1918).
   Mont-Saint-Michel and Chartres. (Privately printed 1904; New American Library, 1961). And *The Education of Henry Adams* (Privately 1907; New English Library, 1966).

Henry Adams, a member of that New England family of Presidents and statesmen, produced between 1889 and 1891 nine volumes of *The History of the United States during the Administrations of Jefferson and Madison,* which asked but left unanswered the question: 'Does greater material progress mean continuing spiritual and moral growth?'.

It was something of a surprise that Adams, a staunch Protestant, should exalt the Roman Catholic visions of Mont-Saint-Michel and Chartres, the former as the highest expression of masculine nature, and the latter as the triumph of feminine nature. He proposed that the twelfth-century renaissance had found and realised the unity of sex and maternity: the religion of beauty rested on the laws of biology. In theology, the idealization of the Virgin Mary was a revolt against the male-centred early Church. The goddess of fertility known to most pagans had to find expression within Christianity, and the blossoming of Marian sculpture, stained-glass and literature fulfilled this primal need.

Adams confused friends and posterity alike with the assertion that the last three chapters of *Mont-Saint-Michel* form, with the last three chapters of his *Education,* his dynamic theory of history. He saw constructive unity in the mediaeval world view, and destructive multiplicity in the twentieth-century world view.

Further reading should include *The Law of Civilization and Decay* (1895; Vintage Books, 1955) by Henry's brother Brooks Adams; and their joint work *The Degradation of the Democratic Dogma* (1919; Harper and Row, 1970), as well as works on medieval architecture such as Émile Mâle's *Religious Art in France: the Twelfth Century* (Princeton U.P., 1978) and *The Gothic Image* (Harper, Row, 1973); and *Abbot Suger on the Abbey Church of Saint-Denis* (Princeton U.P., 1979), edited by Erwin Panofsky and Gerda Panofsky-Sörgel.

CHAIM NACHMAN BIALIK (1873–1934).
  Kithve ('Selected Works'). First published 1926–38. *Selected Poems.* Bilingual edition, with translations by Maurice Samuel (Union of American Hebrew Congregations, 1967).

Bialik, claimed by many to be the leading Hebrew poet of his age, presents an extraordinary picture of a Talmudic student (*Ha-Matmid,* 'The Perpetual Student', is a fine narrative poem written while a lumber merchant at Zhitomir, in the Ukraine) who rejects all avant-garde trends in favour of a call to Zion, for Jewish solidarity in a world of hideous calamity. Taking inspiration from early Hebrew literature, Bialik wrought a major part of the literary Hebrew written today. *Be-Ir ha-Haregah* ('In the City of the Massacre') was a Zionist poem of torment after the Kishinev pogrom of 1903 which ignites fervent sentiment even now. He founded a publishing house in Berlin in 1921, but moved to Tel Aviv three years later.

Stanley Burnshaw and others have edited *The Modern Hebrew Poem Itself* (Holt, Rinehart and Winston, 1965), showing poems in Hebrew, in transliteration and in a literal translation. Other heirs of Bialik can be read in A. Birman's *Anthology of Modern Hebrew Poetry* (Abelard Schuman, 1968). There are Penguin Modern Poets volumes devoted to Yehuda Amichai (1971) and to Abba Kovner and Nellie Sachs (1971). Two collections from T. Carmi have been published by André Deutsch (1964 and 1971), and Carcanet have produced Dan Pagis' *Selected Poems* (1972).

THOMAS HARDY (1840-1928).
> *Jude the Obscure.* First complete edition 1895. Several editions are available, including those from Penguin (by C. H. Sisson, 1978) and Macmillan.

Hardy's greatest novel, and his last important work in this genre (due in some part to the distress caused him by the tragedy of its hero), *Jude the Obscure* deals with the 'deadly war waged with old Apostolic desperation between flesh and spirit'. Jude Fawley, a South Wessex village boy, has a passion for learning, and works to support himself as a stone-mason, but finds the distraction of a 'mere female animal' overwhelming and is disturbed from his course of study. Eventually he attempts to study for the priesthood, but again discovers that his sensuous nature betrays him. The dignity and sympathy that Hardy bestows on a story that might become hackneyed in other hands raises *Jude the Obscure* to a new peak of achievement in the Victorian novel.

Hardy was at the height of his novelistic powers, but as an old man claimed that his poetry would outlive his fiction. *The Dynasts* (1903-6) is an epic poem in the form of a play but, as the author was quick to point out, 'intended for mental performance only'. John Wain has edited *Selected Shorter Poems* (Macmillan, 1966), and there is a Hardy volume in the Penguin Poets series. *Young Thomas Hardy* (1978) and *The Older Hardy* (1980) by Robert Gittings are available in Penguin.

Edward Elgar (1857-1934) occupies a position in Victorian musical life equivalent to Hardy's in literature. Superlative performances of Elgar's music on records include Solti's Symphonies (Decca SXL 6569 and 6723); Boult's *Dream of Gerontius* (2 discs, HMV SLS 987); Barbirolli's Cello concerto (with Jacqueline du Pré) and *Sea Pictures* (with Janet Baker, HMV ASD 655); and Pinchas Zukerman's Violin concerto, with the LPO conducted by Barenboim (CBS 76528).

AHMAD IBN HUSAIN, called AL-MUTANABBI (915-965).
> *Poems.* Edited by A. J. Arberry, with introduction, translation and notes (Cambridge U.P., 1967).

Generally recognised as the greatest poet in Arabic for his mastery of language, and the coherence of his longer works, al-Mutanabbi is repeatedly claimed to be untranslatable. If one learns Arabic to be able to read the Qur'an, then a further reward is waiting in the poems of Mutanabbi (the name means 'would-be Prophet', after his abortive revolt of 933).

Arberry is distinguished for his many contributions to Islamic studies (both in Arabic and in Persian), but this is probably his most outstanding achievement. Al-Mutanabbi broke away from the stereotyped verse forms and images of the traditional school, and became leader of the modern group, who used startling figures of speech, images and puns. The decadence of the modern movement was to lead to a preoccupation with elaborate language for its own sake, but Mutanabbi is still regularly learnt by heart and quoted. Born at Kufa, in Iraq, he was educated mainly in Damascus, and found favour as a writer of panegyrics in the courts of Aleppo, Cairo and Shiraz. He was murdered by bandits on a journey from Shiraz to Baghdad. The best book on Mutanabbi is Taha Husain's *Ma'a al-Mutanabbi* (Dar al-Ma'arif, Cairo, 1962).

HARRY ELMER BARNES (b. 1889).
A History of Historical Writing. (2nd ed., Dover and Constable, 1962).

The critical reader must examine the various styles of historiography at some point, for authors are generally wary of stating their biases or prejudices openly, though many are guilty of harbouring and expressing vested interests and wish to influence their readers to walk the same path. Thus, our view of the enemies of imperial Rome is tainted by the fact that – until Gibbon and his successors offered their alternative readings – the record had been supplied almost entirely by Romans or those antagonistic to the neighbouring peoples such as the Goths, Vandals and Lombards. Until recently our understanding of African history has been limited to the record provided by writers from the colonial powers. Even now we have no adequate corpus in English of historical writings by indigenous South Americans, Burmese or Afghans. A tool such as that by Barnes is therefore required reading for anyone enquiring into the causes of religious or political movements, of dynasties and of social customs, of economic tendencies and industrial innovations. In the course of a lifetime's reading, the critical faculty should be sharpened by investigating the ways in which authors seek to impress their vision of the world upon us and by realizing that no single book or handful of books will be sufficient advice – or imaginative fuel – when so many other possibilities of thought and action exist.

Test your critical awareness against the *Histoire générale de la civilisation en Europe* (1828) by François Guizot (1787–1874), or Jean Froissart's *Chroniques* to the year 1400, translated by Geoffrey Brereton (Penguin, 1978).

Year 22

The Penguin Book of Russian Verse, introduced and edited by Dimitri Obolensky (Penguin, 1962).

Another of the indispensable national anthologies produced by Penguin, Obolensky's collection begins with the *Lay of Igor's Campaign* (*c.* 1185) and concludes with Tvardovsky, Vasiliev and Aliger (b. 1915).

A good introduction and helpful 'Note on Russian Versification', with the usual text and plain prose translation, set the standard by which all subsequent Russian verse anthologies must be judged.

There is a new edition of the book entitled *The Heritage of Russian Verse* (Indiana U.P., 1976).

Borodin's opera *Prince Igor* (first performed in 1890, finished by Rimsky-Korsakov and Glazunov) is available on Decca (4 discs, GOS 562-5) conducted by Oscar Danon. His three symphonies ought also to be explored at this point.

The Aztecs.

The Aztec culture, at once autonomous and totally strange to European criteria, can be studied in a variety of books. For religion, poetry and symbolism there are Miguel León-Portilla's *Aztec Thought and Culture* (Oklahoma U.P., 1967), Laurette Séjourné's *Burning Water* (Thames & Hudson, 1978) and Irene Nicholson's *Firefly in the Night* (Faber & Faber, 1959). For archaeology the best book is Michael D. Coe's *Mexico* (Thames & Hudson and Praeger, 1962), though one may read with profit G. C. Vaillant's *The Aztecs of Mexico* (2nd ed., Penguin, 1978) if one discounts the author's reliance on the false picture presented by L. H. Morgan and Adolph Bandelier and corrects the identification of Classic Teotihuacán with the post-Classic Toltecs.

For social customs, there is Jacques Soustelle's *The Daily Life of the Aztecs* (Penguin, 1964). On art and anthropology, use Ignacio Bernal's illustrated guide to *The Mexican National Museum of Anthropology* (Thames & Hudson, 1968) and

Justino Fernández's *Guide to Mexican Art* (University of Chicago Press, 1969).
The literature of the Aztecs is almost exclusively poetic: see Angel M.
Garibay's *La Literatura de los Aztecas* (Joaquın Mortiz, Guaymas 33–1, México
7, 1964).

The overthrow of the Aztec Empire by the Spaniards is told by Bernal Díaz del
Castillo (1492–1581) in his *Historia verdadera de la Conquista de la Nueva-
España,* first published in 1632 and translated by J. M. Cohen as *The Conquest of
New Spain* (Penguin, 1963). Díaz's book was a response to the *Historia de las
Indias y conquista de México* (1552) by Francisco López de Gómara (1512–72)
and in its turn constituted the major source for W. H. Prescott's classic *History of
the Conquest of Mexico* (3 vols., 1843), in print from the University of Chicago
Press (1966) and in Everyman's Library (Dent and Dutton, 1957).

LEO NIKOLAYEVICH TOLSTOY (1828–1910).
　　Voyna i mir. First published 1863–9. Translated as *War and Peace* by
　　Rosemary Edmonds (Penguin, 1957).

In 1862, Tolstoy married a girl sixteen years his junior and wrote to his cousin in
the following year: 'Never before have I felt my intellectual and even all my moral
faculties so unimpeded, so fit for work. And I have work – a novel of the period
1810–1820, which has completely absorbed me since the beginning of
Autumn. . . Now I am an author with all the powers of my soul, and I write and
reflect as I have never written or reflected before'.

His wife the Countess was kept busy, but happily busy according to her own
journal, trying to decipher the several drafts in order to copy out for serial
publication.

Tolstoy assumes the personae of Pierre Bezuhov and Prince Andrei
Bolkonsky, relating the interwoven histories of the impoverished Rostov family
and the aristocratic Bolkonskys within the historical framework of the period.
Tsar Alexander I and Napoleon Bonaparte stride the stage of *War and Peace*
much as the gods bestride the *Iliad.*

If Pushkin is the poetic genius of nineteenth-century Russia, then Tolstoy is the
genius of prose. Both are ultimately concerned with humanity at large, rather
than exclusively with the Russian people, and that is one reason why both are
avidly read today, as much in English or German as in Russian.

The Bolshoi Opera recording of Prokofiev's opera *War and Peace* is on 4
Melodiya discs (SLS 837), but it is more appropriate now to explore the
composers of Tolstoy's own generation other than Borodin (1833–87):
Balakirev (1837–1910), Mussorgsky (1839–81), and Rimsky-Korsakov
(1844–1908).

WILLIAM BLAKE (1757–1827).
> *The Complete Writings.* Edited by Geoffrey Keynes. Oxford Standard Authors series (Oxford U.P., 1966).

There are many ways of perceiving Blake: as a visionary artist whose autograph can be found in every copy of the *Songs of Innocence* and *Songs of Experience,* every page hand-lettered and cut in reverse on copper before being printed, ornamented and painted in water-colours by the poet and his wife; as a Christian mystic outside the pale of the ecclesiastical tradition; as a social critic; as a prophet; as a painter; as a poet; and as an illustrator of major writers such as Dante, Chaucer and Milton.

In Blake's mythology Urizen stands for a rigid moral authority, and Orc for creative anarchism. *The Marriage of Heaven and Hell* (1790) denies not only authority, but also the existence of matter and the theory of eternal punishment. The *Jerusalem* (1804) expounds a theory of the imagination according to which 'the world of imagination is the world of eternity. It is the divine bosom into which we shall all go after the death of the vegetated body'. Imagination is 'the real and eternal world of which the Vegetable Universe is but a faint shadow'. It is easy to understand the appeal of this form of mysticism to the post-World War II generation coming to uneasy terms with nuclear energy, increased pollution, overpopulation, and urbanisation on a scale greater than ever before known. Blake is seen as a precursor by Allen Ginsberg and adherents of the 'flower power' movement, and his rejection of 'satanic mills' has been understood as a flight from industrialism to rural peace.

Of the many excellent books on aspects of Blake's life and work, one can heartily recommend Northrop Frye's *Fearful Symmetry* (Princeton U.P., 1970), Bernard Blackstone's *English Blake* (Shoestring Press, 1966) and the books by Keynes and Bronowski.

ANTON PAVLOVICH CHEKHOV (1860–1904).
> Plays. The Oxford Chekhov, translated by Ronald Hingley. Vol. 1 (Oxford U.P., 1968): *Short Plays*; vol. 2 (1967): *Platonov, Ivanov, The Seagull*; vol. 3 (1964): *Uncle Vanya, The Three Sisters, The Cherry Orchard, The Wood Demon.*

Chekhov was of peasant origin, but qualified as a doctor and soon became wealthy and well-respected as a writer of comic sketches and farces. His health rapidly deteriorated, and he was forced to spend time recuperating in the South of France and the Crimea.

Through constant application and by the force of his genius, Chekhov raised the art of the Russian short story to a new level, giving it psychological depth and jolting realism based on French Naturalism and native Russian pessimism. A master of pathos, the portrayal of futility in human thought and action, and the humour of self-deception, Chekhov became the greatest dramatist of his country.

His first important play was *Chayka* ('The Seagull', 1896), unaccountably a failure on its first performance but acclaimed when staged two years later at the new Moscow Art Theatre of Stanislavsky and Nemirovich-Danchenko.

Chekhov's major plays reflect the dullness of Russian provincial life, and the empty social round of the longed-for capital city. It is not likely that he saw his serf-owning landlords as a doomed class and the victory of the proletariat as certain, despite Soviet readings in recent years. He was concerned with basic Russian attitudes and weaknesses, and portrayed Madame Lyubov Ranevsky in *Vishnyovy Sad* ('The Cherry Orchard', 1904) not as the dignified matriarch that some Western productions have shown but as 'a comic old woman' clinging to past glories without common sense, business sense, or even any sense or reality. Memorable productions in the West have brought new vigour to *Dyadya Vanya* ('Uncle Vanya', 1897) and *Tri Sestry* ('Three Sisters', 1901).

Or you might prefer to devote a month to the several volumes of *Stories* in the Oxford Chekhov.

PATAÑJALI (*c.* 300 A.D.).

> *Yogasutra.* Of the many commented translations available, one of the best is Swami Vivekananda's *Raja Yoga* in *The Yogas and other works* (Ramakrishna -Vivekananda Center, New York, latest edition), available without commentary in Lin Yutang's *Wisdom of India* (Michael Joseph, 1949). Another, more pedantic, is by J. H. Woods (*The Yoga-System of Patañjali,* reissued by Luzac, 1967).

We know virtually nothing of 'Patañjali': we cannot even state with certainty that 'he' existed, much less that he is certainly the author of the *Yogasutra* commonly attributed to him: it may be a series of ideas passed down to him which he was the first to codify in writing. The aphorisms are not in any sense a philosophical or religious system: they are practical notes towards the attainment of certain psychological states. He does not set out to convert, as the Catholic Truth Society might, but aims to train in certain exercises which will enable the student to pass from ignorance (the *sankhya* concept equivalent to Christian 'sin') towards spiritual enlightenment through processes of meditation and other forms of bodily and mental control.

Geraldine Coster's *Yoga and Western Psychology* (Oxford U.P., 1934) takes an illuminating comparative approach to the subject. Ernest E. Wood's *Yoga* (Penguin, 1956) is a wide-ranging manual. One should beware of books by westerners claiming to 'teach' Yoga as though it were simply a matter of physical fitness, on the one hand, or as though it were a psychic 'science' wholly irrelevant to practical life, on the other.

MARCO POLO (*c.* 1254–1324).

Travels. Originally written in French (*Divisament dou Monde*) at Polo's dictation while a prisoner of the Genoese in 1298–9 and first published in German (*Buch des edlen Ritters und Landfahrers Marco Polo,* 1477). For the specialist, the best edition is that of Sir Henry Yule (*The Book of Ser Marco Polo,* 2 vols., Hakluyt Society, 1903) with a supplement by H. Cordier (1920). For the general reader there is a translation of the *Travels* by Ronald E. Latham (Penguin, 1958), based on the Benedetto edition.

Marco Polo, who travelled east from Venice with his father and uncle in 1271 and did not return until 1295, is the first westerner to give an authentic picture of life in China. Their route was through Persia to the Pamirs, Mongolia, and the Gobi to north-west China, taking a total of four years to reach Shantung. They spent several years at the Court of Kublai Khan, making their way back through southeast Asia and southern India.

The tales are told in a vivid, dramatic style that enhances the wonders of which Polo speaks. He is seldom scornful of unusual customs or traits foreign to Venetian merchants, but does his best to chronicle what he saw with care and accuracy. The physical hardihood of Marco Polo and his companions is amazing, for they travelled on horseback among dozens of tribes, across uncharted deserts and mountain ranges, and repeatedly suffered extremes of heat and cold. Polo's system of measuring distances by days' journeys has proved his calculations remarkably accurate.

Armchair travellers will enjoy illustrated selection from *The Travels of Marco Polo* with a text annotated by Cottie A. Burland, and photographs by Werner Forman (Michael Joseph, 1971).

Several books deal with the traffic in Chinese silks and in reciprocal trade: a good account is that by L. Boulnois in *The Silk Road* (Allen and Unwin, 1966), while for the Japanese viewpoint use Ryoichi Hayashi's *The Silk Road and the Shoso-in* (Weatherhill, 1975).

IVAN ALEXANDROVICH GONCHAROV (1812–1891).

Oblomov. First published 1859. Translated by David Magarshack (Penguin, 1954).

Goncharov's first novel, *An Ordinary Story* (1847), was an analysis of the conflict between the new bourgeoisie (of which Goncharov was a member) and the serf-owning aristocracy.

Oblomov, his second novel, was likewise devoted to an attack on the lazy landowners who thoughtlessly relied on the labour of others. The difference between the two was the writer's increasing maturity, his mordant humour, and the universal figure of Ilya Ilyich Oblomov, as immortal as Quilp or Don Quixote. 'Lying down was not for Oblomov a necessity, as it is for a sick man or for a man who is sleepy; or a matter of chance, as it is for a man who is tired; or a pleasure, as it is for a lazy man: it was his normal condition. When he was at home – and he was almost always at home – he lay down all the time, and always in the same room. . .'

The Precipice (1869), his third novel, was a failure and Goncharov acquired a number of Oblomovian traits in his last twenty-two years, publishing hardly anything at all and accusing the brilliant Turgenev of stealing his plots – even leading a gang who were scheming the ultimate ruin of Goncharov.

KAMO NO CHOMEI (1153–1216).
> *Hojoki.* Written 1212. Translated as *An Account of my Hut* by Donald Keene in his *Anthology of Japanese Literature to the Nineteenth Century* (2nd ed., Penguin, 1968).

Kamo's life was divided by the year 1205, when he left the Court's service, having been an official in the poetry department and a noted player of the *biwa* or lute, and retiring from the world as a Buddhist hermit.

The *Hojoki* is a concise essay permeated with Buddhism on the transience of human life and happiness, and on the serenity he enjoyed in his little hut. 'I naturally feel ashamed when I go to the capital and must beg, but when I return and sit here I feel pity for those still attached to the world of dust. Should anyone doubt the truth of my words, let him look to the fishes and the birds. Fish do not weary of the water, but unless one is a fish one does not know why. Birds long for the woods, but unless one is a bird one does not know why. The joys of solitude are similar. Who could understand them without having lived here?'

Kamo's pessimism reflects the turbulent times of the late Heian period, though he does not mention the fighting between the Minamoto and the Taira which ravaged Japan in his day.

Explore the world of Japanese music on disc and in W. P. Malm's *Japanese Music and Musical Instruments* (Tuttle, Tokyo, latest edition).

Year 23

ARISTOTLE (384–322 B.C.).
> *Ethica Nicomachea*. Text with a translation by H. Rackham in the Loeb
> Classical Library (2nd ed., Heinemann and Harvard U.P., 1934). Translated
> by J. A. K. Thomson as *The Ethics* (Penguin, 1953).

Aristotle's corpus contains three works on morals: the so-called *Eudemian Ethics,*
dedicated to his best pupil, Eudemus; the shorter, eclectic *Magna Moralia*
probably compiled from the moral works of Aristotle by a Peripatetic of the next
generation; and the definitive *Nicomachean Ethics* dedicated to Aristotle's son
Nicomachus who fell in battle while still young.

Ethics is defined by Aristotle as the study of human welfare, showing which
types of conduct are conducive to happiness. A discussion of the moral virtues
leads to the corollary that vices are but the excess or defect of the virtues. The
intellectual virtues are prudence, or practical wisdom, and speculative wisdom.
The highest virtue is the last, happiness consisting in the activity of *theoria,* the
disinterested contemplation of truth. It is to be inferred that the business of
politics is to organize the affairs of state in such a manner that most or all of the
citizens are fitted by nature and by education to attain this end.

The genius of the Greek language is peculiarly fitted for the clear statement of
philosophical and moral ideas, and more than two thousand years have elapsed
without the addition of any significant new concepts to Aristotelian ethics.

FYODOR MIKHAILOVICH DOSTOEVSKY (1821–1881).
> *Prestupleniye i nakazaniye*. First published 1866. Translated as *Crime and
> Punishment* by David Magarshack (Penguin, 1951).

In 1864 Dostoevsky's first wife died, followed by his brother Mikhail. He was
pursued by creditors, lost heavily at gambling, and suffered a further blow when
his monthly magazine *Epoch* was closed by the authorities. He sold all the rights
of his present and future writings to the publisher Stellovsky, and set off for

Wiesbaden with his 'infallible' system for winning at roulette. Having lost everything, he sought a loan from Turgenev, and lost that too. Eventually his friend Wrangel paid his hotel bill in Wiesbaden, and Dostoevsky was free to return, penniless, to Russia. But in the hotel room he had begun work on the immortal semi-autobiographical *Prestupleniye i nakazaniye* which opens as Raskolnikov faces much the same problems that tormented his creator. Before completing it he wrote *Igrok* ('The Gambler', 1866) in a month.

Only the most inspired artists can analyse themselves and their faults with the candour that Dostoevsky reveals. Writing the novel did not purify him of his mania, and he was forced to live in Germany, Italy and Switzerland to evade his many creditors, but the devotion of his second wife, his stenographer Anna, whom he married in 1867, enabled him in the next four years to produce *Idiot* ('The Idiot', 1868–9), *Besy* ('The Devils', 1871–2), and the less successful *Vechny Muzh* ('The Eternal Husband', 1870).

Another work inspired by the gambler's lunacy is Pushkin's *Pikovaya dama* ('The Queen of Spades', 1834; made into an opera by Tchaikovsky, conducted by Mstislav Rostropovich on 4 discs, DG 2740 176).

———————

CHARLES LAMB (1775–1834).
> *Essays of Elia* and *Last Essays of Elia*. First published 1823 and 1833 respectively. World's Classics series (Oxford U.P., 1946).

Carlyle, with his passion for things both Germanic and pompous, regarded Lamb's conversation as 'contemptibly small, indicating wondrous ignorance and shallowness'. The opposite judgment of Lamb's table-talk and occasional essays has been held by most subsequent readers and critics. Cheerful and sociable on the surface, he was prey to nightmares of madness, and did in fact suffer one episode of dementia before Mary Lamb, his sister, killed their mother in a fit of madness and he was forced to devote the rest of his life to her care, resigning his natural inclination towards marriage to stay 'wedded to the fortune of my sister and my poor old father'.

The essays begin with 'The South-Sea House', an establishment with which Lamb had been connected earlier in life, and he signed the essay 'Elia', the name of a clerk in the House. Lamb ranges across the fields of reminiscence and fancy in 'A Dissertation upon Roast Pig', 'All Fools' Day' and 'The Praise of Chimney-Sweepers'.

Lamb's *Letters* (3 vols., Cornell U.P., 1976–8) have been edited by E. W. Marrs.

———————

ISAAC EMMANUELOVICH BABEL (1894–*c.* 1940).
Collected Stories. Translated or revised by Walter Morison (World, 1960; Penguin, 1961).

Traditionally the Cossacks were the sworn enemies of Jews, but Babel first achieved fame with a remarkable collection of stories *Konarmiya*, ('Red Cavalry', 1926), based on his experiences as a supply officer in a Cossack regiment in 1920. Babel was a poor Jew of the Odessa ghetto and his *Odesskiye Rasskazy* ('Tales of Odessa', 1931) are miracles of brief, even laconic anecdotes spiced with humanity and sardonic insights. His literary sources included not only the Talmud and Hebrew traditions, but also French literature (he idolised Guy de Maupassant) and such earthy Russian realists as Gogol. The brutal experiences of his childhood, when his father was humiliated and his father's store looted, all find their corner in one or other of the gnomic, brilliant stories that comprise the whole of Babel's output, except for a couple of less significant plays.

Babel disappeared in one of the purges of 1937 and he died two or three years later of typhus according to one 'eye-witness' – or executed by the firing-squad according to another.

A collected edition, with an introduction by his loyal friend Ilya Ehrenburg, rehabilitated Babel in 1957, and two further editions appeared in 1966. *You Must Know Everything,* translated by Max Hayward (Cape, 1960), consists of diaries and stories by Babel hitherto unpublished, with reminiscences by some friends. The title comes from Babel's first tale, 1915, in which his grandmother cried vehemently: 'Study! Study and you will have everything – wealth and fame! You must know *everything.* The whole world will fall at your feet and grovel before you. Everybody must envy you. Do not trust people. Do not have friends. Do not lend them money. Do not give them your heart!'

NORBERT LYNTON.
The Story of Modern Art (Phaidon Press, 1980).

Either this, or a comparable international survey of movements beginning with the pivotal figure of Cézanne, will be an essential companion to exhibitions of modern art, or national galleries of modern art such as the Metropolitan in New York or the Tate Gallery. Conversely, no gallery can provide a conspectus as wide-ranging as Norbert Lynton's.

Three special surveys published by Thames & Hudson form useful extensions of a general history: *Art Without Boundaries: 1950–70* (1972) edited by Gerald Woods, Philip Thompson and John Williams; *Environments and Happenings* (1974) by Adrian Henri; and *Movements in Art since 1945* (2nd ed., 1975) by Edward Lucie-Smith.

Two currents in twentieth-century art are the sensuous technical virtuosity of a Picasso (illustrations available in numerous monographs; best biography by Roland Penrose, *Picasso: his Life and Work*, Gollancz, 1958), and the intellectual and even cerebral innovations of a Duchamp (1887–1968). On Duchamp, see *The World of Marcel Duchamp* (Time Inc., New York, 1966) and *The Essential Writings of Marcel Duchamp* (Thames & Hudson, 1975).

In music, Picasso has no contemporary equal. Duchamp's inventiveness might perhaps be comparable to that of Anton Webern (1883–1945), whose music forms an instructive contrast to pieces by Alban Berg and Arnold Schoenberg on DGG 2711 014 (4 discs).

IVAN SERGEYEVICH TURGENEV (1818–1883).
   Otsy i deti. First published 1862. Translated as *Fathers and Children* (with *Rudin*, 1856) by Richard Hare (Hutchinson, 1947).

Nothing that Turgenev wrote is ugly or dull. He is one of those novelists whose work is appreciated as keenly abroad (the 'beautiful genius', admired by Henry James) as he is in the Soviet Union. His character was noble and sensitive: the early *Zapiski okhotnika* ('A Hunter's Sketches', published serially, 1847–51; collected in 1852; translated as *Sketches from a Hunter's Album* by R. Freeborn, Penguin, 1967) led indirectly to the emancipation of the serfs in 1861.

The critical reception accorded to *Fathers and Children* was so malicious and wrong-headed, however, that he determined to live abroad, and spent the rest of his life in Baden-Baden (from 1862 to 1870) and in Paris.

Further exploration of the master could lead to the exquisite *Poems in Prose* (1878–82), translated by Evgenia Schimanskaya (Lindsay Drummond, 1945) or to such fine stories as *First Love* (1860; translated by Isaiah Berlin, Penguin, 1978) or *Torrents of Spring* (1872; translated by David Magarshack, Panther, 1965).

A useful biography and critical study combined is Avrahm Yarmolinsky's *Turgenev: the Man, his Art, and his Age* (Collier, 1961, reprinted by Octagon, 1977).

MIRZA ASADULLAH BEG KHAN (GHALIB) (1797 or 1798–1869).
   Divan-i-Ghalib. Edited by Imtiyaz Ali Arshi (1958). Partially translated as *Ghazals of Ghalib: versions from the Urdu* edited by Aijaz Ahmad (Columbia U.P., 1971).

Seven American poets (Fitzsimmons, Hunt, Merwin, Ray, Rich, Stafford and Strand) have collaborated in one of the most successful translation projects of our time. Each of 37 *ghazals* is printed in Urdu script, in a literal English translation, with notes on essential vocabulary, a general explanation, and one or more new renderings. There is a useful introduction.

The Urdu poetic tradition is that of reflection, with varied lyrical effects in a brief compass, verbal complexity and abstract metaphors. Love, the main theme, is invariably generalized: not directed at a specific object. Most of these Urdu poems were completed by the time that Ghalib was 19, during his first six years in Delhi after his departure from Agra, his birthplace. He was a vulnerable man (never having home, books, or children of his own), and his insecurity is frequently evident in his writing.

Ghalib's *Life and Letters* have been edited and translated by Ralph Russell and Khurshidul Islam (Allen & Unwin, 1969).

ALEXANDER ISAYEVICH SOLZHENITSYN (b. 1918).
  Odin den' Ivana Denisovicha ('One Day in the Life of Ivan Denisovich').
  First published 1962, in *Novy Mir.* Translated by Ralph Parker (New American Library, 1963) and by Max Hayward and Ronald Hingley (Bantam, 1963).

In the light of Solzhenitsyn's subsequent move to the West and his detailed, exhaustive three-volume work on Stalinist concentration camps, *The Gulag Archipelago,* Khrushchev's decision to allow the publication of *One Day in the Life of Ivan Denisovich* in the official magazine *Novy Mir* can be seen as a temporary slackening of literary censorship that has once again been tightened.

Shukhov, the ordinary peasant whose normal features can be seen a hundred times an hour on any Moscow street, is a typical victim of a totalitarian machine which neither he nor anyone else can either understand or control. The narrative is plain, and often dry, calm and good-humoured, with none of the hysteria that has sometimes marred Solzhenitsyn's prose.

A different emphasis marks *The First Circle* (translated by 'Michael Guybon', Collins, 1968; Bantam, 1976), also set in Stalinist Russia. Here a much longer, more detailed, but less formally perfect novel portrays three days in the life of a special prison for scientifically-gifted political prisoners. A suffocating vision emerges of a bullying bureaucracy, small-minded envy, colossal inefficiency, and individual heroism on an epic scale.

KUKAI (774–835).
  Kukai and his major works, translated by Yoshito S. Hakeda (Columbia U.P., 1972).

In his *Japan: a Short Cultural History,* G. B. Sansom wrote of Kukai: 'His memory lives all over the country, his name is a household word in the remotest places, not only as a saint, but as a preacher, a scholar, a poet, a sculptor, a painter, an inventor, an explorer, and – sure passport to fame – a great calligrapher'.

Also known by his title, Kobo Daishi, Kukai became the first Japanese to write correct, elegant literary Chinese, a capability much appreciated during the two years (804–6) that he spent in China. He brought back the *Mantrayana* (Sanskrit, 'True Words'), known in Japanese as the Shingon path of Buddhism, esoteric in the sense that the master's teachings are not intended to be passed on in writing, but by word of mouth. The great teacher Hui-kuo (764–805) chose Kukai as his disciple, and Kukai is responsible for several major works, among them the Chinese *Ten Stages of Religious Consciousness.* This was written at the command of 830 of Emperor Junna that each of the six sects should state their beliefs in writing. Kukai's text was both the longest and the most beautiful, written in a poetical style comparable with Alexander Pope's in *The Essay on Man* (1732–4). Esoteric Buddhism became the chief religion practised in Heian Japan, and the stress laid on the learning of Sanskrit by Kukai led to the invention of the Japanese syllabary (*kana*).

For an explanation of 'The Spread of Esoteric Buddhism' see chapter VIII of *Sources of Japanese Tradition,* compiled by Ryusaku Tsunoda and others (vol. 1, Columbia U.P., 1964).

ALEXANDER SERGEYEVICH PUSHKIN (1799–1837).
  Eugene Onegin. First published 1833. Edition with the best commentary (but dead, pedantic translation) is that by Vladimir Nabokov (Revised ed., 4 vols., Princeton U.P. and Routledge, 1975). Best English translation is by Sir Charles Johnston (1977), available from the translator, 32 Kingston House South, Ennismore Gardens, London SW7.

Pushkin's novel in verse, 'something like *Don Juan*' (by Byron) in his own words, is a capital masterpiece which succeeds in its Romantic spirit in devastating the terrain held until 1833 by the classical canons of 18th-century poetics as dictated by Sumarokov and Lomonosov.

The eight 'chapters', or more properly 'canti', of the verse novel each contain some fifty fourteen-line stanzas, ranging from the expression of Pushkin's own poetic theories, parody, and polemics, on the one hand, to the most exquisite songs, such as that of the country girls used verbatim in the libretto for Tchaikovsky's opera *Eugene Onegin* (3 Decca discs, SET 596–8, conducted by Solti). Because the tone of the poem is so varied, the translator's role is crucial, and Sir Charles Johnston has made the best attempt so far. No sequel was ever written, either by Pushkin or any other Russian writer: it remains wholly original, and a delightful experience as the two personalities of Tatiana and Onegin mature throughout the novel.

The same translator has included a version of Pushkin's incomplete 'Onegin's Journey' in his own miscellany, *Poems and Journeys* (1979).

Year 24

Sources of Chinese Tradition, compiled by William Theodore de Bary, Wing-tsit
Chan, and Burton Watson (2 vols., Columbia U.P., 1964).

Starting with the *Shu Ching* ('Book of History') and concluding with authors of
the Chinese communist canon, this nine-hundred-page compendium is
admirably equipped with introductory matter and up-to-date translations by
good authorities.

Among the authors selected for inclusion are Confucius, Mo Tzu, Lao Tzu,
Chuang Tzu, Mencius, Hsün Tzu, Han Fei Tzu, Tung Chung-shu, Ssu-ma T'an,
Ch'ao Ts'o, Ssu-ma Ch'ien, Kuo Hsiang, Hsi K'ang, Tsung Ping, Wang Wei, Ko
Hung, Hui-yüan, Chí-tsang, Fa-tsang, Tao Ch'o, Shen-hui, Han Yü, Ch'eng
Hao, Wang An-shih, Ssu-ma Kuang, Wang Fu-chih, Wang T'ao, Yeh Te-hui,
Sun Yat-sen, Hu Shih, and Li Ta-Chao.

Queste del Saint Graal. Written anonymously *c.* 1225. First edited as a separate
book by F. S. Furnivall 1864. Critical edition by Albert Pauphilet in
Classiques Français du Moyen Âge (1923). Translated by Pauline Matarasso
as *The Quest of the Holy Grail* (Penguin, 1969).

Some readers may prefer to start an exploration of the fascinatingly hybrid Grail
literature with the *Perceval* or *Conte del Graal* (1190) written by Chrétien de
Troyes, and available in a version by R. W. Linker (University of North Carolina
Press, 1960), since this is the source used by many of the later Arthurian writers,
though we now know that Chrétien was elaborating a story already familiar.

However, this anonymously-written spiritual fable in the so-called 'Prose
Lancelot' cycle of Arthurian Romances is unfailingly enjoyable, as long as the
reader keeps it in context. Originally, the Grail vessel was not a Christian relic and
the tradition associating it with Joseph of Arimathea can be traced back no farther
than the apocryphal *Evangelium Nicodemi*. The quest of the Grail can be traced
back to a Celtic myth concerning the journey of a mortal hero to an otherworldly

destination. A maimed king wounded with his own weapon in a land now barren, the dangers to be faced in the quest for the palace, and the question that must be asked and answered if the king is to be healed and the land again made fertile: these are all constant components of the early myth. The legendary material is then reworked and elaborated to fit the society (it might be Brittany or Norman England, Northern Spain or Wales) in which it is newly told. These are the strands of romantic narrative and in this connection one might explore the 19th-century Pre-Raphaelite paintings on some Arthurian theme.

Relevant books include Jessie L. Weston's *From Ritual to Romance* (Doubleday, 1957) and *Quest of the Holy Grail* (Cass, 1964; Haskell, 1973), the symposium *Arthurian Literature in the Middle Ages* (Oxford U.P., 1959) edited by R. S. Loomis, and the wider-ranging *Passion and Society* (Faber & Faber, 1962) by Denis de Rougemont.

Anthology of Chinese Literature, edited by Cyril Birch (2 vols. Vol. 1, Penguin, 1967. Vol. 2, Grove Press, 1965).

Much of this useful anthology will be familiar to those following *A Lifetime's Reading* year by year. For anyone over whom Chinese literature has not yet exercised its fascination, the Birch volumes will prove an appetiser. Alternatively, one might pick up Robert Payne's comparable anthology entitled *The White Pony* (Allen & Unwin, 1949; New American Library, 1960).

Background reading might include J. R. Hightower's *Topics in Chinese Literature* (Harvard U.P., 1962) and Lin Yutang's *Wisdom of China* (Michael Joseph, 1944).

For the artistic background, one might browse through the three volumes of *Chinese Art* from Phaidon Press: *Bronzes, Jade, Sculpture and Ceramics* (1980) by D. Lion-Goldschmidt and J.-C. Moreau-Gobard; *Gold, Silver, Later Bronzes, Cloisonné, Cantonese Enamel, Lacquer, Furniture and Wood* (1981) by R. Soame Jenyns and William Watson; and *Textiles, Glass & Painting on Glass, Carvings in Ivory and Rhinoceros Horn, Carvings in Hardstones, Snuff Bottles and Inkcakes & Inkstones* (1981) by R. Soame-Jenyns.

JANE AUSTEN (1775–1817).
   Pride and Prejudice. First published 1813. Among the many editions available are the 'Oxford Illustrated Jane Austen' volume (latest ed.) and the F. W. Bradbrook edition (Oxford U.P., 1970).

Jane Austen's first novel was the original draft of *Pride and Prejudice,* begun in 1796 and rejected by a publisher in 1797 before its revision in the form we now know. The daughter of the Steventon (Hampshire) rector, she lived an apparently uneventful life. But her command of irony, her stylish ear for conversation betraying every nuance of character, and her gift for gradually unravelling a plot organically, by means of the clash of character with character: every technique of the psychological novelist is already fully operative in *Pride and Prejudice,* a consummation never surpassed in all her subsequent novels.

Jane neglects the surroundings in which people live. Her richest powers are given to dialogue, so that her books are easily dramatised. Her language is pure and undecorated by self-conscious neologisms, archaicisms, or slang. Every character lives and breathes, and one is ultimately confused by the highest art of a novelist: who is really speaking, the character or the author? Jane manages to invest each character with one or more of her own traits: we may be sure that she was as merciless with her own failings as with those of her other targets.

Each of Jane's novels is worth close examination, and will repay re-reading. *Northanger Abbey* (1818) is, however, unusual in being a parody, of Mrs Ann Radcliffe's once fashionable 'Gothick novel' *The Mysteries of Udolpho* (1794). The other major finished works are *Sense and Sensibility* (1811), *Mansfield Park* (1814), *Emma* (1815) and *Persuasion* (1818).

She would have prized Andrew H. Wright's modest and discriminating study *Jane Austen's Novels* (Chatto & Windus, 1961).

LI PO (*also* LI T'AI PO) (701–762 A.D.).
Poems. There is no adequate translation of the 1,000 or so poems written by Li Po. A few appear in Arthur Cooper's *Li Po and Tu Fu* (Penguin, 1973) and others recreated in Ezra Pound's *Cathay* (first published 1915 and since reissued in several forms).

The Chinese poet most loved outside China, he seems to have been born outside the imperial borders (possibly in Central Asia) and spent most of his early life in the westernmost province of Szechuan, his family gaining its livelihood from trading along the Silk Road.

In any event, Li Po felt himself outside the mainstream of Chinese literary life until he was abruptly summoned in 742 to Sian (the former Ch'ang-an) to the Emperor's Court. He quickly achieved the love and respect of the Emperor Hsüan-tsung, but was apparently dismissed in 744 at the instigation of the concubine Yang Kuei-fei and the eunuch Kao Li-shih and thereafter suffered the fortunes and misfortunes of T'ang dynasty exile, amnesties and wanderings. He may have fallen from a boat and drowned while trying to embrace the moon's reflection, but it is more likely that he died of pneumonia.

His poems are technically more varied and daring than those of his contemporaries, relying on the vagaries of Central Asian musical accompaniment for their best effects. Li Po's poetry is personal in tone, often occasional in nature, and compounded of fantasy and a sense of nostalgia that may be superficially literary but serious and even melancholy at its private source.

Arthur Waley's *The Poetry and Career of Li Po* (Allen & Unwin and Macmillan New York, 1950) is unsatisfactory in its lack of sympathy for a particularly elusive personality.

Not a great deal of Chinese atmosphere is reproduced in Gustav Mahler's *Lied von der Erde,* four of whose six songs are translated from Li Po. But the song cycle has its own peculiar beauties and can be enjoyed in the versions conducted by Haitink (Philips 6500 831), by Solti (Decca SET 555), and by Klemperer (HMV SAN 179).

TS'AO HSÜEH-CH'IN (*also* TS'AO CHAN) (*c.* 1715–*c.* 1763).
  Hung-lou meng. Usually translated 'The Dream of the Red Chamber', but ,the latest and best version, by David Hawkes, cites,the author in the *pinyin* romanisation as Cao Xueqin and gives the title as 'The Story of the Stone', translating the original title, *Shih t'ou chi* (5 vols. in progress, of which vol. 1 appeared in 1973, vol. 2 in 1977, and vol. 3 in 1980, Penguin).

The most significant novel in colloquial Chinese, by a writer whose wealthy grandfather had been ruined by confiscation of all property while the boy was only thirteen. The family then moved from Nanking to Peking, living in relative poverty.

Ts'ao Hsüeh-ch'in began to write his novel at the age of thirty, and was still working on at the time of his death. The last forty chapters are believed to have been completed by a certain Kao E, though the climax might easily be inferred from earlier events and from Ts'ao's written outline.

The novel has spawned about as much scholarship in China as have the works of Shakespeare in anglophone countries. The plot is, again as in Shakespeare, not so important as the world view of the author, and the artistry by which he achieves adequate expression of this view. The young man Pao-yü (whose life might be autobiographical) falls in love with Lin Tai-yü, a sweet orphan girl of a branch of Pao-yü's own extended family. Over four hundred other characters are observed in the China of the time, which was the decaying age of a great civilisation. The chapters move with majesty and inevitability through a humanist's view of Chinese history, and the characters never lose their individuality in the long sweep of the novel, the 'education sentimentale' of the Chinese people over the last two hundred years. Ts'ao knew that he must write the novel in colloquial style, but he was also a master of many other styles: the *wen-yen* (literary language) in verse passages of great intrinsic value, and gutter-slang for the voices of peasants and servants. Realist in approach, the *Hung-lou meng* manages to create the effect of a romantic fairy tale in its accurate depiction of a vanished way of life. On Ts'ao's grandfather and the atmosphere of Ts'ao's youth, see Jonathan Spence's absorbing *Ts'ao Yin and the K'ang-hsi Emperor* (Yale U.P., 1966), and of the many studies on the novel itself, Wu Shih-ch'ang's *On 'The Red Chamber Dream'* (Oxford U.P., 1961).

However, the general reader may be content with David Hawkes' 22-page introduction to volume 1 of his masterly new translation.

FEDERICO GARCÍA LORCA (1898–1936).
   Obras completas. Aguilar, Madrid, latest edition. *Three Tragedies*, translated by J. Graham-Luján and R. L. O'Connell (Penguin, 1961).

A painter and pianist of some note, Lorca is nowadays remembered for a magnificent body of poetry and an uneven dramatic output in which three tragedies are outstanding. *Bodas de sangre* ('Blood Wedding', 1933), *Yerma* ('The Barren One', 1934) and *La casa de Bernarda Alba* ('The House of Bernarda Alba', 1936) are authentic Castilian tragedies borrowing themes and imagery from ballads and folklore, and taking their sense of doom from the Attic tragic playwrights. The first may be thought static in its lyrical flights; the second may be thought too melodramatic; but the third – for a cast of women only – achieves a remarkable synthesis of lyric power and dramatic movement.

Next year devote a month to the poetry of Lorca. Either now or at that time, examine the causes, the course and the results of the Civil War, during which Lorca was shot by Nationalist partisans. The best book is undoubtedly Hugh Thomas' *The Spanish Civil War* (2nd ed., H. Hamilton, 1977).

K'UNG FU-TZU (usually latinized as CONFUCIUS) (*c.* 551–*c.* 479 B.C.).
   Lun-yü.('Selected Sayings', often rendered 'Analects' since the time of Legge). The best translation is that by Arthur Waley (*The Analects of Confucius*, Allen & Unwin, 1938) but the older version by James Legge in *Four Books* (Chinese Book Company, Shanghai, 1933) is useful for its text, while Ezra Pound's idiosyncratic *Confucian Analects* (Kasper and Horton, New York, 1952; Peter Owen, 1956) is often memorable for brilliant analogical interpretation.

Of the so-called 'Four Books', one is the work of Mencius; the *Chung Yung* ('Doctrine of the Mean') was probably written by K'ung Chi, grandson of Confucius; and the *Ta-Hsüeh* ('Great Learning') was probably written by a disciple of Confucius called Tseng Shen.

Mencius should be studied separately, but it is appropriate to read the *Chung Yung* and the *Ta-Hsüeh* in the Legge edition with the *Lun-yü*.

Confucius himself is a shadowy figure whom the accretions of late centuries have made virtually unidentifiable. We can no longer speak with certainty, as did earlier generations, of his rising to become Minister of Public Works (in 501 B.C.) and subsequently Minister of Justice. But we do recognise a kernel of authentic teachings: that one should strive to achieve *ren* (true humanity, goodness) in a social framework of *li* (order and correct behaviour) governed by the *te* (virtue, power) of the ruler. As with the contemporary Greek thinkers, Confucius found no place for supernatural beliefs, but based his philosophy on reason and tradition. One should call each thing by its correct name, and honour one's ancestors. The *Lun-yü* were compiled from his better-known sayings by the many disciples he eventually won. A distorted form of Confucianism, stressing formalised behaviour and intricate ritual, became the accepted Chinese system of social intercourse until the Communist uprisings in the present century.

See H. G. Creel's *Confucius and the Chinese Way* (Harper & Row, 1960), formerly entitled *Confucius: the Man and the Myth*.

ALEXANDER IVANOVICH KUPRIN (1870–1938).
   Granatovy braslet. First published 1911. Translated as *The Garnet Bracelet* by
   Stepan Apresyan (Foreign Languages Publishing House, Moscow, n.d.).

In 1902 Maxim Gorki was appointed director of the Znanie ('Knowledge') Publishing House, and it was his brand of socialist realism which has been the official artistic and literary policy of the Soviet state ever since, except for a brief thaw in the time of Khrushchev.

Around him he gathered a group of talented writers who shared his vision to a greater or lesser extent, though several left Znanie to safeguard their artistic integrity against the party line. One such was the currently under-rated Ivan Alexeyevich Bunin (1870–1953), who in 1933 became the first Russian to win the Nobel Prize for Literature and fled to France and the U.S.A. after the Revolution. Another was Leonid Nikolayevich Andreyev (1871–1919), who fled to Finland after the Revolution.

Perhaps the most interesting, with hindsight, is Kuprin, who hated his period in the army from 1890 to 1894 and wrote his short novel *Poyedinok* ('The Duel', 1905; Hyperion, 1977) to expose the brutality and incompetence of the army. The collection entitled *The Garnet Bracelet* includes the famous short novel *Molokh* ('Moloch', 1896) which is a moving insight into the tortured dreams and expectations of Engineer Bobrov. Kuprin too was horrified by the Revolution, and left for France, returning to the Soviet Union in 1937.

For a view of the graphic arts up to the period of the Bolshevik Revolution, see

Camilla Gray's *The Russian Experiment in Art, 1863–1922* (Thames and Hudson, 1969).

Explore the ballet music of Igor Stravinsky (1882–1971), such as *Le Sacre du Printemps* ('The Rite of Spring', conducted by the composer on CBS 72054), *Pulcinella, Petrushka,* and *Apollon Musagète.*

MAO TSE-TUNG (1893–1976).
  Selected Works (Vols. 1–4, 1965; Vol. 5, Foreign Languages Press, Peking, 1977).

By the year 2000, the population of China will have reached one thousand million. Anyone not taking account of the nation's leader during the earliest .decades of its Communist era will risk a myopic view of world events.

It is only fair to point out that Chinese editions (and with them, the authorised translations) of Mao's statements and essays tend to vary according to the political line currently in favour. A clear interpretation of *The Political Thought of Mao Tse-tung* (2nd ed., Penguin, 1969) is by Stuart R. Schram. More controversial is the anti-Maoist line of 'Simon Leys' (Pierre Ryckmans) in such books as *The Chairman's New Clothes* (Allison & Busby, 1977), *Chinese Shadows* (Penguin, 1978) and *Broken Images* (Allison & Busby, 1979).

Corresponding to *The Gulag Archipelago* (3 vols., Collins, 1974–8) of Alexander Solzhenitsyn, in their very different ways, are Amnesty International's *Political Imprisonment in the People's Republic of China* (1978), and the personal story of Bao Ruo-Wang (Jean Pasqualini) told to Rudolph Chelminski in *Prisoner of Mao* (Penguin, 1976).

The much-publicised *Poems* of Mao are not worth attention: they are derivative and banal.

Year 25

MENG TZU ('MENCIUS') (372–289 B.C.).
  Works. Text and translation in J. R. Legge's *The Four Books* (Dover and
  Constable, 1970, but dating to the 19th century). Later versions are by
  James R. Ware, *The Sayings of Mencius* (New American Library, 1960),
  by W. A. C. H. Dobson (University of Toronto Press, 1963), and by D. C.
  Lau (Penguin, 1970), each having its own advantages.

The conversations recorded in which Meng Tzu was the principal speaker
became the thirteenth and last of the Chinese Classics, and deserve urgent
attention because the problems that they confront are with us today – indeed they
are perennial.

Mencius teaches that human nature is innately good, just as Hsün Tzu teaches
that it is innately evil. Mencius reveres the simple virtues of the ordinary man,
and in the full Confucian tradition inveighs against the profit-and-advantage
sought by kings and chieftains in power politics.

The true king is he who has cultivated virtue and justice: acting despotically,
with 'authority' as one's only weapon, will lead to the withdrawal of the mandate
of Heaven. The prosperity of the nation depends on the degree of morality shown
by its citizens, who should be set an example by their leaders.

Mencius never achieved high office, for his recommendations always seemed
too idealistic to the warring and unscrupulous petty kings of contemporary
China. He defends and enhances the historic role of Confucianism in the pursuit
of the golden mean in active politics against the quietism of the Taoists, and the
social revolution implicit in the doctrines attributed to Mo Tzu. Relatively little
needs to be done, for the structure of society itself is sound, according to
Mencius. All that is required is a change of heart on the part of the rulers, and the
citizens would instantly respond with the generosity of their own labour and
imitation of virtuous conduct.

Among the studies in English on this sympathetic Confucian are I. A.
Richards' *Mencius on the Mind: Experiments in Multiple Definition* (Routledge
and Harcourt Brace, 1932) and Arthur Waley's *Three Ways of Thought in Ancient
China* (Allen & Unwin, 1939; Doubleday, 1956).

FEDERICO GARCÍA LORCA (1898–1936).
Obras completas. Aguilar, Madrid, latest edition. Selected poems and the essay *Teoría y juego del duende* introduced and translated by J. L. Gili in *Lorca* (Penguin, 1960).

Continuing the exploration of Lorca's writing from last year, we concentrate now on his poetry. Its rhythms and passion, often deriving from the wide range of Spanish ballads, are untranslatable, and Gili uses the Spanish texts from the *Obras completas* with a plain prose translation for those who have not the time or pertinacity to master Spanish.

The celebrated *Llanto por Ignacio Sánchez Mejías* (1935), written in 1934 on the death of a friend and bullfighter, is cited entire, but each of his other collections is present only in part: *Libro de Poemas* (1921), *Poema del Cante Jondo* (1921), *Canciones* (1921–4), *Mariana Pineda* (1925), *Romancero Gitano* (1924–7), *Poeta en Nueva York* (1929–30), and *Diván del Tamarit* (1936).

Lorca's idiom is unique, for it is both personal and universal, both essentially traditional and in its eclecticism wholly modern. Without incongruity he can use negro rhythms in diction echoing that of Góngora, gipsy feeling with the authentic tone of Andalusian Islamic poetry. He is in revolt against the Spanish bourgeoisie and the Civil Guard, on the one hand, and yet finds keener revolt in his own nature as a homosexual living and working in a society where homosexuality is reviled if discovered.

For a general view of the Spanish poetic scene during Lorca's brief lifetime, see C. B. Morris' *A Generation of Spanish Poets, 1920–1936* (Cambridge U.P., 1969) and the anthology *Spanish Poetry of the Grupo Poético de 1927,* selected by Geoffrey Connell (Pergamon Press, 1977) with texts, introduction and notes but no translations.

One of Spain's leading composers during the time of Lorca was Joaquín Rodrigo, whose work is best heard in the interpretations of Siegfried Behrend (*Concierto de Aranjuez*) and Nicanor Zabaleta (*Concierto de serenata*), both on DGG Privilege 135117; and Pepe and Ángel Romero (*Concierto madrigal,* with Mauro Giuliani's Guitar Concerto) on Philips 6500 918.

The Texts of Taoism translated by James Legge. Sacred Books of the East (2 vols., Dover and Constable, 1962). The *Tao te ching* is also translated by D. C. Lau (Penguin, 1964) and by many others. The *Basic Writings* of Chuang Tzu have been translated by Burton Watson (Columbia U.P., 1964).

Legge's translation does *not* accompany Taoist texts, though some characters are annotated in some detail where they cause more than usual difficulty. The translations include the *Tao te ching* (usually attributed to Lao Tzu (*c.* 570 B.C.) and entitled 'The Way and its Power'), the writings of Chuang Tzu, and the *T'ai Shang Kan Ying P'ien* ('Tractate of Actions and their Retributions').

Taoism teaches the passive, yielding,way of water, which can nevertheless wear away a stone. Both good and evil are contained in the Way, though the Way itself cannot be described in words. Written either during the lifetime of Confucius or afterwards, Taoism is seen as a polar contradiction of the activist and pragmatic instructions of the *Lun Yü* and *Ta Hsüeh.*

Chuang Chou (usually known as Chuang Tzu) lived between about 370 and 286 B.C. and took the Taoist viewpoint to extremes: if the *Tao* is an all-embracing unity, how can one differentiate truly between good and evil, existence and non-existence, sleeping and waking? Earthly possessions and political power are meaningless shells without spiritual content. Man must strive to divest himself of duties, belongings, and influence over others. The 'Way' that things are is the *Tao,* which if left unhindered will fulfil itself in the proper manner. Revolutions and 'progress' are inimical to the *Tao.* So is industrialisation; so is warfare.

The teachings of the Taoists can form a valuable release to someone suffering from nervous or working stress, and much of the recent interest in Chinese philosophy can be traced to a realization by westerners that they have exceeded the golden mean in devotion to material goods and shoddy entertainment, against the spirit of the *Tao.*

See Arthur Waley's *Three Ways of Thought in Ancient China* (Allen & Unwin, 1939; Doubleday, 1956).

JOHN KEATS (1795-1821).
  Poetical Works. Edited by H. W. Garrod for Oxford English Texts (2nd ed., Oxford U.P., 1958).

One of the most powerful English advocates of the Greek spirit in myth and idea was a surgeon who knew no Greek at all: John Keats. His was a lovable personality not unlike that of Lamb, and tinged with a comparable sadness, for he nursed his brother until death in 1818, and he was to die tragically young of consumption, in Italy.

The sonnet on Chapman's translation of Homer, the 'Ode on a Grecian Urn', 'Endymion' and 'Hyperion' all reveal a temperament inspired by Greece, but a style which was to stand as a type of the English Romantic school. Shelley, Wordsworth and Byron all wrote too much, and too uncritically, but in Keats we find an artist unafraid to face the essential difficulties of life and express them in the simplest possible terms, devoid of Wordsworthian pomposity. In *Lamia,* we have something new and challenging in English poetry: a semi-autobiographical work which confronts the evil and destructive as a necessary part of experience.

Keats is not wholly successful, but the attempt is praiseworthy in its audacity.

Keats left the prosaic (which Wordsworth chose to set to verse in *The Prelude* and *The Excursion*) for his letters, which are best read in Hyder Rollins' edition (2 vols., Harvard U.P., 1958), though there is a good selection by Robert Gittings (Oxford U.P., 1970). Gittings is also the definitive biographer: *John Keats* (Penguin, 1979) and one can wholeheartedly recommend a visit to the Keats House, Wentworth Place, Keats Grove, London NW3 2RR, now a museum devoted to the poet's memory.

Chin P'ing Mei, an anonymous 16th-century Chinese novel. First published 1610 or 1611. Translated by Clement Egerton (4 vols., Routledge, 1939; Paragon Book Gallery, 14 East 38th St., New York, N.Y. 10016, 1962). Bernard Miall's abridgment (Lane, 1939; Putnam, 1962) is based on Franz Kuhn's German version, *Kin Ping Meh* (Insel Verlag, Wiesbaden, 1955).

We have only contradictory references to the authorship of the *Chin P'ing Mei,* named after three principal characters: P'an Chin-lien (the 'Golden Lotus' of Egerton's translation), Li P'ing-erh (the 'Lady of the Vase'), and Ch'un-mei. The edition known in the West through the translations by Egerton and Kuhn are unfortunately based on a piecemeal abridgment by a late-Ming editor, whereas the better, more original edition known as the *Chin P'ing Mei tz'u-hua,* is not available in English. Of the hundred chapters, those numbered 53–57 had been lost before printing began, and were supplied by an inferior Suchow hack.

The crucial importance of the novel is its realism in the handling of a merchant's household during its master's rise from obscurity to power and riches, and the detailed descriptions of the six women most clearly associated with Hsi-men Ch'ing, its hero. The eroticism is never obtrusive, but serves to point the true character of each woman in turn. Earlier Chinese novels had tended to idealize a number of stock types: here, the protagonist is a blackguard and a libertine without conscience, and women seek his favour by a variety of methods, some more devious than others. The novelist, never afraid to copy other writings verbatim if they suit his purpose, manages to match the outer turbulence of the times (allegedly in the Sung dynasty but in fact an attack on Ming corruption) with the inner turbulence of the Hsi-men household. The novel has been seen by some scholars as a Buddhist allegory on the vanity of human ambition.

A sequel to the *Chin P'ing Mei,* entitled *Ko Lien Hua Ying* ('Flower Shadows Behind the Curtain'), has been abridged and translated by Vladimir Kean from Franz Kuhn's German version (New English Library, 1963).

JEAN BAPTISTE POQUELIN ('MOLIÈRE') (1622–1673).
  Selected Plays.

Continue the reading of Molière's plays (from Year 5), attending performances if possible, in both French and – if necessary – in translation. Consult the latest edition of W. Grayburn Moore's *Molière: a New Criticism* (Oxford U.P.).

At the same time examine the painters working in France during Molière's lifetime, among them Poussin, Claude, the Le Nain brothers, Georges de la Tour, Millet and Champaigne.

On Poussin there is the splendid 3-volume edition by Anthony Blunt (Phaidon, 1966–8), and on Georges de la Tour the authoritative monograph by Benedict Nicolson and Christopher Wright (Phaidon, 1974).

TU FU (*also* TU KUNG-PU) (712–770 A.D.).
  Poems. There is no adequate translation of the 1,500 or so poems written by Tu Fu. Some appear in William Hung's *Tu Fu* (2 vols., Harvard U.P. and (Oxford U.P.,1952), and rather fewer in David Hawkes' model introduction *A Little Primer of Tu Fu* (Oxford U.P., 1967) and in Arthur Cooper's *Li Po and Tu Fu* (Penguin, 1973).

Tu Fu's status as one of the two or three greatest of all Chinese poets would have struck the man dumb; he believed throughout his life that, a perennial failure in the imperial civil service examinations, he amounted to nothing. His highest administrative post was as Secretary in the Ministry of Public Works, but for most of his life he was a wanderer, a social critic of some pungency (attacking court extravagance, military conscription, and heavy taxation) and a personal poet bewailing poverty and homesickness with poignant artistry.

He believed in the Confucian virtues of practical wisdom, thrift and honesty, forming a fascinating contrast with the Taoist romanticism of his friend Li Po, whose work was more highly praised in their time.

Most of his poems are in the *lü-shih* (regulated verse) style, technically observant of prescribed rhyme patterns, tones, and antithesis. Generally he tends toward the Han ideals of simple classicism, as against the elaborate, often over-refined diction typical of the Southern and Northern Dynasties. He borrows nuances from the ballads, occasionally, and from the *Shih Ching,* but connoisseurs declare that a Tu Fu poem is almost invariably marked somewhere with the master's signature, whether in the atmosphere of calm resignation, or in the bitter indictment of forced absence from home to perform frontier duty.

WU CH'ING-TZU (1701–1754).
Ju-lin wai-shih ('The Unofficial History of Confucian Scholars'). First
published 1768–77. Translated by Yang Hsien-yi and Gladys Yang as *The
Scholars* (Foreign Languages Press, Peking, 1957).

The Scholars is a masterpiece of fiction important on several counts apart from its
high literary merits. First, it is the greatest purely satirical novel from China
second, it reveals the weaknesses of Ch'ing society as no factual account of the
period possibly could (though allegedly set in Ming times); third, it acts as a
masculine equivalent to the feminine *Dream of the Red Chamber,* as it takes place
in a milieu almost exclusively populated by men – the milieu of scholars who
have qualified for office by means of the official examinations.

Wu Ch'ing-tzu himself passed the first stage of the examinations, but failed the
second. Like most Confucians he lamented the (possibly apocryphal) glories of
past kingdoms, contrasting them with the pettiness and corruption of his own
day. However, the novelist's bitterness is transmuted into high good humour and
written out into the admirable character of Tu Shao-ch'ing, whose quasi-comic
trust in those around him is absurdly misplaced. The only true 'hero', one Wang
Mien, conscientiously refuses office and takes to the mountains as a hermit.

Wu visibly mellows as his long novel proceeds: he seems to learn that even
rebels can be cooled down with flattery, and the pure in heart pacified with a
purse. If even the most corrupt inveigh against the system and urge an end to
nepotism, of what use is the advocate of virtue? Of all eighteenth-century novels,
this is possibly the most enduring for its reluctant admiration of the way that
people, gravely or merrily, always seem to muddle through.

ARTHUR SCHOPENHAUER (1778–1860).
Parerga und Paralipomena. First published 1851. Translated in part (from
volume 2), as *Essays and Aphorisms,* by R. J. Hollingdale (Penguin,
1970).

At 21, Schopenhauer received his share of his father's assets and was enabled to
live, write, and enjoy himself as he wished. By the age of 28, having absorbed the
teachings of Plato, Kant and the Upanishads, he had conceived every last detail of
his philosophy which he was to elaborate in six books. The first was *Die Welt als
Wille und Vorstellung* (3 vols., 1819; translated by R. B. Haldane and B. Kemp as
'The World as Will and Idea', 1883) written in Dresden from 1814 and 1818.
Schopenhauer was in no doubt of the book's fundamental wisdom: 'It is inspired
by the spirit of truth', he wrote. 'In the fourth book there are even some
paragraphs which may be considered to have been dictated by the Holy Ghost'.
Public neglect only exacerbated his need for fame and for the disciples he would

obtain. His other books were expansions or footnotes to his major work, and the *Parerga und Paralipomena* can be considered sidelights, for nothing new was to emerge during the last manically-organised 27 years of his life, entirely bound by routine, apart from adventures needed to satisfy his sexual energies.

How then has Schopenhauer come to have such a decisive influence on several subsequent philosophers? First, his pessimism found a ready response among intellectuals oppressed by rising German nationalism and by the blinkers imposed by an orthodox Christian view of the world. Second, his ideas may be expressed in great detail, but they are much easier to follow than those of Kant (the last author in *A Lifetime's Reading* because of his inherent difficulty), and Schopenhauer rejects Hegelian historicism in favour of the value of immediate experience. Third, Schopenhauer is a great prose stylist. Fourth, he challenges the facile 19th-century belief in automatic progress through commercial and industrial growth. Fifth, he taught that intellect is rarely the tool of the will (or, crucially, 'the unconscious' in Eduard von Hartmann's translation) and that we must not seek explanations of political, economic and social events in terms of purely rational behaviour (as some would like) but in terms of individual or collective will, a concept that has gained very wide acceptance in our own times, in viewing such local aberrations as the so-called 'People's Temple' in Guyana or broader phenomena such as the Great-Power arms race.

A typical aphorism is: 'The art of *not* reading is a very important one. It consists in not taking an interest in whatever may be engaging the attention of the general public at any particular time. When some political or ecclesiastical pamphlet, or novel, or poem is making a great commotion, you should remember that he who writes for fools always finds a large public. A precondition for reading good books is not reading bad ones: for life is short'.

This is a good month for concentrating on the music of Schopenhauer's contemporary, Beethoven. If a single set of the string quartets has to be recommended, it would be that of the Italian Quartet (10 discs, Philips 6747 272). There are numerous good performances of the piano and violin concerti. The *Fidelio* to choose would be Klemperer's (3 discs, HMV SLS 5006); the *Missa Solemnis* that of Jochum (2 discs, Philips 6799 001).

CHOU SHU-JEN ('LU HSÜN') (1881–1936).
> *Selected Works* (4 vols., Foreign Languages Press, Peking). Abridged as *Silent China: Selected Writings,* edited and translated by Gladys Yang (Oxford U.P., 1973).

The most important writer of short stories in twentieth-century China, recently elevated amusingly enough to the rank of official apologist of the Chinese Communist Party, was Chou Shu-jen, who assumed the pen-name Lu Hsün.

Abandoning the study of medicine, for which he had gone to Japan in 1902, he returned to China to teach at universities and to write modern vernacular stories as a pointer to the way ahead. His method was to satirise aspects of Chinese life in the traditional way, by attacking current problems under the guise of stories dealing with the past. He spent much time on the translation of Western literature, in particular that of Russia (including Gogol's *Dead Souls*) and endeavoured to found a new Chinese literary school based on Western realism. His most famous story is 'Ah Q cheng-chuan' (The Strange Story of Ah Q), in which a typical villager, mean and self-serving in outlook, is taken to personify the diseases of the spirit which prevented true national progress in China. According to recent Communist orthodoxy, however, Lu Hsün's purpose was not to diagnose and treat endemic Chinese diseases, but merely to undermine the pre-Communist social order, a reading which only prejudiced hindsight can support. In fact it should be recalled that he never joined the Communist Party.

The prose poems of *Yeh-ts'ao* ('Wild Grass', 1927) are mysterious visions combining personal emotions with powerful allusions to external reality: they can be related perhaps to the prose poems of Baudelaire and Blok, but also to the classical Chinese literary tradition. The same weight from the past attaches to Lu Hsün's many essays, conservative in form if innovative in subject matter.

See *Contemporary Chinese Stories* (Columbia U.P., 1944), translated by Chi-chen Wang, and Lu Hsün's own *Chung-kuo hsiao-shuo shih-lüeh* ('Brief History of Chinese Fiction', 1920; translated by Yang Hsien-yi and Gladys Yang, Foreign Languages Press, Peking, 1959).

Year 26

Sources of Indian Tradition, compiled by William Theodore de Bary, Stephen N. Hay, Royal Weiler, and Andrew Yarrow (2 vols., Columbia U.P., 1964).

A compendium of indispensable value, this work is divided into six parts: Brahmanism, Jainism and Buddhism; Hinduism; Islam in Medieval India; Sikhism; and Modern India and Pakistan.

Since five sections are devoted to religious ideologies, this is a good moment to read a balanced introduction to comparative religion, such as A. C. Bouquet's *Comparative Religion* (Penguin, latest edition) or E. O. James' book of the same title (Methuen, 1938).

The sixth section, on modern India and Pakistan (we should not of course forget Bangladesh), considers the opening of India to the West, with extracts from Ananda Ranga Pillai, Abu Taleb, Henry Derozio, Rammohun Roy, Sir William Jones, and Macaulay; the renascence of Hinduism, including selections from Debendranath Tagore, Keshub Chunder Sen, Dayananda Saraswati, Shri Ramakrishna, and Swami Vivekananda; the proponents of nationalism, among them Dadabhai Naoroji, 'Surrender-Not' Banerjea, M. G. Ranade, G. K. Gokhale, B. C. Chatterjee, Bal Gangadhar Tilak, Aurobindo Ghose, and Brahmabandhab Upadhyay; the Muslim Revival under Syed Ahmad Khan and Iqbal; Tagore and Gandhi; Muhammad Ali Jinnah and the founding of Pakistan; and six alternative paths to India's future: the Hindu nationalism of V. D. Savarkar, the national socialism of S. C. Bose, the democratic socialism of Nehru, the radical humanism of M. N. Roy, the national communism of J. C. Kumarappa and Romesh Thapar; and the neo-Gandhian decentralism of Vinoba Bhave.

Cantar de Mio Cid. Composed about 1140 A.D. Text edited by Colin Smith (Oxford U.P., 1972). Translation in verse by W. S. Merwin (Dent, 1959, as *The Poem of the Cid*), and in prose by Rita Hamilton and Janet Perry (Barnes & Noble and Manchester U.P., 1975) facing the Spanish text edited by Ian Michael.

The greatest surviving Spanish epic, equivalent to the Old French *Chanson de Roland*. It is divided into three *cantares:* Exile, The Weddings, and the Insult at Corpes Oakwood. The *Sayyid* ('Lord' in Arabic, corrupted in medieval Spanish to 'Cid') Rodrigo Díaz de Vivar sets out to collect the tribute due to his King, Alfonso VI of Castile, from the subject Muslim King Mu'tamid of Seville. This done, he allies his force with that of Mu'tamid to defeat the Moors of Granada and their ally Count García Ordóñez. Ordóñez spreads the rumour that Rodrigo has embezzled some of the tribute and Alfonso, believing the charge, exiles the Cid.

In Cantar II, the Cid triumphantly seizes Valencia and sends presents to the King of Castile. Finally the Cid is pardoned and grants his daughters Sol and Elvira in marriage to the Infantes of Carrión.

In Cantar III, the Infantes are revealed as cowards, marrying into the Cid's family only for the wealth and power he can bring them. On their way home, the Infantes strike their new brides senseless in the oakwood of Corpes. A nephew of the Cid finds them, and takes the dishonoured brides back to their father, who sues the King for justice.

The great poem's characterisation is remarkably pungent, and the epic drive of the metre is well demonstrated by records and by one's own reading aloud. In the words of C. C. Smith, 'no verse literature could have had a worthier beginning than this'.

Background reading on the Muslims in Spain includes Watt & Cachia's *Islamic Spain* (Edinburgh U.P., 1965), the romanticized *Spanish Islam* by R. Dozy (reprinted by Frank Cass, 1972), and the significant contribution by C. Sánchez-Albornoz, *La España Musulmana* (2 vols., Buenos Aires, 1946).

Bhagavad Gita. First compiled *c.* 200 B.C. Translated by Franklin Edgerton (Harvard Oriental Series, vol. 38, Harvard U.P., and Oxford U.P., 1944; Harper, 1964). With a volume of essays on the *Bhagavad Gita* by Edgerton (Harvard Oriental Series, vol. 39, Harvard U.P. and Oxford U.P., 1944).

Orthodox Hindus do not revere the Sanskrit 'Song of God' as *Sruti* (scriptures revealed directly by God, such as the *Upanishads*) but as *Smriti* (teachings of the prophets or saints); that is, they regard it technically as of secondary revelation. It has nevertheless come to be regarded as the core of Hindu teaching over the past two thousand years by countless millions of Hindus. It is particularly dear to the Krishnaites, with whom the Brahmanic religion – dedicated to the Vedic gods and above all to Indra – originally clashed.

The *Gita* was early incorporated into the great epic *Mahabharata,* but was not an integral part of it, being an interpolated dialogue between the hero Arjuna and his charioteer Krishna, the latter appearing both as an incarnation of the god

Vishnu, and as a human warrior. Arjuna asks about the legality or morality of war, to which Krishna replies with a synthetic but occasionally inconsistent presentation of the main strands of Hindu belief. Krishna tries to solve the contradictions of Arjuna's temporal role as a warrior with the Buddhist conjuration of *ahimsa* (non-violence) and *moksha* (release from attachments). Interpreted allegorically, the struggle is between *jñana* (meditation) and *karma* (action), ending in *bhakti* (devotion).

Most Hindu philosophers and mystics have written interpretations of the *Gita,* one of the best being the *Jñaneshvari* (completed in 1290 A.D.) by Jñaneshvar, the first great Marathi poet, translated by V. G. Pradhan (2 vols., Allen & Unwin, 1967-9). See T. S. Eliot's redaction in 'The Dry Salvages', third of his *Four Quartets* (Faber & Faber, 1944).

Saint AUGUSTINE (354–430).
   Confessiones. Written 397–401. Translated as *Confessions* by R. S. Pine-Coffin (Penguin, 1961).

Aurelius Augustinus was born of a pagan father and a Christian mother in Thagaste, the present-day Suq al-Ahras, in Algeria.

Sympathetic to the Manichees, Augustine was only gradually drawn to Christianity by the influences of his mother, of St Ambrose in Milan, and of tales of conversion such as those of Victorinus (translator of Plotinus) and Ponticianus, a fellow-African in the Emperor's household. In 387 he was baptised and returned to Africa (lamenting the death of his mother on the way, at Ostia) and became a priest, then in 395 Bishop of Hippo. His controversies with the Manichees resulted in his writing a number of books, attempting to refute Manichean dualism and the notion that the Old and New Testaments are contradictory. He also spent much time in argument against the Donatists, who claimed that the efficacy of sacraments depended on the worthiness of their ministers, and against Pelagius, who asserted that human perfection may be attained without divine grace. *The City of God,* issued in instalments between 413 and 426, is an enthralling work of Christian propaganda against the accusation of responsibility for the demise of the Roman Empire, and the fall of Rome itself, which Alaric had taken in 410.

Augustine's style is matched by the depth of his learning and the breadth of his interests. We see with hindsight that his teachings and their influence on later generations were a formidable weapon in the hands of Roman Catholic orthodoxy: without them, the prevailing dogma might well have been Donatism or Pelagianism. The autobiography shows him to have been a boy and youth not by any means given to holiness or chastity: the *Confessions* are in some ways more revealing than those of Rousseau. But it is well to read them with a sophisticated, unobtrusive commentator such as Peter Brown (*Augustine of Hippo*, Faber & Faber, 1969), whose only real (but inexplicable) fault is that he neglects to explain the crucial matter of what Jesus meant to the Bishop of Hippo.

Poems from the Sanskrit. Translated with an introduction by John Brough (Penguin, 1968).

Disappointingly slim without Sanskrit texts, this anthology goes only part of the way towards meeting the need for a substantial collection of Sanskrit poetry with plain prose translations, but it does quote references to the Sanskrit originals (usually in fairly inaccessible editions).

What we are left with is an introduction (pages 11–49), an extract in prose and verse from Kalidasa's *Vikramorvashiya* (pp. 95–105), an extract from Kalidasa's *Kumara-Sambhava* (pp. 107–110), and the anthology proper (pp. 53–157 and 111–139).

If this whets your appetite, there is an excellent *History of Sanskrit Literature* (Oxford U.P., 1920) by Sir A. B. Keith from which further explorations can be made. Sanskrit is a member of the same Indo-European family of languages as English, Welsh, French and Greek, for example, so the effort to learn the language will be facilitated by the recognition of such old friends as *bhratr* (brother) or *naman* (name). Michael Coulson's *Sanskrit* in Teach Yourself Books (Hodder & Stoughton, 1976) is aimed at enabling the private student 'to cope as rapidly as possible with straightforward Classical Sanskrit texts'.

DHANPAT RAY SHRIVASTAV ('PREMCHAND') (1880–1936).
   Godan. First published 1936. Translated as *The Gift of a Cow* by G. Roadarmel (Allen & Unwin, 1958). And *The World of Premchand: a selection of short stories* translated by David Rubin (Allen & Unwin, 1969).

Perhaps the greatest novelist and short-story writer in Hindi, Shrivastav learned his craft while still a schoolmaster and sub-inspector in the Indian civil service, but left in 1921 during the movement initiated and led by Gandhi against co-operation with the British colonial government. He then adopted the pen-name Premchand and began to write principally in Hindi, though he had written his earlier work in Urdu, a language he never abandoned.

Premchand's mission is to raise the material and intellectual level of the Indian peasants, but he simultaneously advocates the values of rural life as against what he interprets to be the decadence of urban life. At the same time he is not afraid to show the cunning peasant, the caste-obsessed and the foolish or the oppression of landlords in a teeming panorama of North India. He feels impelled to call for radical change if British colonialism is to be overthrown, but recognises that the poorest peasants will be the first to suffer in the turmoil of independence revolts.

In three hundred stories and a dozen novels Premchand has created a great fictional portrait of northern India in the first third of the twentieth century. See Madan Gopal's *Munshi Premchand: a literary biography* (Asia Publishing House, 1965).

The plight of India's poor in particular, and those of Asia and the Third World in general, are studied in Gunnar Myrdal's challenging *Asian Drama* (3 vols., Penguin, 1968), brought up-to-date in 1980 by *North-South* (Pan, 1980), also known as the Brandt Report. Compare the urgent economics of overpopulation and famine with the classical economic theories of Adam Smith (*The Wealth of Nations*, 1766) and David Ricardo (*The Principles of Political Economy and Taxation*, 1817), both available in modern annotated editions.

FRANCESCO PETRARCA (1304–1374).
Rime, Trionfi e Poesie Latine, edited by F. Neri and others (1951). *Prose*, edited by G. Martellotti and others (1955). The *Triumphs* written 1352–74 have been translated by E. H. Wilkins (University of Chicago Press, 1962), and *Letters from Petrarch* by Morris Bishop (Indiana U.P., 1966).

Petrarch's Italian poetry is concerned almost exclusively with love for a real or imaginary Laura (who has been identified with a certain Laure, wife of Hugues de Sade). His lifelong dedication to the fashioning of a new Italian poetry was made possible by the financial generosity of the Colonna family. He lived for periods from 1337 at a small house in Vaucluse, near Avignon, but also travelled widely.

About 1338 he began the Latin epic on the exploits of Scipio which he called *Africa* and considered his finest achievement. In 1342, a year after coronation with the laurel wreath at Rome, he began the *Secretum*, a Latin self-examination on his moral and spiritual weaknesses inspired by the *Confessions* of St Augustine, and in 1343 Francesca, his second illegitimate child, was born.

In 1348 he heard news of the death of his Laura and of his patron, Cardinal Colonna. He spent the years 1353–61 as a guest of the Visconti family in Milan, and was subsequently a guest of the Senate in Venice, and of Francesco da Carrara in Padua.

We read Petrarch today for the extraordinary tensions of the *Canzoniere*, 366 poems in mediaeval Italian within the Provençal convention of courtly love lyrics. He fashions a great language from the Tuscan of his day, speaking of his love (which may have been for a married woman) in terms that are often reminiscent of the Christian mystic or the pantheistic pagan. Italians themselves, and indeed other Europeans, long judged Petrarch superior to Dante himself.

See E. H. Wilkins' *Life of Petrarch* (University of Chicago Press, 1961) and Morris Bishop's *Petrarch and his World* (Indiana U.P., 1963).

Listen to *Music from 14th-Century Florence* played by the Early Music Consort of London on Argo ZRG 3257), and enjoy the architecture and technical genius of Filippo Brunelleschi (1377–1446) in Frank D. Prager and Giustina Scaglia's *Brunelleschi: Studies of his Technology and Inventions* (MIT Press, 1970).

Saddharma-Pundarika Sutra ('The Sutra of the Lotus of the True Law').
First compiled in India before 255 A.D. and translated into Chinese by Kumarajiva as *Miao-fa lien-hua ching* (344–413). Translated from Sanskrit into English by H. Kern (Dover and Constable, 1963). Also abridged and translated from Chinese into English by W. E. Soothill as *The Lotus of the Wonderful Law* (Oxford U.P., 1930).

When Ch'ang Chung died in 497 A.D., he held in his left hand a copy of the *Classic of Filial Piety* and the *Tao te ching,* and in his right hand the *Lotus of the True Law,* thus symbolising his desire for the essential harmony of Confucianism, Taoism, and Buddhism.

You will moreover now be familiar with the Chinese tales of how the young priest Tripitaka travelled to India with his friends and disciples Monkey, Pigsy and Sandy to bring back the teachings of the Buddha.

Saddharma-Pundarika Sutra is the heart of Mahayana Buddhism, and is used by all the sects and schools, being the principal sutra of the Nichiren school in Japan, and a significant scripture for the T'ien-t'ai school in China (Tendai in Japan).

Buddha is here no longer the ascetic of history who preached for forty years. He is an eternal being, omniscient and omnipresent, and the setting in which he gives his discourse is uniquely awe-inspiring. Before him are 12,000 arhats, 6,000 nuns headed by his mother, 8,000 Bodhisattvas, 60,000 gods, Brahma and 12,000 dragon kings, and hundreds of thousands of other beings, including angels and demons.

Criticism of such a work will obviously be different from one's appreciation of a work of fiction. It demands a receptive heart and a serene mind, earning both by the sublimity of its vision, and the generosity of its message: salvation, through Bodhisattvas, for all mankind.

See J. Leroy Davidson's *The Lotus Sutra in Chinese Art* (Yale U.P., 1954).

WILLIAM FAULKNER (1897–1962).
The Sound and the Fury. First published 1929 (Penguin, 1964).

The fact that Faulkner chose to set all his best work in the imaginary county of Yoknapatawpha, Mississippi, should not lead one to believe that he is any more a regional writer than is the creator of Macondo, the Colombian Gabriel García Márquez. What these novelists have in common is the unerring ability to create scenes which could well be realistic, on one plane, but on another heighten and condense experience in terms of an oblique language based on a theory of the simultaneity or circularity of time, according to the context.

Sartoris (1929), based on the figure of Faulkner's great-grandfather, begins the Yoknapatawpha sequence, which was to include *As I Lay Dying* (1930, written between midnight and 4 a.m. during six weeks while working as a coal-heaver), *Sanctuary* (1931), *Light in August* (1932, perhaps his most telling novel on Southern racial tensions), *Absalom! Absalom!* (1936), *Go Down, Moses* (1942), *Intruder in the Dust* (1948), the trilogy *The Hamlet, The Town,* and *The Mansion* (1940–59), and *The Reivers* (1962). Many would claim that Faulkner's art benefited from the discipline of the short story, a view for which the *Collected Stories* (1950) provides good evidence. Those without the time or inclination to investigate Faulkner's work in full would enjoy *The Portable Faulkner* (Viking Press, 1967) edited by Malcolm Cowley, arranging Yoknapatawpha extracts in chronological order, with a map and family history of the Compsons.

The Sound and the Fury is a major work of 20th-century literature for its skilful adaptation of Joyce's 'stream-of-consciousness' technique, and the technical virtuosity of the narrative, written by an 'idiot'. It demands and repays re-reading as a demonstration of a great novelist's originality allied to a profound sense of pity.

MOHANDAS KARAMCHAND GANDHI (1869–1948).
Satyana Prayogo. First published 1927–9. Translated from the Gujarati as *An Autobiography: The Story of my Experiments with Truth* by Mahadev Desai (Cape, 1966).

Gandhi's simply-told, honest and often moving autobiography begins in Porbandar and Rajkot in the early 1870s and concludes in 1920, when the Mahatma's struggle against Britain had barely begun. It is nevertheless a brilliant work of compelling originality, and a masterpiece of Gujarati prose style sensitively translated.

There is a very great deal in much of Gandhi's approach to the special problems of India, such as his insistence on rural self-sufficiency as an alternative to industrialism. His ambivalent attitude to the West is constructive, rather than inconsistent, for India does not benefit from wholesale acceptance or rejection of Western ideas and influences, but from selective adaptation on a Gandhian scale.

For the period after 1920, a key work is Jawaharlal Nehru's *Towards Freedom* (Beacon Press, Boston, 1958), earlier entitled *An Autobiography* (John Lane, 1936). Among the hundreds of secondary sources are Louis Fischer's *Life of Mahatma Gandhi* (Collier, 1962 and New American Library, 1965) and B. R. Nanda's *Mahatma Gandhi* (Beacon Press and Allen & Unwin, 1958).

Year 27

THUCYDIDES (*c.* 471–*c.* 400 B.C.).
Historiai. Text first printed by Aldus Manutius in Venice, 1502. Text with a translation by C. F. Smith in Loeb Classical Library (4 vols., Heinemann and Harvard U.P., 1919–23). Translated by Rex Warner as *History of the Peloponnesian War* (Penguin, 1954).

Thucydides was a scholarly specialist whose only subject was the war between Athens and Sparta waged from 431 to 404 B.C. (In fact he stopped short at winter 411). He wrote for those 'who desire an accurate knowledge of the past as a key to knowledge of the future, which in all probability will resemble the past' and made few concessions to personal prejudice, baseless conjecture, or questionable sources.

He is the first indubitably great historian, and his methods have been improved only in detail. Thucydides is methodical, comprehensive, unbiased, and serious in his attitude to the importance of the events he describes. He participated in the war, and was disgraced in 424, spending twenty years in exile, but does not allow such events to deter his narrative from scrupulous honesty.

Thucydides is not, however, a mere annalist: he felt personally involved in the war and its outcome, and records with anguish the gradual deterioration of morals and values as the Greek world is weakened by internecine slaughter. He shows horror as plague strikes Athens, as Corcyra crumbles in revolution, for the loss of dignity and decency. Methodical Thucydides may be: cold and merciless he most certainly is not. He is a model historian, and a thoroughly likeable man. See A. W. Gomme's *Historical Commentary on Thucydides* (4 vols., Oxford U.P., 1944–70), and Sir Dennis Proctor's *The Experience of Thucydides* (Aris & Phillips, 1980).

By the time of Thucydides, Greek vase-painting had become one of the world's most glorious artistic achievements. See John Boardman's *Athenian Black Figure Vases* (Thames & Hudson, 1974) and *Athenian Red Figure Vases: the Archaic Period* (Thames & Hudson, 1975).

KHUSHHAL, KHAN KHATAK (1613–1689).
Divan. Edited by H. W. Bellew (Peshawar, 1869). *Poems from the Divan* have been translated from the Pashto by D. N. Mackenzie (Allen & Unwin, 1965), a work complemented by *The Poems* with translations by Evelyn Howell and Olaf Caroe (Peshawar U.P., 1963).

Khushhal, chieftain of the Pashto-speaking Khatak tribe of Pathans, is considered the Afghan national poet for his position in society coupled with his literary skill. His work in unequal, as is usually the case with men of action, but part of its strength lies in the multiple vision of the author. He was long a warrior chieftain, though he spent time in captivity (where he wrote much of his finest verse), and could be a wine-drinker in one poem and a devout Muslim in the next. He preached forgiveness at one time, and merciless revenge at another. A pantheistic mystic, he was also an unrepentant sensualist.

The Howell-Caroe versions of 26 poems are often poor, missing the tone completely, but they print the original Pashto texts, and offer a valuable introduction. Mackenzie's introduction is too brief, there are no bilingual versions, but the 216 translations provide a much clearer picture of Khushhal's impressively wide range of themes and prosodic variety.

EDWARD MORGAN FORSTER (1879–1970).
A Passage to India. First published 1924. (Penguin, 1979).

Maturity comes as a result of resolving apparent conflicts and contradictions: between male and female, between conservative and radical, between religious groupings, and between nationalities. Forster's wise and thought-provoking novel brings one to an awareness of such conflicts through the personality of the Indian Dr Aziz and the characters he encounters, including the elderly Mrs Moore, the earnest young Adela Quested, his friend Fielding, and the detached Brahmin Godbole.

Forster's prescient analysis of Anglo-Indian differences and their ultimate resolution has contributed another source of interest to a novel – the last major novel that Forster was to write – which was successfully adapted for the stage by Santha Rama Rau.

See Robin J. Lewis' *E. M. Forster's Passages to India* (Columbia U.P., 1979), a study utilising the Forster Papers in King's College, Cambridge.

The Hill of Devi (1953) is a revealing account of Forster's experiences as a private secretary to a maharajah in India, showing the background against which the novel was written. Forster wrote splendid short stories (*Collected Short Stories*, Penguin, 1969) and essays (including *Two Cheers for Democracy*, Penguin, 1970) distinguished for the moderation and clarity of the views expressed.

Forster's other great novel is *Howard's End* (1910; Penguin, 1969), somewhat less successful for being drawn on a much smaller canvas.

Dhammapada. (*c.* 300 B.C.). With introductory essays, Pali text, English translation and notes by S. Radhakrishnan (Oxford U.P., 1950).

The Pali *Dhammapada* which is the best-known of the three recensions extant has no claim to be an original version, and is of no great poetic merit, but its position as a leading text of Hinayana Buddhism is unquestioned.

The basic premiss of the book, in 423 short verses, is that virtuous behaviour and concentrated meditation are more important in the life of man than speculations about the unknowable. *Dhamma* (the Sanskrit *dharma*) can be taken to mean 'law', 'religion', or 'discipline', according to context, while 'pada' means either 'way', 'path' or 'basis'. The title may then be translated 'The Path of Correct Discipline', or 'The Basis of Religion'. The Chinese, who have had a translation since 224 A.D., call the book 'scriptural texts', for it includes passages from a number of canonical books, though it nowhere claims to be the actual words of the Buddha.

The Radhakrishnan edition is recommended not so much for the translation (which depends for some readings on the Max Müller edition of 1881 in the Sacred Books of the East series) as for the Pali text, which enables the sensitive reader to reproduce the sounds of the Buddhists reciting it.

An indispensable companion is Eugene W. Burlingame's edition of the *Buddhist Legends* ascribed to Buddhaghosa (3 vols., Harvard U.P., 1921; Oxford U.P., 1922). This traditional compilation illustrates the occasions and applications for Buddha's preaching each verse of the *Dhammapada*.

Modern Spanish Theatre: an anthology of plays edited and translated by Michael Benedikt and George E. Wellwarth (Dutton, 1969).

The most stultifying effects of an illiberal regime are felt not so much in a poet's privacy or in the novelist's study, but on the theatrical stage, where the playwright – forced by the nature of his craft to accept the verdicts of censors, producers, and audience – cannot see the effects of his tragedies, allegories or parables. They are simply never staged, unless by unofficial audacity or official mistake.

The Franco regime in Spain forced many of the best writers into exile or silence, where murder (in the case of García Lorca) or suicide was not involved. In Arrabal's case, the writer preferred to change his very language – to French.

The anthology above is recommended because its translations range in date from 1913 (the pre-Franquista *Divinas palabras* of Ramón María del Valle-Inclán) to 1963 (an extract from Lauro Olmo's *El cuarto poder* and José María Bellido's *Fútbol*). The other plays included are García Lorca's comedy *La zapatera prodigiosa,* Miguel Mihura's *Tres sombreros de copa,* Rafael Alberti's *Noche y guerra en el Museo del Prado,* Alejandro Casona's *Prohibido suicidarse en primavera,* and Fernando Arrabal's one-act *First Communion.*

Alternative anthologies, in no case duplicating the plays above, are R. W. Corrigan's *Masterpieces of the Modern Spanish Theatre* (Collier, 1967), and G. E. Wellwarth's *The New Wave in Spanish Drama* (New York U.P., 1970). The former includes work by Benavente, Buero Vallejo, Sastre, Martínez Sierra and García Lorca, the latter one play by Sastre and two each by Ruibal, Bellido, and Martínez Ballesteros. See George Wellwarth's *Spanish Underground Drama* (Pennsylvania State U.P., 1972).

ABE KIMIFUSA (ABE KOBO) (b. 1925).

> *Suna no onna.* First published 1962. Translated by E. Dale Saunders as *The Woman in the Dunes* (Knopf, 1964).

Abe trained as a doctor but has never practised, turning to literature instead. An influential avant-garde novelist, he has broken with Japanese tradition as a result of his wide literary interests, ranging from Kafka to communism, and from Rilke to existentialism.

In *Suna no onna,* the hero is an entomologist trapped by villagers at the foot of a dune with a woman. Their joint task is to prevent the dunes from encroaching on the village by shovelling sand continually away. The progress and resolution of the plot allows Abe to present several aspects of liberty and captivity, dependence and self-sufficiency, and the relationships of society to the individual. *Suna no onna* was adapted as a successful film by Horoshi Teshigahara.

A philosophical novelist, Abe is a creator of complex characters, uninterested in movement and action. The novel *Tanin no kao* (1964; translated by E. Dale Saunders as *The Face of Another,* Knopf, 1966) exemplified Abe's approach to the many facets of identity and personality. A scientist's face is disfigured in an explosion so badly that he feels obliged to fit a mask. The mask then begins to assert its own independence.

Though nobody should make the mistake of thinking Puccini's Japan is anything but a fantastic piece of *japonaiserie,* his *Madama Butterfly* (conducted by Karajan, with Freni and Pavarotti on Decca SET 584–6) has a ravishing score surpassed in his own output only by those of *Turandot* (conducted by Mehta, with Sutherland and Pavarotti on Decca SET 561-3), *La Bohème* (conducted by Beecham, with de los Angeles and Björling on 2 discs, HMV SLS 896), and *Tosca* (conducted by Karajan, with Price and di Stefano on 2 Decca discs 5BB 123–4).

FAIZ AHMAD FAIZ (b. 1911).
Poems. Translated by V. G. Kiernan (Allen & Unwin, 1971).

Faiz is one of the world's great poets, and has here been served magnificently by his translator.

The left-hand pages print fifty-four selected poems of Faiz in Urdu script. The right-hand pages offer a sensitive English poetic translation, followed by a literal English translation, followed by a transliteration of the Urdu script in our alphabet. The book thus becomes an excellent instrument for learning Urdu through literature. For those who need background details on the poetry, there is ample introductory material, and also notes on the poems. Any English-language publisher seriously interested in presenting Oriental poetry should have this model at their elbow.

Faiz was educated at the Scottish Mission High School in his native Sialkot (also the birthplace of Iqbal), and studied English and Arabic literature, teaching English literature at Amritsar and Lahore. In 1941 he joined the British Indian Army and rose to high rank in three years. In 1947 he resigned his commission to edit the *Pakistan Times,* but left journalism when Ayyub Khan's military regime seized the paper in 1959. Having spent some years in jail as a political prisoner, he gained the Lenin International Peace Prize in 1962, but the best of his work is intimately romantic, without being either traditional or sentimental. The songs against political oppression are never strident, but convey their message of hope and defiance obliquely, with a heroic wit that succeeds in mocking its target with magnanimity.

One has the inescapable impression that a revolution administered by Faiz would be unprecedentedly benevolent, his power springing from the barrel of water to feed the thirsty.

GÜNTER GRASS (b. 1927).
Die Blechtrommel. First published 1959. Translated by Ralph Manheim as *The Tin Drum* (Penguin, 1965).

One of the great novels of the 20th century, *The Tin Drum* succeeds on every level and, despite its great length, remains spellbinding until the last page. Danzig, the birthplace of Grass, is also the birthplace of his grotesque hero Oskar Mazerath, a retarded dwarf who obsessively plays his toy drum and can shatter glass at a distance with his voice.

The novel is apparently the story of Oskar's family, and of his own early life, including the bizarre suicides of those around him: his mother dies of eating too much fish and his second putative father, Alfred Mazerath, suffocates when trying to swallow his Nazi badge. Oskar's detachment permits Grass, at one remove, to express his disgust with those around him, for there was a massacre of the Jews during the Nazi seizure of Danzig (now Gdansk in Communist and Catholic Poland) when he was a boy of eleven.

Later novels by Grass connected with Danzig include the brief *Katz und Maus* of 1961 and the long and brilliant *Hundejahre* of 1963, also available in English translations by Ralph Manheim. *Der Butt* (1976; translated as *The Flounder*, Penguin and Fawcett, 1979) is a worthy successor.

Grass is a committed Socialist, a prolific playwright and artist. His selected *Poems* (Penguin, 1969) have been translated by Michael Hamburger and Christopher Middleton, but the anthology needs updating.

MALLANAGA VATSYAYANA (c. 3rd century A.D.).
  Kama Sutra. Translated by S. C. Upadhyaya (Taraporevala of Bombay and Charles Skilton, 1961).

The expensive new translation of Vatsyayana, beautifully illustrated, is the first really accurate and scholarly version from the Sanskrit into English.

It ought to replace the much more widely-known and indeed famous translation by Sir Richard Francis Burton and F. F. Arbuthnot, originally produced in 1883 and frequently reprinted since. The Burton version is very readable, and will appeal to many more than the Upadhyaya translation, but Burton is too often inaccurate for his edition to be preferred.

The work is the leading extant statement of early Hindu teachings on the pleasures of eroticism. Vatsyayana states that, although sexual delights are not to be considered a chief end of existence, they must be considered a necessary part of existence. Free of the hypocrisy or obscenity which so often bedevils Western writings on sex, the book deals with matters of social importance, such as elegant deportment, how to court the unmarried, and advice on ways of making love. A knowledge of the *Kama Sutra* is assumed by all later Indian writers, and is considered quite as essential as a knowledge of the *Artha Shastra* ('Treatise on (Material) Prosperity') by Kautilya, or of the *Manu Smrti* ('Laws of Manu').

To anticipate criticism, it might be stressed that Professor A. L. Basham of the University of London has written that the *Kama Sutra* 'cannot be said to support promiscuity or to encourage perversion'.

Many Indian temples possess erotic sculptures of great artistic value, as any good history of Indian art will show. This is a good moment to read Gordon Rattray Taylor's *Sex in History* (Thames & Hudson, latest edition), or a similar work describing comparative sexual *mores*.

ROBERT LOWELL (1917–1977).
   Poems.

The whole output of the Boston-born Robert Lowell is worth careful study, for he expresses a literary facet of the American revolt against materialism opposed to the Blakean, neo-Buddhistic revolt of the Allen Ginsberg school. Lowell's highly sophisticated approach is autobiographical and even affectionately nostalgic, but always technically brilliant.

Imitations (Farrar, Straus, 1961; Faber & Faber, 1962) is a superb series of impressions – not by any means 'mere' translations – from eighteen poets, with special attention to Villon, Baudelaire, Rimbaud, Montale and Pasternak. *Near the Ocean* (Farrar, Straus and Faber & Faber, 1967) also offers poems based on Horace, Juvenal, Dante, Quevedo and Góngora.

But it is of course for his original poetry that Lowell will be remembered. His first truly mature collection was *Poems 1938–1949* (Harcourt Brace and Faber & Faber, 1950). *Life Studies* (Farrar, Straus and Faber & Faber, 1959) mined a rich seam of autobiographical poems, with a prose addition to the 2nd edition of 1968.

Subsequent books have added to the general view that Lowell is a major figure in 20th-century poetry, his deep sense of New England values nicely balanced with an active sympathy towards writers in distant cultures, from Aeschylus (whose *Prometheus Bound* he adapted) and Racine (whose *Phèdre* he adapted) to Voznesensky. Lowell opposed the War in Vietnam and was a consistent opponent of American power politics, as of Soviet power politics.

Notebook 1967–8 (Farrar, Straus, 1969; Faber & Faber, 1970) is a more experimental work, and in subsequent books. there has been a consistent expanding of themes and of technical innovation in this most accomplished of contemporary American poets.

Among the contemporaries of Lowell who are worth some exploration are Yvor Winters, Richard Eberhart, Kenneth Rexroth, John Berryman, Randall Jarrell and Richard Wilbur.

Verse autobiography was the main occupation of Lowell's last decade, in such books as *History, For Lizzie and Harriet, The Dolphin* (Farrar, Straus and Faber & Faber, all 1973), and *Day by Day,* the last appearing in the U.S.A. a few weeks before his death, and from Faber & Faber the following year.

Year 28

VALMIKI (*c.* 3rd century B.C.).
  Ramayana. There is no first-class translation available, the best being the prose rendition of Hari Prasad Shastri (3 vols., Shanti Sadan, 29 Chepstow Villas, London W11, 1952–9). The abridgment by R. C. Dutt in Everyman's Library (Dent and Dutton, 1910) is monotonous, but useful for those interested mainly in the plot.

The *Ramayana* is the earliest, best-loved, and most influential of the great Indian epics. Most of the first book (at least) and the whole of the last book are inferior to the rest, and are probably not by the same author, but by a later devotee wishing to endow the work with a religious framework in which Prince Rama is shown to be a reincarnation of Vishnu.

  The poem in Sanskrit consists of about 24,000 couplets in its presumed original, though many Indian languages have translated and adapted the poem for their own culture area. Book II is a realistic narrative of the events at the court of Rama's father, King Dasaratha, but Books III–VI contain many fantastic elements, and may be based on Rigveda myths, in which Sita, Rama's wife, may correspond to a fertility goddess, and the monkey-host and their king, Hanuman, may correspond to the Maruts, or Vedic storm-gods.

  The Hindu god Vishnu is believed to have saved the world through his own reincarnation six other times, and his seventh reincarnation as Rama, to defeat the demon-chief Ravana, king of the island of Lanka, was yet another example of the power of Vishnu: the poem is thus a text sacred to Hindus, but because it is considered an artificial poem, rather than a scripture, it has been altered by generations of scribes and story-tellers to bring it into line with other court epics. Its influence has been incalculable, from the Old Javanese *Ramayana Kakawin* probably written down in East Java in the 9th century, to the epics of Malaysia, Thailand, Kampuchea, Laos and Vietnam. See Hermann Jacobi's analytical study *The Ramayana* (1893), translated from the German by S. N. Ghosal (Oriental Institute, Baroda, 1960).

  Virtually all the dance dramas and puppet plays of south-east Asia draw on episodes from the *Ramayana,* and to a lesser extent the much longer and more diffuse *Mahabharata.*

Upanishads. (*c.* 1,000–500 B.C.).
> The two best translations are those by R. E. Hume in *The Thirteen Principal Upanishads* (2nd ed., Oxford U.P., 1931); and by S. Radhakrishnan in *The Principal Upanishads* (Allen & Unwin and Harper Row, 1953), the latter incorporating a transliteration of the Sanskrit text.

The simple Vedic hymns are of scant literary importance, and the institutional sacerdotalism of the Brahmanas was responsible for tedious texts such as the *Satapathabrahmana* (translated by J. Eggeling in 5 volumes for the Sacred Books of the East series (1882; Gordon Press, 1974).

But intermediate between the two extremes come the inspired and poetic teachings of the 108 *Upanishads,* of which Deussen has identified fourteen key works as belonging to the oldest, or 'Vedic' stratum: the Aitareya, Brhadaranyaka, Chandogya, Kausitaki, Kena and Taittiriya, the earliest, all in prose; the next 'generation' in verse, consisting of the Isha, Katha, Mahanarayana, Mundaka, and Shvetashvara; and the last 'generation' in prose, including the Maitrayaniya, the Mandukya, and the Prashna.

We know nothing of their authorship beyond the names of some writers who may have been responsible for compiling or revising parts of one *Upanishad* or another. The word *'Upanishad'* may mean 'intimate instruction on mystic doctrines' or 'sessions concerned with connections and correlations': the content may also be (and has been) interpreted in a wide variety of ways, and there are internal contradictions easily accounted for by multiple authorship. The philosophers deal with the responsibilities of the self in the cosmos, with individual salvation, with the vexed problem of the relations of a personal soul or *atman* to the world soul, or the real, or 'God' (*brahman*), or alternatively the identity of *atman* and *brahman.*

Just as Whitehead insisted that Western philosophy was merely a series of footnotes to the dialogues of Plato, so Indian thinkers have likened their own philosophy to a series of footnotes to the various *Upanishads.* Their authors were, as a group, probably in intellectual revolt against the ritualistic brahmins, much as early Buddhism arose as a dissatisfaction with brahminical doctrine and did in fact continue to teach some of the ways of life and thought first adumbrated in the *Upanishads.*

The most orthodox Hindus venerate the *Upanishads* today. For background material, see A. B. Keith's *Religion and Philosophy of the Veda and Upanishads* (Harvard U.P., and Oxford U.P., 1925), and Sarvepalli Radhakrishnan's *Philosophy of the Upanishads* (2nd ed., Allen & Unwin, 1935).

JEREMY BENTHAM (1748–1832).
An Introduction to the Principles of Morals and Legislation. First printed in 1780, and first published in 1789. Several editions in print, including that of Burns and Hart (Athlone Press, 1970).

A genius who read widely at the age of three, was nicknamed 'the philosopher' at five, and took his B.A. at fifteen, Bentham inherited wealth and was able to devote his whole life to studying, reading and writing, choosing principally the fields of government, morals and law.

Bentham coined such neologisms as 'international', 'codification', and 'utilitarianism', and due to his clearsightedness and relative lack of prejudice or vested interest was able to criticise existing institutions with such acumen and persuasiveness that much of the progress he desired has already been achieved. He defined good government as the promotion of the greatest happiness of the greatest number of citizens, realizing that in a pluralistic society it is impossible to satisfy everyone. Since happiness serves as the underlying motivation for human behaviour, morals and legislation must take happiness as their ultimate criterion of success. The individual must always subordinate his own selfish interest to the interests of the greatest number.

Bentham's logical approach to law led him to attack in the *Fragment on Government* (1776) the organic approach to the growth of law favoured by Blackstone, and it was this *Fragment* that formed the basis for his classic work. Criminal law and procedure and civil procedure benefited from Bentham's approach, above all in the legal revolution of 1873 in which law and equity were united.

Bentham has always enjoyed disciples among the logically-minded, from his ardent follower Étienne Dumont of Geneva, to J. S. Mill, who popularized the utilitarian ideas enunciated by Bentham. See Elie Halévy's *Growth of Philosophic Radicalism* (3rd ed., Faber & Faber, 1972).

Contemporary Indonesian Poetry, edited and translated by Harry Aveling (University of Queensland Press, St Lucia, Queensland, 1975).

Indonesia is a great nation of thousands of islands, and many millions of people speaking hundreds of different languages. The *lingua franca* selected in 1928 to be the official language of the country was Malay, subsequently known internally as Bahasa Indonesia, or 'the Indonesian language'. The first generation of writers in the new mother-tongue was called the *Pudjangga Baru* generation, after their leading magazine, and these poets are represented in Burton Raffel's *Anthology of Modern Indonesian Poetry:* Amir Hamzah, S. · T. Alisjahbana, Aoh Kartahadimadja and J. E. Tatengkeng. The Generation of 1945 included an indisputable master, Chairil Anwar, as well as Rivai Apin, Asrul Sani, and Siti Nuraini, and the later Sitor Situmorang and Toto Sudarto Bachtiar. The new generation, with whom Raffel concludes his anthology, includes W. S. Rendra, also an important actor and playwright, and Ajip Rosidi, also a publisher.

Aveling's selection is drawn from the poetry of the years from 1967–73, after Sukarno's Guided Democracy had come to an end. Rendra's long visit to America had inspired a popular, sensational type of verse based on American negro rhythms, social rebellion at all levels from that of the silenced intellectual to that of the exploited prostitute, and a gutter-Indonesian immediately accessible to the mass audience he wished to contact. Other poets in this varied and exciting anthology include Rosidi, Sastrowardojo, Toeti Heraty, Taufiq Ismail, Goenawan Mohamad, and Sapardi Djoko Damono. The Aveling anthology is recommended for those learning Bahasa Indonesia, because it is bilingual, unlike the Raffel. A successor, *Arjuna in Meditation* (Writers' Workshop, 162–92 Lake Gardens, Calcutta 45, India), translates selected verse of three younger poets: Abdul Hadi W. M., Darmanto Jt, and Sutardji Calzoum Bachri.

At the same time one could also recommend the other Indonesian literature in the same Asian and Pacific Writing series from the University of Queensland, and Harry Aveling's collection of Indonesian short stories *From Surabaya to Armageddon* (Heinemann, 1976).

Literature may be a new phenomenon in Indonesia (if one ignores the remarkably rich oral literature, only a tiny proportion of which has ever been set down in writing), but art has been a living impulse for over two thousand years.

A. J. Bernet Kempers' *Ancient Indonesian Art* (Van der Peet of Amsterdam and Harvard U.P., 1959) is neatly complemented by Claire Holt's *Art in Indonesia* (Cornell U.P., 1967), which includes an illustrated analysis of the more modern aspects of art, predominantly in Java and Bali, where the Hindu pictorial sculptural and architectural influences have remained strong.

Explore Bali personally if at all possible, or otherwise vicariously in books such as J. A. Boon's *The Anthropological Romance of Bali, 1597–1972* (Cambridge U.P., 1977), C. Hooykaas' *Balinese Temple Festival* (Kluwer, Boston, 1977), *Dance and Drama in Bali,* (Oxford U.P., 1974), by Beryl de Zoete and Walter Spies, and Belo's *Traditional Balinese Culture* (Columbia U.P., 1970). Balinese culture is a remarkable synthesis of fossilized medieval Hindu civilisation and traditions acquired over the centuries from Java, with a foundation of nature-worship. When I was advising the Government of the Republic of Indonesia on national library development, it was decreed that Bali should not be subjected to the standardisation implied by television, and so there is still no television on Bali.

PIO BAROJA (1872–1956).
Las Inquietudes de Shanti Andía. First published 1911. Translated by
Anthony Kerrigan in *The Restlessness of Shanti Andía and other writings*
(University of Michigan Press, 1959).

Baroja, born in San Sebastián on the northern coast of Spain, described himself
as 'seven-eighths Basque and one-eighth Italian' to show that he had no love for,
and claimed no affinity with, the Castilian majority. He believed the German and
English to be superior racial types, and in his writing took mainly French models
in his fiction, and Germans (Kant, Nietzsche and Schopenhauer) in his ideas.

Baroja is a superlative autobiographer in the eight-volume *Memorias* (1955),
and the best of his fiction is dominantly autobiographical until about 1912, when
his creative energy and, his powerful nihilism are at their height. His themes are
poverty, injustice, and hypocrisy. He demands compassion from his characters
and from the reader in a real world where so little is shown by officialdom.
Though never poor, he took pleasure in mingling with social outcasts and the
disadvantaged as if in restitution for their neglect by society and government at
large. González-Ruano once described him as 'resembling a beggar dressed in a
suit snatched from a corpse'.

Las Inquietudes de Shanti Andía is the first volume of a tetralogy entitled *El
Mar:* the others are *El laberinto de las sirenas* (1923), *Los pilotos de altura* (1929),
and *La estrella del Capitán Chimista* (1930). Anthony Kerrigan has added two
stories, four essays and sketches, and the play *La leyenda de Jaun de Alzate* (1922),
as well as a useful introduction.

The badly-arranged *Obras completas* of Baroja (8 vols., 1946–51) contain all
his significant work, though they are very far from complete. Almost as much as
Pérez Galdós, Baroja cries out for a systematic translation programme.

CHAIRIL ANWAR (1922–1949).
Complete Poetry and Prose, edited and translated by Burton Raffel (State
University of New York Press, Thurlow Terrace, Albany, New York
12201).

In a bilingual edition of the poems, and a translation of the prose, Burton Raffel
has presented us with the rounded figure of the most important poet that
Indonesia has yet produced.

As the leading writer of the Generation of 1945, Anwar died tragically young of
simultaneous typhus, syphilis and tuberculosis. He composed a number of
poems about death when he realised how near it was, but his Western-inspired
writings are imbued with a sense of joyous vitality and immediacy that seem to
overpower his suffering.

He translated Rilke, Marsman and Slauerhoff, bringing over into Indonesian a brilliance and precision which it had hitherto lacked. Born into a fairly prosperous family in Medan, North Sumatra, he moved with them to Jakarta in 1940, only beginning to write with full maturity and insight following the Japanese occupation in 1942. Altogether he produced only about seventy poems in the seven years remaining to him, but whereas other writers formed groups and movements, Chairil moved quietly and introspectively alone. It was only with the publication of three collections between 1949–51 that Indonesians realised how great a poet they had lost: a surprising visionary, and a master of a language that had never before been made to yield such nuances, such power.

This is an appropriate month to explore the music of Indonesia on gramophone records, and in particular the gamelan styles of Central Java and Bali.

Mediaeval Latin Lyrics, translated by Helen Waddell (Penguin, 1952).

Nobody – any more – can consider the great body of mediaeval songs in Latin even slightly dull or uninteresting. The masterpieces may in some cases be marked 'Anon.', but the true heart of secular passion, for life, liberty, nature, and love is unmistakeable in the originals and in the facing translations of Helen Waddell. She confessed herself beaten by Gottschalk, the finest two lyrics of Fortunatus, by Hildebert, and Gautier de Châtillon: which of her admirers can pick up the gauntlet?

The Wandering Scholars (Penguin, 1954) is her essential companion to the anthology. It began as a study of those *vagantes* whom we know from their extant songs, but ended as a history of mediaeval lyric, and there are more translations (with texts in an appendix). *More Latin Lyrics* (Gollancz, 1977) is another superb collection of translations. Use Latham's revised *Mediaeval Latin Word List* (Oxford U.P., 1965).

We do not know what many mediaeval songs actually sounded like, though the Early Music revival is producing some spectacular new discoveries, but the settings of the mediaeval *Carmina Burana* by Carl Orff are splendid in their way, especially in the recording conducted by Rafael Frühbeck de Burgos on HMV SAN 162.

The Romanesque art of northwestern Europe, dating roughly from 1050 to 1175, can be studied in the first volume of Henri Focillon's *The Art of the West in the Middle Ages* (Phaidon Press, 1963; Vol. 2 *Gothic Art*) and in Hanns Swarzenski's *Monuments of Romanesque Art* (2nd ed., University of Chicago Press and Faber & Faber, 1974).

KAUTILYA (*c.* late 4th century).
> *Artha Shastra.* Text, translation and study of R. P. Kangle (3 vols.,
> Bombay, 1960–5).

The author of this manual of early Indian statecraft may have been the Kautilya
(or Vishnugupta, or Canakya) who served as prime minister to Chandragupta
Maurya, King of Magadha (Bihar) from about 322 to about 299 B.C. In its extant
form, however, the book dates from the early fourth century A.D.

Rediscovered as recently as 1909, the book reversed earlier views on the strict
moral code of early Indian rulers, in fact recognising no good other than the
ruthless seeking and keeping of power by the king. The *Artha Shastra* is generally
viewed as the definitive Indian prose work on political craft, the verse summaries
being in all probability later interpolations. Among the subjects considered are
the education of a ruler, how to administer the realm and the law courts, how to
deal with treason and curb the power of the nobility, and how to conduct war and
diplomacy.

See M. V. Krishna Rao's *Studies in Kautilya* (Delhi, 1958), and compare the
writings of Kautilya with those of Machiavelli in Renaissance Europe and Nizam
ul-Mulk in 11th-century Iran.

TAKASUE NO MUSUME, called 'LADY SARASHINA' (1008–*c.* 1065).
> *Sarashina nikki.* Editions by Miyata Kazuichiro (Kyoto, 1931) and by
> Nishishita Kyoichi (Tokyo, 1964). Translated by Ivan Morris as *As I
> Crossed a Bridge of Dreams* (Penguin, 1975).

Subtitled 'Recollections of a woman in eleventh-century Japan', this translation
offers another glimpse into the great Heian period which also gave us Murasaki's
The Tale of Genji and *The Pillow-Book of Sei Shonagon,* two other masterpieces by
women.

Lady Sarashina was tenuously related to the Fujiwara family, but she herself –
though distinctly aristocratic by temperament and sensitivity – played little part
in the political turbulence of the time, being too timid and gentle. She was a
talented poetess, and much of the emotion shown throughout her notebook is
clearly due not so much to fashionable sentimentality as to authentic sensibility.
Though married – very late by Heian standards – and a mother, we learn but little
of her family: her notebook is full of impressions of her travels (though she is an
inaccurate guide) and of poems occasioned by these and by events and feelings
that overwhelmed her, often on looking out of a window or reading a novel.

European literature has virtually no parallels to the notebook of Lady
Sarashina: the closest poetic spirit that comes to mind is that of Emily
Dickinson.

What kind of novel did Lady Sarashina pore over? Possibly she read most of the extant literature of the time, but the most poignant will have been *Kagero Nikki*, by one of her aunts, known as 'Michitsuna's Mother', just as we know Lady Sarashina as 'Takasue's Daughter'. *Kagero Nikki* is the autobiographical account of a woman's jealousy of her husband's infidelities and her wretchedness at his neglect of her. The book has been expertly translated by Edward Seidensticker as *The Gossamer Years* (Tuttle, Tokyo, 1965).

BALDASSARE CASTIGLIONE (1478–1529).
   Il Libro del Cortegiano. First printed by Aldus in Venice (1528). Edited by Ettore Bonora (U. Mursia, Milan, 1972). Translated as *The Book of the Courtier* by George Bull (Penguin, 1976). The 1561 translation by Sir Thomas Hoby reprinted in Everyman's Library is the one drawn on by Shakespeare for the figure of Polonius in *Hamlet*.

Set at the ducal court of Urbino in 1506, two years before the death of Guidobaldo da Montefeltre (whose consort was Elisabetta, of the Gonzagas), Castiglione's masterpiece is in the form of a discussion among members of that distinguished court on the ideal qualities of a courtier.

With the *Orlando Furioso* of Ariosto, though much shorter and more natural than the epic, it can be said to represent the Italian Renaissance idea of the perfect gentleman, though the virtues it recommends are similar to those advocated by Aristotle long before in the *Nicomachaean Ethics*. The 'gentleman' ('caballero' in Spain; 'honnête homme' in France) must be as capable in arms as in letters, practising honesty, magnanimity, and good manners. He should be a connoisseur of the arts, and practise all sports and games. His speech should be concise and to the point, courteous and unaffected. Towards ladies he should be punctilious, and as careful of his own honour as of theirs.

The 'characters' given speech in the *Cortegiano* include Pietro Bembo (whose discourse on platonic love is especially memorable), Cardinal Bibiena, the Fregoso brothers, Pietro Aretino, Giuliano de' Medici, and Ludovico da Canossa.

Imitators of Castiglione appeared in their dozens, for the genre was of great significance as the rising middle class emulated the manners and attitudes of the aristocracy.

See *Castiglione* by J. R. Woodhouse (Edinburgh U.P., 1978).

Those curious about the Venetian Pietro Bembo (made a Cardinal in 1539) should read his *Gli Asolani* (1505) a neo-Platonic dialogue on love translated by R. B. Gottfried (Indiana U.P., 1954; reprinted by Arno, 1976).

Year 29

Sacred Writings of the Sikhs, revised by George S. Fraser (Allen & Unwin and Samuel Weiser, 625 Broadway, New York, N.Y. 10012, 1973).

The bulk of this important contribution to comparative religion is taken up by selections from the *Adi Granth,* the most important Sikh scripture. There is a complete *Adi Granth* available from Munshiram Manoharlal, P.O. Box 5715, 54 Rani Jhansi Road, New Delhi.

Sikhism was founded by Guru Nanak in the fifteenth century as a bridge between Islam and Hinduism, preaching non-violence. However, by the time of the fifth guru, Gobind Singh, the Sikhs were being persecuted by the ruling Moghuls of India and were forced to take up arms to protect themselves. See W. H. McLeod's *Guru Nanak and the Sikh Religion* (Oxford U.P., 1968) and Khushwant Singh's authoritative *History of the Sikhs* (2 vols., Oxford U.P., 1964–6).

W. G. Archer has written a well-illustrated account of *Paintings of the Sikhs* (H.M.S.O. for the Victoria and Albert Museum, 1966).

GUY DE MAUPASSANT (1850–1893).
  Oeuvres complètes (16 vols., Piazza, Paris, 1968). *Complete Short Stories* (3 vols., Cassell, 1970).

The France that we know from the naturalistic pages of Maupassant's stories is the Third Republic of 1870 to 1890. His literary associates could hardly have been more august: his early mentor was the disciplined stylist Flaubert, who was himself driven to surpass the novels of Balzac, and Maupassant found great inspiration in the work of Zola, who brought out Maupassant's *nouvelle* 'Boule de Suif' in 1880 as part of a book of war stories.

Apart from three hundred masterly short stories, Maupassant produced three volumes of travel sketches, four plays, and six novels, of which perhaps *Une Vie* (1883) and *Pierre et Jean* (1888) are the most moving. The former concerns the loneliness and despair of a deceived Norman woman; the latter is a study in jealousy also valuable for a statement in the preface of the writer's own aims.

Pierre and Jean is a translation by Martin Turnell (New English Library, 1962), and *Une Vie* is available, as *A Woman's Life,* in a version by H. N. P. Sloman (Penguin, 1965).

Among the most useful studies of Maupassant in English are Francis Steegmuller's *Maupassant* (1954; reprinted by Greenwood Press, 1978) and Michael Lerner's *Maupassant* (Braziller, 1975).

Listen to the Requiem (on CFP 40234, conducted by Cluytens), and the songs and piano music of Gabriel Fauré (1845–1924).

A Celtic Miscellany: Translations from the Celtic Literatures by Kenneth Hurlstone Jackson (Penguin, 1971).

Choosing to exclude modern writings which are no longer characteristic of traditional Celtic thought and feeling, Professor Jackson has also presented very little in Breton, Cornish and Manx, but has concentrated on the older Irish, Welsh, and to a lesser extent Scots Gaelic literatures.

Unfortunately no parallel texts are given, but there is a pronouncing index of names and a valuable section of notes. The greatest handicap to a reader trying to form a picture of the development of Celtic literatures is that the versions are given not in chronological order, but in a cross-classified mixture of genre and subject, so that sections are divided as follows: Hero-tale and adventure; Nature; Love; Epigram; Celtic Magic; Description, Humour and Satire; Bardic Poetry; Elegy; and Religion.

The background to the six Celtic languages has been set down, with grammatical material, by D. B. Gregor in *Celtic: a Comparative Study* (Oleander Press, 1980), while *Celtic Art* by George Bain (Constable, 1977) and *The Celts* by Nora Chadwick (Penguin, 1970) can be recommended as useful introductions to the art and history of the Celts respectively.

JAMES BOSWELL (1740–1795).
   The Life of Samuel Johnson. First published 1791. G. Birkbeck Hill's edition, revised and enlarged by L. F. Powell, is published in 6 volumes (Oxford U.P., 1934–64). A popular abridgment has been made by J. E. Shepard: *Everybody's Boswell* (Bell, 1949).

Sir Sidney Lee asserted that 'the longest biography in the English language is also the best. Boswell's *Life of Johnson* is indeed reckoned the best specimen of biography that has yet been written in any tongue'.

Anyone termed a 'Boswell' can be considered a loyal amanuensis meticulous in preserving a subject's wit and wisdom on all occasions and in all company. But Boswell also wrote a good deal more, including amusing and perceptive journals of a tour with Johnson to the Hebrides, in London (1762–3), in Holland (1763–4), in Germany and Switzerland (1764), and in Italy, Corsica and France (1765–6). Vain, snobbish, priggish, and a compulsive scribbler, Boswell had many faults, but all are redeemed by his supreme literary gifts, which make his wenching, boozing and duplicity seem all the more endearing for being so candidly described.

Johnson not only wrote the satire *Rasselas* (1759), and the monumental *Lives of the English Poets* (1779–81), but the first scrupulous attempt at a comprehensive *Dictionary of the English Language* (2 vols., 1755; reprinted in 1 volume by Times Books, 1980).

HUNG SHENG (1646–1704).
   Ch'ang-sheng Tien. First performed *c.* 1688. Translated by Yang Hsien-yi and Gladys Yang as *The Palace of Eternal Youth* (Foreign Languages Press, Peking, 1955).

The poem *Ch'ang hen ko* ('The Everlasting Sorrow') by Po Chü-i and a story by Ch'en Hung are the basis for Hung Sheng's great opera in fifty acts, which is usually considered one of the finest Ch'ing lyric dramas.

Set in T'ang times, at the Court of the Emperor Ming-huang, the play traces the course of intrigue at the Court, the Emperor's flight, and also his love for his concubine Yang Yu-huan. Apart from the fascinating music, the particular interest of this work is the idealised romance of which Europe considered itself the only exponent. Extraordinary fidelity within romantic love is however by no means a monopoly of the Western tradition, as Hung Sheng and many other writers who dealt with the same theme have shown.

FRANÇOIS, *Duc de* LA ROCHEFOUCAULD (1613–1680).
   Réflexions ou sentences et maximes morales. First authorised edition 1665 (Paris), following a clandestine edition of 1664 (The Hague). The Classiques Garnier edition (Paris, 1957) is accompanied by the *Oeuvres choisies* of Vauvenargues. The World's Classics edition (Oxford U.P., 1940) has a translation of *The Maxims,* as the compilation is usually known, by F. G. Stevens facing the text. For an English version alone, use the *Maxims* translated by L. W. Tancock (Penguin, 1959).

The best authority for La Rochefoucauld's life and times is his own *Mémoires,* printed clandestinely in 1662, and in an authorized edition two years later.

He was an aristocrat who married at fifteen and had become a professional soldier on active service at sixteen. He pursued political intrigue with little success in an age when disagreement with the policy of the Government (*sc.* King Louis XIII) was construed as sedition, and generally punished by either execution or exile. La Rochefoucauld found himself at odds first with Cardinal Richelieu, and later (on the accession of Louis XIV at the age of three and the Regency of the Queen Mother) with Cardinal Mazarin. La Rochefoucauld took part in the rebellion called La Fronde (1648–53) against Mazarin, and was twice compelled to vanish from the scene. He was probably acquainted with the *Leviathan* of Thomas Hobbes, and his *Maximes* betray a certain degree of cynicism. According to La Rochefoucauld, all that a person does, whether apparently virtuous or apparently vicious, is guided by self-interest, chance, good or ill fortune, and vanity. 'So-called virtue', he begins, 'is often simply a mixture of activities and interests which good fortune or our own industry enables us to show to good advantage. It is thus not always courage that moulds a hero, nor modesty a chaste woman'. The hundreds of admirably brief aphorisms which follow can be said to elaborate this general view of human nature in a wide variety of ways. His clear-sighted realism places him in the line of thinkers running from Machiavelli to Nietzsche, and he cannot be ignored.

RENÉ KARL WILHELM JOSEF MARIA RILKE (1875–1926).
Sämtliche Werke, edited by R. Sieber-Rilke and E. Zinn (1955–1963).

Like Goethe, Rainer Maria Rilke (he preferred the German form of his first name) can be appreciated only by those with a continuous and loving acquaintance with the German language and its sonorities. No translation is excellent: Leishman and Spender are pedestrian, and the new *Duino Elegies* version by David Young (W. W. Norton, 1980) may be an improvement, but suffers the fatal flaw of abandoning the Rilkean long line in favour of the triadic line (here entirely inappropriate) favoured by William Carlos Williams.

However, for those who must have an anglicised Rilke (born in Prague of Bohemian and Alsatian stock, he spent several years in Paris as secretary to Rodin the sculptor and was as at home on the Adriatic at Duino as in the Swiss Valais, so he must be considered an international poet in all but language), there are the translations by G. Craig Houston and J. B. Leishman of *Selected Works* (2 vols., Hogarth Press and New Directions, 1960–1), supplementing the Leishman versions of Rilke's *Poems 1906–1926* (Hogarth Press and New Directions, 1959).

For the *Duino Elegies* one would now prefer the Young version above, though the bilingual version by C. F. MacIntyre (University of California Press, 1961) must be considered MacIntyre has also produced a bilingual *Sonnets to Orpheus* (University of California Press, 1960), which ranks above the translation by M. D. Herter Norton (Norton, 1942). The Penguin *Selected Poems* (1964) uses some Leishman translations, but the omissions are too important for the book to be of any real use, and there are no originals.

To set Rilke in context, read C. M. Bowra's *The Heritage of Symbolism* (Macmillan, 1943), for essays on Valéry, Rilke, Stefan George, Alexander Blok, and W. B. Yeats.

MIKHAIL YEVGRAFOVICH SALTYKOV (using the pen-name SHCHEDRIN and hence usually known as SALTYKOV-SHCHEDRIN, 1826-1889). *Gospoda Golovlyovy.* First published 1876. Translated by Natalie Duddington as *The Golovlyov Family* for Everyman's Library (Dent and Dutton, 1955) and, rather better, by A. R. MacAndrew as *The Golovlovs* for Signet Classics (New American Library, 1961), and by Samuel Cioran (Ardis, 1976).

Saltykov was of aristocratic descent, and worked in the War Office until he was exiled to Vyatka for a satire, *Zaputannoye delo* (1848). His satirical fables, *Skazki* (1884–5), which have dated less than his radical journalism, have been translated by Vera Velkhovsky (1941, as *Fables;* reprinted by Greenwood, 1976) and by Dorian Rottenberg (Foreign Languages Publishing House, Moscow, as *Tales* n.d.).

Saltykov-Shchedrin is however best known for the *Gospoda Golovlyovy,* tracing the fifteen years of decay and corruption within a family of country nobles. The hypocrite Porfiri (Judas or Iudushka) has become an eponymous figure in Russia, just as have Tartuffe in France and Uriah Heep in England.

KABIR (*c.* 1430–*c.* 1518).
Kabir. Vol. 1, by Charlotte Vaudeville (Oxford U.P., 1974).

An attempt at a critical evaluation and translation of the authentic utterances of the Eastern Hindi poet-weaver of Benares who was brought up by a Muslim but found no satisfaction (as he put it) in Ka'aba or Kailash, but taught that God was accessible more easily to the washerwoman or carpenter than to the professional holy man, of whatever religious persuasion. Many of his mystical songs have been assimilated into Sikh scriptures. *One Hundred Poems of Kabir* (Macmillan, 1974) is a reworking by Rabindranath Tagore through a Bengali translation, and has been criticised for its inaccuracies and failure to represent Kabir's ecstasy by Robert Bly, but Bly's own few versions in *The Fish in the Sea is not Thirsty*

(Rainbow Bridge, P.O. Box 40208, San Francisco, CA 94140) and *Try to Live to See This!* (Ally Press, P.O. Box 30340, St. Paul, MN 55175, 1976) have also been adversely criticised.

LUCIUS ANNAEUS SENECA (*c.* 4 B.C.–65 A.D.).
   Moral Essays. Text with a translation by John W. Basore in the Loeb Classical Library (3 vols., Heinemann and Harvard U.P., 1928–1935).

Having enjoyed the letters of Seneca in Year 11, it is now time to explore the more extended essays often called *Dialogi,* which deal with many of the same topics at greater length, although only *De Providentia* among the *Moral Essays* is addressed to the Lucilius of the letters. The *De Clementia* is of particular interest because it was written for the young prince Nero who had just completed his eighteenth year, and its careful compound of exhortation and flattery will greatly intrigue those who have become familiar with the period, especially since we can only guess at the contents of the missing section, believed to be more than half of the whole.

Seneca's fellow-Spaniards Martial and Quintilian also made a career in Rome, and might be explored at this point. Marcus Fabius Quintilianus (*c.* 35 – *c.* 95 A.D.) is the author of a textbook on rhetoric which is also an exposition of how the Roman citizen should acquire the art of persuasive public speaking so that all sectors of the community can be represented. The *Insitutionis Oratoriae* (4 vols., Heinemann & Harvard U.P., 1953) includes a translation by H. E. Butler. Marcus Valerius Martialis (*c.* 40 A.D.–*c.* 104 A.D.) is the author of twelve books of *Epigrams* (2 vols., Heinemann & Harvard U.P., 1919–20) which give a witty, acid verdict on contemporary personalities. The Ker translations are literal, as usual with Loeb Classical Library editions, and others are preferable in parts, particularly Peter Porter's *After Martial* (Oxford U.P., 1972), and the examples in *Martial and the Modern Epigram* (Cooper, 1927) by Paul Nixon.

Another Spaniard, the Emperor Trajan, established Mithraism as the religion of the Roman Empire about 100 A.D. See Franz Cumont's *The Mysteries of Mithra* (2nd ed., 1911, reprinted by Dover and Constable, 1956) and *Oriental Religions in Roman Paganism* (1911, reprinted by Dover and Constable, 1956).

Year 30

An Anthology of Sinhalese Literature up to 1815, selected by the Unesco
National Commission of Ceylon. Edited and with an introduction by
C. H. B. Reynolds (Allen & Unwin, 1970).

Theravada Buddhism was always the dominant theme and mood of Sinhalese
literature until the British captured Kandy in 1815.

The Sinhalese prose version of the Milinda-Questions (see *Milindapañha* later
in this chapter) by Hinatikumbure Sumangala dates from the eighteenth century,
thus attesting the essential continuity of Sinhalese culture.

Graffiti found on the Mirror Wall of the rock fortress at Sigiriya are the earliest
known literary inscriptions in Sri Lanka (6th–9th centuries), but the tradition
rose to its peak in the 12th to 14th centuries as regards prose, and in the
15th–16th centuries as regards verse.

Dance and Magic Drama in Ceylon by Beryl de Zoete (Faber & Faber, 1957)
makes a useful companion to the Reynolds anthology, as does the Unesco album
published in the same year: *Ceylon: Paintings from Temple, Shrine and Rock.*

GIUSEPPE TOMASI, *Principe di* LAMPEDUSA (1896–1957).
  Il Gattopardo. First published 1958. Translated by Archibald Colquhoun as
  The Leopard in Fontana (Collins, 1969).

Sicily has produced numerous important writers – Verga, Pirandello, and more
recently Brancati and Sciascia. *I Viceré* (1894) by the Neapolitan Federico De
Roberto, translated by Archibald Colquhoun as *The Viceroys* (1962), was a
historical novel penetrating into the lives and minds of an aristocratic Sicilian
family through three generations.

Lampedusa was likewise an aristocrat. He interrupted his studies at the age of
twenty to serve in World War I, and managed to escape (at a second attempt)
from the Poznan concentration camp. He served in the army until 1925, but
refused to collaborate with the fascists, retiring to a life of study and meditation.

As a critic, he was too fastidious to publish anything during his lifetime, but the novelist Giorgio Bassani found the MS of *Il Gattopardo* after the Prince's death, and immediately recommended its publication. Three years later another Lampedusa appeared: four stories and a few essays on French literature of the 18th century collectively known as *Racconti*. Three of the stories, and eight chapters of autobiography, were translated by Colquhoun as *Two Stories and a Memory* (Penguin, 1966).

The Leopard opens as the Kingdom of the Two Sicilies is about to fall, in May 1860. It can be construed as an elegy for a long-lost Sicily, or (and?) a demonstration of the theory that Sicily does not change in essentials, despite national upheavals in politics or social *mores*. The central figure, Don Fabrizio, lives through the events which brought Garibaldi to power and led to the rise of the Italian middle classes.

CHANDIDAS (15th century).

> *Shri-Krishna-kirtana*. First published 1916. Translated by Deben Bhattacharya as *Love Songs of Chandidas* (Grove Press and Allen & Unwin, 1967).

The Bengali poet Chandidas, of whom almost nothing is known, was a Brahmin temple-attendant who wrote on the love between Krishna and Radha in the form of a dramatic dialogue. A third protagonist is the old woman go-between Barai.

An original feature of this Vaishnava poetry is the indication that Radha was married at the time of her infatuation with the god Krishna, who is no papier-mâché figure, but a lustful and even cruel youth who stops at nothing to achieve the conquest of Radha.

A legend is told that Chandidas (also spelt 'Candidas') was enamoured of a washerwoman, Rami. He openly declared his love for her, and was excommunicated from the Brahmin caste, a fate he bore with cheerful fortitude, glorifying Rami with the title 'Mother *gayatri*', the most sacred formula in brahminical Hinduism.

Compare Chandidas with the Marathi poet-saint Tukaram (1598–1649). His religious hymns have been translated by N. J. Fraser and K. B. Marathe in *The Poems of Tukaram* (3 vols., Madras 1909–15) and to greater effect by Dilip Chitre in *Delos* (no. 4, 1970) and *Modern Poetry in Translation* (no. 32, Autumn–Winter 1977).

LUCIAN (*c.* 115–*c.* 180).
Works. Text with a facing translation by Austin Morris Harmon (vols. 1–7) and M. D. Macleod (vol. 8) in the Loeb Classical Library (8 vols., Heinemann and Harvard U.P., 1913–36). Translations by H. W. Fowler and F. G. Fowler (4 vols., Oxford U.P., 1905) and (judiciously abridged) by Paul Turner (Penguin, 1961).

A native of Samosata (Samsat in present-day Syria), Lucian was a Roman citizen who wrote not in the demotic Greek current in his day, but in the classical Attic Greek common six centuries earlier.

He did not take the Christians at all seriously, unfortunately for his mediaeval reputation, but Erasmus and More gleefully took up his wit and common sense. More's version of Lucian sold more than twice as many editions as *Utopia* in his own lifetime, and Erasmus was sternly rebuked by Luther as 'the modern Lucian'. No writer indeed influenced Erasmus more than did the sly Syrian.

Lucian is consistently funny, especially about the perennially fascinating themes of life and death. His Charon, for instance, emerges from the Underworld to find out why his passengers are so unwilling to cross the Styx: after his tour of inspection he goes back more mystified than ever.

Our satirist pokes fun at the Stoics, the Cynics, the Pythagoreans and all the other schools of the time, but probably his most enjoyably sustained satire is the parody of Herodotus which in the form of a *True History* takes us to the Moon, where the inhabitants have beards above their knees, use artificial private parts ('which seem to work quite well'), and sweat milk. Given the sensational popular success of such pseudo-scientists as Erich von Däniken in the twentieth century, it seems that nothing changes.

Milindapañha ('The Milinda-Questions') (*c.* 2nd-1st centuries B.C.). Translated from the Pali by T. W. Rhys Davids (2 vols., Dover and Constable, 1963, reprinting the Sacred Books of the East edition of 1890–4) and by I. B. Horner (2 vols., Pali Text Society, 1963).

Just as Gandharan art represents the meeting of Greek paganism and Indian Buddhism, so the *Milindapañha* is a perpetually fascinating encounter between the Greek Menandros, King of Bactria in the 2nd century B.C., and the Buddhist monk Nagasena (or Dhitika, according to the Sarvastivadins).

The civilized wit and enlightenment which both men bring to their dialogues is particularly Greco-Buddhist, though one need not lend absolute credence to the work's conclusion: that the King adopted Buddhism.

One of the best studies of the *Milindapañha* is Caroline A. F. Rhys-Davids' *The Milinda-Questions* (Routledge, 1930).

SANDOR PETÖFI (1823–1849).
   Petöfi. Translated by Anton N. Nyerges. Edited by J. M. Értavy-Baráth (Hungarian Cultural Foundation, P.O. Box 364, Stone Mountain, GA 30086, 1973).

The national poet of Hungary began writing at the age of fifteen, neglecting his studies to join a group of strolling players. His father, a poor butcher, refused to have any more to do with the boy, who often faced starvation.

His first collection of poems appeared – to adverse reactions – in 1844, and he turned to translation (including Shakespeare's *Coriolanus*) and to editorship. In 1845 he produced the poetic narrative *János Vitéz* (translated by W. N. Loew as *János the Hero*, 1920), but subsequently found his best themes in political republicanism and love lyrics for his bride. The 'Nemzeti Dal' of 1848 is a stirring Hungarian anthem in the style of the 'Marseillaise'. He met his death while serving as aide-de-camp to General Bem, Commander-in-Chief of the Transylvian army, at the Battle of Segesvár, nowadays known as Sighişoara, Romania.

See *Rebel or Revolutionary? Sandor Petöfi as revealed in his diary, letters, notes, pamphlets and poems,* selected by Béla Köpeczi (Corvina Press, Budapest, 1974).

Hungarian folk music is well known, and can be explored on a number of records. Béla Bartok not only studied and collected songs and dance-music, but extended the tradition by his own genius. Try his string quartets, the Concerto for Orchestra, the exquisite Romanian folk dances, and the piano concerti.

BIBHUTIBHUSAN BANERJI (1894–1950).
   Pather Panchali ('Song of the Road'). First published 1929. Translated by T. W. Clark and Tarapada Mukherji (Allen & Unwin, 1968).

Banerji wrote in Bengali, but his finest novel is known all over India and indeed throughout the world, for it was made into a superb film by Satyajit Ray in 1958.

Set in Nishchindipur, a faithful mirror of Banerji's own native village north of Calcutta, the novel is a miraculous evocation of the childhood of Opu and his sister Durga. Their father is a gifted but impecunious singer and family priest who never earns enough to keep his family in any comfort. The picture of rural India, which virtually no outsider can ever penetrate, is both detailed and tellingly selective.

Banerji himself left the village to obtain a good education and become a teacher. He translated Scott's *Ivanhoe* into Bengali and wrote over fifty books of unequal quality. *Pather Panchali* ranks as one of the major works of Indian literature.

FRANCIS BACON, *1st Baron Verulam* (1561–1626).
   The Advancement of Learning and *New Atlantis.* First published in 1605 and
   1626 respectively. World's Classics (Oxford U.P., 1906). And *Essays.* First
   published in 1597, then definitively in 1625. World's Classics (Oxford U.P.,
   1937).

Even if one does not agree with the school of Herbert Lawrence (*The Life and
Adventures of Common Sense,* 1769) that Bacon wrote the plays attributed to the
actor Shakespeare, one must respect the literary genius of the essayist and thinker
who rose to become Lord Chancellor under James I in 1618.

'I have taken all knowledge to be my province', stated Bacon quite simply,
proposing 'a total reconstruction of sciences, arts and all human knowledge. . . to
extend the power and dominion of the human race. . . over the universe'. His
general essays are still of great appeal too, but we read him today chiefly for *The
Advancement of Learning,* greatly expanded within his majestic plan as *De
Augmentis Scientiarum* (1623) and the *Novum Organum,* which was a new method
for acquiring true knowledge. Bacon carefully and shrewdly attacked the
Aristotelian and scholastic methods of thinking; his work was influential above
all on the thought of Locke, Boyle, Leibnitz and Huygens.

The unfinished *New Atlantis* is a fable dealing with an imaginary Pacific island
called Bensalem, and with Solomon's House, a college of natural philosophy.

This might be an appropriate moment to explore writing by some of Bacon's
contemporaries, among them Lyly, Drayton, and Nash, and the music of John
Dowland (1563–1626).

BILHANA (*c.* 1040–1095).
   Caurapañcasika. Translated by Barbara Stoler Miller as *Phantasies of a
   Love-Thief* (Columbia U.P., 1971).

A Sanskrit poet born in Kashmir, Bilhana spent most of his settled life, after early
travels in Southern India, at the Court of King Vikramanka or Vikramaditya VI in
Kalyana, near Bombay. As court poet (*vidyapati*) he composed the official epic
Vikramankadevacarita, but he is' best loved for the lyric verses of the
Caurapañcasika, fifty strophes all beginnning with the words rendered as 'even
now I think about. . .', and all concerned with the poet's forbidden love for a
princess. The subject gave rise to the legend that Bilhana was in fact enamoured
of a princess, in whose praise he wrote the work, and that he was imprisoned for
his daring, but released and given the hand of the princess because of his poetic
skill.

Okagami ('Great Mirror') (*c.* 1200). Translated by Joseph K. Yamagiwa (Tuttle, Tokyo, 1978) and by Helen C. McCullough (Princeton U.P., 1980).

Of the five important *rekishi monogatari* (historical stories) written in classical Japanese and describing aspects of court life in pre-Edo times, the two best known are the *Okagami,* and the earlier and longer *Eiga monogatari.*

The *Okagami* is the most satisfactory as a work of literature, leaning on Chinese historiographical practice. After succinct biographies of the emperors from 851 to 1036, the main part of the work is taken up by accounts of the Fujiwara leaders and their families. The work concludes with a miscellany. The form of the book is a narrative related by a man aged 150, who had thus lived through much of the age he describes, interrupted by his 140-year-old friend, and a rather younger attendant.

The *Okagami* has been attributed to Tamenari, himself a member of the powerful Fujiwara clan. Tamenari was a court official attached to the Mikado Sutoku (1124–1141) who in later life retired to a hermitage on Mount Ohara, near Kyoto.

Year 31

DESIDERIUS ERASMUS (c. 1469–1536).
  Colloquia familiaria. First published 1518–1533. Translated as *Colloquies* by
  Craig R. Thompson (University of Chicago Press, 1965). And *Moriae
  encomium*. First published 1511. Translated as *In Praise of Folly* by Betty
  Radice (Penguin, 1971).

Erasmus of Rotterdam was one of the great European scholars of his day, and his
Latin dialogues and essays on contemporary themes, the *Colloquies,* were
influential in the course of the Reformation for their satire on corrupt
monasticism, though Erasmus attacked Luther for splitting the Church so
disastrously.

A deeply thoughtful man of letters, he detested the accretions of medieval
ecclesiastical superstition on the body of New Testament doctrine. His *Moriae
encomium,* also known as the *Laus stultitiae* ('The Praise of Folly' punningly
also reads 'The Praise of (Sir Thomas) More', his personal friend. Educated at
Deventer, then at Paris, he was equally at home in Louvain (1502–4), in Italy
(1506–9), and in Cambridge (1511). Erasmus spent much of the next decade in
the Netherlands but settled in Basle in 1521 until he felt oppressed by growing
religious sectarianism and departed in 1529 for Freiburg im Breisgau
(1529–35).

This would be an appropriate moment to read a selection of Luther's work,
such as *Reformation Writings* (Lutterworth Press, 1937), or selections from
Calvin's *Institutes,* Commentaries and Tracts such as *On the Christian Faith*
(Bobbs-Merrill, 1957), edited by John T. McNeill.

Concentrate on the paintings, drawings and woodcuts of the Hungarian-born
Albrecht Dürer (1471–1528), the paintings of Lucas Cranach (1472–1553) and
Mathis Gothardt Nithardt, called 'Grünewald' (c. 1475–1528), and the career of
Hans Holbein the Younger (1497–1543).

The Emperor Maximilian I set up magnificent courts at Vienna, Innsbruck and
Augsburg, and employed both Dürer and Burgkmair. Music of Maximilian's
courts is played by the Early Music of Consort on Argo ZRG 3783, including

works by Ludwig Senfl and Heinrich Isaac.

FRIEDRICH HÖLDERLIN (1770–1843).
Poems and Fragments. Translated by Michael Hamburger (University of Michigan Press and Routledge, 1967).

Born in the same year as Beethoven and Hegel, Hölderlin was to become an intimate of Schiller and Goethe, studied Kant's philosophy, knew Schelling, and attended lectures by Fichte.

Physically delicate, and highly-strung mentally, eventually insanity was delayed for some time by his falling in love in 1796 with Madame Gontard, to whose son he was tutor. Mme. Gontard, the 'Diotima' of Hölderlin's poetry, was beautiful and intelligent: he identified her with the spirit of classical Greece idealised by the Weimar thinkers as the ultimate in earthly harmony and wisdom.

Hölderlin's best poetry ranges from the prophetic exaltation of his patriotic a memorable epistolary novel *Hyperion, or The Hermit in Greece* (1797–9), translated by Willard R. Trask (New American Library, 1965).

Hölderlin's best poetry ranges from the prophetic exaltation of the patriotic songs to the Klopstockian devotion to the poet's craft, and its quasi-religious significance to the poet himself and to mankind in general. His influence on George and Rilke was incalculable.

Explore the paintings of Hölderlin's contemporary Caspar David Friedrich (1774–1840) in the monograph by Helmut Börsch-Supan (Braziller, 1974) or in Linda Siegel's *Caspar David Friedrich and the Age of German Romanticism* (Branden Press, 21 Station St., Brookline, MA 02147, 1979).

JAKOB ROSENBERG.
Rembrandt: Life and Work (4th ed., Phaidon Press, 1980).

It is of little lasting value to obtain volumes of the complete paintings, etchings, and drawings by Rembrandt if they are unaccompanied by a detailed and sympathetic commentary. The works of Benesch are exemplary, but Professor Rosenberg of the National Gallery of Art (Washington, D.C.) has produced the best short introduction, beautifully illustrated in monochrome.

For the background, see Paul Zumthor's *Daily Life in Rembrandt's Holland* (Weidenfeld & Nicolson, 1962), and Kenneth Clark's *Rembrandt and the Italian Renaissance* (John Murray, 1966).

I cannot resist commending at the same time Rosenberg's *On Quality in Art* (Princeton U.P. and Phaidon, 1967), distinguished not so much for the first part, on the critical acumen of Vasari, Roger de Piles, Reynolds, Théophile Thoré, and Roger Fry, but for the second, in which he brings authoritative judgment on the Berensonian scale to master drawings from the fifteenth century to twentieth.

As well as the extended visit to Amsterdam's Rijksmuseum, where Rembrandt and all other major Dutch artists can best be enjoyed, make time to visit the Rembrandt House ('Het Rembrandthuis'), Jodenbreestraat 4–6, Amsterdam, with its fine collection of etchings and drawings. This is the house where Rembrandt lived from 1639 to 1659, finally leaving it insolvent, when it was publicly sold.

BLAISE PASCAL (1623–1662).
   Les Provinciales, ou les Lettres Escrites par Louis de Montalte à un Provincial de ses Amis. First published in Cologne (false imprint, i.e. Paris) 1656–7. Translated as *The Provincial Letters* by A. J. Krailsheimer (Penguin, 1967). And *Les Pensées.* first published posthumously in a selection made by a group of Jansenists in Paris, 1670. Translated by A. J. Krailsheimer (Penguin, 1966).

An infant prodigy in mathematics and pure science, Pascal early solved problems in the infinitesimal calculus which had defeated Galileo, Descartes and Fermat.

But he is remembered as the first great French prose stylist after Montaigne, and as the chief apologist for the 17th-century ascetic movement called Jansenism, which aimed at reform within the Roman Catholic Church. Its centre was the monastery of Port Royal, where Pascal's sister Jacqueline became a nun. Pascal went to live at Port Royal late in 1654, and produced a series of ironic letters against the Jesuits in defence of the Jansenists: they were triumphant in their purpose, and even to this day the Jesuits have not recovered from Pascal's barbed charges of casuistry in *Les Provinciales.*   .

Les Pensées is not a systematic work of this kind, but a series of reflections aiming to establish the truth of Christianity against the scepticism of Montaigne, or traces of rationalism in Descartes. Pascal challenges scepticism with a suggested 'pyrrhonism', which is sceptical of scepticism itself, faith and revelation justifying each other in a circular fashion at a level deeper than scepticism.

The Krailsheimer versions of these peculiarly challenging texts are unlikely to be superseded within the next generation.

A Thousand Years of Vietnamese Poetry, translated by N. N. Bich, B. Raffel, and W. S. Merwin (Knopf, 1975).

Vietnamese poetry has been written in Chinese characters (up to the 19th century), in the Chu Nom characters (from the 13th century) deriving from Chinese, and in the romanised script known as Quoc Ngu invented by Christian missionaries in the 17th century. John Balaban, an American poet who recorded oral poetry on tape in the late 1960s and the early 1970s, suggests that Vietnamese oral tradition can be traced back to Mon-Khmer times over a span of four thousand years. There are thus four strands in Vietnamese literary history, vigorous from the Buddhist Ly Thai Tong (999–1054) to the Communist Ho Chi Minh.

The background to Indo-Chinese conflict, domestically and with the invasions of the French and then the Americans, should be examined in a balanced history.

BARUCH (later BENEDICT DE) SPINOZA (1634–77).
Ethica. First published posthumously in the *Opera posthuma* (1677) edited by Lodewijk Meyer. Translated with the *De intellectus emendatione* by A. Boyle in Everyman's Library (Dent and Dutton, 1910).

Bertrand Russell considered the Amsterdam-born son of a family of Jewish exiles from Spain 'the noblest and most lovable of great philosophers. Intellectually, some others have surpassed him, but ethically he is supreme. As a natural consequence, he was considered, during his lifetime and for a century after his death, a man of appalling wickedness. He was born a Jew but the Jews excommunicated him. Christians abhorred him equally; although his whole philosophy is dominated by the idea of God, the orthodox accused him of atheism'.

To earn a living, he learnt how to grind lenses, and studied the theory of optics, and became the focal figure in a small philosophical club which met first to discuss the ideas of Descartes: it was almost certainly for these kindred spirits that Spinoza composed his *Ethica.* In metaphysics he is close to Descartes, and in psychology close to Hobbes, but his ethical system was original.

Using a system of 'geometric' proofs that we now find quaint, Spinoza finds that all is ruled by absolute logical necessity: there is no free will. Astonishingly, he suggests that 'the human mind has an adequate knowledge of the eternal and infinite essence of God', but human passions distract us from seeing and understanding: thus it is that strife, love, and hate complicate our lives. One should live free from deep passions and from fear. 'A free man thinks of nothing less than of death: his wisdom is that he meditates not on death, but on life'.

Spinoza wrote other works, including a treatise on the rainbow, the *Tractatus Theologico-Politicus* which argues for religious toleration and a rational approach to Biblical criticism, and a Dutch monograph on the relations between God and man written between 1658 and 1660: the *Korte verhandeling van God, de Mensch en deszelfs Welstand* (translated by A. Wolf, 1910).

EMIL M. CIORAN (b. 1911).
   Précis de la décomposition. First published (by Gallimard, like all other French originals by Cioran) 1949. Translated by Richard Howard as *A Short History of Decay* (Viking Press and Blackwell, 1975). And *La tentation d'exister.* First published 1956. Translated by Richard Howard as *The Temptation to Exist* (Quadrangle, 1972). And *La chute dans le temps.* First published 1964. Translated by Richard Howard as *The Fall into Time* (Quadrangle, 1972). And *Le mauvais démiurge.* First published 1969. Translated by Richard Howard as *The New Gods* (Quadrangle, 1974).

A philosophical essayist and aphorist of style and brilliance, Cioran has derived some of his insight from a study of Nietzsche but (as a personal friend) I can assert that Cioran finds more significance in Spanish fatalism, and the Spanish sense of death, even if his favourite books are Dostoevsky's *The Possessed,* and the *Macbeth* of Shakespeare. By origin a Rumanian, Cioran is the son of a Greek Orthodox priest, but has lived in Paris since 1937. He wrote in Rumanian until 1947, when he realized the absurdity of writing in a language dead to him.
   Of Cioran, the distinguished poet St.-John Perse has written: "his lofty thought is one of the most rigorous, independent and interesting in Europe today". Cioran has chosen the aphorism not because of any sympathy towards that form, but because for him the aphorism is the key principle of knowing: that every profound idea will sooner or later be neutralised by its opposite, and may even have generated that opposite. Cioran is a man of pure intellect who realizes the fallibility of pure intellect, and considers all possibilities of men at the end of their tether, including suicide, philosophical nihilism, abnegation of the will in general religion or particular gods. No other writer of our time has conveyed in such exquisite language the 'inconvenience of being born' (translating the title of a collection of notes published in 1973 and translated by Howard as *The Trouble with Being Born,* Viking Press, 1976).

FRANCISCO GÓMEZ DE QUEVEDO Y VILLEGAS (1580–1645).
Sueños. First published 1627. And *Historia de la Vida del Buscón.* First published 1626.

Quevedo hated his mother, a lady-in-waiting to the Queen, and despised himself for carrying around his club foot, to be mocked at in an age not noted for delicacy. His vitriolic temperament ensured that, despite the high quality and great quantity of his writings, he would be shunned by the masses and indeed by many of his peers. His satirical poems show no trace of gentleness in their mockery, but he reserved his bitterest arrows against humanity and its hypocrisies for the novel *El Buscón* (now available with the anonymous *Lazarillo de Tormes* in *Two Spanish Picaresque Novels,* translated by Michael Alpert, Penguin, 1969), and the *Sueños.* These 'Visions' or 'Dreams' vary in effectiveness, the finest being 'El mundo por de dentro' ('The World Within'), in which an old man guides Quevedo through the largest street in the world, known as Hypocrisy, where almost everyone who has ever lived can be identified. Each set of appearances hides its contrary: a widow's mourning, female 'beauty', and aristocratic wealth. The name of the old man is Disillusion.

Poetry of the Netherlands in its European Context, 1170–1930, illustrated with poems in original and translation, by Theodoor Weevers (Athlone Press, 1960).

'Poetry' is understood by Professor Weevers here in its Teutonic sense which incorporates medieval secular fiction such as *Van den vos Reinaerde,* which became Caxton's *Reynard the Fox,* and Goethe's *Reineke Fuchs;* and also the drama of Joost van den Vondel (born at Cologne in 1587) and the mystical poetry of Guido Gezelle (1830–99).

The Dutch and Flemings are perpetual losers in the objective assessment of world literary classcis, for readers as well as writers tend to be multilingual, while the French, British and Germans tend to neglect or underestimate literature from the Low Countries in either Dutch or Flemish. It is unfair to dismiss the novel *Max Havelaar* (2 vols., 1860, but best ed. by G. Stuiveling, 1949) by Eduard Douwes Dekker, writing as 'Multatuli' about colonial conditions in Indonesia (the then Netherlands East Indies); or the poetry of Hendrik Marsman (1899–1940). Professor Weevers' choice is apt, and beautifully translated in several instances. It should be supplemented by an anthology of literature from the Low Countries since 1930, such as the Dutch issue of *Modern Poetry in Translation* (no. 27–28, Summer, 1976). Anyone who has studied German at all thoroughly will find Dutch and its cognate Flemish easy to read, with practice.

Early music in the Low Countries can be enjoyed in *The Art of the Netherlands*

(3 discs, HMV SLS 5049), played by the Early Music Consort of London.

For the artistic background, see *Dutch Art and Architecture 1600–1800* by Rosenberg, Slive and ter Kuile (Penguin, 1977).

YOSHIDA NO KANEYOSHI ('KENKO') (1283–1350).

Tsurezuregusa. Written between 1330 and 1332. Translated by Donald Keene as *Essays in Idleness* (Columbia U.P., 1967).

Two hundred and forty-three prose passages varying from a few lines to two pages, the *Essays in Idleness* were the largely secular essays or ideas of a Japanese Buddhist priest whose way of life was totally removed from the mystical or ascetic solitude common to most medieval priests.

The *zuihitsu* ('follow-the-brush') genre of which these essays form a distinguished part is the genre to which the *Pillow Book of Sei Shonagon* of c. 1000 also belongs. But whereas Sei Shonagon lived for the present, and sought to give her work an air of fashion, of being up-to-the-minute, Kenko shows his affection for the past, and laments a decline in standards both moral and political. His work can be compared to that other mirror for the perfect gentleman, the *Cortegiano* of the Renaissance Italian Castiglione. Both abjure affectation, believing that discretion is the soul of virtue. Both are arbiters of taste as well as of conduct.

Kenko is however as delicate as Castiglione is robust. Where the Italian praises (in words not so different from those which the half-mocking Cervantes put into the mouth of Quijote) the equal necessity of cultivating arms and letters, Kenko advocates a feeling for the evanescence (the 'ah-ness') of things.

Year 32

ROBERT, *Edler von* MUSIL (1880–1942).
Der Mann ohne Eigenschaften. First published incomplete 1930–43; revised
incomplete edition 1952. Translated by E. Wilkins and E. Kaiser as *The
Man Without Qualities* (3 vols., Pan, 1979).

Ulrich, the 'man without qualities', is a partly-autobiographical figure who rejects
an active part in the shallow Austria of 1913–4, looking on in Proustian
absorption at the foibles and petty doings of his friends and acquaintances. On
the surface are the Prussian industrialist Arnheim (based on Rathenau), Graf
Leinsdorf, his friends Walter and Clarisse, Diotima, and Direktor Leo Fischl.
Below the surface of society are dark shapes such as the sex-murderer
Moosbrugger. Book Two sees Ulrich falling in love with his married sister
Agathe, a symbol not only of a return to the womb, but also of the world of illicit
passions, and social hypocrisies.

Musil was driven to produce a masterpiece to end all masterpieces, and he
could perhaps see the irony of dying before he could finish the giant novel. He
saw imperial Austria collapsing around him as he wrote, and viewed the ruins
with a bitterness not devoid of a certain nostalgia. In his sense of witnessing the
rapid decadence of society, he is reminiscent of Hofmannsthal and Rilke, but
really there is no writer in German but Thomas Mann capable of such
meticulously written analysis. More urbane than Joyce, and more direct than
Proust, Musil is a novelist who demands the closest attention.

The same translators who performed such prodigies with his long novel have
also tackled his shorter works: *Die Verwirrungen des Jünglings Törless* (1906;
Young Törless, Penguin, 1961); and *Five Women* (Dell, 1966).

THOMAS STEARNS ELIOT (1888–1965).
Collected Poems, 1909–1962 (Faber & Faber and Harcourt Brace, 1963).

The central poetry of our time remains that cycle begun with 'Prufrock', and running from 'The Waste Land' and 'Ash Wednesday' to the 'Four Quartets'. Conservative in mood and philosophy, Eliot's work was experimental in its unexpected juxtaposition of slang and religious imagery, conversational throwaways and striking similes. While 'The Waste Land' (first published in *The Criterion,* a magazine Eliot had founded in 1922) concerned itself with man's need for salvation at every period and against every background, 'Four Quartets' was more specifically Christian, appearing in sections from 1936, nine years after Eliot had become a British subject and a member of the Church of England.

Eliot was influential also as a critic, a friend of poets (notably of Pound in his early years), and the poetry editor of Faber & Faber; under his guidance the publishing of British poetry became a serious preoccupation of Fabers. He was awarded the Nobel Prize for Literature in 1948.

DENIS DIDEROT (1713–1784).
La religieuse. First published 1796. Translated by Francis Birrell as *Memoirs of a Nun* (Elek, 1959). *Dialogues.* First published 1796–1830. Translated by F. Birrell (1927, reprinted by Kennikat, 1971). *Le neveu de Rameau.* First published in a German translation by Goethe, 1805; first French publication in 1823. Translated by L. W. Tancock (Penguin, 1966). *Jacques le fataliste.* First published 1796. Translated as *Jacques the Fatalist and his Master* by J. Robert Loy (Norton, 1978).

Diderot's most lasting contribution was his editorship of the monumental *Encyclopédie ou Dictionnaire raisonné des sciences, des arts et des métiers* (17 vols. of text and 11 vols. of plates, 1751–72). Diderot worked on the *Encyclopédie* for twenty years, transforming the concept from that of a mere translation of Chambers' *Cyclopaedia* of 1728 into a vastly more ambitious compilation of original essays from over 100 contributors, some of high eminence, such as Voltaire, Rousseau, Buffon, d'Holbach, Montesquieu. The work also featured careful explanations of technical processes written by craftsmen and artisans. The work was imbued with a spirit of enquiry and scepticism far removed from mediaeval encyclopedias such as that of Isidore of Seville, notable principally for their credulity. Diderot himself wrote at least six hundred articles, realising that it would be his most effective tool for enlightenment in an age dominated by the clergy and the Crown. The *Encyclopédie* was indeed banned by royal decree for several years from 1759.

Extracts from the *Encyclopédie* are available (2 vols., Dover and Constable, 1959; and Harper & Row, 1967) but the present value of the text is severely limited, and readers are recommended to sample the pleasures of Diderot's dialogues and fiction, in particular the amusing anti-clerical satire of *La religieuse,* with its attack on forced vocations and the unhealthy environment of a convent.

DAVID FARRANT BLAND.
A History of Book Illustration: the Illuminated Manuscript and the Printed Book (2nd ed., Faber & Faber, 1969).

If most of our reading lives are concerned with texts, that is no excuse for failing to take into due account the place of illumination in the manuscript and illustration in the printed book.

David Bland's general account might be supplemented with David Diringer's *The Illuminated Book* (Faber & Faber) in its edition of 1967 revised with Reinhold Regensburger. The evolution from manuscript to book is shrewdly charted by H. J. Chaytor in *From Script to Print* (Cambridge U.P., 1945; reprinted by Folcroft, 1966) and with an even greater time-span, from oral tradition to the present age, by Marshall McLuhan in his debatable but always stimulating *The Gutenberg Galaxy* (University of Toronto Press, 1962) and *Understanding Media* (McGraw-Hill, 1964).

Though few may own an illuminated manuscript of their own, many outstanding facsimile editions are available, and are works of excellence in their own right: these include the *Rohan Book of Hours* and others from Thames and Hudson. John Harthan's *Book of Hours* (Thames & Hudson, 1977), describes and illustrates many surviving examples of these exquisite works that show the passing of the seasons. Appropriate musical accompaniment would be *The Four Seasons* of Vivaldi (Argo ZRG 654), and *The Seasons* by Haydn (3 discs, DGG 2709 026) and by Glazunov (with other music, HMV ASD 2522).

Birds Through a Ceiling of Alabaster: three Abbasid poets, translated with an introduction by G. B. H. Wightman and A. Y. al-Udhari (Penguin, 1975).

The Abbasids, who created their capital of Baghdad in 750, were ultimately responsible for driving the Umayyads out of the Muslim East and the founding of the Umayyad empire in southern Spain.

Abbasid poetry emerged from a century of Umayyad growth, and came to full maturity with the poets whose works have been selected for this volume (unfortunately without facing originals): Abbas ibn al-Ahnaf (born in 750), Abdullah ibn al-Mu'tazz (861–908), and the superlative Abu 'l-Ala al-Ma' arri *(973–1057)*.

Abu 'l-Ala, from the Syrian countryside, is unquestionably the most intriguing of these poets, and has never ceased to attract criticism ranging from anathema to hagiography. For he was an unbeliever in a culture where race and religion are always assumed to be identical. Moreover from the age of four he was blind and, after failing to establish a poetic reputation in Baghdad, became a recluse within his own home, thus justifying his claim to have experienced 'three nights'.

In *Studies in Islamic Poetry,* R. A. Nicholson observes that Abu 'l-Ala's work 'should be weighed by the standard which we apply to the *Divina Commedia* or the *Paradise Lost*. He sits below Dante and Milton, but he belongs to their school'.

The Zend-Avesta.
> Translated for the Sacred Books of the East series by J. Darmesteter and L. H. Mills and first published 1880-87 (reprinted in 3 vols., by Motilal Banarsidass, Bungalow Road, Jawaharnagar, Delhi 7, India, 1965).

It is due to the traditional tolerance of India that we possess the ancient literature of the Parsi people, also called dualists, Mazdaists, and Zoroastrians. Their original home was Iran, but after the Battle of Nihavand in 642 the defeated Zoroastrians were compelled to flee or to accept Islam. Those who fled preferred in the main to settle in western India, though their numbers have gradually diminished with marriage to members of more dominant religions, in particular Hinduism and Islam.

Briefly, Zoroastrianism teaches that the world of the good principle, Ahura Mazda, was invaded by the evil principle, Angra Mainyu, and the world has since been the scene of perennial conflict between the two, which can be resolved only when at the appointed time a son of the lawgiver, named Saoshyant, will appear. He will destroy Angra Mainyu, the dead will be resurrected, and everlasting happiness will be the lot of mankind. Until that time, the duties of men are laid down in the *Zend-Avesta*, holy books compiled in a language akin to Sanskrit.

The Zend-Avesta (the words mean 'commentary' and 'the law') was probably first written down in the 3rd or 4th centuries A.D., though the original teacher Zoroaster probably lived about 600 B.C., when the hymns known as *Gathas* were composed.

Difficulties of language and interpretation arise because, except for a short period, in Iran the teachings were passed down by a persecuted minority. They were ridiculed by Christians, and suppressed by Muslims. They are of particular significance as the conjunction of proto-Aryan and proto-Semitic religious ideas, but should not be passed over by anyone interested in comparative religion.

MICHELANGELO BUONARROTI (1475–1564).
> *Rime.* First published 1623. Best edition by E.N. Girardi (1960). Translations by Creighton Gilbert (*The Complete Poems and Selected Letters*, Random House, 1963) and by Joseph Tusiani (*The Complete Poems*, Honor Books, 1960, omitting the letters, but including more poetry than Gilbert's version).

Subsequent critics (Girardi and Binni) have refuted Croce's claim that – as one might be excused for believing – Michelangelo did not take poetry seriously. He approached the art in fact with a full awareness of its contemporary state and his own need for verbal expression, using the genre to work out his feelings of homosexual and heterosexual love, his worries about time and decay, and his intellectual and spiritual doubts.

As to the quality of Michelangelo's poetry, it would remain quite remarkable, even if we had no understanding of his stature as painter or sculptor. See R. J. Clements' study *The Poetry of Michelangelo* (New York U. P., 1965; Peter Owen, 1966). The *Drawings* are available in one volume edited by Ludwig Goldscheider for the Phaidon Press, and the *Paintings, Sculptures, Architecture* in another.

The sublimity of Michelangelo is equalled in music perhaps only by Giovanni da Palestrina (*c.* 1525-1594). Performances to be recommended are those conducted by Willcocks (Argo ZK 4), Guest (Argo ZRG 690), and McCarthy (Oiseau-Lyre SOL 269).

ERNST ROBERT CURTIUS (1886-1956).
Europäische Literatur und lateinisches Mittelalter. First published 1948. Translated by Willard R. Trask as *European Literature and the Latin Middle Ages* (Pantheon and Routledge, 1953).

The career of Curtius was divided into roughly two major periods. During the first he believed that his task was 'to make modern France understood in Germany through studies of Rolland, Gide, Claudel, Péguy (*Die literarischen Wegbereiter des neuen Frankreich*, 1919); of Barrès (1922) and Balzac (1923); of Proust, Valéry, Larbaud (*Französischer Geist im neuen Europa*, 1925). This cycle ended with a study of French culture (*Einführung in die französische Kultur*, 1930).

In 1932 Curtius changed direction with a polemical anti-Nazi pamphlet, *Deutscher Geist in Gefahr*, pleading for a new humanism which should learn from the Latin Middle Ages, from Augustine to Dante. Just as the European vernacular languages led to regional diversity and nationalism, so a reversion to Latinity would offer a basis for reunification, at least on the literary and cultural levels. Curtius and his mentor Gustav Gröber (1844-1911) saw the interaction of Latin and vernacular composition from the earliest Middle Ages; scholars such as Gaston Paris, by contrast, could assert that the 'clercs . . . restèrent sans influence sur la poésie vulgaire qu'ils dédaignaient'. The issue – broadly speaking between classics and romantics – is still not yet resolved, except that opponents tacitly take their case as proven. The great work of Curtius, specifically written for lovers of literature and not for other scholars, should be read with two books by Erich Auerbach: *Mimesis* (1946; English version by W. R. Trask, Princeton, 1953) and *Literatursprache und Publikum in der lateinischen Spätantike und im Mittelalter* (1958; English version by Ralph Manheim, Routledge, 1965).

This is an obvious moment to explore Vulgar Latin, in a manual such as Grandgent's *Introduction to Vulgar Latin* (Hafner, 1907), and an anthology such as Manuel C. Díaz y Díaz's *Antología del latín vulgar* (latest edition, Gredos, Madrid).

DECIMUS JUNIUS JUVENALIS (JUVENAL) (*c.*60-*c.*140 A.D.)
Satires. Text with a facing prose English translation (and with the *Satires* of Aulus Persius Flaccus) by G. G. Ramsay in Loeb Classical Library (Heinemann and Harvard U.P., 1950). Translations in verse by Charles Plumb (Panther, 1968), Rolfe Humphries (Indiana U.P., 1958), and Peter Green (Penguin, 1967).

Despite Gilbert Highet's stimulating study *Juvenal the Satirist* (Oxford U.P., 1962) we really know very little of the life of Juvenal. Indeed like most satirists he was somewhat discreet about his own private circumstances, and Professor Highet builds too secure a fabric on shaky biographical foundations.

Juvenal's worth is clearly demonstrated by his vitriolic diatribes on contemporary Rome, never equalled even by Johnson's *Vanity of Human Wishes* or Swift's acid pamphlets. The vivid epigrammatic hexameters sting women and senators, coxcombs and idlers, the cynical rich and the vicious poor.

The satires of Persius, by contrast, are more in the nature of homilies: against poetasters, against sloth, on prayers acceptable to the gods, on the duty of virtue in those accepting public office, and on the recognition of our passions and superstitions. Apart from the bilingual Loeb edition, the only freely accessible translation of Persius is that by William Gifford (1802) in Everyman's Library (Dent and Dutton, 1954) as revised by John Warrington.

MO TZU (*c.*470-*c.*391 B.C.)
Basic Writings. Translated by Burton Watson (Columbia U.P., 1963).

Steeped in the doctrines of Confucius, which he is on a number of counts eager to refute, Mo arrives at a crucial moment in Chinese thought – after the death of Confucius, and before the birth of Mencius.

Mo taught universal love, in a time of bitter warfare, four centuries before Christianity, and in a more extreme way, for whereas Jesus led his disciples against the temporal rule of the Romans and the sacerdotal rule of the Sanhedrin, Mo taught that all men should 'identify with their superiors' in the interest of state unity and common ideals. Conversely, rulers have a duty to 'honour the worthiest': in other words, to ignore the dictates of hereditary posts and titles in favour of giving each post to the man worthiest to occupy it, regardless of birth or wealth.

Other appealing aspects of Mo-ist ideas are moderation in expenditure, and in grief at funerals. Why then did Mo-ism not thrive? In his time, and after it, the Chinese held fast to the Confucian idea that one should pay particular respect to one's parents and grandparents: that loyalty should be graded according to one's nearness by blood or marriage. Mo Tzu's claim that each of us is equally to be respected and loved undermined Confucian ancestor-worship, and was consequently unacceptable. And his appeals for frugality in private and public life went unheeded in an age of sophistication. Mo also favoured a return to primitive religion in the sense of fearing ghosts and other spirits, but he was preaching to an age of materialism, divided very much between Taoist quietism and Confucian ethics.

Year 33

Kalevala.
The national epic of Finland compiled in its present form by Elias Lönnrot. First published in 1835 and definitively revised in 1849. No verse translation is recommended; use instead the prose version of F. P. Magoun, Jr. (Harvard U.P., 1963).

Lönnrot (and his predecessor Zakarias Topelius) took a disparate mass of orally-preserved folk songs, and welded them into a Homeric whole to create an epic of genuinely traditional material.

Rather like the Chinese *Monkey, Kalevala* ('The Songs of Kaleva') begins with the creation of the world, and the birth of a semi-divine hero, in this case Väinämöinen. It closes with the departure of the hero and the arrival of Christianity. Like the Indian *Mahabharata*, the main body of the epic is concerned with a struggle between two forces, in this case Kalevala (a mythical country equated with the land of the Finns) and Pohjola ('Northland'). The three heroes of Kalevala woo the Maid of the North, who is eventually won by the smith Ilmarinen. Other episodes show the attempt to steal the Sampo (source of prosperity) from Pohjola and the tragic incest of Kullervo. 'Recited in the original language', observes Kenneth Rexroth, 'the *Kalevala* has a gripping sonority and haunting cadences quite unlike those of any other great poem in any language'. Longfellow distorted the cadences while imitating them in his *Song of Hiawatha*, which he wrote after reading a German version of the *Kalevala*.

Sibelius, the national composer, is only one of many Finns to have been inspired by Lönnrot's conflation of Finnish traditional songs.

JOHN STUART MILL (1806–1873).
Utilitarianism. First published in book form 1863. Reprinted many times, including Collins (1962, with *On Liberty* and *Representative Government*). And *Autobiography.* First published 1973. Reprinted many times, including Oxford U.P. (1971).

Mill's father, James, educated his son so rigorously that the boy could read Greek at the age of three, was conversant with Plato and Herodotus at eight, and at twelve had embarked on Aristotle's *Logic*, Adam Smith and Ricardo. Despite this unhealthy, unbalanced life, J. S. Mill was able to follow his father to the India Office, and to begin a series of deeply-thought writings, from 1851 with the added pleasure and stimulus of a charming and brilliant wife.

Unfortunately his wife died just before *On Liberty* appeared. He then produced *Utilitarianism* (appearing serially, 1861) and *Representative Government*. Mill realised, beyond Bentham and his own father, that the greatest good of the greatest number is a principle indivisible from the liberty of the individual. Mill's view of tyranny included an intolerant majority, asserting that 'the sole end for which mankind is justified in interfering with liberty of action is self-protection'. His eloquent arguments for freedom of thought and action led to many of the safeguards that the British people enjoy today.

The autobiography of such a man makes absorbing reading; luckily, Mill was a gifted writer with sufficient humility to see his own imperfections as well as those of the Victorian society of his later years.

HENRIK IBSEN (1828-1906).
> *Brand*. First published 1866. And *Peer Gynt*. First published 1867. Translated by Michael Meyer, the former published by Methuen (1967) and the latter by Hart-Davis (1963). Meyer's slightly abridged versions are preferable to the versions of other translators.

The essentially Nordic vision of these two plays, with their very different heroes conceived in a spirit of rebellion against the bourgeoisie, is all the more extraordinary if we consider that both were composed in Rome, where Ibsen had been living since 1864 on a travelling scholarship. *Brand* and *Peer Gynt* earned him an official pension, and made his name as a European dramatist, not merely as a playwright from remote Norway.

Ibsen's years from the age of eight were disfigured by the poverty and humiliation caused by his father's bankruptcy. Both Brand and Peer can be understood in partly-autobiographical terms, as Ibsen wrote out of the facets of his own nature. These two plays come from his first, Romantic period, and should be read before the realistic plays of the middle period which gained him the most widespread respect as a stage craftsman: such plays include *A Doll's House* and *The Pillars of Society*. Ibsen's last period is that of symbolism and allegory, represented by *The Wild Duck* and *The Master Builder*, the latter dating from 1892.

On Ibsen, see Ronald Gray's *Ibsen: a Dissenting View* (Cambridge U.P., 1977) on the last twelve plays; John Northam's more general critical study *Ibsen*

(Cambridge U.P., 1973); and Edvard Beyer's *Ibsen: the Man and his Work* (Taplinger, 1980).

Enjoy the music of Edvard Grieg (1843-1907), especially the suites from *Peer Gynt* (many first-rate performances available, including those of von Karajan, Leppard, Beecham and Susskind); the Lyric Pieces for piano played by Emil Gilels (DGG 2530 476); and the Piano Concerto played by Curzon (Decca SXL 2173) or by Bishop-Kovacevich (Philips 6500 166).

GUNNAR EKELÖF (1907-1968).

> *Dikter.* First published 1965. And subsequent collections of poems: *Diwan över Fursten av Emgión* (1965), *Sagan om Fatumeh* (1966) and *Vägvisare till underjorden* (1967).

Ekelöf was the son of a wealthy Swedish stockbroker who died, insane, of syphilis, while Gunnar was still a boy; his mother showed Gunnar little affection. So the highly original corpus of Ekelöf's poetry was born: surreal and mystical at times, intellectual and dispassionate at others. He was obsessed by music and by Oriental religions, including esotericism. During a séance he was told that his spiritual persona was in Persia, a certain Prince of Emgión, and he wrote the *Diwan* thirty years later, beginning it in Istanbul in 1965. Together with *The Tale of Fatumeh*, this forms the eccentric choice for the Auden-Sjöberg *Selected Poems* (Penguin, 1971), following the more evenly balanced Bly-Paulston *Late Arrival on Earth* (Rapp & Carroll, 1967) and the Rukeyser-Sjöberg *Selected Poems* (Twayne, 1966).

Ekelöf is one of the most exciting European poets of the century, attempting to resolve ultimate questions of reality and identity in poetic styles always appropriate to the theme.

MICHEL DE MONTAIGNE (1533-1592).

> *Essais.* First published 1580. Definitive edition 1588. Edited by Pierre Michel for Livre de Poche (3 vols., Gallimard et Librairie Générale Française, 1965). *Complete Works*, including the travel journal and letters, edited by Donald M. Frame (Stanford U.P., 1957). The Everyman's Library translation is impossibly antiquated (the Elizabethan Florio version is unluckily as famous as it is inaccurate) and J. M. Cohen's selection for Penguin is injudicious.

Montaigne's most appealing essay, the *Apologie de Raimond Sebonde*, is a plea for tolerance which would find ample echo in the thought of the Victorian J. S. Mill.

Elsewhere Montaigne sounds a welcome note of scepticism in an age when the certainties of Aristotelian science were rapidly being eroded by experiment, observation, and scientific speculation. Over the door of his library, Montaigne inscribed 'I do not understand; I pause; I examine' His motto was not a statement or fashionable exhortation, but 'What do I know?'. Montaigne's style is conversational to the point that, within an hour, one feels at home by his fireside, as if one were listening to an old friend. 'Essai' literally meant 'attempt' or 'trial effort', and in this modest manner he strove to articulate the story of his life and opinions without giving offence.

See Donald M. Frame's *Montaigne: a Biography* (Harcourt Brace, 1965).

HJALMAR SÖDERBERG (1869-1941).
> *Doktor Glas.* First published 1905. Translated as *Doctor Glas* by P. B. Austin (Tandem, 1970). And *Selected Short Stories*, translated by C. W. Stork (1935).

From his earliest *Historietterna* ('Little Histories') of 1898, Söderberg became established as a leading writer, his neat, memorable stories lingering in the memory to evoke upper-middle-class Stockholm at the turn of the century. Learning quickly from Freud's discoveries, *Doktor Glas* analyses in the first person the state of mind of a doctor who murders the husband of a patient with whom he has become infatuated. Söderberg is a pessimist in the line of Strindberg and Brandes, but in his fiction greater than either. The play *Gertrud* (1906) was also successful, but for the last quarter century of his life he wrote mainly essays, against the systematic falsification of history by Christians and other sceptical essays, and against the Nazis. His second wife was Danish, and he lived during this latter period in Denmark.

Most of Söderberg's writings on religion have not been translated, but they are urbane, witty, and frequently so accurate that they deserve a hearing.

SEXTUS PROPERTIUS (c.50-c.16 B.C.).
> Works. Text with a facing English prose translation by H. Butler in Loeb Classical Library (Heinemann and Harvard U.P., 1912). Translations cannot be recommended: the best available is by Constance Carrier (Indiana U.P., 1963) and the worst by A. E. Watts (Penguin, 1966).

Propertius, essentially untranslatable in contradistinction to Juvenal whom we read last year, benefits from the Loeb or Oxford Classical Text edition with the prose guide by Butler. Ezra Pound's *Homage to Sextus Propertius* is in no sense a translation, but an admirable paraphrase emphasising irony and playful humour at the expense of the duller rhetorical flavour common to most Roman conventional elegies.

The first of Propertius' books of elegies, that is to say love poems dedicated to the fair Cynthia, attracted the attention of the patron Maecenas, and the young Umbrian – trained at Rome to practise law – found himself a honoured writer whose self-pity and egocentrism were to mark a new phase in the Latin love lyric: he may be considered the direct forerunner to Petrarch and Dante in their love songs. It is plain that during the five years of his devotion to his beloved Cynthia (identified by some scholars with one Hostia, grand-daughter of the epic poet Hostius), Propertius cast aside many of the formulae then considered necessary to the elegy, forging new sounds and a new intensity for emotions no longer conventional.

KNUT PEDERSEN (later KNUT HAMSUN) (1859-1952).
  Sult (1891; translated by Robert Bly as *Hunger*, Pan, 1976). And *Mysterier* (1892; translated by Gerry Botham as *Mysteries*, Pan, 1976).

Hamsun attacked the Scandinavian realists of his time (among them Ibsen) for their superficial preoccupation with social problems and their neglect of the unconscious. However unjust his accusation, remembering that Brand and Peer Gynt are subjective creatures, it led Hamsun to write a literature new to Scandinavia in its emphasis on the egocentric male hero, who is the scantily-disguised Hamsun. Of peasant stock, Hamsun came from north Norway, and his greatest novels (*Sult* and *Mysterier* as well as the later *Pan* and *Victoria*) show the grim realities of violence and prejudice in that part of the country. There are grounds for considering Hamsun a nihilist, and it is possible that, in many cases where the hasty reader detects overweening arrogance, the author is writing with irony, which might appear even stronger with hindsight.

He won the Nobel Prize for Literature in 1920, the year in which his novel *Markens grøde* (1917) was translated into English as *The Growth of the Soil*. This ambivalent book seems to advocate a return to the rural life of an earlier generation, yet the picture Hamsun paints elsewhere of life in the country seems to suggest that we are better off in the more intellectually stimulating life of the city.

JOHN DONNE (1572-1631).
  Poems. First collected 1633. Edited by Sir Herbert J. C. Grierson (2 vols., Oxford U.P., 1912) Superseded in part by Dame Helen Gardner's editions of *The Divine Poems* (O.U.P., 1952) and *Elegies and the Songs and Sonnets* (O.U.P., 1965), and Wesley Milgate's edition of the *Satires, Epigrams, and Verse Letters* (O.U.P., 1967).

No English poet has been subject to more somersaults of favour or disfavour than Donne, the taste in his poetry corresponding roughly to the English taste for wit.

Born a Roman Catholic, he was ordained an Anglican priest in 1615, and many of his poems are filled with religious imagery, much of it outlandish and even shocking. It has been said that he wrote 'all his poems ere he was twenty-five years old', and his earliest poems are certainly among the most individual in English. Even more than Shakespeare, Donne made the intellectual framework of the poem an integral part of its poetic texture. He took the empty pastoral rhetoric of the time and shook out its platitudes, opening with colloquial directness even when the body of the poem becomes linguistically complex. But his major technical innovation was the metaphysical conceit, described (disapprovingly) by Johnson as '*discordia concors*', the discovery of occult resemblances in things apparently unlike, the most heterogeneous ideas yoked by violence together'. Nowadays, informed by Donne and his heirs, we tend to feel that poetry might indeed possess that metaphysical licence.

See J. B. Leishman's *The Monarch of Wit* (Hutchinson,1967), R. C. Bald's *John Donne: a Life* (O.U.P., 1969), and John Carey's *John Donne: Life, Mind and Art* (Faber & Faber, 1981).

Brennu-Njáls Saga.
> Written about 1280. Edited by Einar Ólafur Sveinsson (Reykjavik, 1954). Translated as *Njal's Saga* by Magnus Magnusson and Hermann Pálsson (Penguin, 1960).

The tragedy of Njal Thorgeirsson, burnt alive with his family in his home by a confederacy of enemies, is a central moment in early European literature. Like most sagas (or epics, as they are known outside Scandinavia), the story of Njal begins simply, with characters of flesh and blood. Gradually, however, they become victims of their weaknesses, such as envy or passion, and set out on the road to calamity from which there is no turning back.

The popularity of *Njal's Saga* in medieval Iceland may be judged from the fact that more vellum manuscripts of this story (twenty-four in all) have survived than of any other. The saga describes events three hundred years earlier, about 980, but the first extant MS. dates from about 1300, so it is roughly two stages away from the original. Its author is unknown, but he must have written in the next generation but one after that of Snorri Sturluson (q.v.), the greatest writer of his day.

For the context, see for example the *Edda and Saga* (Thornton Butterworth, 1931) of Bertha S. Phillpotts, and the more recent *Origins of Icelandic Literature* (Oxford U.P., 1953) by Gabriel Turville-Petre.

Year 34

HENRIK IBSEN (1828–1906).
  Samfundets Støtter. First published 1877 and translated as *The Pillars of Society*. And *Et Dukkehjem*. First published 1879 and translated as *A Doll's House*. The recommended versions are those of Michael Meyer (Hart-Davis, 1963-5).

Realistic plays such as these afford one view of the evolving Ibsen. We have already seen the fantastic side of his nature, exemplified in *Brand* and *Peer Gynt*, and one should make time for examples of his allegorical drama, such as *Rosmersholm* and *John Gabriel Borkman*.

  Hedda Gabler (1890; translated with *The Wild Duck* by Michael Meyer, Norton, 1977) stands on its own as a passionate view of the need for each individual to realise his (or in this case her) potential. Ibsen is perennially interesting as a playwright for his ambiguous attitude to the bourgeoisie: he fully appreciates the economic significance of the middle class in creating modern society, but carefully points out that individual members of that class, as indeed of all classes, are subject to strains which lead inevitably to deceit, hypocrisy, and finally in extreme cases to breakdown.

  See Edvard Beyer's *Ibsen: the Man and his Work* (Souvenir Press, 1978) and the biography *Henrik Ibsen* (Penguin, 1974) by Michael Meyer.

JEAN COCTEAU (1889-1963).
  Les enfant terribles. First published 1929. Translated by Rosamond Lehmann (Penguin, 1969).

Active not only in films (*La belle et la bête*, 1945; *Orphée*, 1949; and *Le testament d'Orphée*, 1959), but also in the theatre, ballet, art, and music, Cocteau made a name early in his career as a poet, but it is possible that it is for his fiction that he will be remembered.

His play *Les parent terribles* (1938; translated by Charles Frank as *Intimate Relations*, in *Four Plays*, MacGibbon & Kee, 1962) is a moving yet amusing psychological drama, using a household twisted with deceit as a backcloth to the chaste love of Michael and Madeleine.

Les enfant terribles, Cocteau's best novel, weaves extraordinary patterns around the lives of four young people who live in a world of their own. Cocteau himself made a memorable film of the book in 1950.

Steegmuller's *Cocteau* (Macmillan, 1970) is one of the most sympathetic studies of a man who has seemed as at home working in ceramics or glass as acting on the stage or composing music. A friend of Honegger and Stravinsky, Picasso and Dufy, Apollinaire and Cendrars, Cocteau can be seen as a web of connections with French civilization in our time. But it must be said that he was taken by surprise when elected to the Academie Française in 1955.

Listen to the music of Cocteau's French contemporaries, including 'Les Six' (as designated by the critic Henri Collet in *Comoedia*, 16 January 1920): Arthur Honegger, Darius Milhaud, Georges Auric, Louis Durey, Francis Poulenc, and Germaine Tailleferre.

ARMAS EINO LEOPOLD LÖNNBOHM (EINO LEINO) (1878-1926).
Helkavirsiä. Two collections, first published in 1903 and 1916 respectively. The first collection, of eleven poems and six legends, has been translated as *Whitsongs* by Keith Bosley (Menard Press, 23 Fitzwarren Gardens, London N19 3TR, 1978).

The young Lönnbohm, early adopting the pseudonym Leino, was recognised from his Helsinki university days as a promising poet. He built on the *Kalevala*-tradition, having absorbed the poems of Heine and the Finland-Swedish output of J. L. Runeberg, as well as the darker Germanicism of Nietzsche and Goethe.

His masterpiece, the first volume of *Whitsongs*, consists of dramatic diptychs in which a problem is first set out, and then resolved. Unmistakeably Scandinavian in its heavy alliteration, complex metre, archaic vocabulary, and urgently vivid economy of description and narration, each poem seems to run to its climax.

Leino's complete poems have been edited by Aarre M. Peltonen (1964), and a facsimile of the original *Whitsongs* has been produced by Otava of Helsinki (1977).

Finnish ceramics and glass since World War II have earned a worldwide reputation, and can be enjoyed in several illustrated books.

HENRY FIELDING (1707-1754).
   Tom Jones: the History of a Foundling. First published 1749. Many times reprinted, among the best editions being that of R. P. C. Mutter (Penguin 1970).

Fielding forsook the theatre to ridicule the prim and prudish *Pamela* (1740) of Samuel Richardson, in the apprentice-work *Apology for the Life of Mrs Shamela Andrews* (1741). But within a decade Fielding had become the most famous English novelist on his own account: for *Tom Jones*, a work in which incident is carefully balanced with motivation and dialogue. The modern English novel of adventure stems from Fielding's *Tom Jones,* whose hero is not the black or white caricature of earlier novelists but a real human being of passion, thoughtlessness and changing moods.

   Each of the eighteen books of the novel is preceded by an introductory essay: a procedure later adopted by Thackeray and George Eliot, among others.

   We love Fielding for his hatred of hypocrisy (Square in *Tom Jones*), pedantry (Thwackum), and despotism (Squire Western). A noble, forthright man who helped to stamp out hooliganism while justice of the peace for Westminster, Fielding is a writer whose vigorous prose style is not matched until the narrative of Charles Dickens.

AUGUST STRINDBERG (1849-1912).
   Plays. Translated by Michael Meyer (2 vols., Secker & Warburg, 1975).

Strindberg is one of the most complex personalities in Swedish literature. Married three times, he persistently railed against all women. Some of his fiction is tranquil – even charming – but many of the expressionist plays are vicious to the point of savagery. He has been called stark and humourless, but only by those who do not appreciate the high spirits of *Hemsöborna* (1887), translated as *The People of Hemsö* by E. H. Schubert (Cape, 1959). At once an aristocrat and a socialist, Strindberg was at one time a confirmed Nietzschean, and at another an anti-Nietzschean.

   He is read today for his plays, which are still often performed. A good one-volume selection is cheaply available in the translations by Elizabeth Sprigge: *Six Plays* (Doubleday, 1955), which contains *The Father, Miss Julie, Easter, A Dream Play* and *The Ghost Sonata*, chronologically, in addition to the monologue *The Stronger*. The widely-acclaimed Meyer versions are generally, however, agreed to be the best so far.

   The Father and *Miss Julie* belong to the so-called 'naturalist' phase of Strindberg's art, while *A Dream Play* and *The Ghost Sonata* are 'expressionist' plays. But these labels mean little, for Strindberg is the creator of a body of work which cannot usefully be categorised in conventional terms. Like his extraordinary autobiographies-cum-novels and his letters, the plays are the utterings of a genius only intermittently in control of his artistic powers. It is interesting that Bernard Shaw gave his Nobel Prize money towards a fund for translating all of Strindberg's drama, a project still not completed. The Americans and British have always tended to value Ibsen more highly than Strindberg, as F. L. Lucas does in *The Drama of Ibsen and Strindberg* (1962), a judgement which may be due for revision.

The introspective films of Ingmar Bergman are sophisticated descendants of Strindberg's plays, understating where Strindberg's expressionism tends to strident overstatement.

HAN FEI TZU (*c.*280-233 B.C.).
    Complete Works. Translated by W. K. Liao (2 vols., Probsthain, 1939-59).
    or *Basic Writings*. Translated by Burton Watson (Columbia U.P., 1964.
    Watson translates here nos. 5–10, 12–13, 17–18, and 49–50 of the fifty-five
    sections).

Han Fei's writings constitute the fullest statement of the so-called Legalist system of government, which has never been adopted overtly by tyrants, but has always been practised by them to a greater or lesser degree. Briefly, in the name of stability it justifies the rejection of all theoretical morality in favour of a clearly-defined and harsh series of laws and punishments, and the belief that these controls are valid above family ties.

Han Fei's ruthlessness was bitterly opposed by Confucians and Taoists alike. He was a nobleman – unlike Confucius, Mo, Mencius and his own teacher Hsün Tzu – who belonged to the lower gentry. His writings came to the notice of the King of the Ch'in kingdom soon to become Emperor of the Ch'in dynasty and hence of all China, and the ruler obviously derived great benefit from them, but still chose to attack the philosopher's state of Han. The Han ruler decided to send Han Fei as his ambassador to Ch'in; while there, the minister Li Ssu prevailed upon the King of Ch'in to seclude Han Fei, and the trapped philosopher saw that he was unable to extricate himself without suspicion and drank the poison sent him.

A number of the passages in the classic are clearly by later writers, and one is an interpolated attack on Han Fei which has survived as an integral part of the corpus!

TARJEI VESAAS (1897-1970).
> *Is-slotten.* First published 1963. Translated by Elizabeth Rokkan as *The Ice Palace* (Peter Owen, 1966). And *Baten om krelden.* First published 1968. Translated by Elizabeth Rokkan as *The Boat in the Evening* (Peter Owen, 1971).

The Norwegian rural novelist Vesaas, less important as a playwright and poet, produced a very varied body of fiction and benefited as early as 1946 from a 'state artist's salary' which enabled him to live without financial worries yet did not involve keeping to a particular party line as it would have in a totalitarian state.

The publishers Peter Owen have consistently promoted the work of Vesaas in English, and all these translations are worth reading. Vesaas is particularly sensitive on the relationship of his characters to landscape, and on the peculiarities of human psychology which lead to a craze for power, expecially in the case of Fascism. *The Seed* (1940; translated by K. G. Chapman, Peter Owen, 1966) shows how madness can grip an island community. *The Ice Palace,* far superior, is told by an identical twin whose sister was trapped in a frozen waterfall and drowned when the ice melted. *The Boat in the Evening,* his last work, was explicitly described as the summation of his life's experience.

Vinje, Telemark, is the part of Norway to explore if you wish to understand the background to the life and work of Vesaas.

SØREN KIERKEGAARD (1813–1855).
> *Enten-Eller.* First published 1843. Translated by D. and L. Swenson and W. Lowrie as *Either/Or* (Princeton U.P., 1944). And *Stadier paa livets vej.* First published 1845. Translated by W. Lowrie as *Stages on Life's Way* (Princeton U.P., 1939).

Just as one reads Hitler's *Mein Kampf* or Freud's *Introductory Lectures* without being a professional politician or psychoanalyst, so one reads Kierkegaard without being a professional theologian. As much as Pascal, and perhaps more than Heidegger, Kierkegaard made original contributions to the way we look at fundamental questions of life and religion.

His childhood was deeply unhappy, in the company of a father haunted by fear after having once cursed God, and away from the healthy companionship of other boys. He reacted against stern parental control while an undergraduate in his native Copenhagen by a kind of instinctive dissipation which he later repented. He rejected the girl he loved (Regine Olsen) because he 'was an eternity too old for her' and rejected holy orders: two types of life which would have quietened his torment. *Either/Or* presents two 'stages' of a possible life, the ethical and the aesthetic. *Stages on Life's Way* presents the third 'stage', the religious, as not only the highest of the three, but also that stage which is inevitably to be chosen by the human soul.

Many other writings of Kierkegaard are worth urgent consideration today for their brilliant, nervous style and for the dazzling inconsistencies which echo the common reader's own. He detested the church establishment, which replied in kind by ignoring his work. It is only in the last half-century that he has been rediscovered, and more justly valued. Many of his theories have been absorbed into modern schools of thought, such as existentialism, and church modernism.

While reading Kierkegaard, it is illuminating to listen to the Danish composer Carl Nielsen (1865–1931). His six symphonies, three concerti and tone poems are available on 8 discs (HMV SLS 5027) conducted by Herbert Blomstedt.

CHINUA ACHEBE (b. 1930).
 Things Fall Apart. (Heinemann Educational, 1958; Astor-Honor, 1959).

Exceptional value for money, the African Writers series (whose founding editor was Chinua Achebe) began with this splendid Nigerian novel. Like his later *Arrow of God* (Heinemann Educational, 1965; Doubleday, 1969), the book is concerned primarily with the impact on tribal life of the white people, centred on the experience of Okonkwo, a strong, respected, hardworking Ibo with a slight stammer. We sympathise with his struggle to overcome the example of his father's laziness, and the bad weather which spoils his early yam harvests. Deceptively simple in narrative style, the novel shows Nigeria in many of its facets, and could be read in conjunction with the novels of Onuora Nzekwu (b. 1928), the later novels of Cyprian Ekwensi (b. 1921), and those of T. M. Aluko (b. 1920).

Achebe was born in Ogidi, not far from Onitsha. And if one associates the writers above with a strictly literary tradition, the folk literature of Onitsha Market is no less evocative of Nigerian life. Onitsha market literature (studied in a book of that title by E. N. Obiechina, Heinemann Educational, 1972) is a genre consisting of short stories, folk history, and moral guidance expressed in simple terms in such chapters as 'Sundry Advice About Life' from the pamphlet *No Condition is Permanent* by Okenwa Olisa, the self-styled 'Master of Life'. My own favourite, which has to be read aloud to be enjoyed to the full, is Miller O. Albert's *Rosemary and the Taxi-Driver.* Peter Stockham used to import Onitsha market literature for Dillon's University Bookshop in London, but these booklets are now becoming scarce.

It would be misleading to suggest that the only good African fiction is emerging from Nigeria. One thinks of the Kenyan James Ngugi ('Ngugi wa Thiong'o') and his *Petals of Blood* (Heinemann Educational, 1977); *L'enfant noir*

(1953; translated by James Kirkup as *The African Child,* Collins, 1959) and *Le regard du roi* (1954; translated by James Kirkup as *The Radiance of the King,* Collins, 1956) by Camara Laye of Guinea; the novels of Alexandre Biyidi of the Cameroons written as 'Mongo Beti'; and the novels of the South African Thomas Mofolo (1877–1948) writing in Sotho.

SNORRI STURLUSON (1178–1241).
> *Heimskringla.* First published 1697. Translated and edited by Lee M. Hollander (University of Texas Press, 1964).

An account, in sixteen poetic sagas, of the royal history of Norway up to 1177, the *Heimskringla* is a masterpiece by the Icelandic historian Sturluson (or Sturlason), who was brought up at Oddi in southern Iceland by the wealthy and powerful Jón Loptsson.

His gifts include brevity, vividness in dialogue and description, and brilliance in the organisation of material found in earlier writers. If one ignores the convention of bestowing a semi-divine, semi-mythical origin on the royal genealogies (found from Mexico to Assyria, and from India to Japan), Sturluson cannot be faulted on the plausibility of much of the narrative, with cause and effect clearly demonstrated.

Snorri also wrote the *Edda* (just before the *Heimskringla*; first published 1665) as a manual of the art of the *skald* (bard, or poet) amply illustrated by examples and prefaced by a valuable retelling of Norse myth. It is possible that he may also be the author of *Egil's Saga.*

The *King Harold's Saga* translated by Magnusson and Pálsson (Penguin, 1966) forms a part of the vast *Heimskringla* cycle, but can be read independently.

For a truer perspective of Germanic myth, we should remember that the Anglo-Saxon *Beowulf* and the Teutonic *Nibelungenlied* both owe their origins to the tales of Snorri Sturluson.

For background reading, there is G. Turville-Petre's *The Heroic Age of Scandinavia* (Hutchinson, 1951), or *Northern Sphinx* (McGill-Queen's University Press, 1977) by Sigurdur A. Magnusson.

Year 35

Anthology of Japanese Literature to the Nineteenth Century, introduced and
    compiled by Donald Keene (Penguin, 1968).

A function of Donald Keene's sampler is to enable the reader to judge which of
the many Japanese classics he chooses to pursue, for only the specialist will be
able to read them all. Professor Keene opens with the *Manyoshu,* and attempts a
balanced coverage between the Heian period (794–1185), the Kamakura period
(1185–1333), the Muromachi period (1333–1600) and the Tokugawa period
(1600–1868). We have already read Kamo no Chomei's *Hojoki* (1212) in Year
22.

    For those attempting to read the Japanese originals, numerous grammars and
dictionaries are available. I recommend the carefully-graded *Manual of Japanese
Writing* (3 vols., Yale U.P., 1969) by Hamako Ito Chaplin and Samuel E. Martin.
If you simply want to get around provincial or rural Japan, where foreign
languages are not widely spoken, the *Teach Yourself Japanese* (English U.P.,
1958) by C. J. Dunn and S. Yamada requires no mastery of written Japanese. But
then of course you can read nothing whatsoever while there, from the original
classics to modern shop signs.

    Aspects of Japanese culture which might be studied at this point include
Bonsai (miniature trees), in Kan Yashiroda's *Bonsai* (Faber & Faber, 1960); or
the tea ceremony, in Okakura Kakuzo's *The Book of Tea* (1906; reprinted by
Dover and Constable, 1962).

GEORGE BERNARD SHAW (1856–1950).
    Man and Superman. First published 1903. (Penguin, 1971). And *Saint
    Joan.* First published 1924. (Penguin, 1969).

Although I should always advocate acquiring *The Complete Plays* and *The
Complete Prefaces* in one volume each, as bedside books, there are many readers
who feel that the Shavian paradox is too facile, and the humour dated. Much in

the *Prefaces* can be enjoyed today, but even more has lost its topical resonance, for Shaw was a political animal before he was a dramatist, and too many of his characters take up stage postures which they are never allowed to drop. *Man and Superman* (some would prefer the *Heartbreak House* of 1917 for its greater maturity) is chosen as an example of Shaw's theory that a 'Life Force' with positive assistance can raise the human race to higher levels of intelligence, common sense, and idealism.

Saint Joan is another of his major plays, for its idiosyncratic view of a historical character. Read with John Osborne's *Luther* or Brecht's *Life of Galileo* at the back of one's mind, it offers insights into the personality of the subject as well as into that of the author.

Specialists will make out a case for *The Doctor's Dilemma, Candida,* and *Pygmalion,* but it is doubtful if many will recommend today the large-scale *Back to Methuselah,* too long to retain the interest.

Shaw was a passionate advocate of Wagner in his influential music criticism, and in particular of the *Ring* in his *Perfect Wagnerite.* Explore as much as you can of Wagner's music, beginning with *Der Fliegender Holländer,* the exquisite *Tannhäuser, Lohengrin, Die Meistersinger von Nürnberg,* and *Parsifal.*

IHARA SAIKAKU (1642–1693).
> *Koshoku ichidai onna.* First published 1686. Partially translated by Ivan Morris in *The Life of an Amorous Woman and other writings* (New Directions, 1963; Corgi, 1964).

Saikaku was a popular novelist writing in the Osaka of the Tokugawa shogunate, and is also remembered for his poetry and plays. His experiences travelling the Japanese countryside added realism to his fiction which has been compared by Ivan Morris to that of Defoe, in both style and subject-matter.

Fashionable fiction concentrated on warlike themes (*bushido*), but Saikaku was one of those who sought to indicate an alternative path for Japanese society: the *chonindo,* or way of the townspeople. The merchant class thrived under a stable central government based on insularity. Thus, five years before the birth of Saikaku, the repression of the Christian rebellion of Shimabara had led to an exclusionist policy decreeing that no Japanese could leave the country and prohibiting the construction of ocean-going ships. This remained official policy for two hundred and fifteen years, so the literature of the age is one of our few ways of understanding Tokugawa Japan. Saikaku is best known for his erotic novels (*koshokubon*) and for his urban novels (*choninmono*), and the Morris translation above prints extracts from four such works, including 14 of the 24 chapters from *Koshoku ichidai onna.*

Complete versions of Saikaku are also available: the *Nihon eitaigura* as *The*

Japanese Family Storehouse, by G. W. Sargeant (Cambridge U.P., 1959), and *Koshoku gonin onna* as *Five Women Who Loved Love* by W. T. de Bary (Tuttle, 1956; New English Library, 1962). See also *The Life of the Amorous Man* (translated by K. Hamada, Tuttle, 1964) and *Worldly Mental Calculations* (translated by B. Befu, University of California Press, 1976).

The first master of the Japanese woodcut was Ihara Saikaku's contemporary Hikishawa Moronobu (1638–1714), and the last Hiroshige (1797–1858). Good general surveys include James Michener's *Japanese Prints* (Tuttle, 1963), and Jack Hillier's *Japanese Colour Prints* (2nd ed., Phaidon Press, 1981).

Ch'an and Zen Teaching, edited, translated and explained by Lu K'uan Yü (Charles Luk) (3 vols., Rider, 1960–62).

It is misleading to consider Ch'an Buddhism (or 'Zen' as it is, more familiarly, known in Japan) a religion, because it lacks a church, priests, gods and dogmas. it is more accurately thought of as a stripping away of preconceptions, prejudices, illusions, dogmas, and methods of thinking which the student has acquired in the course of instruction at home, at school, and in the world. Most of these ideas are wrong, but whereas the method of the Greeks was to refute these errors by logic, and the methods of modern scientists are hypothesis followed by observation and experiment, the method of Zen is sudden enlightenment, which may be achieved by any one of a thousand ways, and is probably never the same for any two pupils.

Charles Luk's anthology includes many of the main classics, but one should draw special attention to the Platform Sutra (or 'Altar Sutra') of the Sixth Patriarch (vol. 3, pp. 15–102). Other translations are by P. B. Yampolsky (Columbia U.P., 1968) and by Wing-tsit Chan (*The Platform Scripture: the basic classic of Zen Buddhism* (St John's U.P., Jamaica, N.Y., 1963).

The Japanese value Sesshu (1420–1506) as the greatest of all their artists, and the Long Landscape Scroll (1486) as his masterpiece. *Sesshu's Long Scroll: a Zen Landscape Journey* is available in scroll form (Tuttle, 1959) with an introduction and commentary by Reiko Chiba.

MARIE-RENÉ-AUGUSTE-ALEXIS LÉGER ('ST. -JOHN PERSE') (1887–1975). *Oeuvre poétique.* Gallimard, 1953. Bilingual editions have been produced by T. S. Eliot (*Anabasis,* Faber & Faber, 1959) and by R. Fitzgerald (*Birds* and *Chronique*), L. Varèse (*Eloges and other Poems*), D. Devlin (*Exile and other Poems*), W. Fowlie (*Seamarks*), and H. Chisholm (*Winds*), all published in 1968 by Princeton U.P.

Born in Guadeloupe, Léger studied law and passed the diplomatic service examination, reaching the level of ambassador in 1933. The Vichy government revoked his nationality and confiscated his properties on the fall of France in 1940, when he sought refuge in the United States, and was given a post at the Library of Congress.

The poetry of Perse is in the declamatory *vers-libre* style of Paul Claudel, with generalisations and abstractions that give the effect of living at several removes from reality. Declamatory poetry being at source a matter of tone, Perse became a master of eloquence, of musical expression. Like Baudelaire, he is therefore untranslatable, since his manner is far more crucial than his matter. But given the excellent bilingual editions above, readers should be able to absorb the extraordinary qualities of an abstract, hyperliterary French which seems timeless because it is never colloquial. There is a piquant contrast with the discursive poems of Pound, such as the *Cantos,* in which the message is breathlessly emphasised from many directions in succession, like the famous passage against usury: Perse seems to have no message at all, but to attain the quality of pure music.

In this connection listen to the atmospheric compositions of Claude Debussy (1862–1918) and Maurice Ravel (1875–1937).

MATSUO MUNEFUSA (BASHO) (1644–1694).
Oku no Hosomichi. Translated by Nobuyuki Yuasa in *The Narrow Road to the Deep North and other travel sketches* (Penguin, 1966).

Basho perfected the art of welding together in one sequence the prose vignette known as *haibun* and the evocative 17-syllable poem known as *haiku.* His technique, based on brevity and insight, might be contrasted with the verbal cataracts of Pepys, his near contemporary, or with the discursive and prosaic travel writings of Cobbett (*Rural Rides,* 1830).

Basho is capable of rendering a mood distinctive in a few words, where Pepys will take a page, and he can also educe the spirit of place more individually than can Cobbett. But his true originality lies in the unity of prose-and-poetry, neither subservient to the other.

He is the first great writer of *haiku,* which can be studied in Harold Henderson's *An Introduction to Haiku* (Doubleday, 1958) and the voluminous *Haiku* translated by R. H. Blyth (4 vols., Kamakura Bunko, Tokyo, 1949–52).

And just as Basho perfected the unity of prose and poem, so his successor Yosa no Buson (1716–1783), in calling for a 'return to Basho', was not only a brilliant poet but a great painter (see the *Buson* volume with introduction by William Watson in the Faber Gallery, Faber & Faber, 1960). Buson spent his dying night, his strength failing after a long journey, composing *haiku,* the last of which

looked forward to Spring:
> 'White plum-blossom in the night –
> I thought I saw the light of dawn'

He died at dawn on Christmas morning.

Japanese painting during the Edo period achieved its apogee in the decorative style of Tawaraya Sotatsu and Ogata Korin, whose work is explored by Hiroshi Mizuo in *Edo Painting: Sotatsu and Korin* (Weatherhill, 1972).

GEOFFREY CHAUCER (*c.* 1340–1400).
> *The Canterbury Tales.* Written between 1386 and 1400 in ten fragments, but never finished. Translated into modern English by Nevill Coghill (Penguin, 1951).

About 17,000 lines long, chiefly in heroic couplets, Chaucer's great poem belongs to his third and final period, after he had absorbed and outgrown the early French influences and the intermediate Italian influences.

After a fascinating Prologue, with its detailed picture of contemporary life, Chaucer describes how thirty-one pilgrims (if we include himself) assemble at the Tabard Inn, Southwark, before setting off for the shrine of Thomas Becket, at Canterbury. The plan was for each pilgrim to tell two stories on the way out and two on the way back, but Chaucer completed only twenty-three tales altogether. He knew the tales of Boccaccio, and the French *fabliaux,* while most of the stories derive ultimately from the Orient, being common property among travellers on the Continent, many of them pilgrims such as one might find even today in French or Spanish monasteries on the way to Santiago de Compostela.

Do not leave Master Chaucer without reading the beautiful, tragic yet also witty love-story *Troilus and Criseyde* (written between 1380 and 1385; annotated text by R. K. Root, Princeton U.P., 1926; modern English rendering by Nevill Coghill, Penguin, 1971). There is not much doubt that Chaucer's version improves on Boccaccio's (in *Filostrato*); it is also arguably superior to the versions of Henryson, Shakespeare and Dryden.

UEDA TOSAKU (UEDA AKINARI) (1734–1809).
> *Ugetsu monogatari.* First published 1776. Translated and edited by Leon M. Zolbrod (University of British Columbia Press, Vancouver, and Allen & Unwin, 1974).

Made famous in the West by the 1953 film directed by Kenji Mizoguchi, *Ugetsu monogatari* ('Tales of a Clouded Moon' is one acceptable version of the title) is a collection of nine supernatural tales drawn from Chinese and earlier Japanese sources, and not unlike the stories of M. R. James, though more delicate. The governing moods are those of suspense and night-time. Demons, ghosts and spirits conjure the same world as that of the No theatre, and the extensive notes provided by Leon Zolbrod are as crucial as those to No plays.

We now have as good a translation of Ueda's vigorous *Harusame monogatari* ('Tales of the Spring Rain'), first published in the year of his death (University of Tokyo Press, 1975).

The brilliant artist, calligrapher and poet Gibbon Sengai (1750–1837) has been introduced to the English-speaking world by Daisetz Teitaro Suzuki in *Sengai, the Zen Master* (Faber & Faber, 1971).

Manyoshu. Many printed editions, one of the best being that of 1643. Of the 4,516 poems, one thousand are translated in *The Manyoshu* by Nippon Gakujutsu Shinkokai (Columbia U.P., 1965, with the texts in *romaji*; and without *romaji* texts, 1969). Complete translation by J. L. Pierson, Jr. (E. J. Brill, Leiden, 1929 onwards).

The *Manyoshu* ('Collection for a Myriad Generations') was probably edited in its final form by Otomo Yakamochi, who died in 785, and included a majority of poems written during the previous two centuries. The subject-matter is as varied as one might expect in such a vast compilation, from poems in praise of drunkenness, to those in grief at parting or at the death of a loved one.

The poetic styles, easily appreciated by the modern western reader, are the five-line *tanka* still widely adopted; the longer *choka* more often than not accompanied by the envoi or *hanka;* and the pair of tercets or *sedoka.* The pervading atmosphere is one of simplicity combined with sincerity.

Ralph Hodgson, an English poet, revised the original committee-approved drafts of the translations. Professor Keene has written in his foreword: 'Collaboration between Japanese and Western scholars has often been urged as the best solution to the eternal problem of how to produce translations of difficult works which are at once accurate and of literary distinction but, as far as I know, *The Manyoshu* is the only successful example of such collaboration'.

The principal critical work in English on the anthology is Robert Brower and Earl Miner's *Japanese Court Poetry* (Stanford U.P., 1961).

For the archaeological background, see Namio Egami's *The Beginnings of Japanese Art* (Weatherhill, 1975).

EPICTETUS (c. 55–135).

> *Discourses*. Text with an English translation by W. A. Oldfather in the Loeb Classical Library (2 vols., Heinemann and Harvard U.P., 1935–8). Translated, with the *Enchiridion* and fragments, as *Moral Discourses*, by Elizabeth Carter, in Everyman's Library (Dent and Dutton, 1910).

By origin a Phrygian slave, Epictetus was recognised as a great and good man by his master, who set him free. His pupil Arrian, historian of the exploits of Alexander the Great, collected the *Discourses* of Epictetus and published them after his death.

It is likely that the extant writings of the greatest Stoic of his time were saved for posterity because of their usefulness in the advocacy of Christianity: certainly the 'Divine Providence' to which Epictetus entrusted himself could conceivably be equated with the God of the monotheistic religions. Yet the essence of the teachings of this noble writer, whose writings in Greek have 'done more good than Plato's' in the view of Origen, are essentially practical, and have very little theological content. Epictetus argues against concentrating on the externals of life (such as riches, luxurious beds, or too much food) in favour of austerity and economy, modesty, and a tranquil mind undisturbed by fear, envy or hatred. Moral philosophy, if seriously studied and practised, can be the source of true contentment, conquering even the dread of death. How practical was the doctrine of Epictetus can be seen in the example of the Stoic Emperor Marcus Aurelius, who ruled from 161 to 180.

See J. M. Rist's *Stoic Philosophy* (Cambridge U.P., 1969), which treats Epictetus in the context of the whole Stoic school. Rist points out that Stoicism arose at a moment when Aristotle dominated the intellectual climate, and draws attention to the fundamental difference of outlook represented by the divergent psychological theories of Posidonius and Chrysippus.

Year 36

The Penguin Book of Japanese Verse. Translated with an introduction by
Geoffrey Bownas and Anthony Thwaite (Penguin, 1964).

With a thorough introduction, this anthology of Japanese verse in English
translation can be wholeheartedly recommended. The earliest poet included is
the Emperor Ojin (reigned 270–312) and the latest is Tanikawa Shuntaro (born
in 1931).

As if this were not enough, Penguin then published in 1972 a complementary
anthology, *Post-War Japanese Poetry,* edited and translated by Harry and Lynn
Guest and Kajima Shozo. This latter volume begins with Yamazaki Eiji (b. 1905)
and ends with the concrete poet and graphic artist Ishii Yutaka. It is particularly
valuable for its coverage of those modernists influenced by European and
American poets who have apparently disowned their Japanese heritage, but it
will be recalled that hundreds of Japanese poets wrote in Chinese or absorbed
Chinese models in earlier centuries, so that adaptation to a strange milieu is
nothing startling in Japanese literary history.

An ideal accompaniment to the anthologies might be a study of landscape
gardening in Japan or Hideo Haga's *Japanese Folk Festivals Illustrated* (Miura,
Tokyo, 1970; distributed by Japan Publications Trading Co., 175 Fifth Avenue,
New York, N.Y. 10010).

THOMAS DE QUINCEY (1785–1859).
Confessions of an English Opium-Eater. First published 1822, but definitively
revised, 1856. Many current editions, including that by Alethea Hayter
(Penguin, 1971).

Browsing through the fourteen-volume De Quincey collected edition by David
Masson (1889–90) is a constant pleasure, for this most underrated of English
writers was incapable of writing a dull or inelegant line.

He is best remembered for a frank and frequently nightmarish account of his gradual enslavement by opium to reduce physical suffering and nervous exhaustion. De Quincey explains how, after eight years of taking an increasing daily dose, he realised that he was near to dying from its effects, and determined to give it up.

Fashionable advocacy of drugs during our own century by such writers as Aldous Huxley (*The Doors of Perception* and *Heaven and Hell*; Panther, 1977) and the extremist Timothy Leary (*The Politics of Ecstasy*, Granada, 1970) have made the warnings of De Quincey again significant. We are aware that society has a responsibility to cure suffering while avoiding the likelihood of addiction. Poetic, graphic or dramatic visions 'enjoyed' while under the grip of drugs are frustratingly illusory, for frequently the addict is incapable of transferring the visions to paper or canvas. Moreover – and this must be the cardinal defect of drug-taking – the visions are often so horrifying that the sufferer is permanently unbalanced, disrupting the lives of friends and family as well.

Experimentation with drugs has produced no works of outstanding literary merit, but only peripheral sketches such as the work of the Belgian Henri Michaux.

Twenty Plays of the Nō Theatre, edited by Donald Keene, with the assistance of Royall Tyler (Columbia U.P., 1970).

The No (or Noh) play is a *Gesamtkunstwerk* in the sense of comprising music, drama, poetry, dance and mime, and arose in Japan in the fourteenth century. Strictly speaking the No play is only what is performed (No = performance); as read in a book it is known as *yokyoku*.

The creators of this major art form, using elements which already existed, were Kan'ami Kiyotsugu (1333–1384) and his son Zeami Motokiyo (1363–1443), under the patronage of the Shogun Ashikaga Yoshimitsu (1358–1408). Zeami refined the No play for the court taste, and nearly half of the 240 plays in today's No repertory are his. The protagonist is a god, demon, or ghost, in most plays, and the deuteragonist a priest who summons the visions which the audience will see. The No plays are more poetic and less dramatic than Western plays, and their weight of allusion and literary reference is so great that a good deal of preparation is necessary if one is to enjoy them fully. They are certainly best *approached* through translations and commentaries, even if the No experience itself is incommunicable through the printed page.

Both the puppet theatre of Japan and the Kabuki theatre are deeply influenced by No practice. Ueda Akinari and many other novelists are imbued with No traditions, and Mishima Yukio produced in 1956 the *Kindai Nogakusha* (*Modern No Plays*).

Though the best versions of No currently in print are those recommended above, Arthur Waley's *The No Plays of Japan* (Allen & Unwin 1921; Tuttle, Tokyo, 1977) is a useful adjunct.

ISAAC BASHEVIS SINGER (1904–1980).
> *The Family Moskat.* First published 1950. Translated from the Yiddish by A. H. Gross (Bantam, 1965; Penguin, 1980).

Dedicated to I. J. Singer, the novelist's older brother, Singer's best novel, which has been compared to Thomas Mann's *Buddenbrooks,* is a saga of three generations set in Poland in the first half of the present century. From 1935 Singer lived in the U.S.A., a refuge after the family's departure from the Warsaw ghetto. All his books were written in Yiddish, and stem from an ultra-orthodox Jewish background, though they have a timeless quality which enables the reader to share in a world now long vanished. Many of his stories and novels are set in seventeenth-century or nineteenth-century Poland, but Singer's historical vision is effortlessly convincing.

Other books by Singer worth exploring are *In My Father's Court* (1956; English translation, Penguin, 1980), reminiscences of a rabbinical court in Lublin, and the short stories in *The Séance* (Penguin, 1974). Singer's influence has been widespread: see for instance the works of the Québec-born novelist Saul Bellow (who has translated Singer), such as *Henderson the Rain King* (Viking, 1959; Penguin, 1966) and *Herzog* (Viking, 1964; Penguin, 1969), and of the Labrador short-story writer Rached Gold (also of Polish ancestry), such as *Alaskan Sneeze* (University of Toronto Press, 1965) and its sequel *Wet Handkerchiefs* (University of Toronto Press, 1967).

Hekigan Roku. Compiled about 1000. Translated as *The Blue Cliff Records* by R. D. M. Shaw (Michael Joseph, 1961).

Christmas Humphreys, President of the Buddhist Society, has explained that the ideal translator of the *Hekigan Roku* must be a master of T'ang Dynasty Chinese, must have a very wide knowledge of Zen Buddhism, and must possess intuitive insight into the meaning of the stories and the comments on them by the Abbot Set-cho. Since Dr Shaw possesses these three qualities in a high degree, *The Blue Cliff Records* is potentially an excellent tool for enlightenment, but as in all studies the reader must make the culminating step. Just as the Copenhagen Interpretation implies that it does not *matter* what quantum mechanics is about, but only that it works, so it is impossible to define the *Hekigan Roku* in external terms, but it may well be that it can be observed to work, in the sense that it assists the right reader to realise that not everything can be understood in a linear or logical way. There is a residue that is never grasped, as in Wagner's *Ring* or Chinese celadon, and it may be that it is this residue which the best minds and the best painters have sought, occasionally coming across it, perhaps by accident. Zen Buddhism is a path to such an accident.

PÄR LAGERKVIST (1891–1974).
Evening land/Aftonland. First published 1953. Bilingual edition, translated by W. H. Auden and Leif Sjöberg (Wayne State U.P., 1975; Souvenir Press, 1977).

Lagerkvist was awarded the Nobel Prize in 1951, having achieved international renown with the novels *Dvärgen* (1944; translated by Alexandra Dick as *The Dwarf,* 1953; Hill & Wang, 1958) and *Barabbas* (1950; translated by Alan Blair, Chatto & Windus, 1952; Bantam, 1968).

In fact he is a versatile writer, equally successful in the autobiographical *Gäst his verkligheten* (1925; translated as *Guest of Reality* by A. Masterton and D. W. Harding) and the fantasy *Det eviga leendet* (1920; translated by R. B. Vowles in *The Eternal Smile and other stories,* Random House, 1953).

A talented playwright (*Seven Plays,* University of Nebraska Press, 1966), Lagerkvist also earned respect as a poet. Influenced by Darwinism, he rejected the religious bigotry of his provincial home in southern Sweden, and in his poetry gradually came to terms with a concept of life without religious meaning or religious hope. Full acceptance of life, with all its uncertainties and disappointments, marks *Aftonland.* Serenity and reconciliation with the notion of a personal God are the eventual themes of these brooding, often melancholy poems that are occasionally shot through with exhilaration. The poems are not all obscure, or even profound: they are the bare statements of a searcher after the eternal truths – a poetic equivalent of Hermann Hesse's novellas.

Lagerkvist was a recluse, never granting interviews. One of the few studies of his work is R. D. Spector's *Pär Lagerkvist* (Twayne, 1973).

Explore post-war Scandinavian architecture in illustrated monographs if you cannot travel to see the achievement for yourself.

KAWABATA YASUNARI (1899–1972).
Yukiguni. First published in book form 1947. Translated by Edward Seidensticker as *The Snow Country* (Secker & Warburg, 1957). And *Sembazuru.* First published 1949–51. Translated by Edward Seidensticker as *The Thousand Cranes* (Secker & Warburg, 1959). Published together by Knopf (1972).

The Nobel Prize was awarded to Kawabata in 1968 for 'his narrative mastery, which with great sensibility expresses the essence of the Japanese mind'. But in fact Kawabata was never interested in plot: his strength lies in precise characterisation and the evocation of mood. A profoundly lonely, melancholy writer, he lost his parents while still an infant, and his grandfather in adolescence. Moving restlessly from one part of Japan to another, never settling and rarely completing a novel, he eventually committed suicide without explanation.

Yukiguni, to which Kawabata wrote a number of possible conclusions, describes the visits of a Tokyo man to a winter resort, where he forms a relationship with the geisha Komako. The mood of the book is ambiguous, for the reader finds the episodes characteristic of modern times in their disjointed pointlessness, while there remains a Buddhist conception of the evanescence of our sensual world.

Sembazuru, another essentially Japanese creation, is set in post-War Japan, a period when Kawabata felt himself 'to be no longer living, a corpse buried under autumn leaves'. A young man seeks the company of his late father's mistress and, after she dies, that of her daughter. He finally loses all the companionship he cherishes, and the only woman to stay with him is one he detests.

There is no doubt that Kawabata is a writer to approach in middle life, for he is capable of overthrowing the illusions of youth, and of creating despair in the aged.

Mabinogion. Translated by J. Gantz (Penguin, 1976).

It was Lady Charlotte Guest who first used the word *Mabinogion* to describe twelve Welsh tales drawn from a variety of sources, but principally from two manuscripts, 'The White Book of Rhydderch' (*c.* 1320) and 'The Red Book of Hergest' (*c.* 1400). The first four tales, by a single 11th-century author, deal with the story of Pryderi, son of Pwyll, prince of Dyfed, while describing four branches of the Mabinogi (Pwyll, Branwen, Manawyddan and Math); the next two are drawn from other early British myths (the Dream of Maxen Wledig and the Story of Lludd and Llevelys); five more describe the exploits of Arthur; while the last is on Taliesin.

Thus, though the language and sources are Welsh, the subject matter is largely English and Irish. Laymen are divided in their loyalties between the archaic style of translation adopted by Guest, and the more colloquial, mundane usage favoured by her successors. In either case the book provides escapist reading for those interested in the mythology of Britain. The narrative art is high indeed, the dialogue realistic, and the style both lively and dignified.

SEI SHONAGON (*c.* 966–after 1008).
Makura no soshi. Translated as *The Pillow Book* by Ivan Morris with a separate *Commentary* (both Oxford U.P., 1967; Penguin, 1971).

Sei's diary is a precious document not only in itself, but also as a rare evocation of a period otherwise known to us best through the fictional veil of Lady Murasaki Shikibu's *Tale of Genji.* The pillow-book covers the period from 991 to 1000, when Sei was lady-in-waiting to the Empress Sadako, beginning when the Empress was fifteen and ending when she died in labour ten years later.

The Heian of the day (now known as Kyoto, literally 'the capital') was a society closed not only to the outside world (China being the only foreign country at all familiar by reputation) but also to the past, which was held to be of little value, and to the future, which was of no interest. The passionate involvement with the pleasures of the passing moment or 'floating world' led to the formation of a society in which the cardinal virtues were fine calligraphy and excellence in the blending of perfumes. Science, mathematics, and philosophy were of no account: the Court calendar was filled with rituals such as mimes and processions.

The *Pillow Book* (only a quarter of which was translated in the otherwise excellent Waley version now superseded) is amusing for its observations on nature and striking little poems as well as for the acid comments on men and women Sei found in her narrow circle. The wealth of literary and other allusions in this classic ensures that the Morris commentary is appreciably longer than the translation.

MARCUS ANNIUS VERUS, *later Emperor* MARCUS AURELIUS ANTONINUS (121–180, ruled 161–180). *Works.* Text with English translation by C. R. Haines in the Loeb Classical Library (Heinemann and Harvard U.P., revised ed., 1930). Translations by M. Staniforth (*Meditations,* Penguin, 1969) and by J. Jackson in World's Classics (*Thoughts,* Oxford U.P., 1906).

Carefully selected from a Spanish aristocratic family by the Emperor Hadrian, Marcus Aurelius was groomed to become a future Roman Emperor, as we know from extant correspondence between Marcus and Fronto. He became a convinced Stoic, practising what Epictetus had preached. However, due to a series of accidents beyond his control, the rule of Marcus Aurelius was marked by catastrophes: war with Parthia, plague brought back by his armies who had fought in the East, and the invasion of the northern barbarians in 166. The rest of his noble life was spent in trying to strengthen the Danube border defences, and time which he dearly wished to devote to meditation was sacrificed to military tactics. The *Meditations,* in Greek, were written in army camps.

He realises the tragic triviality of human affairs in the incalculable vastness of time and space, but on the positive side accepts the need to act rationally both as a man and as an Emperor, in pursuit of short-term and medium-term goals. Marcus Aurelius is one of the wisest men who has even been called upon to rule an Empire: much of what he writes is relevant even today.

———————————

Year 37

The New Oxford Book of American Verse, chosen and edited by Richard Ellmann (Oxford U.P., 1976).

The Ellmann anthology supersedes F. O. Matthiessen's *The Oxford Book of American Verse* (1950), which was representative of poetry in the U.S.A. from the time of Anne Bradstreet (1612–72) to the beginning of the twentieth century.

The Ellmann volume brings the picture up to Amiri Baraka, formerly LeRoi Jones (b. 1934), who is also a gifted playwright and novelist.

An alternative book, cheaper but inevitably less comprehensive, is Geoffrey Moore's *The Penguin Book of American Verse* (Penguin, 1977), which manages to include a poet as young as James Tate (b. 1943).

You might prefer to spend the month exploring history and the growth of the present American way of life. This would begin by examining the Constitution and *The Federalist* (first published in book form, 2 vols., 1788) by 'Publius', a pen-name concealing the names of Alexander Hamilton, James Madison and John Jay (Dent and Dutton, 1961). To set these essays in perspective, read a general survey such as Frank Freidel and others' *American History* (4th ed., Knopf, 1975). Do not miss the pleasure of reading Alexis de Tocqueville's *Democracy in America,* edited by H. S. Commager for World's Classics (Oxford U.P., 1946).

ANTOINE-FRANCOIS, *l'Abbé* PRÉVOST (1697–1763).
> *Mémoires et aventures d'un homme de qualité.* 7 vols. 1728–31. Vol. 7,
> *Histoire du Chevalier des Grieux et de Manon Lescaut.* Frequently reprinted.
> Translated by L. W. Tancock (Penguin, 1949).

The translator of Richardson into French, Prévost had been ordained in the Benedictine Order in 1726, but fled when the first four volumes of his novel appeared in 1728. Later reconciled with the Church, he nevertheless devoted the rest of his life to literature, and is best remembered nowadays for the sentimental picaresque novel *Manon Lescaut.* The only link with the inferior volumes which preceded it is 'the man of quality' to whom the story is told.

The young Chevalier, an autobiographical character, meets when seventeen the charming Manon, who is about to enter a convent against her will. She escapes with him and is established as his mistress. When his aristocratic family discover what has happened, they cut off his money. As an aristocrat he may not work and so chooses to gamble, leading to debt and eventually to murder. Meanwhile the delicate and adorable Manon is faithless to him, because she is morally incapable of fidelity: their passion ruins them both. Eventually, des Grieux's father manages to secure Manon's deportation to America, as a prostitute. Des Grieux himself accompanies her, and is present as she dies in a 'deserted plain near New Orleans'. Though the ineluctability of fate connects the novel to the tragic drama of Racine, the wildness of the passions anticipates the Romanticism of Victor Hugo.

The over-simplified operatic versions of Puccini (*Manon Lescaut*, 2 discs, HMV SLS 962, conducted by Bartoletti) and Massenet (*Manon*, 3 discs, HMV SLS 5119) have their own appeal, though Massenet's heroine dies before setting foot on the boat which is to deport her.

JOHN RUSKIN (1819–1900).
    Praeterita. First published 1885–9 (Hart–Davis, 1949).

Ruskin's autobiography was never completed, but we have ample supplementary material in his voluminous letters and diaries.

Among the themes which dominated his life and writings were the supremacy of Turner over his predecessors, a theory fully worked out in *Modern Painters* (3rd ed., 5 vols., 1846–60); the excellence of the Pre-Raphaelites, with whose feelings of morality in art he identified himself; the connected passion for Gothic art and the morality of the Gothic period, outlined in *The Stones of Venice* (1851–3); and – again related – the theory that high morals in art must be applied to society, so that harmony should exist between the artefact, its maker, and the maker's individual role in the commonwealth, as described in *Unto this Last* (1862) and *Munera Pulveris* (1872). Ruskin taught his ideas in working-men's institutes.

As well as following Ruskin's appreciation of Turner and the Pre-Raphaelites in the Tate Gallery and elsewhere, one can trace the socialist thread in nineteenth-century British intellectuals through histories of the growth of the Mechanics' Institutes and the Labour Party, and the career of William Morris & Company, the Society for the Protection of Ancient Buildings, and the Socialist League.

See John D. Rosenberg's compilation *The Genius of John Ruskin* (Routledge, 1979). There is a good introduction to *Turner* by Graham Reynolds (Thames &

Hudson, 1969) and the Tate Gallery's *Turner, 1775–1851* (1974) makes a useful companion to the standard *Life of J. M. W. Turner, R.A.* (2nd ed., Oxford U.P., 1961) by A. J. Finberg.

QUINTUS HORATIUS FLACCUS (HORACE) (65–8 B.C.).
   Odes. Text with English prose translation (including *Epodes*) by C. E. Bennett in Loeb Classical Library (including the Centennial Hymn, 2nd ed., Heinemann and Harvard U.P., 1927) and in English verse translation by James Michie (Penguin, 1967).

Horace experienced the decline of the Roman Republic, its downfall, and the birth of the Empire under Augustus. He joined Brutus, and was stranded without possessions when the cause of Brutus collapsed.

Virgil restored the young man's fortunes, however, by introducing him to Maecenas, the man whose name has subsequently become synonymous with enlightened partronage. As well as helping him to publish his first book of *Satires,* Maecenas gave Horace the farm which ensured his material security. After the death of Virgil, Horace became the most respected Roman poet, and even now perhaps it is true to say that wherever Virgil is revered, Horace is loved. The Emperor Augustus was even named by Horace as his heir.

The themes of Horace are the brevity of life and the need for moderation in all things to make the ideal citizen. His irony is tantalising: we do not know what to make of it even now. Epicurean in his beliefs, he paid conventional lip service to the gods of the Roman Pantheon. The witty *Epistles,* on morality and literature for the most part, are overshadowed by the brilliant *Odes,* 'the most translated and the most untranslatable' of classics. He adapts Greek metres for the genius of Latin in such a way as to challenge any translator: Crashaw, Milton, Congreve, Johnson, Coleridge, Cowper and Swift. For our times, James Michie has proved the best of the idiomatic translators.

See Eduard Fraenkel's *Horace* (Oxford U.P., 1957) and L. P. Wilkinson's *Horace and his Lyric Poetry* (2nd ed., Cambridge U.P., 1951).

OSCAR WILDE (1854–1900).
   Works. (Spring Books, 1963).

It would be careless to read the first four plays in this collected Wilde and then ignore the other 775 pages, for Wilde is a talented story-teller and essayist whose ideas may be mutually inconsistent, but are rarely less than elegantly expressed. *The Picture of Dorian Gray* (1891) is an autobiographical novel of tragic intensity, and *De Profundis,* the prose letter to 'Bosie', his homosexual friend Lord Alfred

Douglas, is the cardinal document in that scandal which broke upon the public in 1895 with Wilde's defeat in the case brought against the Marquess of Queensberry for criminal libel, and his imprisonment, with hard labour, for two years.

Yet all those who knew him agreed that Wilde was a talker whose epigrams and neat anecdotes were worth all his carefully-considered writings together. That is why we still read and act his plays, and in particular those four comedies of the 1890s which remain equally popular today: *Lady Windermere's Fan,* successfully produced in 1892 by George Alexander (1893), *A Woman of no Importance* (1894), *The Importance of being Earnest* and *An Ideal Husband* (both 1899).

Another authentic Wilde is to be found in the 1,098 unexpurgated *Letters* edited by Rupert Hart-Davis (1962; *Selected Letters,* Oxford U.P., 1979).

JAMES JOYCE (1882–1941).
> *Ulysses.* First published in Paris, 1922. First unlimited edition, 1937. Current edition published by Faber & Faber and Random House.

Possibly the most influential novel of the twentieth century, *Ulysses* tells – in the stream-of-consciousness technique which was to culminate in *Finnegans Wake* – the story of a day in Dublin in June 1904. Extremes of parody, fantasy, and realism take narrative fiction to its uttermost limits, but the prose style is still intermittently recognisable from *A Portrait of the Artist as a Young Man* (1918). The protagonist is still Joyce himself, or Stephen, surnamed Dedalus, and the deuteragonist Leopold Bloom, an advertising representative. Molly Bloom, Leopold's wife, is the unseen presence throughout the book whose long monologue closes the book in a psychological and literary *tour de force.*

As the title suggests, the books follows the course of Homer's *Odyssey.* Stephen is Telemachus, Bloom Odysseus, and Molly Penelope. But there are literally dozens of other parallels, levels of symbolism, and myths which have gradually been unravelled by commentators in the two succeeding generations. Two of these essential companions are Stuart Gilbert's *James Joyce's "Ulysses"* (Faber & Faber, 1930) and Frank Budgen's *James Joyce and the Making of "Ulysses"* (Indiana U.P., 1960).

NIKOLAI SEMYONOVICH LESKOV (1831–1895).
> *Sobraniye sochineniy.* 11 vols., 1956–8. *Selected Tales* translated by David Magarshack (Secker & Warburg and Farrar, Straus, 1962).

The son of a minor civil servant, Leskov was brought up by his aunt, an English Quaker, after the death of both parents. After being employed by the English firm of Scott and Wilkins to travel all over Russia on business, Leskov took up journalism and made ample use of his hoard of remembered sayings, phrases and dialect words in stories that reflect on most levels of Russian society. Self-taught, he claimed that unlike most Russian writers of his generation he had learned to know the people by growing up in their midst: 'I have therefore no need either to put them on a pedestal or to trample them underfoot'. This is why his language retained its appeal long after the stilted prose of the aristocracy had died of boredom. Leskov tells many of his stories through characters who played a principal part in them, in language that remains lifelike even when grotesque or comic. As a man he was wise and sensible, full of good humour, and exceptional in adhering to none of the hare-brained eccentricities marring Russian intellectual life in the nineteenth century.

One of his typical tales is *The March Hare,* finished in 1895 and the last he wrote, 'trying to show that ideas can be fought only with ideas and that violent measures for the suppression of ideas are likely to produce the most unexpected results'. Less typical is the story *Lady Macbeth of Mtsensk District* (1865), which Dmitri Shostakovich made into an opera, warmly praised on its première (Leningrad, 1934) but denounced as formalist, muddled, bourgeois, and even leftist(!) in 1936, when it was withdrawn. Re-edited by the composer in 1956 as *Katerina Ismailova,* the work is available in its original form (conducted by Rostropovich, 3 discs, HMV SLS 5157) and in its revised form (conducted by Provatorov, 4 discs, HMV SLS 5050).

See Hugh McLean's *Nikolai Leskov: the Man and his Art* (Harvard U.P., 1978).

ABOLQASIM MANSUR BIN HASAN FIRDAUSI (or FERDOWSI)
(*c.* 940–1020).
Shahnameh. Composed between about 980 and about 1010. Translated into prose by Reuben Levy as *The Epic of the Kings* (Routledge & Kegan Paul, 1967).

Told in metrical, rhymed verse, this epic tells the story from mythical times up to the death of the Sassanian Shah Yazdegerd III in 651 and the Arab invasion of Iran which supplanted Zoroastrianism with Islam.

Firdausi is traditionally thought of as an Isma'ili Shi'a, finishing his epic during the reign of the Sunni Sultan Mahmud of Ghazna (999–1030), a known patron of literature. But legend has it that the Sultan rewarded the poet's achievement meagrely, possibly as a result of religious differences.

The *Shahnameh* is divided in most manuscripts into fifty chapters, each devoted to a single reign, but many of the chapters deal more with heroes than with kings, and particularly with the Iranian national hero Rostam. The conception remains Zoroastrian in its conflict between the spirits of good and evil which struggle to dominate the world. A curiosity of the book is that Firdausi believes that Fate is inexorable and blind, yet constantly explains that one should fight against it.

Stirring battle-scenes alternate with descriptions of nature and lyrical episodes of human love. Beyond everything else, however, lies Firdausi's conviction that Iran is in a very real sense of microcosm of the world, and that its ruler must be hereditary to partake of the divine authority which ensures justice and mercy, order in the state, stability, and prosperity.

The *Mahabharata* and the *Iliad* do not overshadow this magnificent creation, which has inspired many later writers and all succeeding generations of Iranians.

Great miniaturists have given their best endeavour to illustrate Firdausi, Nizami, Hafez and Sa'di. Most monographs on Persian painting can be enjoyed from this point of view, among them Stuart Cary Welch's *Wonders of the Age: Masterpieces of Early Safavid Painting, 1501–1576* (Fogg Art Museum, Harvard University, 1979).

BENITO PÉREZ GALDÓS (1843–1920).
Nazarín. First published 1895. *Halma.* First published 1895. *Misericordia.* First published 1897.

This trilogy within the *Novelas españolas contemporáneas* cycle deals with the difference between true and false religion: between the ideals of Christianity and the Roman Catholic Church's practice, together with observations on how the Church treats those who come into conflict with it, and the reactions of common people to the truly good, innocent, and unworldly.

'Nazarín', as the priest Nazario Zajarìn is known, emulates the poverty and chastity of Christ in a poor district of Madrid in the 19th century. He gives away all he collects in charity, and takes into his home the fugitive la Andara, who has killed another woman. She burns down the home to cover her tracks and escapes. Nazarín is accused of complicity in la Andara's crimes and of consorting with her illicitly, and is forbidden to celebrate Mass. The adventures of Nazarín and his disciples on the road are not only a serious parody of Christ and his disciples, but also of Quijote and Sancho Panza, calling into question yet again the traditional values of society.

Halma and *Misericordia* follow *Nazarín* in taking a single Christ-like protagonist (the wealthy Doña Catalina and the poor servant Benina respectively) and examining the methods by which they pursue and fulfil their ideals. Pérez Galdós uses the naturalistic background and sordid characters of nineteenth-century city and country life, just as Zola did, but his books possess the extra dimension of moral idealism, and are also often witty. Not one of these three books appears to have been translated, so that if you still wish to depend on English translations of Galdós you will have to make do with the more superficially appealing social satires in the same cycle: *La de Bringas* (1884; translated by Gamel Woolsey as *The Spendthrifts,* New English Library, 1962) and *Miau* (1888; translated by J. M. Cohen, Penguin, 1966).

See also Sherman H. Eoff's *The Novels of Pérez Galdós* (Washington University St Louis, 1954).

WALLACE STEVENS (1879–1955).
Collected Poems (Knopf, 1954; Faber & Faber, 1955).

'One of the unchallenged masters of modern poetry', in the words of Stanley Kunitz, Stevens was an assiduous innovator (in such poems as 'The Search for Sound free from Motion', page 268 of this edition) and an explorer who taught a generation that music and colour were as integral to a complete poem as meaning or sequence.

In life, Wallace Stevens was vice-president of the Hartford Accident and Indemnity Company from 1934 and maintained that 'it gives a man character as a poet to have this daily contact with a job'. It also gave him the necessary security to pursue his pure poetry without thought of awards or academic tenure, journalism or such drudgery as prose translation.

Stevens will always be less popular than his contemporary Robert Frost, for example, for he is never afraid to reduce the expression of his ideas to that minimum which is expressed by the correct sounds: 'a poem need not have a meaning and like most things in nature often does not have'. This makes an exposition in prose a precarious exercise, but often any help at all is to be welcomed, and good guides are Ronald Sukenick's *Wallace Stevens; Musing the Obscure* (New York U.P.; University of London Press, 1967) and Lucy Beckett's *Wallace Stevens* (Cambridge U.P., 1977).

Paradoxically, most of the poems can be appreciated only intellectually: that is, the idea to be grasped has no relationship to the concrete; while at another level even that idea is simply the figure of a dance where the overall impression of the dance is more significant than its individual steps.

For those who can appreciate the genius of Stevens, *Opus Posthumous* (Knopf, 1957; Faber & Faber, 1959) and *The Necessary Angel* (Knopf, 1951; Faber & Faber, 1960) will be required reading. His daughter Holly selected and edited the *Letters* (Knopf, 1966; Faber & Faber, 1967).

The American architect who stands out among the contemporaries of Stevens in Frank Lloyd Wright (1869–1959). As a writer he was egotistic and biased, as *An Autobiography* (Horizon, 1976) amply proves. But *The Work of Frank Lloyd Wright* (Horizon), and his far-ranging *The Future of Architecture* (Horizon, 1953) reflect his startlingly novel approach.

———————————

Year 38

BENITO PÉREZ GALDÓS (1843–1920).
> *Fortunata y Jacinta.* First published 1886–7. Translated by Lester Clark (Penguin, 1973).

The longest and greatest of the novels which Pérez Galdós created in successful emulation of the Dickens canon. (He had translated *The Pickwick Papers* into Spanish, and claimed Dickens as a master).

The novel is solidly based on the experience of the middle classes in Madrid from the revolution of 1868 up to the Bourbon restoration, and the gallery of minor characters rivals those in *Anna Karenina* or *Great Expectations:* Don Plácido Estupiñá, Feijóo, Doña Lupe, and Guillermina Pacheco.

The characters of the title are mistress and wife, respectively, to the selfish Juanito Santa Cruz. The marriage of Juanito (like that of Maxi Rubín and Fortunata) is sterile, while the illicit relationship is fertile, an example of the symbolism which Pérez Galdós uses in many cases to underlie the more overt of his comments. The crises arises when Juanito deserts Fortunata for a new mistress, Aurora. In her fury, Fortunata rises from her childbed and assaults Aurora, but suffers from a haemorrhage which she realises will cause her death. She sends the child to her former rival Jacinta. 'A forest of interconnecting novels' makes *Fortunata y Jacinta* a superlative example of that realistic fiction which Balzac produced in French and Trollope, for example, produced in English. Only Flaubert, and intermittently Dickens, reached the heights of *Fortunata y Jacinta.*

JAYADEVA (12th century A.D.).
> *Gitagovinda.* Translated by Barbara Stoler Miller as *Love Song of the Dark Lord* (Columbia U.P., 1977).

Jayadeva of Orissa based his poem (probably originally in Sanskrit, although some scholars believe it was written in a dialect and only later put into Sanskrit) on Book X of the *Bhagavata Purana*.

The eroto-religious theme is the familiar story of the love between Radha and Krishna, for which see W. G. Archer's invaluable *The Loves of Krishna in Indian Painting and Poetry* (Allen & Unwin, 1957; Grove Press, 1958).

Jayadeva's pulsating story verges on the epic and the dramatic, for Krishna is not the disembodied Father God of Christianity but a compound of the spiritual and physical. It can be read as a devotional allegory, or accompanied by music and painting or (less historically) as a work of sensuality apart from religious connotations.

The interpolated songs, with melodic patterns (*ragas*) and rhythmic cycles (*talas*), are intended for performance by artists representing the God Krishna, his beloved Radha, and the woman who acts as go-between. The twelve elaborate songs are linked by recitative in classical Sanskrit metres. Altogether the poem represents the height of Sanskrit literary art, and it is worth learning *devanagari* script and the Sanskrit language itself for the nobility and sensuous beauty of the *Gitagovinda*.

Some readers prefer the older translation by George Keyt (Dar al-Kutub, Bombay, 1947), as beautiful as it is accurate.

SAMUEL PEPYS (1633–1703).
   Diary. Edited by R. Latham and W. Matthews (9 vols., Bell, 1970–76).

Due to his eminent position in the Admiralty following the Restoration of the Stuarts in 1660, Pepys wrote his frank and entertaining diary in cipher. It covers nearly ten years, from 1 January 1660 up to 31 May 1669, when his eyesight was rapidly failing. He did, however, write a second diary of a trip to Tangier in 1683–4 which has been edited by R. G. Howarth as *The Letters and Second Diary of Samuel Pepys* (Dent and Dutton, 1932).

The key to his diary's cipher was discovered by Lord Grenville and passed to an undergraduate, John Smith, who transcribed the diary. It was then 'edited' and expurgated by Lord Braybrooke and published in 1825. But the Pepys we know is the writer of the *Diary* edited in its full form by Henry B. Wheatley (10 vols., 1893–1905) and only recently superseded.

The library that Pepys formed – and he was a discerning bibliophile with adequate resources to pursue his hobby and a remarkable taste for collecting ephemera such as ballads and chapbooks – remains open to the public almost as Pepys left it in Magdalene College, Cambridge.

Pepys is a lovable man precisely because he was at pains to admit to his foibles and follies. Though a married man and a caring husband, he was not above extra-marital affairs and minor misdemeanours. As Secretary to the Admiralty he was in an enviable position to describe at first hand the Court, the Civil Service, the everyday life of London, and his visits to the provinces. But even Pepys did not choose to tell the whole truth, and to restore the balance one should read Sir Arthur Bryant's *Samuel Pepys* (3 vols., Collins, 1967).

This is an appropriate moment to study the English Civil War, and the personality of Cromwell. In architecture, this is the period of the rebuilding of St Paul's Cathedral after the Great Fire of 1666. Note the importance of the founding of the Royal Society in 1660 for the progress of science and technology, leading to the Industrial Revolution. The Society of Friends was founded by George Fox (1624–1690).

GAIUS PETRONIUS ARBITER (d. *c.* 65 or 66 A.D.).

> *Satyricon.* Text with a translation by M. Heseltine in the Loeb Classical Library (with W. H. D. Rouse's version of Seneca's *Apocolocyntosis,* Heinemann and Harvard U.P., 1936). Translated by John Sullivan (Penguin, 1965).

It is often forgotten that the *Satyricon* we read today consists of merely parts of Books XV and XVI: all the rest is tragically lost, and we cannot estimate the value of the rest, for we can infer so little about it. The fragments that remain have been compared with the low Latin of Plautine comedy, with the outrageous good humour of Rabelais, and with the malicious satire of Apuleius, but the real comparison is with the satires of the Cynic philosopher Menippus of Gadara (3rd century B.C.), whose works are almost wholly lost, but can be imagined from the imitations by Lucian and Varro.

Petronius tells in a mixture of prose and verse how Encolpius and his friend Ascyltos (with the boy Giton) explore the low taverns of Campania and Magna Graecia. The most remarkable scene is the Cena Trimalchionis, or Banquet given by a certain Trimalchio at Cumae, where Petronius was to commit suicide. The picaresque novel is also of enormous interest for the observations of the disreputable Eumolpus on epic poetry and against rhetorical extravagance in contemporary verse. The language is extraordinarily lifelike and dramatic, with such touches as 'olim oliorum' ('absolutely *ages* ago'), and the characters are so memorable that they have become proverbial even though they occur fleetingly in a truncated fragment.

J. P. Sullivan's *The "Satyricon" of Petronius: a Literary Study* (Faber & Faber, 1968) is comprehensive enough for the reader dissatisfied with the incomplete manuscript, except that he unaccountably omits reference to the Pompeian wall paintings which are gross enough to please the crude taste of Petronius, ironically called Nero's 'elegantiae arbiter'.

EUGENE O'NEILL (1888–1953),
   A Long Day's Journey into Night. (Yale U.P. and Cape, 1956).

O'Neill's achievement has been to weld American personalities and occasions, scenes and passions, into timeless tragedy which – if translated into classical Greek or Swedish – might pass for a new work of Euripides or Strindberg.

Many of his plays remain formless, or strike the spectator as misshapen, for O'Neill could not write effective comedy, lacked poetry as notably as did Shaw himself, and failed to communicate any great ideas. The greatness of the prose, as each accusing thrust stabs home, is that we are as near the heart of truth, or reality, as humankind can possibly bear. The Tyrone family, in *A Long Day's Journey into Night,* learns on one fatal day that the mother of the young James and Edmund has returned to drugs after agonising abstinence, and her younger son Edmund (*alias* Eugene O'Neill) has learned that he is suffering from tuberculosis. Old James Tyrone, her husband, is a drunken miser, while his elder son is a drunken womaniser. Recriminations against each lead to spoken and unspoken recriminations against fate, and it seems that only Edmund is blameless, until we learn that it was his difficult birth that originally led the family doctor to prescribe morphine to his mother. So even he is guilty. Nobody who ever saw it will forget the Jason Robards-Fredric March performances in New York, or the Gwen Frangcon-Davies performance in the abridged version at the Globe, London.

Almost as riveting are *Mourning becomes Electra* (Random House, 1931; Cape, 1932) and *The Iceman Cometh* (Random House, 1946; Cape, 1947). O'Neill won the Nobel Prize in 1936, before his best work was staged.

Among the best introductions to O'Neill's life and work are *O'Neill* (Cape, 1962) by Arthur Gelb, and *O'Neill: Son and Playwright* (Dent, 1969) by Louis Sheaffer.

Pre-Columbian Peru.

Introductions to the Incas and other pre-Columbian peoples of Peru range from the Spanish accounts to the nineteenth-century *History of the Conquest of Peru* by W. H. Prescott (first published 1847) and Nathan Wachtel's recent, authoritative *The Vision of the Vanquished: the Indians of Peru before the Spanish Conquest* (Harvester Press, 1977). John Hemming's *Conquest of the Incas* (Macmillan; Harcourt Brace, 1970) is recommended, as is *Peoples and Cultures of Ancient Peru* (Smithsonian Institution, 1979) by L. G. Lumbreras.

If you can read Spanish, try to obtain the accounts by Francisco López de Jérez (1504–39) and by Felipe Guamán Poma de Ayala (1526?–1615), the latter discovered as recently as 1908, in the Royal Library, Copenhagen. The selective

Incas of Pedro Cieza de León has been translated by Harriet de Onís (University of Oklahoma Press, 1959), while books I–IV of Agustín de Zárate's *Historia* has appeared in a version by J. M. Cohen (*The Discovery and Conquest of Peru*, Penguin, 1968). 'El Inca' Garcilaso de la Vega (1539–1616), not to be confused with the poet Garcilaso de la Vega, is the subject of J. G. Varner's *El Inca* (University of Texas Press, 1968). His *Obras Completas* are available in the Biblioteca de Autores Españoles (4 vols., Madrid, 1960), and abridged in English by Maria Jolas (Avon, 1961).

For the archaeologist's view, try G. H. S. Bushnell's *Peru* (Thames & Hudson, 1963) or Rafael Larco Hoyle's *Peru* (Nagel, Muller, Hippocrene Books, 1966). The most pleasantly discursive travel guide is George Woodcock's *Incas and Other Men* (Faber & Faber, 1965).

The society of the Incas is studied in Louis Baudin's *A Socialist Empire* (Van Nostrand, 1961) or *Daily Life in Peru under the Last Incas* (Allen & Unwin, 1961; Macmillan, 1962). A subject in bizarre contrast to that of Jean Descola's *Daily Life in Colonial Peru, 1710–1820* (Allen & Unwin, 1968).

Peruvian literature is more alive today than ever, with such figures as Julio Ortega and Mario Vargas Llosa, Enrique Verástegui and Abelardo Sánchez León proving worthy successors to the novelists of the previous generation: Ciro Alegría and José Maria Arguedas.

JOSEF ŠKVORECKÝ (b. 1924).

> *Zbabelci*. Written in 1948–9 and first published 1958. Translated as *The Cowards* by Jeanne Němcová (Penguin, 1972). And *Bassaxofon*. First published 1967. Translated as *The Bass Saxophone* (with *Legenda Emöke*) by Káča Poláčková-Henley (Pan, 1980).

A *cause célèbre* on its first publication, and soon banned in Czechoslovakia, Škvorecký's earliest novel is a magnificent evocation of a small Czech town during and after the Russian 'liberation' of Czechoslovakia from Nazi occupation, and the attitudes of the bourgeois parents, and their children.

The foreword to *The Bass Saxophone* is as absorbing as the two novellas which follow, for Škvorecký, now a freelance writer exiled in Canada, explains how jazz became for him and for his friends a means of self-expression when words were banned. In fact, the authorities soon sensed that jazz was taking the place of 'seditious' literature and denounced it as a form of protest. When popular mass art becomes mass protest, Škvorecký observes, 'the ideological guns and sometimes even the police guns of all dictatorships are aimed at the men with the horns'. *The Bass Saxophone* is jazz-like like in its variations, departures from a main theme, digressions, hypnotic loops and laconic jokes for those in the know.

A Count Basie record makes appropriate accompaniment to the story.

DEMOSTHENES (384?–322 B.C.).

Philippics, Olynthiacs, and Minor Public Orations. Text with translations by J. H. Vince in the Loeb Classical Library (Heinemann and Harvard U.P., 1930). Selected *Political Speeches* from Demosthenes and Aeschines are translated by A. N. W. Saunders in Penguin Classics (Penguin, 1975) and thirteen of Demosthenes' *Public Orations* translated by A. W. Pickard-Cambridge in Everyman's Library (Dent and Dutton, 1963).

The oratory of Demosthenes can be divided into the private speeches and the public. Although fewer than half of the surviving private speeches are thought to be authentic, it was the success of Demosthenes in these which brought him into the limelight as a public prosecutor and politician.

The early political speeches, from 354 to 351, support Eubulus and the concept of the balance of power in Athenian foreign relations. From 351 to 344 come the city-states against the threat from Philip of Macedon. In 344 the impeachment of his arch-rival Aeschines failed, but so narrowly that from now on, until 338, the anti-Macedon faction prevailed. Demosthenes' greatest speech is the Third Philippic of 341. The alliance of Thebes was achieved, but too late.

Demosthenes is the greatest orator of Greece, with a forceful personality imbued with sincerity and moral strength. He was an able analyst of current politics, and skilled in argument and all the rhetorical devices named by the Syracusan Corax and his pupil Teisias in their treatises.

For an understanding of his mind, see Pickard-Cambridge's *Demosthenes and the Last Days of Greek Freedom* (Oxford U.P., 1914), and for the legal background (but without, inevitably and infuriatingly, a resolution of any of the cases), see Kathleen Freeman's *The Murder of Herodes* (Macdonald, 1946), with speeches by Demosthenes, Lysias, Isaeus, and Antiphon.

The *Letters* of Demosthenes have been edited by J. A. Goldstein (Columbia U.P., 1969).

MARINA IVANOVNA TSVETAYEVA (1894–1941).

Selected Poems. Translated by Elaine Feinstein (Penguin, 1974).

Tsvetayeva, like her great contemporary Anna Akhmatova, belonged to the literary world of the last pre-revolutionary decade, that is from about 1908 to 1917, which also included Bely, Blok, Bryusov, Mandelstam and Sologub. Her father was a professor at Moscow University and her mother had been half-Polish and half-German, which gave the young Marina an insight into German literature and a love for Goethe's homeland that was transformed into contempt and hatred with Hitler's invasion of Czechoslovakia.

Her own poetry is very difficult, and is often intelligible only in the light of letters to friends, or knowledge of old Russian folk customs. Further, she admitted to more *personae* than those of Pessoa, for there are '*seven* different poets one could isolate in my work, not to speak of the different kinds of prose, from the driest thought to the most vivid depiction. That is why I am so difficult as a whole to encompass and to comprehend'.

Suffering alike under the Soviet Government and among the emigrés in Berlin, Prague and Paris, she was often famished, constantly persecuted, and finally committed suicide by hanging. Most of her work remains unpublished, and due to its intensely personal nature is unlikely ever to appear in the Soviet Union, at least in the form in which it was written. The individuality of her diction is almost impossible to translate, but the versions by Elaine Feinstein based on literal drafts prepared by Angela Livingstone (whose *Notes* are also helpful) go some way to bridging the gap for those unwilling to learn Russian.

See also Simon Karlinsky's *Marina Cvetaeva* (University of California Press, 1967), with literal translations alongside the Russian poems quoted.

MARY ANNE CROSS, *née* EVANS ('GEORGE ELIOT') (1819–1880).
Middlemarch: a Study of Provincial Life. First published 1871–2 in instalments. Edited by W. J. Harvey (Penguin, 1968).

The moral authority which we have recognised in John Ruskin's writings on art and society emerges again in the novels (and the letters) of Mary Ann Evans, the Victorian novelist who used a male pen-name (as did the Brontë sisters) to secure publication.

She was liberated from bigoted religious views by a Coventry man, Charles Bray, before becoming a contributor to the *Westminster Review* in 1850 and its assistant editor from the following year to 1853. In 1854 she went to live with the writer and intellectual George Henry Lewes, and remained with him until he died in 1878. In May 1880 she married John Walter Cross.

George Eliot's early novels are centred around her home district of Nuneaton and the people that she knew. These novels are *Scenes of Clerical Life* (1858); *Adam Bede* (1859) based on her own father; *The Mill on the Floss* (1860) based on her brother and herself; and *Silas Marner* (1861), in which George Eliot first allows her invention free rein.

Discovering her creative independence, she published novels dealing with Savonarola's Florence (*Romola*, 1863); politics (*Felix Holt, Radical*, 1866); and the Jewish people (*Daniel Deronda*, 1876). But her abilities reached their peak in *Middlemarch*, where she returned to her familiar Warwickshire and filled her novel with a Dickensian array of characters, though without the grotesque element that places a Dickens novel apart from real life. Dorothea Brooke, another autobiographical character, marries an elderly pedant, while in a parallel plot the ambitious young Tertius Lydgate marries a beautiful but empty-headed young woman. High humour may be lacking in George Eliot, but essential humanity abounds in a work that never loses sight of the true purposes of life and finds the characters wiser at the end through their varied experiences.

See also *The George Eliot Letters,* edited by Gordon S. Haight (7 vols., Yale U.P., 1952–6).

Year 39

The Penguin Book of Latin American Verse, edited by E. Caracciolo-Trejo
(Penguin, 1971).

Arranged by country, this unsurpassed anthology selects the best poems from
Argentina, Bolivia, Brazil, Chile, Colombia, Cuba, Ecuador, Guatemala,
Mexico, Nicaragua, Peru, Puerto Rico, Uruguay and Venezuela. Each poet has a
brief biography, and all poems or extracts are translated in prose at the foot of the
page. With a cover painting by Diego Rivera, the book is further enhanced by a
history of poetic movements in Latin America from Andrés Bello to Octavio
Paz.

The reader is warned that the majority of Latin American poetry anthologies
are biased, uncritical, pietistic, and badly-edited, so the Caracciolo-Trejo book is
unreservedly to be welcomed.

LU YU (1125–1210).
   Chien-nan shih-kao. Definitive collection of poems published 1220. Partly
   translated, together with excerpts from the *Ju Shu-chi* ('Diary of a Journey
   to Shu') by Burton Watson in *The Old Man Who Does as He Pleases*
   (Columbia U.P., 1973).

Lu Yu, known in China by his pen-name Fang-weng, 'the old man who does as
he pleases', is the most celebrated poet of the Southern Sung (1127–1280),
corresponding to the pre-eminent Su Tung-p'o in the Northern Sung
(960–1126).

His poems are divided roughly into two categories: those which reflect his
indignation at the peaceful policy which induced the Chinese to accept the
continuing presence and rule of the invading Jurchen non-Chinese minority
from Manchuria; and those which manage to avoid bitter reflection, and deal
instead with daily pleasures of existence. Most of his ten thousand surviving
poems and miscellaneous prose pieces were written after the age of forty, for he is

recorded as having destroyed his juvenilia.

The journey up the Yangtse, on his way to a new official post, is translated in part by Burton Watson, but lacks the originality and piquancy of the handful of poems which continue to resonate in the mind long after they are read.

Grieving until he fell sick unto death for his subservient and disunited country, Lu penned the following lines 'To Show to My Sons':

'In death I know well enough all things end in emptiness;
Still I grieve that I never saw the Nine Provinces made one.
On the day the king's armies march north to take the heartland,
At the family sacrifice don't forget to let your father know'.

Modern Czech Poetry.

Since the publication of *Modern Czech Poetry* (1945; reprinted by Arden, 1979), an anthology translated by Ewald Osers and J. K. Montgomery, there have been a number of significant publications.

Three Czech Poets (Penguin, 1971) is a translation of selected poems by Nezval, Bartušek, and Hanzlík translated by Ewald Osers and George Theiner.

Jaroslav Seifert's *The Plague Column* (1979) and *An Umbrella from Piccadilly* (1981) are translations by Ewald Osers (Terra Nova Editions, 27a Old Gloucester St., London WCl 3XX).

Miroslav Holub's *Selected Poems* (Penguin, 1967) are translated by Ian Milner and George Theiner, while Vladimir Holán's *Selected Poems* (Penguin, 1971) are translated by Jarmila and Ian Milner.

At last the poetry of Nezval (1900–1958) has been put on open sale in Czech bookshops, but one cannot find there the work of the other writers, for they are all outside the officially-approved stream of socialist realism.

Vitezslav Nezval reacted against his own proletarian-style verse of the 1920s after contact with surrealism, and evolved that 'poetism' which exalts fantasy, free association and word-play against one-track propaganda.

Seifert was born in 1901 in Žižkov, a suburb of Prague, and joined the Social Democrat Party, from which the Communist Party later seceded.

His more recent work has been elegiac in tone, taking past love as his principal theme, and urban Prague for his dominant landscape. It has been forced to circulate in *samizdat* form despite (or in view of) the fact that the political content is negligible. But then, in a totalitarian state, even not talking in political terms can be construed as a political act if one is under suspicion.

The Plague Column is the monument in the centre of Hradčany Square, the stronghold overlooking the Vltava and the 'modern' city which dates back to the time of Charles IV, like the castle itself. Seifert uses the Column allegorically in ways that a Czech reader can easily understand, but even here images of past human love and human beauty recur stubbornly and with exactly-modulated pathos.

Holán, born in 1905, was excluded from participation in Prague literary life, including publication, from 1948 to 1963, and the poetry of those fifteen years is marked by a new maturity, culminating in the *Noc s Hamletem* ('A Night with Hamlet'), a marvellous sequence of dramatic dialogues which Holán wrote with the spirit of Hamlet during those cruel years.

Holub, born in 1923, a clinical research pathologist, wrote no poetry until he was 30, and then his purpose was to repeat in poetic terms what he was achieving in science: the discovery of facts about emotions and levels of meaning inexpressible in numbers or prose.

Antonín Bartušek (1921–1974) worked as an art historian at the State Institute for Ancient Monuments, and was poetically silent during the Stalinist period. His work is ambiguous, wavering between dream and waking, the real and the fantastic.

Josef Hanzlík, born in 1938, employs a personal, allusive tone in yet another alternative to the prescribed realism of contemporary Czechoslovakia.

See the issues no. 5 (1969) and no. 35 (1978) of *Modern Poetry in Translation* devoted to Czech poetry, and the broader *New Writing in Czechoslovakia* edited by George Theiner (Penguin, 1969).

HENRY DAVID THOREAU (1817–1862).
> *Walden, or Life in the Woods.* First published 1854. Many current editions, of which the best is *The Variorum Walden* (Twayne, 1962), annotated by Walter Harding, Secretary of the Thoreau Society.

The writing and action behind the publication of *Walden* is almost identical to that behind *A Lifetime's Reading,* for Thoreau experimented to discover how far the 'higher potentialities of a human being can be developed, when one lives deliberately'. Spiritual awakening, for Thoreau, can be achieved in numerous ways, one of which is to respect and revere the natural world. Exploration and travel might, if one so desired, be restricted to the few square miles in the vicinity. He lived at Walden Pond for two years, but wrote an ideal account, following the seasons from summer to spring. *Walden* is not a naturalist's book: it has nothing in common with Gilbert White's observations at Selborne, for example. It was written to find parallels between Man and the world about him, and led to a variety of conclusions, many of which would be shared by ecologists today, such as the desirability of vegetarianism, and the need for a balance between species.

Thoreau also taught and practised opposition to the state on moral grounds. He refused to pay poll tax to a government which had not abolished slavery, and his *Civil Disobedience* of 1849 was to inspire Gandhi in a South African jail, and Martin Luther King in the U.S.A.

B. F. Skinner's *Walden Two* (Collier-Macmillan, 1962) is a renewed call for the sanity and humanism of Thoreau in a world dominated by the urge to unlimited growth and unrestricted technological applications, whether appropriate or inappropriate. Another text for our times of which Thoreau would have approved is E. F. Schumacher's *Small is Beautiful* (Blond & Briggs, 1973).

WILLIAM BUTLER YEATS (1865–1939).
Collected Poems (Definitive ed. Macmillan, 1956).

Yeats began by writing in Irish, but English translations were soon demanded, and it was in English that his poems – of which the finest were written after the age of fifty – were eagerly awaited, for Yeats was a truly popular poet in the manner of W. H. Davies the 'super-tramp', or Walt Whitman.

He consistently advocated a return to Celtic roots by studying folklore and producing such books as *Irish Fairy and Folk Tales* (Modern Library, 1918), and many of his poems are imbued with oriental esotericism.

His best book, found complete in the *Collected Poems,* is *The Tower* (1928), the tower in question being that of Ballylee, not far from the small Irish town of Gort, where Yeats spent many happy and productive summers. It is now open as a Yeats Museum.

His marriage to Georgie Hyde-Lees in 1917 marked a period when he turned from a posturing pre-Raphaelitism to an urgent, spare lyric of sinewy grace. Though he was tone-deaf, his original drafts are in many cases more impressive than heavily-revised versions. He was also influenced by the alleged mediumship of his wife to compose a symbolic system published as *A Vision* (1925) and employed in many subsequent poems. He won the Nobel Prize in 1923.

There are many excellent accounts of Yeats, for he had a wide circle of friends (see Richard Ellmann's *Eminent Domain: Yeats among Wilde, Joyce, Pound, Eliot and Auden* (Oxford U.P., 1967) and he was a man of action, serving as senator of the Irish Free State from 1922 to 1928. His plays were well received, but are less impressive than his poetry.

See Richard Ellmann's *Yeats: the Man and the Masks* (Dutton, 1948) and *The Identity of Yeats* (Oxford U.P., 1954).

JAROSLAV HAŠEK (1883–1923).

Osudy dobrého vojáka Švejka. Written 1920–3 and left unfinished. Translated as *The Good Soldier Schweik* by Sir Cecil Parrott (Penguin, 1974).

Hašek was an anarchistic alcoholic and hoaxer who delighted in deceiving police, law, and all established authority both in person and in print. Like his anti-hero Švejk (a name usually germanicised to Schweik), he ran a dog-stealing business, and edited a fortnightly called *The Animal World* in which he frequently wrote articles on imaginary animals.

The projected six-volume novel, his masterpiece, was completed only as far as volume four, and it was clumsily and unworthily concluded by Karel Vaněk. The book was predictably banned to the armies of Czechoslovakia, Hungary and Poland, for it poked fun at patriotism, courage, and all the high-sounding abstract nouns by which military authorities grace violence. Josef Švejk is a compound of the ignorant, shrewd and resourceful in peasant psychology, and was taken up with alacrity as a model of the cunning working man by Bertolt Brecht in his play *Schweyk im Zweiten Weltkrieg* ('Švejk in the Second World War', 1943).

The novel is based on Hašek's own life in the Austro-Czech army in 1915, before he joined the free Czech armies in Russia, but it is timeless because, although it is obvious that fun is being poked at the Austrian occupiers, in the last analysis the book is a defence of human eccentricity against the apparently overwhelming tide of authority.

If Hašek is the most universal of Czech writers, then Antonin Dvořák is unquestionably the most universal of Czech composers. His symphonies are available in a splendid set conducted by István Kertesz (7 discs, Decca D 6 D 7).

Portuguese Voyages (1498–1663), edited by Charles David Ley. Everyman's Library (Dent and Dutton, 1953).

It may be that of all the colonial powers, the most enlightened were the Portuguese, though the myth that they rejected racialism cannot be supported.

Their contributions to modern geography, to seamanship, and indeed to modern cuisine can hardly be overestimated. They revealed to the astonished western world not only Madeira and the Azores but the Cape Verde Islands, the coasts of Brazil and Africa, and the sea passages to India, Malaya, the great archipelagos now collectively known as Indonesia, China and Japan.

The leaders and pioneers included household names such as Prince Henry the Navigator and Vasco da Gama as well as Diogo Cão, Cadamosto, and Dias.

My own favourite travel writer in Portuguese is Fernão Mendes Pinto (*c.* 1510–1583), whose *Peregrinação* was published posthumously, in 1614, long after most of the classics had appeared: the *Décadas* of Joâo de Barros, the *História* of Castanheda, the *Crónica de D. Manuel* by Damião de Góis, and the *Tratados* of António de Galvão and of Fr. Gaspar da Cruz. There are numerous editions in Portuguese, but no complete version, apparently, in print in English though three came out between 1614 and 1700. One might recommend in lieu of a complex text Maurice Collis' *The Great Peregrination* (Faber & Faber, 1949).

A companion to the Ley anthology of Portuguese voyages is C. R. Boxer's *The Portuguese Sea-borne Empire, 1415–1825* (Hutchinson, 1969). The historiographical approach of Boxer is the sweeping panorama, omitting what the author might consider the trivia of everyday life. He is an opponent of the school of the Brazilian historian and anthropologist Gilberto Freyre, whose works are considered later in *A Lifetime's Reading*.

Like Water, Like Fire: an Anthology of Byelorussian Poetry from 1828 to the Present Day. Translated by Vera Rich (Allen and Unwin, 1971).

A number of tub-thumping, poetically valueless verses mar this collection, but there are some poems which amply justify a pioneering view of poetry in Byelorussia, which was incorporated in the U.S.S.R. in 1917.

One prizes the satire of Francišak Bahuševič (born in 1840) and sparks from the national poet, Janka Kupała (1882–1942). The style of the translation is to keep as close as possible to the metre, rhythm and diction of the original, a method which will please traditionalists and leave others cold. It certainly seems to work more effectively with nineteenth-century poems.

The choice of recent poetry follows the official line, including no dissident voices, which leads to imbalance. In compensation, there is a good deal of historical commentary to set the poems in context.

Alternatively, one might spend the month with *Modern Bulgarian Poetry* (Sofia Press and the International Writing Program of the University of Iowa, 1978) selected by Bozhidar Bozhilov and translated by Roy McGregor-Hastie. Or with *Reading the Ashes* (University of Pittsburgh Press, 1977), an anthology of modern Macedonian poetry compiled and edited by Milne Holton and Graham W. Reid.

FYODOR MIKHAILOVICH DOSTOEVSKY (1821–1881).
  Idiot. First published 1868–9. Translated as *The Idiot* by David Magarshack (Penguin, 1955).

Having rejected eight versions of a plot outline, Dostoevsky started to write the final version on 18 December 1867 'and on 5 January I already sent off five chapters of the first part to Moscow'. Again, 'Yesterday, 11 January, I sent off two more chapters'. The finale of the first part was written by inspiration, and cost him two epileptic fits, one after another.

Strands in the work include *Othello,* Dostoevsky's own epilepsy and other autobiographical elements, Holbein's painting of The Deposition of Christ in the Basle Museum, the ideal of a Christian drawn not from arid Bunyanesque allegory but from the teeming life of contemporary Russia, and an obsession with the portrayal of many types of reality according to psychological observation, both outward and inward.

The novel was composed as Dostoevsky always composed, at fever pitch and without preconceptions as to the behaviour of characters and their interaction but only as to the main idea. In *The Idiot,* as Dostoevsky wrote to the poet Apollon Maykov, 'the idea is the representation of a perfect man. Nothing in my opinion can be more difficult, especially nowadays'.

Though Dostoevsky confessed himself 'disgusted' at some of the details in the earlier parts of the novel, as a whole it is a triumph of the imagination.

New Writing in Yugoslavia, edited by Bernard Johnson (Penguin, 1970).

Though this anthology of Yugoslav literature since World War II offers no texts in the original Serbo-Croat, Slovene, or Macedonian, it is still the most balanced and useful introduction to its field.

The arrangement is not by language, chronology, religion, or area, but by currents of theme and style, a method that works better than any other would have done. The situation of Yugoslav writers is unique in Eastern Europe for the high degree of creative freedom allowed them, though explicit sex and criticism of the regime are still forbidden. Thus, Solzhenitsyn, Zamyatin's *We* and Pasternak's *Dr Zhivago* are translated into Serbo-Croat and placed openly on sale, though they cannot be found in Moscow.

Writers in Yugoslavia are to be found almost exclusively in the cities, principally in Zagreb and Belgrade.

Of the thirty-seven contributors, perhaps the best-known are Miodrag Bulatović (author of the novel *Crveni petao leti prema nebu,* 1959, translated by E. D. Gov as *The Red Cockerel,* Corgi, 1965); Ivan Lalić, whose selected poems of 1956–1969 were translated by Charles Simic and C. W. Truesdale as *Fire Gardens* (New Rivers Press, 1970); and Vasko Popa, whose *Selected Poems* (Penguin, 1969) have been translated by Anne Pennington.

Year 40

JONATHAN SWIFT (1667–1745).
Travels into Several Remote Nations of the World. By Lemuel Gulliver.
First published 1726. Many current editions, including one in Carl Van
Doren's *Portable Swift* (Penguin, 1977).

Most of the output of Swift he considered ephemeral, dealing with topical issues
in satirical pamphlets, yet even so his polemics remain readable today. These
include *The Battle of the Books* (1704), in which Swift joined the controversy of
the day to decide the relative merits of ancieᴜ writers (among them Homer,
Plato and Aristotle) and the moderns (including Milton, Dryden and Hobbes);
and *The Drapier's Letters* (1724) in which the now-notorious Dean of St Patrick's,
Dublin, attacked the English policy of debasing the Irish currency.

Gulliver's Travels is a triumph of devastating satire in the form of sustained
imaginative fiction, divided into four parts. In the first part, the surgeon Gulliver
is shipwrecked on the island of Lilliput, whose inhabitants are six inches high.
This is not inconvient to them, however, for everything else is on the same scale.
To Gulliver, the emperor's pomp and the feuds of the citizens appear ridiculously
petty. Religious animosities at hand are satirized in the dispute over whether to
break eggs at the broad end or the narrow. In part two Gulliver's condition is
reversed, for he looks tiny among the towering Brobdingnagians, but the English
politicians and sectarians are again made to seem ludicrously disputatious by the
wise King of Brobdingnag. In part three Gulliver finds himself on the flying
island of Laputa and the continent Lagado, where the butt of Swift's satire are
philosophers and scientists. The philosophers are completely ignorant of
practical affairs, and the scientists are involved in schemes of no value to
mankind. In part four, Swift describes the country of the wise horses or
Houyhnhnms, which he contrasts with the behaviour of Yahoos, or brutes in
human form.

While Swift has often been considered a misanthropist, it might be more
accurate to think of *Gulliver's Travels* as a warning: if we can avoid these pitfalls of
vanity and enmity, concord and reason may eventually prevail.

Polish Post-War Poetry, selected and translated by Czesław Miłosz (Penguin, 1970).

Miłosz, awarded the Nobel Prize for Literature in 1980, has chosen for the most part poems published since the abolition of censorship in 1956, and those not written in the traditional syllabo-tonic verse ('feet' within a line of counted syllables), which are impossible to translate satisfactorily into English. The first writer included is Leopold Staff (1878–1957) and the last Urszula Kozioł (b. 1935).

The two dominant voices are those of Tadeusz Różewicz (b. 1921) and Zbigniew Herbert (b. 1924).

Adam Czerniawski has translated selected poems by Różewicz as *Faces of Anxiety* (Rapp & Whiting, 1969). The parallel with Samuel Beckett's theatre of the absurd is almost exact, though Różewicz is better known for his poems than for his plays. A nihilist humanitarian, he has rejected all ideology, and considers art itself as quite insufficient to express the desperation of the human spirit during and after a cruel war. He has been influential with the current generation of young Polish writers.

Zbigniew Herbert, by contrast, cynically expects no revolution to emerge from the pages of a poetry book: his strategy is ironic paraphrase, for his early work was banned first by the Nazis who occupied Poland and then by the Communists who drove the Nazis out, and it was only in 1956 that Herbert's first book was published. In the 'Elegy of Fortinbras', Fortinbras the commissar mourns Hamlet the dreamer, meditating that at the funeral 'there will be no candles no singing only cannon-fuses and bursts/crêpe dragged on the pavement helmets boots artillery horses/drums drums I know nothing exquisite/those will be my manoeuvres before I start to rule/ one has to take the city by the neck and shake it a bit. . .' The *Selected Poems* of Herbert are translated by Czesław Miłosz and Peter Dale Scott (Penguin, 1968). Herbert was introduced to the West by A. Alvarez, who has written *Under Pressure* (Penguin, 1965) on poetry in Eastern Europe and the U.S.A.

NATSUME KINNOSUKE (NATSUME SOSEKI) (1867–1916).
  Kokoro. First published 1914. Translated by E. McClellan (University of Chicago Press, 1956; Peter Owen, 1968).

Soseki was sent to be adopted at the age of two, but was taken back when his adoptive parents separated seven years later. The knowledge of this rejection clearly coloured the rest of his life, for he chose to reject his Chinese-centred upbringing for the study of English at Tokyo University and (after he had spent some time teaching in Tokyo and the provinces) he rejected the English society into which he was thrust for two years on taking up a Japanese government scholarship in 1900. He used the time in England to read intensively, developing a theory and technique of the novel which enabled him to achieve in Japan what European realists and descriptive writers had already achieved.

On his return to Japan he was offered an academic appointment, but in 1907 took the almost unprecedented step of resigning to take up a post with the *Asahi Shimbun* newspaper as a fiction-writer and literary editor. As a man he was emotionally unbalanced: according to some actually insane. He was a convinced lifelong Buddhist, but it is in *Kokoro* (literally 'Heart') that all of the strands come together, with his previously-hinted homosexuality. The first part of the novel tells of an encounter at the resort of Kamakura between a student and an older man, the Master *(Sensei)*. The Master is attracted to the student, but keeps aloof. In the second part the narrator-student visits his dying father, but outrageously deserts the bedside when he receives a message that the Master too is dying. The third part is the full text of the message, where the Master reveals a previous homosexual relationship.

Soseki then wrote an explicitly autobiographical novel: *Michikusa* (1916; translated as 'Grass on the Wayside', University of Chicago Press, 1968; Peter Owen, 1969), dealing with the breakdown of his marriage in the period before he turned to writing as a career.

Soseki, with Shimazaki Toson, can be considered a forerunner of the contemporary novel in Japan, having released psychological realism from the bonds of convention.

Poems of Black Africa, edited and introduced by Wole Soyinka (Heinemann Educational, 1975).

This is the most intelligent and comprehensive of African poetry anthologies in English. Boundaries of authorship, period, region and style are eliminated: Soyinka's approach is thematic, and he has selected examples to illustrate such themes as 'Ancestors and Gods' or 'Mortality' from both traditional and modern literary sources. Only in this way is it possible to discover how far modern African authors have remained within their tradition. Translations are mainly from the French and Portuguese, though Yoruba, Swahili, Zulu and Bakiga are also represented.

Wole Soyinka is an important Nigerian poet and playwright perhaps best known for the play *Kongi's Harvest* (Oxford U.P., 1967). His hilariously satirical poem *Telephone Conversation* is one of the poems in the less extensive but equally enjoyable *Modern Poetry from Africa* edited by Gerald Moore and Ulli Beier (Penguin, 1963), and all the books on African and other literatures by Ulli Beier are worth acquiring.

For a bilingual anthology of a major African language it would be hard to improve on *Poetic heritage: Igbo traditional verse,* compiled and translated with an introduction by Romanus N. Egudu and Donatus I. Nwoga (Nwankwo-Ifejika & Co., 10 Ibiam St., Uwani, P.O. Box 430, Enugu, Nigeria, 1971).

An Anthology of African and Malagasy Poetry in French, edited by Clive Wake (Oxford U.P., 1965) should be accompanied by A. C. Brench's *Writing in French from Senegal to Cameroon* (Oxford U.P., 1967) and updated by the francophone poetry of Africa anthology in *Modern Poetry in Translation* no. 37–38, Winter 1979).

The principal visual art in Black Africa is sculpture, and there are many excellent introductions to the subject, among them William Fagg's *Tribes and Forms in African Art* (Methuen, 1966) and *African Art* by Michel Leiris and Jacqueline Delange (Thames & Hudson, 1968).

If you are more interested in African history than in African literature, then a major book to investigate is the *General History of Africa,* the second volume of which is devoted to *Ancient Civilizations of Africa* (Unesco, Heinemann and University of California Press, 1981).

JAMES COOK (1728–1779).
   The Journals of Captain James Cook on his Voyages of Discovery. First
   published 1773–1784. Edited by J. C. Beaglehole. (4 vols. and portfolio
   of charts, Hakluyt Society, 1955–1974).

Cook's first voyage, in the *Endeavour* (1768–1771) was round the Cape of Good Hope to Australia and New Zealand. The second, in the *Resolution* and *Adventure* (1772–1775) took Cook and his men to the South Pole and round the world, discovering to the West many Pacific islands. The third, in the *Resolution* and *Discovery* (1776–1780), was to discover the Northwest Passage, via the Pacific Ocean, during the course of which Cook was murdered in Hawaii.

One of Cook's many achievements was to inform the West about much of the Pacific then uncharted, and another was to pave the way for the British colonisation of Australia and New Zealand. It was he who demonstrated that there is no great southern continent, the 'fact' of which had up till then been assumed and taught. But he suggested the existence of antarctic land masses on the other side of the gigantic ice patches, a view proved true as late as the nineteenth century.

As a seaman and humanitarian Cook was a notable pioneer, insisting on proper food and conditions for crews under his command, and putting into effect the suggestion first made by James Lind in 1775 that limes should be available on board at all times to counteract scurvy. It is this precedent that caused British sailors to be called 'lime-juicers' or 'limeys'.

Readers keen to sample the adventures of Cook without investing in the sumptuous Hakluyt Society set listed above might try the selection edited by John Barrow in Everyman's Library (Dent and Dutton, 1969) or that edited by A. Grenfell Price as *Explorations of Captain James Cook in the Pacific* (Dover and Constable, 1968).

The artistic background is described in *Oceania and Australia* by A. Bühler, T. Barrow and C. P. Mountford in Art of the World (Methuen, 1962).

ADAM BERNARD MICKIEWICZ (1798–1855).
Pan Tadeusz. First published 1834. Translated by W. Kirkconnell in Everyman's Library (Dent and Dutton, 1966).

The national poet of Poland was born a Russian subject in Lithuania among peasants who spoke White Ruthenian. He attended a Dominican secondary school and the best Polish university of the period – Wilno.

Mickiewicz's first two poetic collections in 1822 (*Ballady i romanse*) and 1823 (*Poezye II*) revealed an important new poet of the Romantic school, reviled by the classicists of Warsaw and hailed by the young. Arrested with other young men for 'spreading unreasonable Polish nationalism', Mickiewicz was compelled to leave Poland and live in Russia. The result was predictably to exacerbate nationalistic unrest in Poland, where the young poet was seen as a hero.

His poetic inspiration culminated in the epic poem *Pan Tadeusz,* a vast portrayal of life among the Polish squires in the Lithuania of 1811 and 1812, viewed with nostalgia. Written in verse of thirteen-syllable lines, the standard Polish metre, it reads as vividly today as ever. There is a verse translation by K. Mackenzie (Polish Cultural Foundation, 9 Charleville Road, London W14, 1964), but it may be that English prose treatment gives a more authentic ring to the story, which is essentially narrative.

Later in life Mickiewicz wrote little, for he was depressed by his wife Celina's mental illness and became obsessed with the mysticism of Böhme and Böhme's disciple Louis-Claude de Saint-Martin. Before reading Saint-Martin's *Des erreurs et de la vérité* (1775), Voltaire had said: 'S'il est bon, il doit contenir cinquante volumes in-folio pour la première partie, et une demi-page pour la seconde'. After reading it, Voltaire observed: 'Je ne crois pas qu'on ait jamais rien imprimé de plus absurde, de plus obscur, de plus fou et de plus sot'.

The pervasive nature of Mickiewicz's influence may be judged from *Adam Mickiewicz in World Literature,* a symposium edited by Wacław Lednicki (University of California Press, Berkeley, 1956; reprinted by Greenwood Press, 1976).

RICHARD BRINSLEY SHERIDAN (1751–1816).
  Plays. Edited by Joseph Knight in World's Classics (Oxford U.P., 1951).

Sheridan is today remembered for *The Rivals* (1775), a failure when first produced, and for *The School for Scandal* (1777), which has held the stage for two centuries without losing an iota of its appeal.

The 'rivals' are Captain Absolute, son of the comically irascible Sir Anthony Absolute, and the docile rustic Bob Acres, who believes that his rival is a certain 'Ensign Beverley'. Both intend to marry Lydia Languish, the niece and ward of Mrs. Malaprop. Sheridan injected more than a customary dose of fun into *The Rivals* with such straight-faced malapropisms (from the French *mal à propos,* 'inappropriate') as 'a nice derangement of epitaphs' for 'a nice arrangement of epigrams'. Shakespeare used this device, but Sheridan derived it from Winifred Jenkins in Smollett's novel *The Expedition of Humphry Clinker* (1771).

The School for Scandal coruscatingly mocked the tendency of the leisured classes to murder reputations on suspicion, for the truth was often nearer to the worst imputation than to the best. The scandalmongers, Sir Benjamin Backbite, Lady Sneerwell, and Mrs Candour, provide a comic thread through the play, but the main plot concerns two brothers, Charles and Joseph, and their relations with a rich uncle, Sir Oliver Surface, who returns home from India unexpectedly and tests his nephews' characters.

A great deal of light is shed on Sheridan and his times by his *Letters,* edited by Cecil Price (3 vols., Oxford U.P., 1966).

Sasuntsi Davith. The Armenian national epic, translated as *Daredevils of Sassoun* by L. Surmelian (Allen & Unwin, 1966). Also translated in prose by Mischa Kudian as *The Saga of Sassoun* (Kaye & Ward, 1970), and in French verse by F. Feydit (Paris, 1964).

The pulsating history of Armenia from the foundation of Urartu, the original nation state on Armenian soil (*c.* 824–*c.* 585 B.C.), to the genocide by the Turks in 1915, followed by absorption within the Soviet Union and Turkey, forms material for a dozen possible epics, so it is hardly surprising that the greatest monument of Armenian literature is an epic, variously rendered 'David of Sassoun' or 'The Daredevils of Sassoun'.

Four generations of the town and castle of Sassoun are the heroes: the founding twins Sanasar and Balthasar; Meherr the Elder, son of Sanasar; David, son of Meherr the Elder; and Meherr the Younger, son of David. It is the last hero who plunges into the Underworld, promising to return to the world when peace and justice prevail once more. Armenia was christianized as early as 301, by St Gregory the Illuminator. The nucleus of the historical *Sasuntsi Davith,* however, dates back to the Islamic invasions, when Christianity's survival was threatened. Other elements are mythical, and yet others utopian, but the result is surprisingly unified if one considers its oral tradition.

Léon Surmelian has also compiled forty Armenian folk-tales in the fascinating *Apples of Immortality* (Allen & Unwin, 1968).

Background reading would certainly include D. M. Lang's *Armenia, Cradle of Civilization* (2nd ed., Allen & Unwin, 1978), while the archaeological aspects are treated in depth in *Urartu* by Boris B. Piotrovsky (Barrie & Rockliff, 1969).

SŁAWOMIR MROZEK (b. 1930).
> *Tango.* First performed in Polish 1964. Translated by Nicholas Bethell (Cape, 1968). And *The Ugupu Bird.* Translated (from three Polish books) by Konrad Syrop (Macdonald, 1968).

Tango was the first full-length play that the Polish dramatist wrote, though his short plays had already delighted Polish audiences with their witty barbs aimed at recognisable targets. *The Police,* for instance, first performed in 1958, shows the dismay among the police when the last ageing revolutionary signs the act of allegiance. To ensure the survival of the political police, a sergeant decides to go to jail himself.

Tango is much more complex, being based on a deliberately confused and anarchic approach to the Hamlet story, borrowing from surrealism and of course from the Polish political situation, since in Poland almost everything *finit en politique.*

The Ugupu Bird consists of seventeen stories, each revolving a single idea or devoted to parody. In *Ad Astra,* for example, a group of brilliantly-inspired and unfailingly industrious young authors undermines the existing Writers' Union, while *Check!* describes the activities of part-time human chess-pieces.

Satire also runs through the 'play in 77 scenes' called *Vatzlav* (Cape, 1972), a brilliant political fable with a cast of absurd characters who are again all too recognisable.

Romanian Poems: a bilingual anthology, by Sever Trifu and Dumitru Ciocoi-Pop (Dacia Publishing House, Cluj, 1972). And *Poesía rumana contemporánea,* translated into Spanish by Darie Novăceanu (Seix Barral, Barcelona, 1972).

Romanian poetry is undervalued in the Anglo-Saxon world, and there is no excellent anthology in English to represent the whole field.

The Trifu/Ciocoi-Pop collection has mediocre versions, and covers only the period from the ageless patriotic folk ballad *Miorița* ('Little Ewe-Lamb') to

Nicolae Labiş (1935–1956).

By contrast the Romanian/Spanish anthology compiled by Darie Nováceanu concentrates on twelve major poets, and does not attempt to reproduce exactly the cadences of the original, because Romanian pronunciation can easily be learnt by speakers of Romance languages. The first poet included is Tudor Arghezi (1880–1967) and the last Dumitru M. Ion (b. 1945).

The most important 19th-century poet of Romania is the Hölderlin-like Mihai Eminescu (1850–1889), who virtually created Romanian as a vehicle for important literature with his contemporaries, the playwright Ion Luca Caragiale (1852–1912) and the writer of fiction Ion Creangă (1837–1889).

Apart from Arghezi (nominated for the Nobel Prize in 1964), the most remarkable 20th-century poet from Romania is Nichita Stanescu (b. 1933). His *The Still Unborn about the Dead* (Anvil Press, 1975), translated by Petru Popescu and Peter Jay, is a volume of selected poems in which Stanescu attempts, as he puts it, to describe humanity from outside, as a leaf might observe, and to show that man is only one part of the world. It seems to be the duty of a poet to illuminate that part of reality which scientific terminology cannot grasp, though he also tries obliquely to penetrate the mysteries of logic and philosophy. Stanescu's finest achievement so far seems to be the eleven *Elegies* of 1966, with the anti-elegy or twelfth elegy, a kind of Judas to the eleven disciples of the remaining elegies.

Year 41

ANNA COMNENA (1083–c. 1153).
> *Alexiad.* Completed after 1148. Translated from the Greek by E. R. A. Sewter (Penguin, 1969).

If one can forgive a biographer and historian the lack of a sense of humour, then Anna is one of the most remarkable chroniclers of the Middle Ages.

The *Alexiad* is essentially a life and justification of her father, the Byzantine Emperor Alexios I (1081–1118), but we also learn much of the Byzantine Court, the Crusades, and much else from the prose epic, written in a good attempt at 'classical' Greek.

As the betrothed of Constantine Ducas, Anna counted on eventually succeeding to the imperial throne, but Constantine's death led to her younger brother John's becoming heir. Anna married Nicephoros Bryennios, descendant of an unsuccessful pretender, and bore him several children. When her father died, Anna (and possibly her mother Irene Ducas) were suspected of being concerned in a plot to assassinate John, and were confined to a convent where Anna compiled the (admittedly-biased) portrait of an age which would otherwise be almost shadowy.

MOSES BEN JACOB BEN EZRA (c. 1055–c. 1138).
> *Selected Poems.* Bilingual edition, with translations by S. de Solis-Cohen (Jewish Publication Society of America, Philadelphia, 1934).

Granada is a city which exemplifies to some people the glories of Islamic architecture, and to others the gypsies who have retained to this day a quarter of their own.

To Moses ben Ezra, and to his distinguished Jewish family, however, it was a home where the family was persecuted in 1066 (leading to Moses' temporary departure, perhaps to Lucena) and from which he was driven, destitute, after the Berber invasion of 1090. Living in Christian Spain, he longed for the south, writing a poignant poem to his friend, the writer Judah Ha-Levi.

His youthful Hebrew poems on friendship, love, wine, and the pleasures of springtime, reflect a comfortable and affluent life. Moses also wrote a manual in Arabic on Hebrew poetry, *Kitab al-muhadara wa 'l-mudakara* (translated into Hebrew in *Shirat Israel* by B. Halper, 1924).

Seven of his lyrics are to be found in David Goldstein's anthology *The Jewish Poets of Spain, 900–1250* (Penguin, 1971).

This is a good moment to enjoy the Judaic Hellenism of Philo (*c.* 30 B.C.–*c.* 45 A.D.), a member of the Jewish mission sent to Rome to implore Gaius to refrain from imposing Emperor-worship. Philo Judaeus' works are available in the Loeb Classical Library (11 vols., Heinemann and Harvard U.P., 1929–62), and there is a good *Introduction to Philo Judaeus* (Blackwell, 1962) by E. R. Goodenough. Loyal equally to his Alexandrian Greek heritage and his Jewish background, Philo taught contemplation towards a mystical vision of the divine and had a prolonged influence on mediaeval scholasticism and the neo-Platonic tradition.

GIOVANNI BATTISTA VICO (1668–1744).
Principi di una Scienza Nuova intorno alla Natura delle Nazioni. First published 1725. *The New Science of Giambattista Vico,* revised translation of the 3rd ed., 1744, by T. G. Bergin and M. H. Fisch (Cornell U.P., 1968; abridged in Cornell Paperbacks, 1970).

It is odd to reflect that writers as different as Arnold Toynbee and James Joyce could feel kinship with a Neapolitan professor of rhetoric whose work was almost completely neglected outside Italy until W. E. Weber's German translation appeared in 1822 and the French version by Jules Michelet five years later. The principal attraction for Toynbee and Joyce was the notion that human history passes through clearly-defined cycles, from barbarism to a spiritual and intellectual awakening, and finally to full humanity, then regressing to barbarism.

But Vico was a many-sided genius who shed disconcertingly novel spotlights on many aspects of philosophy, rhetoric, aesthetics, and historiography. In his own time he represented a Catholic reaction to the Cartesian idea that perfect knowledge of the world we live in depends solely on the perfection of our mathematical knowledge. He taught that we are nearer to understanding ourselves and our forebears through the study of history that we are to understanding the physical and chemical universe through the study of purely mechanical and mathematical phenomena. He showed how epic and narrative poetry from oral tradition could reveal aspects of philological and historical development. His view of natural law – opposed to those of Grotius and Pufendorf – was probably wrong, but accidentally fertile in leading him to discoveries anticipating those of modern linguists, psychologists and anthropologists. His *Autobiography* is not to be relied upon (he even gets his year of birth wrong!) but remains a fascinating insight into an original mind of high distinction. There is a translation by M. H. Fisch and T. G. Bergin (Cornell U.P., 1944).

The best survey of his thought is Benedetto Croce's *La filosofia di Giambattista Vico* (Laterza, Bari, 1911), translated by R. G. Collingwood as *The Philosophy of G. B. Vico* (1913). While Croce is the subject of an independent section in *A Lifetime's Reading,* Collingwood is not, so it is relevant here to stress his elegant *Autobiography* (1970), *The Principles of Art* (1963), and *The Idea of History* (1961), all published by Oxford U.P.

SAMUEL BECKETT (b. 1906).
> *Molloy. Malone meurt. L'Innommable.* Trilogy of novels first published respectively in 1947, 1951 and 1953. Translated into English as *Molloy* (with Patrick Bowles), *Malone Dies* and *The Unnamable* (in one volume, Calder, 1966). And *En attendant·Godot.* First published 1952. Translated as *Waiting for Godot* (Faber & Faber, 1956).

The above novels and 'tragicomedy in two acts' were produced in the years 1947–9, Beckett's most creative period. From 1937, when he settled permanently in France, Beckett wrote most of his work first in French, and then translated it into English. A third dimension in his work is Irish, for while he abandoned Dublin, where he was born, educated, and where he taught for some time, the parochial intellectual atmosphere affected him deeply and probably permanently.

He has constantly poked fun at critical exegesis of his work, as in the famous passage from *Fin de partie* (*Endgame*) in which Hamm asks 'We're not beginning to. . . to. . . mean something?' swiftly·answered by Clov, laughing sardonically: 'Mean something! You and I, mean something! That's a good one!' Beckett's characters – note – do not deny that they mean anything, any more than they assert it. But the weight of critical opinion has come down heavily on the side affirming that Beckett's plays and characters *do* mean something, a point on which every reader will feel free to make up his own mind. Beckett's own work has subsequently become more minimal in length and language, cutting down on the number of characters, and turning inward to their own memories, which may be false or falsified. The predicament of the individual takes up the centre of the stage, as it does in the thought of the Romanian philsopher Emil Cioran – who also lives out exile in Paris.

See Deirdre Bair's exhaustive but controversial biography *Beckett* (Pan, 1980). There is much excellent critical work, beginning with *Samuel Beckett: a critical study* by Hugh Kenner (Calder and Grove Press, 1962).

VLADIMIR ILYICH ULYANOV ('LENIN') (1870–1917).
Selected Works (3 vols. Lawrence & Wishart, 1964). And *What is to be Done?* Translated from *Chto delat'?* (first published in Russian by Dietz of Stuttgart, 1902) by S. V. and P. Utechin (Panther, 1970).

The three-volume selection is almost as interesting for its omissions as its inclusions, since even Communist 'classics' are not immune from silent excisions and abridgments. The complete *What is to be Done?* is a version from the book, subtitled 'burning questions of our movement', which was to become the cornerstone of the Bolshevik Movement. There were several reasons for its popularity, including the clarion call for unity among the warring revolutionary factions, a plan for extensive revolutionary action, and the listing of definite jobs to be carried out. A professional corps of ideolgists was proposed, devoting to the revolution not only their spare evenings (as was then the case) but their whole lives. It is fascinating to note that as early as 1902 Lenin was quoting Lassalle's doctrine of 1852 that 'A party becomes stronger by purging itself'. One does not need a particularly long memory to recall how efficiently that doctrine has been practised by each succeeding generation.

Among the numerous background books of every political colour, one might pick out David Shub's biography *Lenin* (Penguin, 1966).

Among the composers who were trying to forge an individual style during an age of conformity were Rachmaninov (1873–1943), Prokofiev (1891–1953), and Shostakovich (1906–75).

SHOTA RUSTAVELI (*fl.* 1200).
Vepkhis-tqaosani. First critical edition 1712. Translated in prose by R. H. Stevenson as *The Man in the Panther's Skin* (State University of New York Press, 1977). There is an uninspired, archaic verse translation by Marjory Wardrop published by Progress Press in Moscow – not recommended.

Legendary as his life is, there is no doubt of the literary achievement of Rustaveli, for his romantic epic in 1669 rhymed quatrains is still the greatest work of Georgian literature. The poem was subversive of medieval church dogma, and no manuscripts are extant before those dated to the 17th century, but among the common people and their poets *The Man in the Panther's Skin* is irreplaceable.

Ingoroqva has identified the poet with Prince Shota III (1166–1250), Duke of Hereti, who lived at Rustavi. The author was certainly a man of wide learning, for there are numerous classical and Arabic allusions, and the courtly-love ideal bears comparison with that of the troubadours and Minnesänger of western Europe, or that of the Persian court poets. There are no specifically Georgian characters or landscapes, yet the atmosphere throughout is as Georgian as the productions of the Tbilisi-based Rustaveli National Theatre which caused such a sensation at the Edinburgh Festival when offering Shakespeare's *Richard III* and Brecht's *Caucasian Chalk Circle.*

The fantastic plot recalls episodes from the *Arabian Nights* or the books of chivalry ambiguously derided by Cervantes in the *Quijote.* 'The Man in the Panther's Skin' is the Indian Prince Tariel, who has gone mad after losing Princess Nestan-Darejan. He is joined in his quest by Avtandil, a knight frustrated in his love for the Arabian Princess Tinatin, daughter of King Rostevan. How the two knights seek Nestan-Darejan, find her in the demon-country, and rescue her, is told with brilliant technical polish.

Recent Georgian poetry can be enjoyed in *Modern Poetry in Translation* no. 18 (1974).

Background reading could include D. M. Lang's *The Georgians* (Thames & Hudson, 1966) and *The Arts of Ancient Georgia* (Thames & Hudson, 1979) by Rusudan Mepisashvili and Vakhtang Tsintsadze.

MIGUEL DE UNAMUNO (1846–1936).
Del sentimiento trágico de la vida en los hombres y en los pueblos. First published 1913. Translated by Anthony Kerrigan as *The Tragic Sense of Life in Men and Nations* (Princeton U.P. and Routledge, 1973).

Unamuno is a highly significant writer whose fiction, essays, poetry and plays have all been influential on subsequent writing in Spanish. Himself a Basque, Unamuno was for many years Rector of Salamanca University, and came to identify himself with Castile as well as with the Basque Provinces. Influenced successively by Hegelian dialectic, Spencer and Comte, Kierkegaard, William James and Henri Bergson, he arrived at the theologically unorthodox position that the idea of God is not the cause but the consequence of man's yearning for eternal life. He suggested that immortality is attainable precisely by those who desire it strongly enough. Man differs from the animals not so much in his capacity for reason as in his capacity for feeling, and it is feeling, he maintains, that made possible Kant's leap from the *Kritik der reinen Vernunft* to the *Kritik der praktischen Vernunft.* His conclusion is to reject all systems, rationalism as well as Roman Catholicism, and to adopt the attitude of doubt and wonder.

Anthony Kerrigan has made equally distinguished translations from many other works in a projected nine-volume *Selected Works* of Unamuno from Princeton and Routledge, and all are valuable: *Our Lord Don Quixote* (1968), *The*

Agony of Christianity and Essays on Faith (1974), *Novela/Nivola* (a philosophical 'novel', 1976), and *Ficciones: Four Stories and a Play* (1976).

ROBERT GRAVES (b. 1895).
  Collected Poems (Cassell, 1965; Doubleday, 1966).

Graves is for many the outstanding British lyric poet of the twentieth century, allying fastidious craftmanship with extreme fidelity to the Muse. He has earned his living from unusual historical novels, such as the series of Claudius and the politics of Rome, and possesses an enviable reputation as a critic, basing his opinions on his own practice and repudiating the idea that valid critical opinions can be based on anything other than trial and error. He praises the Muse, dismissing all other verse, purpose-built, as Apollonian. 'True poetic practice' (he declares in that eccentric, rewarding 'historical grammar of poetic myth' *The White Goddess,* Faber & Faber, 1961) 'implies a mind so miraculously attuned and illuminated that it can form words, by a chain of more-than-coincidences, into a living entity – a poem that goes about on its own (for centuries after the author's death, perhaps) affecting readers with its stored magic'.

The *'Collected' Poems* is nothing of the sort, but a radically-pruned selection of those essential – often very brief – encounters with the Muse by which Graves chooses to be remembered.

Those who pursue the medieval tradition of courtly love will find themselves constantly astonished at its renaissance in the work of Robert Graves.

The best English prose of World War I is probably Graves' *Goodbye to All That* (1929; Doubleday, 1957; Penguin, 1969) and the best poems probably those of Wilfred Owen (*Collected Poems;* Chatto & Windus, 1963; New Directions, 1964). It was the latter which inspired Benjamin Britten's moving War Requiem (conducted by the composer, 2 discs, Decca SET 252–3).

THEODOR FONTANE (1819–1898).
  Effi Briest. First published 1895. Translated by Douglas Parmée (Penguin, 1967).

Only Fontane specialists will want the whole of the *Nymphenburger-Ausgabe* of the *Sämtliche Werke* (29 vols., 1959–74) but anyone with an interest in literature would derive immense pleasure from his best novel, *Effi Briest,* written between 1891 and 1893. The muted realism is most effective, and the detrimental influence of Sir Walter Scott is for once in the background.

Effi's tragedy is all the more poignant because it is the mundane plight of so many girls of seventeen, married too early and never allowed to mature as a separate personality.

Fontane wrote a good deal of fiction, but was celebrated for his ballads from the publication of his first edition of *Gedichte* (1851) to the fifth (1897). His autobiography is divided between *Meine Kinderjahre* (1894) and *Von Zwanzig bis Dreissig* (1898); collectively it might be compared with the next generation's *Eine Kindheit* (1922) and *Verwandlungen einer Jugend* 1928) by Hans Carossa (1878–1956), the partly fictional reminiscences of an army doctor with strong literary appeal.

A pleasant introduction to Fontane's fiction is Alan R. Robinson's *Theodor Fontane* (University of Wales Press, 1976).

Spend some time with the symphonies of Anton Bruckner (1824–96), preferably the set conducted by Haitink (12 discs, Philips 6717 002).

Modern Hungarian Poetry.

There is a choice of anthologies: Th. Kabdebó's *One Hundred Hungarian Poems* (Albion Books, Manchester, 1976), and the rather better *Modern Hungarian Poetry* edited by Miklós Vajda (Columbia U.P., 1977).

There is regrettably no collection available in English by Lajos Kassák (1887–1967) but we have the *Works* of Attila József (1905–1937, Hungarian Cultural Foundation, P.O. Box 364, Stone Mountain, GA 30086, 1973) and József's *Selected Poems and Texts* translated by John Batki (Carcanet Press, 1973).

The *Selected Poems* of Gyula Illyés (b. 1902) (Chatto & Windus, 1971) appeared in the U.S.A. as *A Tribute to Gyula Illyés* (Occidental Press, 1968).

Sándor Weöres (b. 1913) and Ferenc Juhász (b. 1928) are represented by *Selected Poems* (Penguin, 1970), translated respectively by Edwin Morgan and David Wevill.

Miklós Radnóti (1909–44) has been translated by Emery George in *Subway Stops* (Ardis, 1978) and by George Gömöri and Clive Wilmer in *Forced March* (Carcanet New Press, 1979).

János Pilinszky (b. 1921) has been translated by Ted Hughes and János Csokits in *Selected Poems* (Carcanet Press, 1976) and by Peter Jay in *Crater* (Anvil Press, 1978).

László Nagy, another important poet of the Juhász generation, has been translated by Tony Connor and Kenneth McRobbie in *Love of the Scorching Wind* (Oxford U.P., 1973).

Explore the history and politics of Hungary in the twentieth century in an up-to-date survey.

Year 42

GIOVANNI VERGA (1840–1922).
> *I Malavoglia.* First published 1881. Translated as *The House by the Medlar Tree* by Eric Mosbacher (Grove Press, 1953). *Novelle Rusticane.* First published 1883. Translated as *Little Novels of Sicily* by D. H. Lawrence, 1925; reprinted by Greenwood Press, 1976). *Mastro Don Gesualdo.* First definitively published 1889. Translated by G. Cecchetti (University of California Press, 1980).

The Sicilian Verga was at home both in his native city of Catania, below Mount Etna, and in the village of Vizzini where his family owned land. His first novels were mistaken attempts to find a voice in Milan, Florence and Naples, but it was only when he discovered the little world of Sicily that his true voice was heard. The *Novelle Rusticane* are longish short stories interspersed between two major novels, the first and second of a projected pentalogy to be collectively entitled *I Vinti*, 'the Defeated'. The aim was to present a 'phantasmagoria of life's struggle, extending from the ragpicker to the Minister of State and the artist, assuming all forms from ambition to avarice, and lending itself to a thousand representations of the great, grotesque play of mankind, the providential struggle guiding humanity through all appetites, high and low, to its conquest of truth'.

Verga's technique was *verismo,* or realism. After Manzoni he is considered the most important Italian novelist, for he achieved his aims as far as the two published volumes allowed. A pessimist, he views each individual as essentially isolated from family, community, and even from personal fulfilment due to the innate waywardness of the human character. It is Verga's successful stage play *Cavalleria Rusticana* (1883) from which the Mascagni opera of 1890 is derived (with Leoncavallo's *I Pagliacci,* 3 discs DG 2709 020, conducted by Herbert von Karajan).

Though all the best studies of Verga are in Italian, including G. Ragonese's *Interpretazione del Verga* (Palermo, 1965), see Alfred Alexander's *Giovanni Verga* (Grant & Cutler, 1972). The fields around Vizzini are still very much as they were in Verga's day, for those interested in the pilgrimage.

JACOBUS DE VARAGINE (*c.* 1227–1298).
> *Legenda Aurea.* Written before 1264, and edited by T. Graesse 1846.
> Translated as *The Golden Legend* by Granger Ryan and Helmut Ripperger
> (2 vols., Longmans, Green, 1941) and as *La Légende Dorée* by J. –B.
> M. Roze (2 vols., Garnier-Flammarion, 1967).

The art galleries and museums of the Christian world are full of paintings, and the great Western books full of references, which need to be interpreted in the light of what people, from princes to paupers, believed about their faith, which was the central fact of many lives. Virtually the only patron of the artist, until the rise of the Renaissance nobility and bourgeoisie, was the Church, and the Church demanded that subjects be treated in a definite manner, iconography determined by tradition. Much of that tradition derives directly or indirectly from the *Legenda Aurea,* the most popular 'lives of the saints' of the Middle Ages. It is an attempt to make theology a matter of martyrs and heroes, Good triumphing inevitably over Evil. Virtually all of the anecdotes are invented, and many are based on pagan or secular heroes of fact or fiction, with only a change of name and a devotional perspective.

A Dominican who rose to become Archbishop of Genoa in 1292 (and began a *Chronicon genuense* the following year), Jacobus assembled his materials in the order of the liturgical calendar. His style is deliberately easy to read, and the book's rapid diffusion all over Christian Europe through the medium of the international language, Latin, ensured that it was one of the first books ever printed (notably by William Caxton: see *The Golden Legend of William Caxton,* 7 vols., 1900). The *Legenda Aurea* is an indispensable source for an understanding of how the medieval clerisy viewed their saints and martyrs.

Some of the most wonderful religious music is in the styles of the Ambrosian and Gregorian chant which can be enjoyed on DGG Archive 2533 284 and Decca Turnabout TV 34070S respectively.

GUILLAUME DE LORRIS (*c.* 1212–*c.* 1237) *and* JEAN DE MEUN (c. 1237–*c.* 1305).
> *Le Roman de la Rose.* The Lorris section composed about 1237; the Meun
> section about 1275–80. Edited by Ernest Langlois (5 vols., 1914–24).
> Translated as *The Romance of the Rose* by Harry W. Robbins, and edited
> by Charles W. Dunn (Dutton, 1962).

If one were to set Ovid's *Ars Amatoria* in thirteenth-century France, one would find many resemblances to the poem of Guillaume, who wrote four thousand lines of octosyllabic couplets in celebration of the ideals of courtly love then prevalent in France.

Entering a garden by courtesy of Oiseuse (representing Idleness), the poet finds other allegorical characters, such as Doux Regard and Largesse, before falling in love with a rose. The God of Love now teaches him the precepts of courtly love, by which he must abide if he is to achieve his heart's desire. His attempts to reach the Rose are helped or hindered by conflicting emotions of the lady, such as Danger or Bel Accueil. An alarm is sounded when the poet tries to kiss his lady, and a chaperone appears.

Jean de Meun drastically altered the style and content when adding eighteen thousand lines much later. He intrudes his vigorous personality upon the continuation of the allegory, expressing his own views on medieval life and thought, culminating in the doctrine that everything in accordance with Nature is good, and everything out of harmony with Nature is evil. His pages are filled with a gallery of types, from a startlingly malicious attack on women in direct contrast with the atmosphere of Guillaume's lines, to satires on magistrates, nobles, and mendicant friars, later a favourite target of Rabelais. The English *Romaunt of the Rose* attributed (at least in part) to Chaucer is a modified translation and paraphrase of the Lorris part, and about a sixth of the Meun part.

For general background reading one can do no better than Joan Evans' *Life in Medieval France* (3rd ed., Phaidon Press, 1969), with appropriate illustrations.

LAURENCE STERNE (1713–1768).
The Life and Opinions of Tristram Shandy, Gent. First published in 9 vols., 1760–1767. Introduced by Christopher Ricks (Penguin, 1967).

A huge practical joke of a book, as witty and frenetic in its way as Rabelais's *Gargantua* was in his, *Tristram Shandy* is an unfinished 'autobiography' of a man not born until the end of volume three, and still an infant in volume six!

Sterne filled it with table talk, parodies of his contemporaries, opinions on hundreds of matters more or less irrelevant, a Rabelaisian tale of the German pedant Slawkenbergius and his treatise on noses, and (in volumes seven and eight) travel notes on France and Bohemia.

The main characters, apart from the ubiquitous if for the most part unborn, author, are his father Walter, full of crazy ideas, and his uncle Toby, who spends much time in attacking fortified towns, at least in his overheated imagination.

Who knows how Shandy would have finished, if Sterne had lived to tell the tale? As it is, he finished neither that masterpiece, nor the equally famous *Sentimental Journey through France and Italy, by Mr. Yorick, 1768* (1768; edited by Graham Petrie, Penguin, 1967), written partly to answer the plain, phlegmatic *Travels through France and Italy* (1766) of Sterne's rival Tobias Smollett, known thenceforth to Sterne enthusiasts by the epithet 'Smelfungus'. The grumpy Smollett had not bothered to forget himself in the beauties of his surroundings, a fault for which Sterne made up in his own tour.

Sterne took holy orders without any real religious convictions, teaching in *The Sermons of Mr. Yorick* (1760–1769) that benevolence and simple morality are all that can reasonably be required of the ordinary person.

One of the best studies of Sterne is *The Life and Times of Laurence Sterne* by Wilbur Cross (3rd ed., Russell and Russell, 1967) but my favourite is Henri Fluchère's *Laurence Sterne,* translated by Barbara Bray (Oxford U.P., 1965).

Hungarian Short Stories. With an introduction by A. Alvarez. World's Classics (Oxford U.P., 1967). And *Folktales of Hungary* by Linda Degh. Translated by J. Halász (2nd ed., University of Chicago Press, 1969).

Try to obtain a regular subscription to the English edition of the *New Hungarian Quarterly,* and the current catalogue of translations from Kultura, P.O. Box 149, Budapest 62, Hungary.

Hungarian is related to no other West European language except, loosely, to Finnish, so the need to translate is ever-present in the minds of the authorities. However, since the régime is totalitarian, much of the best literature appears only overseas or secretly, so it is essential to review the U.S. and British national bibliographies, as well as *Encounter* and *Index to Censorship,* for dissident writings.

There is a saying that nine of Hungary's ten million people are writers, and most of the others are also able to spin a folk tale, as the Halász compilation suggests. The 'literary' story and the folk tale in Hungary have a common basis in cunning and sophistication: to defy corruption one must know all the tricks possible, or be so innocent that no amount of deceit or guile can do harm. Hence, the Hungarian writers and readers reserve their sympathy for the Švejk-like exploited, and their bitterness for the exploiters.

Mór Jókai (1825–1904) is the first author represented, and Ferenc Karinthy (b. 1921) is the latest, in the World's Classics selection.

See Linda Degh's *Studies in East European Folk Narrative* (University of Texas Press, 1978).

WANG SHOU-JEN (WANG YANG-MING) (1472–1529).
Instructions for Practical Living, and other neo-Confucian Writings. Translated by Wing-tsit Chan (Columbia U.P., 1963).

A formidable scholar who attained the highest possible commendation at the state examinations, Wang spent most of his life in the civil service, achieving high office on several occasions.

On retirement, he chose to devote himself to the study of philosophy, and propagated four concepts within the Confucian mainstream, against the dominant ideas of Chu Hsi and towards the tradition of Mencius. The first concept, of *ren* (or *jen*), might be construed as humanism, equating the human philosopher in microcosm with the universe as macrocosm. The second concept equates principle with the mind, so that the innate 'good' knowledge of the human being derives from the original or universal mind. The principle of 'heaven' or of the highest good is thus the moral law of both man and universe.

It follows that men do not need to study the classics in detail, as Chu Hsi had stated: poor and rich, labourers and leisured classes alike can attain wisdom simply by following the dictates of the innate 'good' knowledge, turning aside those things which are known to be evil by experience or observation.

Finally, knowledge and action are indivisible: 'knowledge is the beginning of action; action is the fulfilment of knowledge'. Thus, filial piety is known to be desirable, but only by carrying it out can one really understand its meaning.

See Carsun Chang's *Wang Yang-ming* (St John's University Press, Jamaica, New York, 1962).

AKUTAGAWA RYUNOSUKE (1892–1927).
  Rashomon and other stories. Translated by Kojima Takashi (Bantam, 1959).

Rashomon was first published in 1915; together with *Yabu no Naka* (*In a Grove,* it formed the basis of the great Akiro Kurosawa film *Rashomon* which won so many international prizes in 1951.

The technique, known to Akutagawa from Browning's *Ring and the Book,* is to tell a story in the words of each protagonist and each witness in such a way that the reader chooses his own sequence of events in which to believe, based on the conflicting statements.

Akutagawa wrote in all some hundred and fifty short stories in eight volumes, distinguished for their psychological subtlety, paradox, irony, and (in the water-gnome tale *Kappa,* 1927) broad allegory.

It was after the early publication of *Rashomon* that Akutagawa chose to become a *protégé* of Natsume Soseki (q.v.) and fell under the influence of the anti-naturalist Mori Ogai (1862–1922), author of *The Wild Geese* (translated by Kingo Ochiai and Sanford Goldstein, Tuttle, 1958).

JUDAH HA-LEVI (*c.* 1075–after 1140).
> *Selected Poems.* Bilingual edition, with translations by N. Salaman (Jewish
> Publication Society of America, Philadelphia, 1928).

Spain produced a number of important Arabic and Hebrew books, as well as
those in the dominant Romance languages and Basque.

Born in Tudela, Ha-Levi was educated in Granada, where he met Moses ben
Ezra and earned a living as a doctor. Since Jews and Judaism were despised in a
milieu not unlike that depicted in Shakespeare's *The Merchant of Venice,* Ha-Levi
took it upon himself to write in Arabic, between 1130 and 1140, the *Kitab al-
huyya wa 'd-dalil fi nusr ad-din ad-dalil* ('The Book of the Proof and Defence of
the Despised Religion'). This resumes the familiar mediaeval debate between
religions, and ends with the vindication of Judaism. To resolve the apparent
discrepancy between the God-given land of Israel and the current situation of
Jews in the Diaspora, Ha-Levi called for unity among Jews and a return not to a
misty Zion of legend but to the Jerusalem of actuality. To put his beliefs into
practice he made a pilgrimage to Palestine and there lost his life in circumstances
which are not certain – according to one account he was murdered by an Arab at
the moment of entering the Promised City.

Ha-Levi is represented by more poems than is any other writer in David
Goldstein's anthology *The Jewish Poets of Spain, 900–1250* (Penguin, 1971).

The story of the Jews can be explored further in an important classic: the works
of Flavius Josephus (parallel text and translation, 9 vols., Heinemann and
Harvard U.P., 1926; translation of *Jewish War* by G. A. Williamson, Penguin,
1959).

JAMES JOYCE (1882–1941).
> *Finnegans Wake.* First published 1939 (New ed., Faber & Faber, 1950).

The intoxication of sound-and-flurry which comes from the initial impact of
reading *Finnegans Wake* makes it a disastrous influence on young writers, for
they have still to learn the formal structures which underlie this apparently
anarchic prose epic.

Finnegans Wake does have a pattern: it is divided into four parts (Parents, Sons,
People, and *Ricorso* in the Viconian sense) and is set in Dublin in circular time,
the first word in the book continuing from the last.

Joyce's verbal exuberance demands that the book be read aloud, and the more
languages you have at your disposal, the more resonances – intended and
unintended – will occur to your ear. Read it page by page with Joseph Campbell
and Henry Morton Robinson's *A Skeleton Key to Finnegans Wake* (Harcourt
Brace, 1944; Faber & Faber, 1947) and any other keys you can find to unlock the

treasury, such as the volumes of *Census* by Adaline Glasheen.

Preparation for *Finnegans Wake* might include the very different books which he wrote earlier, all more or less concerned with Dublin and its people. The first is *Dubliners* (short stories, 1914), followed by *A Portrait of the Artist as a Young Man* (autobiographical novel, 1916); read too the parody *A Portrait of the Artist as a Young Dog* by Dylan Thomas (Dent, 1940), and of course *Ulysses* (1922).

The major biography *James Joyce* by Richard Ellmann (Oxford U.P., New York, 1959) may be amended by later chroniclers in detail, but never replaced as a comprehensive portrait of the artist.

LUDOVICO ARIOSTO (1474–1533).

Orlando Furioso. Begun about 1503 and first published 1516. First definitive edition 1532. Critical edition by S. Debenedetti and C. Segre (Mondadori, Milan, 1964). Translated by Barbara Reynolds in verse (2 vols., Penguin, 1975–7) and by Guido Waldman in prose (Oxford U.P., 1974).

The major Renaissance epic poet spent most of his life at the ducal court of Ferrara, first with Cardinal Ippolito d'Este (1503–17) and then with the latter's brother Duke Alfonso I (1518–33).

Matteo Boiardo, Count of Scandiano and himself a diplomat in the service of the Ferrarese court, had died in 1494 with his epic poem *Orlando Innamorato* unfinished. Ariosto set himself the specific task of continuing the epic, and surpassed Boiardo in many ways. Roland, Charlemagne and other figures of the French *chansons de geste* enact exploits of love and adventure more familiar from Arthurian sources. Ariosto's ideals help to form, and are formed by, such Renaissance concepts as the need to subdue passion by prudence, the supremacy of *virtus* over fate, and the power of love as a spur to courage and virtue. Ariosto shows how overwhelming romantic love can make a man insane (*furioso*) and incapable of rational action or conversation. Social and political acts, for Ariosto, are equally threatened by the insanity of irrationality due to belief in fate or dominating passions. Overt description, irony and metrical irregularity are among Ariosto's methods, and he never falls into the trap of rhythmical dullness that mars a good deal of Tasso's later *Gerusalemme Liberata*.

Ariosto's influence has been enormous. To take the case of one composer alone, Handel used episodes from the *Orlando Furioso* in *Alcina* (3 discs, Decca GOS 509–11, conducted by Bonynge), *Ariodante,* and *Orlando*.

Enjoy Venetian art of the period, especially the paintings of Giorgione (*c.* 1478–1510), Titian (*c.* 1477–1576), and the architecture of the Florentine Sansovino (1486–1570).

Year 43

'CURRER BELL' (CHARLOTTE BRONTË) (1816–1855).
Jane Eyre. First published 1847. Edited by Q. D. Leavis (Penguin, 1966).

Jane Eyre is the first plain heroine in a major British novel, written like those of her sisters and of 'George Eliot' under a pseudonym. *Jane Eyre,* based in part on Charlotte's own experiences, remained a central novel in the English tradition, appearing in the same year as Emily's equally significant *Wuthering Heights.*

The sisters' mother had died in 1821, leaving five daughters and a son, Branwell. Four of the daughters were sent to a boarding-school for the daughters of the clergy at Cowan Bridge (recalled as 'Lowood Asylum' in *Jane Eyre*), a move which may have caused her sisters Maria ('Helen Burns') and Elizabeth to contract the consumption from which they died.

From 'Lowood', where she taught for some time, Jane was appointed governess of Mr Rochester's daughter at Thornfield Hall. Though the finale of the book has passed into the language, it cannot be exempted from the charge of sentimentality. The overall impression of *Jane Eyre,* however, is that of a finely-wrought work of art based in authentic experience, and deriving from a fine, generous and sensitive spirit.

The classic *Life of Charlotte Brontë* (1857) by Mrs Elizabeth Cleghorn Gaskell will never be superseded, but in *The Brontë Story* (Heinemann, 1953) Margaret Lane sought to complement Mrs Gaskell's book.

Jean Rhys has imagined the early life of Mrs Rochester of Thornfield Hall in her novel *The Wilde Sargasso Sea* (Norton and André Deutsch, 1966).

PINDAR (c. 518–c. 438 B.C.).
The Odes, including the principal fragments. Text with a prose translation
by Sir John Sandys in the Loeb Classical Library (Heinemann and Harvard
U.P., 1915). Translated into free verse by Richmond Lattimore (2nd ed.,
University of Chicago Press, 1976).

Writing in literary Dorian Greek, Pindar is remarkable among authors of his
period in that at least a quarter of his verses are believed to have survived. These
are mainly *epinikia,* or choral odes in honour of a victor at one of the games
festivals, pre-eminently that of Olympia. Commissioned by the family or town of
the victor from a poet (Simonides, Bacchylides and Pindar are the most
celebrated), the *epinikion* was performed on the victor's return home. The form
was that of three stanzas forming triads and comprising three parts: the victory
itself, a mythical variation of the theme, and a eulogy of the victor, usually
accompanied by a moral conclusion.

The odes are divided according to the Games celebrated: the Olympian, the
Pythian, the Nemean, and the Isthmian.

Strength and beauty, grandeur and musicality: Pindar's poetry lacks all the dull
flattery normally connected with commissioned paeans of praise. His word
inversions are daring, and his metaphors equally striking; even traditional myths
are not immune from his original handling and bold, driving similes.

Recent attempts to set Pindar to music must be praised, for his odes were never
performed without it.

C. M. Bowra's *Pindar* (Oxford U.P., 1964) is by the editor of the Oxford
Classical Text volume of Pindar, but Gilbert Norwood's *Pindar,* the Sather
Classical Lectures for 1943–4, remains indispensable and has been reprinted by
the University of California Press in 1974.

RENÉ DESCARTES (1596–1650).
*Discours de la Méthode pour bien Conduire sa Raison & Chercher la
Verité dans les Sciences.* First published 1637. Translated, with *Meditations,*
and the Letter-Preface to the *Principles of Philosophy,* by Arthur Wollaston
(Penguin, 1960).

The most influential teacher of Descartes was the enquiring Montaigne,
asserting neither 'I know' or 'I don't know', but asking 'What is it that I know?'.

Descartes abandoned medieval scholasticism, with its gullible acceptance of
traditional lore, and stressed instead the value of a critical intelligence. The
Discours suggests a truth that even now our schoolteachers fail to instil: that
before one learns anything at all, one should discover the true methods of study,
such as logic, the use of reference books, and the need to verify what one is told by

observation and experiment. Descartes' celebrated 'cogito, ergo sum' implied that men exist objectively because they are capable of formulating the concept of their own existence. He believed that truth is finite in the finite consciousness of men but infinite in the infinite consciousness of God. He saw the material universe as reducible to extension and local movement. He applied modern algebraic arithmetic to classical geometry and thus created analytical geometry. His shrewd and penetrating speculations laid the foundations for fresh discoveries in many fields from biology to optics.

But his old teachers, the Jesuits, resented his anti-Aristotelian views expressed in French and savouring too much of an independent outlook; prudently he published his next *Meditations* on metaphysics in Latin and dedicated the book to the Theological Faculty of the Sorbonne, but he was still attacked on all sides, almost as hysterically as was Galileo, his older contemporary. Cartesian thought led not only to modern science and philosophy, but to the *Encyclopédie* of Diderot and his collaborators, and to the *Esprit des lois* of Montesquieu. It is only in the present century that scientists are beginning to join Vico, questioning Descartes' assumption that the universe may not be explicable entirely in mathematical terms.

ALESSANDRO MANZONI (1785–1873).
   I Promessi Sposi. First definitive edition 1840–2. Edited by M. Barbi and F. Ghisalberti 1942. Translated by Archibald Colquhoun as *The Betrothed: a Tale of XVII Century Milan.* Everyman's Library (Dent and Dutton, 1956).

Manzoni is not only one of the giants of Italian literature, with a descriptive power rivalling that of Dickens, but the founder of the Italian historical novel in emulation of Sir Walter Scott, and a pillar of Italian Romanticism, following his conversion to the Roman Catholic faith, and his return after five years in France, in 1910.

I Promessi Sposi, set in and around Milan between 1628 and 1631, focusses on the lives of the young couple Renzo Tranaglino and Lucia Mondella. Before the betrothed pair can be married, Don Rodrigo, the local lord, threatens to abduct and marry Lucia, but they escape before his wishes can be carried out. The rest of the book is a brilliant evocation of the Duchy of Milan under Spanish administration, with fine characterization of the peasants at the centre of the book and a detailed description of the effects of the terrible plague of 1629–30. Manzoni's prose style is unaffected, and – unlike that of so many of his contemporaries – has not dated. The moral stance is that of simple Christianity, which Manzoni portrays at three hierarchical levels: Lucia the peasant, the Capuchin friar Padre Cristoforo, and the Cardinal of Milan, Federigo Borromeo.

Colquhoun's *Manzoni and his Times* (1954) was reprinted in 1979 by Hyperion Press Inc., 45 Riverside Av., Westport, Conn. 06880.

It was for Manzoni that Giuseppe Verdi (1813–1901) wrote his Requiem Mass (2 discs, HMV SLS 909, conducted by Giulini). This is an appropriate moment to enjoy Verdi operas that you have not heard before, in particular *Rigoletto, Il Trovatore, La Traviata, Un Ballo in Maschera, La Forza del Destino, Don Carlo, Aïda, Otello* and *Falstaff.*

BHARTRHARI (7th century A.D.).
Poems. Translated by Barbara Stoler Miller (Columbia U.P., 1967).

Bhartrhari is the author of three 'hundreds' or 'centuries' of short verses, in known in classical Sanskrit as *Śatakas.* The Sanskrit text, and Hindi and English translations, are to be found in the edition by Purohit Gopi Nath: *The Nitiśataka, Śringaraśataka and Vairagyaśataka* (2nd ed., Venkateshwar Press, Bombay, 1914), but the versions by Miller are more idiomatic.

The three collections are devoted respectively to conduct, love, and renunciation. A fine lyric poet, Bhartrhari shows the dilemma of a man torn between sensuality and asceticism. He reputedly took the ascetic's robe seven times, seven times returning to normal life; but one can discount the number seven, replacing it by 'several'.

Barbara Stoler Miller's *Hermit and the Love-Thief* (Columbia U.P., 1978) includes poems by Bilhana (c. 1040–1095) as well as by Bhartrhari.

SEAN O'CASEY (1884–1964).
Three Plays: Juno and the Paycock, The Shadow of a Gunman, The Plough and the Stars. First published in 1925, 1925 and 1926 (Macmillan, 1957; St Martin's Press, 1960).

A Protestant from the slums of Dublin, O'Casey was a self-educated dramatist who learnt all he knew from the life of Dublin and the boards of the Abbey Theatre. His three greatest plays reflect the experience of poverty and violence, but transmute the tragedy into compassion by means of splendid characterisation, and a brilliant use of Dublin slang and dialect.

Sean O'Casey's *Three More Plays* (Macmillan and St Martin's Press, 1965) comprise *The Silver Tassie, Purple Dust,* and *Red Roses for Me.* His controversy with the Abbey Theatre, over the first of these, a play against war, led to his voluntary exile in England. But his artistic roots were in Ireland, and the plays he wrote abroad were less effective, his aggrieved tone becoming distressingly strident and partial.

O'Casey's urban realism may be contrasted with the rural romanticism of J. M. Synge (1871–1909), whose most important plays, *The Playboy of the Western World* (1907) and the one-act tragedy *Riders to the Sea* (1904) have been reprinted together (Allen & Unwin, 1962).

The two Irish writers may also be contrasted in their prose: the testy, often unreasonable but always fascinating autobiography of O'Casey collectively known in its American edition as *Mirror in My House* (6 vols. Macmillan, 1939–54); and Synge's *The Aran Islands* (with *Four Plays* in the World's Classics edition of Robin Skelton, Oxford U.P., 1962) and *The Autobiography*, constructed by Alan Price from the MSS. (Dufour, 1967).

VLADIMIR NABOKOV (1899–1977).
   Ada or Ardor: a Family Chronicle (McGraw-Hill, 1969; Penguin, 1970).

A supremely exuberant work of art by the Russian emigré who rose to fame on the disreputable reputation of *Lolita* (Fawcett, 1959; Corgi, 1969), an erotic but not pornographic novel, *Ada* is an American idyll. In part possibly a wild parody of F. Scott Fitzgerald's *The Great Gatsby* (1925) and of Tolstoy's *Recollections* (translated by Aylmer Maude in World's Classics, Oxford U.P., 1937) – though with the witty hoaxer and teaser Nabokov nothing is certain – *Ada* is a brilliantly-written evocation of an America that never was.

Nabokov came from a wealthy, aristocratic pre-revolutionary Russian family, and his hero in *Ada*, Dr Van Veen, is the son of the wealthy and illustrious Baron 'Demon' Veen, of Manhattan and Reno. The nucleus of the novel is the romance between Van Veen and Ada, the daughter of Marina, Daniel Veen's wife. But the presence of Nabokov himself never allows the plot to run consecutively: his ear for the elusive sound which must precede vulgar meaning is no less acute than his lepidopterist's keen eye for a butterfly.

Nothing Nabokov wrote is dull or predictable, and one would not consult his 'autobiographical' *Speak, Memory* (2nd ed., Putnam, 1966; Penguin, 1969) for factual information of his life. Neither can subsequent biographies be altogether trusted, for disentangling his wily half-truths proves beyond the capacity of Andrew Field, for instance, in *Nabokov: His Life in Part* (Hamish Hamilton and Little, Brown, 1967).

Pale Fire (Weidenfeld & Nicolson, 1962) is a brilliant spoof of academic criticism and scholarship in general. *Bend Sinister* (McGraw-Hill, 1973; Penguin, 1974) is a novel of a philosopher and his son set in a totalitarian state.

T'AO CH'IEN (365–427).
The Poetry of T'ao Ch'ien. Translated with commentary and annotation by J. R. Hightower (Oxford U.P., 1970).

T'ao Ch'ien, also known as T'ao Yüan-ming, served the Chin dynasty in the tradition of his great-grandfather, Duke of Ch'ang-sha, but retired at the age of forty to devote himself to farming. His life is often cited as an example of the rejection of official honours in favour of simplicity and integrity: a European commonplace from Horace to Fray Antonio de Guevara's *Menosprecio de corte y alabança de aldea* of 1539.

For twenty-two years T'ao Ch'ien experienced all the hardships of a peasant's life, including insect pests and crop failure, while exchanging visits and poems with distinguished scholars.

His main poetic medium was the *shih* studied in Burton Watson's *Chinese Lyricism* (Columbia U.P., 1970). A hundred and fourteen of his poems are in the five-word *shih* metre, while only three are *fu,* and a further nine are written in the older four-word metre. He avoided the conventional poem, or set-piece, concentrating on aspects of his own life which were treated in a manner compounded of Taoist and Confucian elements. He saw man as a part of nature, understanding the value of Taoist quietism, but balanced this with a respect for Confucian practicality, filial piety, and social stability; he was never pompous, enjoyed wine and good company, and regarded death with composure.

T'ao Ch'ien's prose must be mentioned, for the humorous *Wu liu hsien-sheng chuan* ('Gentleman of the Five Willows') and the *T'ao-hua yüan chi* ('Peach Blossom Spring'), an ancestor of Shangri-la fiction, found in Birch's *Anthology of Chinese Literature.* (Penguin, 1967).

IVY COMPTON-BURNETT (1892–1969).
A God and his Gifts (Gollancz, 1963; Simon & Schuster, 1964).

There is no reason for choosing one of Dame Ivy's novels before another, for with the exception of one or two hesitant early experiments, all are equally successful, and almost interchangeable. However, in a postcard dated 6 April 1956, she told me that her books she liked best then were *A House and Its Head* (1935) and *Manservant and Maidservant* (1947), noting that 'no character in my books is drawn from life, though in some cases an actual person or a portrait or even a face in the fire may give an impetus to imagination'. Her dialogue may be artificial, but Dame Ivy invested almost the whole of her creative genius into direct speech. These are shadows with brilliant voices. Every page crackles with electricity from head-on collisions in words, gradually revealing old crimes or moving inexorably to new ones.

All the novels are set in an English country house in the generation before World War I, and involve entanglements and passions within the family and – to a much more limited extent – outside it. The following brief snatch from *A God and his Gifts* occurs near the beginning of the novel, between the formidable Hereward, and his lover Rosa who has just rejected the opportunity to become the wife he feels he must have. Instead, he is now resigned to marrying Ada Merton.

> "Rosa, I shall be a good husband".
> "You may be what you mean by the words".
> "I will see that Ada finds me what she should".
> "In time she must find what you are. There is no escape".

The surface is polished, but the nerves beneath are raw. Astringency is there: crudely open antagonism rarely. Younger members of a family are invariably as measured and ironic in their replies as the older members, and servants as composed in subtle repartee as their masters. While one can relax for long periods during a Jane Austen novel, there is no moment to drop guard in a Compton-Burnett. One should not read many one after another, for the novels (like the Jeeves stories of P. G. Wodehouse) are apt to merge in the memory, but there is a high level of technical accomplishment – and an awareness of the greater world – which marks an Ivy Compton-Burnett novel as a work of enduring quality. There is a limited edition of her *Collected Works* (19 vols., 1972) available from International Publications Service, 114 E. 32nd St., New York, N.Y.10016.

GOTTFRIED VON STRASSBURG (*fl.* 1210).
> *Tristan.* Composed in the years up to 1210, but unfinished. Edited by F. Ranke (1930). Translated with the surviving fragments of *Tristram* of Thomas by A. T. Hatto (Penguin, 1960).

Gottfried, the supreme verse stylist of his day on the borders between France and Germany, wrote in Middle High German but was also adept at French and familiar with Latin, French and German literature, being one of the Strasbourg intelligentsia, though not a nobleman.

His life of Tristan, in which Yseult makes a relatively late appearance, is based on an inferior French poem by Thomas, who revised about 1160 the first-known version of the story, compiled about a decade earlier, possibly in Anglo-Norman, from a source which might originally have been Celtic.

Only the first five-sixths of the Gottfried poem survive, miraculously complemented by the last sixth of the poem that Thomas wrote in the literary French of the Angevin court. Hatto's decision was to translate the 20,000 lines of short rhyming couplets into modern English prose, thus:

Ez zimet dem man ze lobene wol,
des er iedoch bedürfen sol,
und laze ez ime gevallen wol,
die wile ez ime gevallen sol.
'A man does well to praise what he cannot do without.
Let it please him so long as it may'.

If that rendering seems flat, then the alternative of finding four English end-rhymes for every verse seems dauntingly difficult, and ultimately self-defeating if it makes the poem boring.

Wagner's opera *Tristan und Isolde* was written to his own libretto, and stresses the element of fateful romantic love. Versions available on five discs each include those conducted by Herbert von Karajan (HMV SLS 963) and by Georg Solti (Decca D41D5).

Year 44

The Maya.

The peoples collectively named 'Maya' seem to us as paradoxical as we should seem to them. They were good mathematicians, being among the first to recognise the zero, and recognised the positional system which permits calculations with numbers higher than a million; but they never thought of fractions, or weights and measures. They built good roads, but did not know the wheel and never used beasts of burden. In astronomy they invented a solar calendar not inferior to our own; but they did not know glass, so had no conception of optics; nor had they any mechanical way of measuring the passage of time, not even the sundial or hourglass.

In addition to relevant sources already mentioned in the entry for Aztecs (and remembering that the Maya cultural region includes not only parts of present-day Mexico and Guatemala, but also inland Belize), one should consult Ferdinand Anton's *Art of the Maya* (Thames & Hudson, 1970) and, for the difficult literature, *La Literatura de los Mayas* by Demetrio Sodi M. (Joaquín Mortiz, Guaymas 33–1, Mexico 7, 1964).

But the major books to have at one's side are *The Maya* (2nd ed., Thames & Hudson, 1980) by Michael D. Coe and Herbert J. Spinden's *A Study of Maya Art: its subject matter and historical development*. With a new introduction and bibliography by J. Eric Thompson (Dover and Constable, 1975).

EZRA POUND (1885–1972).
   The Cantos (New Directions and Faber & Faber, 1970).

Pound's background was as varied as his interests, or indeed his later life. Born in Idaho, he never returned to live in the American West. He studied Romance languages at Hamilton College and the University of Pennsylvania, but at this time became an admirer of Walt Whitman's metrical innovation and grand vision. In his early years, Pound appreciated Browning's method (in *Sordello* and similar works) of invoking medieval figures, and anticipated his later preoccupation with translations by producing a series of immature versions in the manner of Dante Gabriel Rossetti.

Pound left the United States in 1908 to seek his literary fortune in Venice and London, becoming European correspondent of the Chicago magazine *Poetry,* recognising the genius of Eliot and Marianne Moore, among many others, and helping Yeats in that difficult transition between his early style and the mature achievement. After a brief period as an Imagist (with his friend Hilda Doolittle, Richard Aldington, and T. E. Hulme), he turned to the Vorticism espoused by Wyndham Lewis and the magazine *Blast.* The early *Cantos* shows the influence of Whitman, Browning, and Vorticist aesthetics, but Pound later found threads in an alleged Jewish conspiracy to defraud the world by usury (see the great Canto XLV); the differences between good and bad government (drawing on Jefferson and Confucius); and the connections (which Pound believed necessary) between goodness in the individual, a state of excellence in poetry, and just administration, including control over the banks. The curious theories, together with an often abrupt use of anecdote, make the work difficult to comprehend, and Pound himself – as an old man whose word was not necessarily to be taken seriously – was accustomed to depreciate the *Cantos* as 'a botch' and 'a mess'. 'I knew too little about so many things. I've read too little and I read very slowly', he said to Daniel Cory (*Encounter,* May 1968), but he inspired countless readers with his enthusiasms for the poetry of Arnaut Daniel, the No plays of Japan, and the thought of Confucius, in his often erratic translations.

Pound's shorter poems are more immediately accessible, and can be found in *Collected Shorter Poems* (Faber & Faber, 1968). *The Literary Essays* of Ezra Pound, edited by T. S. Eliot (New Directions and Faber & Faber, 1954) are always thought-provoking.

To accompany a reading of the *Cantos,* which are a poetic commentary on the course of civilization and its faults, one might read Pound's invigorating comments on how to think and how to read in such seminal books as *The Spirit of Romance* (1910; Peter Owen, 1953; New Directions, 1968), *The A.B.C. of Reading* (1934; New Directions, 1960; Faber & Faber, 1961), and *Guide to Kulchur* (1938; Peter Owen, 1967; New Directions, 1968). The last was 'written for men who have not been able to afford an university education or for young men, whether or not threatened with universities, who want to know more at the age of fifty than I know today'.

Readers who find Pound too easy to be intellectually challenging might explore Louis Zukofsky's *A* (University of California Press, 1978), a poem equally long but linguistically more abstruse than the *Cantos.*

MARIANO AZUELA (1873–1952).
  Los de abajo. First published in El Paso, Texas, 1916. Standard edition
  published by Pedro Robredo (Mexico City, 1938). Translated as *The
  Underdogs* by Enrique Munguía Jr. (1929; reprinted by New American
  Library and New English Library, 1967).

Azuela was a doctor who served during the Mexican Revolution of 1910, and
wrote *Los de abajo* (1916), *Los Caciques* (1917), and *Las Moscas* (1918) as a
result.

Influenced by French naturalism in the evocation of a great national disaster
through the accumulation of separate incidents, Azuela is a novelist steeped in
pessimism. He feels an overwhelming sense of grief at the fate of the poor, and
indignation at the behaviour of their oppressors. Technically, his style is simple
and his plots are both convincing and elaborate. Motivation is clear, and the
peasant is nowhere idealized.

In *Los de abajo,* a rebel peasant called Demetrio Macías escapes from his
village before government troops arrive, and leaves for the Revolution. After the
capture of Zacatecas he joins other victorious rebels in pillaging and rape.
Returning for home leave, the newly-promoted 'General' Macías is ambushed
with his followers at the very place where he and his friends had cut down
government troops at the beginning of the novel.

Violence breeds only violence, according to Azuela, and its futility should be
demonstrated by those who, like him, fought under Pancho Villa.

Los Caciques and *Las Moscas* have been translated by Lesley Byrd Simpson as
Two Novels of Mexico (University of California Press, 1956).

The background can be studied in the classic of anthropology by Robert
Redfield, *Tepoztlán: a Mexican Village* (University of Chicago Press, 1930) and in
J. Rutherford's *Mexican Society during the Revolution: a Literary Approach*
(Oxford U P., 1971).

British writers have generally failed to rise to the challenge of understanding
Mexico: from D. H. Lawrence's *Mornings in Mexico* (1927) and often bathetic
novel *The Plumed Serpent* (1926), to Graham Greene's *The Lawless Roads* (1939)
and *The Power and the Glory* (1940; called *The Labyrinthine Ways* (Knopf, 1946) in
the U.S.A. and often considered one of his two best novels with *The Heart of the
Matter*), and Evelyn Waugh's forgettable *Robbery Under Law* (1939).

OCTAVIO PAZ (b. 1914).
  El Laberinto de la Soledad: vida y pensamiento de México (2nd ed., Fondo
  de Cultura Económica, Avenida de la Universidad 975, Mexico 12, 1959).
  With *Posdata* (4th ed., Siglo XXI Editores, Gabriel Mancera 65, Mexico 12,
  1970). And *Configurations* (New Directions and Cape, 1971).

Paz is one of Mexico's leading poets and intellectuals. A career diplomat, from 1943 until his resignation in 1968 in protest against repression of Mexico's student movement, Paz has served in the U.S.A., Europe, Japan, and Switzerland, adding an international voice to the predominantly inward-looking literature of Mexico.

But *The Labyrinth of Solitude* (translated by Lysander Kemp, Grove Press, 1962; Allen Lane, 1967) is devoted wholly to the Mexican spirit, which Paz sees, in somewhat Blakean terms, as threatened by technology and commerce. Paz follows the Mexican philosopher Samuel Ramos (1897–1959) in believing that the repeated rewriting of the Constitution is a theoretical rejection of pragmatism, making reality itself illegal. Ramos suggested sincerity as the virtue to be cultivated by Mexicans, and psychoanalysis as a method towards self-realization. In his *Posdata,* Paz shows that successive Mexican governments have preserved the authoritarian mode of rule from the Spanish *conquistadores* (and the Aztecs before them), and proposes a critical use of the imagination to overcome false values.

As a poet, Paz is the author of numerous books from which several translators have selected the bilingual *Configurations,* ranging from *Piedra de Sol* of 1957 to *Blanco* of 1966. Paz's *Poemas* (1935–1975) were published by Seix Barral of Barcelona in 1979. He has translated not only Blake, but also Rimbaud and Hölderlin, with whom he feels a special affinity. Yet Paz has also experimented with surrealism and concrete poetry, and has perhaps come closer than anyone else since Goethe in the *West-östlicher Divan* to a reconciliation in words between Western and Eastern modes of thought and expression in the collection *Ladera Este* of 1969.

See *The Poetic Modes of Octavio Paz* by Rachel Phillips (Oxford U.P., 1972), and *Octavio Paz* by Jason Wilson (Cambridge U.P., 1979).

CHU HSI (1130–1200).
Chin-ssu lu. First published during the compiler's lifetime. Translated by Wing-tsit Chan, from the printed *Chu Tzu i-shu* datable to about 1717, as *Reflections on Things at Hand: the neo-Confucian Anthology* (Columbia U.P., 1967).

Just as Wang Yang-ming represents the idealistic aspect of neo-Confucianism, so Chu Hsi represents the rationalistic aspect.

His compilation, the forerunner of the *Hsing-li ta-ch'üan,* or the 'Great Collection of neo-Confucianism', has had an incalculably deep influence on aspects of Chinese thought and behaviour for over seven centuries.

The good man is serious in mind and righteous in behaviour. The foundation of all truth and value is *li* (variously rendered as 'principle' or 'virtue'), a word not mentioned in the Confucian *Analects*. Phenomena should be investigated, and seriousness should be cultivated: two doctrines owing much to the influence of Ch'an (Zen) Buddhism. Neo-Confucianism elevated the 'Four Books' (*Analects, The Great Learning, The Doctrine of the Mean* and the works of Mencius) above the five classics which were all compiled *after* the time of Master K'ung (Confucius). These so-called classics were the Spring and Autumn Annals, the Book of Odes, the Book of History, the Book of Changes, and the Book of Rites (lost, and replaced by the *Li Chi*). The sixth classic, the Book of Music, was lost before the 3rd century B.C. and replaced by the *Chou Li*.

As an example of the investigation recommended, when Yin-T'un (1071–1142) asked about the methods of study, he was told 'that to study one must read books. One need not read many. The important thing is to know their essentials. If one reads a great deal without knowing the essentials, he is but a bookstore. Because as a youngster I was greedy and read a great deal, I have forgotten much of it now. One must explore and experience the real meaning of the Sage, remember it, and then exert every effort to put it into practice'.

PIERRE CORNEILLE (1606–1684).
The Chief Plays. Translated by Lacy Lockert (New ed. Princeton U.P., 1957).

Like Descartes and Molière, Corneille was educated at a Jesuit school, and the Latin-biased training shaped the young dramatist in many ways, from the discipline of verse composition at an early age, to concepts of order, and plots from Roman history and legend. For twenty-two years he was employed both as an advocate in the Ministry of Forestry and as a registrar of the movement of shipping at Rouen, writing plays in his spare time. His 'years in the galley' can be forgotten, for the conversation pieces and realistic comedies were not marked by any special gifts, apart from a sense of dialogue. Neither did his first tragedy *Médée* (1635) bring him any great success. *L'Illusion Comique* (1636) was unusual for its time in being a comedy without buffoonery or coarseness.

But the first evidence of Corneille's greatness is *Le Cid* (1636–7), which aroused the envy of fellow-playwrights and drew down on him accusations of clumsiness and plagiarism. The famous riposte 'Je ne dois qu'à moi seul toute ma renommée' was ill-judged and untrue, for he had indeed taken the course, normal then and earlier, of deriving the structure of a play from a predecessor, in this case Guillén de Castro's *Las Mocedades del Cid* (1618). If *Le Cid* shows the apotheosis of honour (the hero winning two duels, a practice which Richelieu had outlawed in France and was furious to see glorified on stage), then *Polyeucte* was a tragedy of Christian martyrdom, *Horace* the triumph of patriotism, and *Cinna* a play in praise of generosity. Lockert's English blank verse translations of these four plays are supplemented by the inferior *Rodogune* (1645) and *Nicomède*

(1651).

The two volumes of Corneille translated by John Cairncross in Penguin contain *Le Cid, Cinna,* and *L'Illusion Comique;* and *Polyeucte, Nicomède,* and *Le Menteur* respectively.

A convenient French text is that in Classiques Garnier.

The last two decades before Corneille's death saw the building of the great Palace of Versailles. See Ian Dunlop's *Versailles* (Hamish Hamilton, 1970) and Jacques Levron's *Daily Life at Versailles in the 17th and 18th Centuries* (Allen & Unwin, 1968).

This is the period of the Marquise de Sévigné (1626–96), whose letters were first published in 1725 (best edition in the 'Grands Écrivains de la France' series, supplemented by the *Lettres inédites* published by Capmas). There is a *Selected Letters* translated by H. T. Barnwell in Everyman's Library (Dent and Dutton, 1960).

ALEJO CARPENTIER (1904–1980).
Los Pasos Perdidos. First published in Mexico City, 1953. Translated as *The Lost Steps* by Harriet de Onís (Penguin, 1968).

A Cuban novelist and short-story writer of Franco-Russian parentage, Carpentier was imprisoned in 1927 for signing a manifesto against the dictator Machado. He escaped from Cuba with a false passport and worked as a journalist in Paris until 1939. After World War II he again went into exile, this time to Venezuela, where he ran a radio station and lectured at a university. With the Cuban Revolution of 1959, Carpentier was appointed Vice-President of the National Cultural Council and was responsible for a vigorous programme of publications, ranging from literacy readers to experimental poetry. *El Recurso del Método* (1974) is a novel satirising Latin American dictators (in this case Gerardo Machado) comparable with Miguel Ángel Asturias' *El Señor Presidente* (1946, but written much earlier) against the Guatemalan dictator Estrada Cabrera, and with Gabriel García Márquez's *El Otoño del Patriarca* (1975).

The Lost Steps is a sophisticated work of art told by a Latin-American composer living in New York, who takes his French mistress on a journey to the jungle to find primitive musical instruments for a museum. The dialogue is slight, and the psychological motivation of the characters does not preoccupy Carpentier. He aims instead to evoke the multiple contrast between New York, the derivative city (in this case Caracas), and the primitive life of the jungle. The land and the symbolism are evoked with delicacy.

CESAR VALLEJO (1892–1938).
> *Obra poética completa*. First published 1968. There is no complete translation available, but Clayton Eshleman has translated *Poemas Humanos* (Grove Press, 1968; Cape, 1969) and (with José R. García) also *The Complete Posthumous Poetry* (University of California Press, 1978). David Smith has translated *Trilce* (Mushinsha Books, 1973, distributed by Small Press Distribution, 1636 Ocean View Ave., Kensington, CA 94707). Álvaro Cardona-Hine has translated *Spain, Let this Cup Pass from Me* (Red Hill, 1972, also distributed by SPD).

Vallejo wrote some fiction and essays, but he is valued on a par with Pablo Neruda for his contribution to Latin American poetry.

He was born in the Andean town of Santiago de Chuco, in northern Peru, and there quickly established a reputation with his first two books, *Los heraldos negros* (1919) and *Trilce* (1922). Then in 1923 he left Peru for Paris and never returned. Having become a Communist, he ended a period of poetic silence lasting almost fifteen years after the Fascist uprising in Spain in July 1936 by energetically revising and writing the poems that comprise *Poemas Humanos* and *España, aparta de mí este cáliz*, both published in 1939. The latter has a propagandistic tone, but the former is of great significance. Dominated by an existential pain exacerbated by events in Spain (where he spent a month in 1937 travelling between one ruined city and another), Vallejo is the most important poet of death since Baudelaire. His political convictions are anything but strident here: having passionately embraced the ideology of the Russian Revolution, he eventually comes to feel that any revolution is insignificant in the face of all-consuming death, and places his trust in the efficacy of poetic truth. The bitter ferocity of many poems is witness to the fire in his soul which cannot be set down in calm order, for events do not warrant calm or order.

See Jean Franco's *César Vallejo* (Cambridge U.P., 1976).

HASAN IBN ALI TUSI, NIZAM AL-MULK (1018–1092).
> *Siyasatnama*. Written 1086–1091. Translated by Hubert Darke as *The Book of Government, or Rules for Kings* (Routledge & Kegan Paul, 1960).

The Saljuqs, fierce Turkish nomads, took control of the Persian province of Khurasan in 1034, under Chaghri Beg, whose brother Tughril Beg conquered the neighbouring lands until Saljuq sovereignty extended from the Egyptian border to Chinese Turkestan and India.

Nizam al-Mulk was chief minister of Chaghri Beg's son Alp Arslan, and tutor to the latter's son, Malikshah. Nizam's use of Persian in literature and in matters of state proved crucial to the prosperity of the language, which survived and was an instrument in dealings with the West. His *Siyasatnama* is one of the immense number of oriental and occidental treatises on statecraft collectively known as *De regimine principum,* exemplified in Europe by the book of that title written in 1284 by Egidio di Colonna for Philip the Fair of France, and culminating in the *Idea de un príncipe político cristiano* (1640) by Diego de Saavedra Fajardo. Nizam advocated contacts with learned and prudent men, and managed to attract to court the astronomer and mathematician Umar Khayyam best known in the West for the quatrains (*Rubaiyyat*) paraphrased in English by Edward Fitzgerald (1859).

Nizam founded libraries for scholars and reorganised the old *medresehs* or religious seminaries into state schools, attracting to them distinguished scholars by the expedient of raising teachers' salaries, and arranging for poor pupils to receive state grants. Nizam was also responsible for establishing Baghdad's first university, called after him the Nizamiyyah.

It was there that al-Ghazzali taught before abandoning academic theology in favour of asceticism.

Nizam's great work was completed after his murder (by one of the Batini assassins he had denounced in the *Siyasatnama*) by the scribe Muhammad Maghribi, who appended information on political conditions.

See Tamara Talbot Rice's *The Seljuks in Asia Minor* (Thames & Hudson, 1961).

JUAN JOSE ARREOLA (b. 1918).

> *Confabulario Total, 1941–1961.* First published 1962. Translated by George D. Schade as *Confabulario and other Inventions* (University of Texas Press, 1964).

The fables and satires of the Mexican Arreola are less celebrated than they deserve, possibly because they are even more concise and laconic than those of Borges the Argentinian, who has also written a bestiary. It may be that Arreola's apocryphal biographies are inspired by *Les Vies Imaginaires* (1896) of the erudite and creative Parisian Marcel Schwob, and there are hints too of Kafka and Orwell, but it is also true that many of these brief anecdotes and stories could have been written by no other hand.

The 'Baby H.P.' of 1952, for instance, is in the form of an advertisement for 'a very light resistant metal that adapts itself perfectly to the infant's delicate body by means of comfortable belts, bracelets, rings and brooches'. All the child's energy is then converted into a reusable store of electricity. There are reassurances as to possible electrocution or the attraction of lightning bolts and sparks. . .

Since there is nothing specifically Mexican about Arreola's tales, it is instructive to read his own *La Feria* (1963; translated by John Upton as *The Fair*

(University of Texas Press, 1977), in which childhood memories of his home town Ciudad Guzmán are mingled with fragments from the Old Testament and colonial archives.

Contrast Arreola's cosmopolitan approach to the semi–autobiographical fiction of his exact contemporary Juan Rulfo, also from the province of Jalisco: the stories in *El llano en llamas* (1953; translated as *The Burning Plain* by G. D. Schade, University of Texas Press, 1968) and the haunting novel *Pedro Páramo* (1955; translated by Lysander Kemp, Grove Press, 1959). The hero Pedro is obsessed with the years from Porfirio Díaz's regime to that of Obregón: all the other characters are dead, surviving merely as voices.

Year 45

HENRY WALTER BATES (1825–1892).
  The Naturalist on the River Amazons. First published 1863. Available in
  Everyman's Library (Dent and Dutton, 1969).

Bates spent seven and a half years collecting specimens and studying the wild life
in the *sertão* or wilderness of the Amazonian hinterland, suffering at various
times from ague, overwork (six days a week) and climatic exhaustion, and bad,
insufficient food.

  In the circumstances it is remarkable that he was able to gather no fewer than
eight thousand unrecorded varieties of insect, as well as previously unknown
butterflies, birds and plants. The legendary exploits of this courageous traveller
were modestly recorded in a model travel chronicle which even the most efficient
modern expeditions could not hope to surpass.

  The background to the man's life and work can be found in George
Woodcock's *Henry Walter Bates, Naturalist of the Amazons* (Faber & Faber,
1969).

  Excellent illustrations and an up-to-date text make *The Amazon* by Tom
Sterling (Time-Life, 1973) an excellent companion to Bates, while the
anthropological background is supplied by Gerardo Reichel-Dolmatoff in
Amazonian Cosmos (University of Chicago Press, 1974).

JOÃO GUIMARÃES ROSA (1908–1967).
  Sagarana. First published 1946; definitive ed., 1956. Translated by Harriet
  de Onís (Knopf, 1966). *Grande Sertão: Veredas.* First published 1956;
  definitive ed., 1958. Translated as *The Devil to Pay in the Backlands* by
  James L. Taylor and Harriet de Onís (Knopf, 1963).

The Brazilian novelist Guimarães Rosa won instant acclaim for his first cycle of
stories, set in the backlands of Minas Gerais, his native state.

  A country doctor, Rosa began his literary career as a poet, and his striking use of language enlivened all his subsequent fiction. Having participated in the revolution and civil war of 1930–3, Rosa was appointed to the diplomatic service, and spent time in Europe and Bogotá before becoming chief of the Frontiers Division within the Foreign Office, living in Rio de Janeiro. Extravagant in diction, he is elementally vital and sympathetic to all living things: a latter-day Melville in this, as he is comparable to Faulkner in his concentration on one part of the country to be explored.

Grande Sertão: Veredas is an epic which transcends its Brazilian *locale* to become universal in its appeal. Rosa's contemporary, Jorge Amado, has called it 'one of the greatest books our literature has produced – brutal, tender, cordial, savage, vast as Brazil itself, the image of Brazil drawn by a writer with a consummate mastery of his craft'. See J. S. Vincent's *João Guimarães Rosa* (Twayne, 1979).

Also from Minas Gerais is the ironic and witty post-modernist poet Carlos Drummond de Andrade (b. 1902), a selection from whose work has been translated by Virginia de Araujo as *The Minus Sign* (Carcanet New Press, 1981).

THOMAS PAINE (1737–1809).
   Rights of Man. First published 1791. Edited by H. Collins (Penguin, 1969).

The son of a small farmer of Thetford, in Norfolk, Paine was dismissed from his poet as an excise-man in 1772 for agitating in favour of a pay increase, and sailed for America, returning in 1787.

In 1790, Edmund Burke published his influential *Reflections on the Revolution in France* (edited by Conor Cruise O'Brien, Penguin, 1969). The Dublin-born Whig politician argued that, even if the *ancien régime* had been as wholly corrupt as was claimed, the methods of the revolutionaries guaranteed no real liberty and should be repudiated, for Burke foresaw the catastrophe that might occur if similar methods were applied in Britain. A settled constitution without interference by the mob was essential to liberty and democracy.

Tom Paine, a Quaker radical, subtitled his reply 'an answer to Mr. Burke's attack on the French Revolution', and formulated in even more firm and cogent terms the absolute priority of fundamental human rights, no matter what horrors were to be endured before those rights could be obtained. The book was prohibited by the Government of the day, but when his printer refused to sell any more copies, Paine found another and sales continued to rise. It was in fact far more moderate in tone than Paine's subsequent defence of Deism *The Age of Reason,* and Pitt could say that Paine was right, 'but what am I to do? As things are, if I were to encourage Tom Paine's opinions we should have a bloody revolution'.

In this connection, one should read Alexis de Tocqueville's *L'Ancien Régime et la Révolution* (1856), translated by S. Gilbert as *The Ancien Régime and the French Revolution* (Collins, 1966), and some of the many studies on the Revolution by modern scholars such as Cobban, Lefebvre, and Sorel.

This is an appropriate moment to study *The English Constitution* (1867) by Walter Bagehot, Editor of *The Economist* from 1860 to his death in 1877.

ORLANDO & CLAUDIO VILLAS BOAS (b. 1916 and 1918 respectively).
Xingu: the Indians, their Myths (Farrar, Straus and Giroux, 1973; Souvenir Press, 1974).

The brothers Villas Boas, including a third, Leonardo (1920–61), were among the military expedition known as 'Brazil's March to the West', and arrived at the headwaters of the Xingu in 1946. In 1961 the Xingu National Park was created, to protect the Xingu Indians, and in 1968 the Park was enlarged to about 30,000 square kilometres, equivalent to 11,500 square miles.

The purpose of the Villas Boas brothers was to respect the Indian 'and to guarantee his existence according to his own values. Until we, the "civilized" ones, create the proper conditions among ourselves for the future integration of the Indians, any attempt to integrate them is the same as introducing a plan for their destruction. *We* are not yet sufficiently prepared'. Their book is packed with unusual myths (and others readily identifiable with universal myths) and possesses a glossary, as well as authentic Xingu drawings.

It will be instructive to compare the attitude of the Villas Boas to that of Christian missionaries in Africa, or to that which dictated the massacre of Tasmanian aborigines.

WALT WHITMAN (1819–1892).
Leaves of Grass. First published 1855. New and comprehensive edition by Emory Holloway. Everyman's Library (Dent and Dutton, 1947).

Whitman repels the modest man, who finds the posturing and noisy declamation offensive. The extravert, however, is attracted by Whitman's exuberance and appetite for life, even if he finds the language is inflated. Preaching liberty, fraternity and equality, Whitman's songs are for himself, it is true, and celebrate his own personality, but in doing so they celebrate also his kith and kin, his workmates and contemporaries the land of America, its animals and its seasons.

The breakdown of the rigid distinction between prose and verse in Whitman caused concern among conservatives, but the technique was finally vindicated in Ezra Pound's *Cantos*. The incantatory sound of Whitman has inspired such poems as *Howl* by Allen Ginsberg, published in 1956.

If the first American Declaration of Independence of 1776 was political, then the second, *Leaves of Grass,* is spiritual, calling for brotherhood in democracy. The preface to the first edition states that the poems are saturated 'with a vehemence of pride and audacity of freedom neeessary to loosen the mind of still-to-be-formed America from the folds, the superstitions, and all the long, tenacious and stifling anti-democratic authorities of Asiatic and European past'.

Whitman reflects the aggressive individuality of the backwoodsman or Congressman, and his popularity in the U.S.A. has waxed and waned according to each American generation's level of belief in its own individuality.

See Roger Asselineau's *The Evolution of Walt Whitman* (2 vols., Harvard U.P., 1960–2).

GILBERTO FREYRE (b. 1900).
Casa-Grande & Senzala. First published 1933. Translated as *The Masters and the Slaves* by Samuel Putnam (2nd ed., Knopf, 1956). And *Sobrados & Mucambos.* First published 1936. Translated as *The Mansions and the Shanties* by Harriet de Onís (Knopf, 1963; Weidenfeld & Nicolson, 1966). And *Ordem & Progresso.* First published 1959. Translated as *Order and Progress* by Rod. W. Horton (Knopf, 1970; Secker & Warburg, 1972).

Freyre's magnificent work of scholarship on the history of Brazil cuts across the borders of sociology, social anthropology, social psychology, and economic and social history, to interpret social development in cultural and historical – rather than merely ethnic terms.

As a historian, he has certain shortcomings. He generalises, for example, from the patriarchal north-east of Brazil and the social life of its sugar plantations in the 16th and 17th centuries. He was responsible for the view, only now being reversed with accumulating documentation, that slavery was less vicious in Pernambuco and the Recôncavo of Bahia than in other countries, enlarged into the questionable thesis (of *O Mundo que o Português Criou,* 1940), that Portuguese colonists have been more racially tolerant than have other Europeans.

But the great sweep of Gilberto Freyre's historical research has been of immeasurable value to Brazilians in obtaining a perspective of their lives and activities. One might also derive benefit from his articles collected in *Tempo de Aprendiz* (2 vols., Instituição Brasileira de Difusão Cultural S.A., 1979).

A great sociological study of the previous generation was created by Euclides Cunha (1866–1909) in *Os Sertões* (1902), translated by Samuel Putnam as

Rebellion in the Backlands (University of Chicago Press, 1957).

TOKUTOMI ROKA ('TOKUTOMI KENJIRO') (1868–1927).
   Omoide no ki. First published 1901. Translated as *Footsteps in the Snow* by
   Kenneth Strong (Allen & Unwin, 1970).

A Christian and a socialist, Kenjiro met Tolstoy and attempted to model his life
on that of the eccentric Russian, attacking the family system as being essentially
selfish and backward.

Omoide no ki (literally, 'Recollections'), is a semi-autobiographical novel
dealing with the adventures of a young provincial Japanese of aristocratic family
who escapes from his cloistered home environment in the 1880s to make his
career as a writer and libertarian in Tokyo. He is drawn into a Christian milieu,
but is repelled by the bigotry of many missionaries as well as by the inequalities of
Meiji life. In his reforming zeal, Kenjiro has been thought of as a Japanese
Dickens, and it is true that his style is vigorous, but his characters are less varied
than those of Dickens, and his sentimentality more open.

These faults are more evident in his first novel, which caught a popular mood
and assured financial independence for Kenjiro, *Hototogisu* ('The Cuckoo',
1898; translated as *Namiko* by S. Shioya and E. F. Edgett, 1904).

THEOPHRASTUS (*c.* 372 B.C.–*c.* 287 B.C.).
   Characters. First published 319 B.C. Text with a facing translation by
   J. M. Edmonds in the Loeb Classical Library (Heinemann and Harvard
   U.P., 1929). Translated (with the plays and fragments of Menander,
   341–290 B.C.) by Philip Vellacott (Penguin, 1967).

A distinguished Greek philosopher and successor to Aristotle as president of the
Peripatetics, Theophrastus studied under Plato, deriving from his mentor that
lifelong interest in classification and typology which was to lead to his extant
treatises on botany, the *Enquiry into Plants* and the *Aetiology of Plants,* as well as
to his amusing typology of good and bad human characters. A supreme
polymath, Theophrastus was reputed to have lectured and written on every
discipline in the Peripatetic School curriculum from ethics to mathematics.

The series of 'good' characters has been lost, but we have the thirty 'bad'
characters,such as 'Ostentation', 'Brutality', and 'Stupidity'. Concise, droll and
probably aimed at individuals known to the author's audience, these sketches
have been translated into many languages, and imitated by John Earle in his
Microcosmographie (1628) and by 'Hudibras' Butler in his *Genuine Remains*
(1759).

The best translation is that into French by Jean de La Bruyère (1645–1696), who published his much longer and more comprehensively satirical *Caractères* in 1688 (translated as *Characters* by J.Stewart, Penguin, 1970).

La Bruyère pours scorn on the follies and vanities of men, women, and institutions, like Theophrastus often referring in thinly-veiled irony to individuals notorious for a given foible. His style is pithy and direct, with a rich vocabulary always appropriate to the occasion. It seems likely that La Bruyère found many of his 'characters' in the comedies of Molière: certainly one cannot appreciate 'good society' and its detractors in 17th-century France without understanding these satirists in prose and drama.

CHARLES-LOUIS DE SECONDAT, *Baron de* MONTESQUIEU (1689–1755).

> *De l'Esprit des Loix.* First published 1748. Edited by J. Brethe de La Gressaye 1950–61. Translated by T. Nugent as *The Spirit of the Laws* (Hafner, 1949).

Montesquieu was born into a noble family with a legal background, and he himself was trained in law at Bordeaux and Paris, inheriting his uncle's office of President of the Bordeaux *Parlement* in 1716. In 1721 he published anonymously the *Lettres Persanes* which purport to be a correspondence showing the reaction of two visitors from Persia to the strange ways of the French, much as *Gulliver's Travels* (1726) will give the British a view of themselves as seen by the King of Brobdingnag.

Montesquieu believes that his country is in sharp decline, and his next book is not afraid to give a warning anticipating that of Gibbon to the British in 1776–88. This book is *Considérations sur les Causes de la Grandeur des Romains et de leur Décadence* (1734; translated by D. Lowenthal, Cornell U.P., 1969).

But Montesquieu is remembered above all for the *magnum opus* which carries the arguments of the *Considérations* from ancient Rome to the domain of the abstract principle. The *Esprit des lois,* as it is commonly known in modern French usage, was begun in 1743 and took four years to write. The first of its six sections deals with law in general and different kinds of government; the second, with the means of government; the third, with climate and its effect on national character; the rest of the book is devoted to economics, religion and types of legal system. The book offers no panacea as guiding principles in law as in life, and concludes that the most judicious mode of government is a liberal, benevolent monarchy limited by constraints to safeguard the liberty of every citizen. As a result of its critical examination of the French monarchy it had to be published in Geneva, but proved immensely popular, and formed a theoretical justification for the American, French and even the Russian Revolutions.

PUBLIUS OVIDIUS NASO (OVID) (14 B.C.–17 A.D.).
Ars Amatoria. Text with an English prose translation by J. H. Mozley in the Loeb Classical Library (with other poems, Heinemann and Harvard U.P., 1929). Modern verse translation by Rolfe Humphries (Indiana U.P., 1958).

According to Ovid, he was banished from his influential position in the social and literary life of Rome in 8 A.D. because of one poem and one mistake. The mistake was unmentionable, and has consequently been assumed to have had a connection with the Emperor Augustus or his close family, such as the Emperor's profligate daughter Julia. The poem was the erotic *Ars Amatoria,* an elegiac poem in three books, of which the first two show how a man may win and retain a woman, and the third how a woman may win and hold a man. The *Remedia Amoris,* also in the Loeb volume, shows how an affair can be brought to an end.

Ovid's unflagging powers of wit and invention make these poems among the most amusing and sophisticated of antiquity. They give us a remarkable portrait of Rome, and Ovid's flippant libertinism can be traced again and again in medieval poetry, including the Goliardic poets and Juan Ruiz, Archpriest of Hita.

Ovid's *Tristia* lament the last night he spent at Rome, the dreaded voyage to Tomi (now Constanza, on the Black Sea coast of Romania), and the years of exile.

The first to put *The Art of Love* into English was Thomas Heywood (1600); the second was Francis Wolferston of the Inner Temple, a man otherwise unfamiliar to us, who took advantage of the more tolerant Restoration times to publish his version. Dryden translated Ovid in part, as did Congreve.

Year 46

ALEXANDER SERGEYEVICH PUSHKIN (1799–1837).
> *The Captain's Daughter and other stories.* Translated by Natalie Duddington in Everyman's Library (Dent and Dutton, 1933).

Pushkin is still considered by many to be the greatest of Russian poets, although the twentieth century has provided us with several other writers of comparable stature.

He is also, however, one of the outstanding exponents of the Russian *novella*, as the five examples in the present selection prove. The first in chronological order is *Peter the Great's Negro* (1828; an Abyssinian whose grandson he claimed to be); followed by 'The Station-Master', one of the five *Tales of Belkin* (1831); the melodramatic *Queen of Spades* (1834) which provided the plot for Tchaikovsky's opera (3 discs, HMV SLS 5005, conducted by Khaikin); the short novel *The Captain's Daughter* (1836); and *Dubrovsky* (1841).

See Henri Troyat's *Pushkin: a Biography* (Allen & Unwin, 1974).

TORQUATO TASSO (1544–1595).
> *Gerusalemme Liberata.* First published complete 1581. Translated by Edward Fairfax (1600; Centaur Press, 1962; South Illinois U.P., 1962).

Bernardo Tasso (1493–1569), father of Torquato, tried to harmonise the adventure romance of Ariosto with the serious intentions of the Virgilian epic in *Amadigi* (1560), based on the famous Spanish novel of chivalry *Amadís de Gaula*.

Torquato, naturally influenced by his father's success, emulated it with *Rinaldo* (1562) before embarking on his most ambitious work, devoted to the 'liberation' of Jerusalem by the Christian Crusaders, which was complete by 1575. The great epic poem was written while Torquato was court poet to Alfonso II, Duke of Ferrara. Constant rewriting, marred by religious interpolations and ill-conceived allegorical additions, turned the poem into a shadow of itself, the

Gerusalemme Conquistata (1593), published after Torquato had completed and published his father's *Floridante* (1587).

Jerusalem Delivered, in the Elizabethan translation of Fairfax, is too coldly calculated for most readers: why should anybody write a huge poem an imitation of Virgil's *Aeneid* in the sixteenth century, inventing hundreds of imaginary events in a pseudo-historical setting the poet had never visited? It is true that the rhyme-scheme is mechanical, and few of the characters come alive. But if one has to point to indisputable excellence there is the world of action and crowded canvases that, as Camerini has said, endow *Gerusalemme Liberata* with the same kind of visionary power in an earthly context which the *Divina Commedia* possesses beyond the confines of our earth. And if one can identify with that strange impulse that leads Christians or Muslims to holy war, the poem is stirring indeed.

See C. P. Brand's *Torquato Tasso* (Cambridge U.P., 1965).

This is the period of the madrigals of Monteverdi (1567–1643) and the splendid Venetian festival music of Giovanni Gabrieli (1557–1612).

HERBERT READ (1893–1968).
   The Contrary Experience: Autobiographies (Faber & Faber, 1963). And *The Green Child.* First published by Heinemann, 1935 (Penguin, 1969).

Nobody can appreciate the English artistic scene in the twentieth century without studying the works of Herbert Read: not only his general books like *The Meaning of Art* (first published in 1931) and *Education through Art* (Faber & Faber and Pantheon, (1974), but also his monographs on Ben Nicholson and Barbara Hepworth. He was a distinguished poet, and his writings on anarcho-syndicalism were always thought-provoking. As a literary critic he ranked with T. S. Eliot, being especially sympathetic to the writings of the English Romantics.

But many would agree that his most engaging creations were his autobiographical writings which began as early as 1933 with *The Innocent Eye;* and his only full-length novel, *The Green Child.*

In the first part of the fable, Olivero returns to his native village (much as Read always came back to his native Yorkshire from living elsewhere and travelling from China to Cuba), meets the Green Child, and disappears together with her, when 'hand in hand they sank below the surface of the pool'. The second part, in reality not as separate from the first as a hasty reading might lead one to expect, deals with President Olivero and the green people. It is a fictional Utopia very different from Aldous Huxley's satirical *Brave New World* or George Orwell's horrific *1984.*

The first part of *The Green Child* might be compared, in its fantasy of childhood, with Alain-Fournier's *Le Grand Meaulnes* (first published in 1913, the year before he was killed in action; translated by F. Davison, Penguin, 1978), and with Rafael Sánchez Ferlosio's exquisite *Industrias y andanzas de Alfanhuí* first published in 1952, and translated by R. M. Donald (Purdue U.P., 1975).

Herbert Read has written eloquently on the sculpture of his great friend and fellow-Yorkshireman Henry Moore (b. 1898), who is probably the most important sculptor produced in Britain. See Herbert Read's *Henry Moore* (Thames & Hudson, 1966) and *Henry Moore: Sculpture and Environment* by Moore and David Finn (Abrams, 1977).

VIDYAPATI THAKUR (1352–1448?).
Love Songs. Edited by W. G. Archer and translated by Deben Bhattacharya (Allen & Unwin and Grove Press, 1963).

'Vidyapati' means 'master of true knowledge', so the name has been used by a number of writers and it is virtually impossible to disentangle the authentic songs from those by later poets, for it was long accepted practice for writers to sign their work with the names of illustrious predecessors, such as the celebrated Vidyapati and Chandi Das.

The body of work commonly ascribed to Vidyapati includes eight works in Sanskrit, and verses on the love between Krishna and Radha in Maithili, a dialect of Bihari spoken in Mithila, between Bihar and West Bengal. Vidyapati's approach differs from that of most of his contemporaries (and of his great predecessor Jayadeva), for whereas they wrote of love as an exclusively masculine passion, in which the woman was to be subjugated, Vidyapati was able to evoke the feminine response to sex and the feminine nature which needed true fulfilment in its own right. The allegorical method, by which Radha's yearning for Lord Krishna can be seen as a complementary duality comprising the Supreme Being of the Seventh Heaven, succeeds as nobly in Vidyapati as it does in the Christian terms of lover/Beloved in St John of the Cross. Even now, the songs of Vidyapati are widely loved and widely performed, especially in Bihar and Bengal.

Aspects of life in Vidyapati's region can be studied in *The Art of Mithila* by Yves Véquaud (Thames & Hudson, 1977), particularly enlightening for a view of matriarchal society in which only the girls and women paint, and where the linear time of the West is incomprehensible, for the *Ramayana* story is played out everywhere, with everyone a character in the living drama.

See also Jeremiah P. Losty's *Krishna: a Hindu Vision of God* (British Library, 1980).

PIERRE CARLET DE CHAMBLAIN DE MARIVAUX (1688–1763).
Le Paysan Parvenu. First published 1735–6, but left unfinished. Translated by L. W. Tancock as *Up from the Country* (Penguin, 1980).

This psychological novel of Marivaux (his *Vie de Marianne* of 1731–41 is the other, also unfinished) anticipates the middle class novels of Henry Fielding, for just as Tom Jones could be any young buck of the time, so could Jacob, the 'hero' of *Le Paysan Parvenu.* Arriving in Paris from Champagne, Jacob uses his wits and intelligence as well as his good looks to rise to become a farmer-general of taxes, and marries a Countess.

High birth and good breeding count more in the fiction of Marivaux than in Fielding's, and the Frenchman tends to be more subtle in his treatment of the various modes of love, but outrageous comedy appears in both writers. Farce occasionally penetrates Marivaux's smooth narrative, as in the scene in Madame Rémy's home. Extraordinary figures abound, among them the talkative Madame d'Alain and the blunt Bono.

The excellent Penguin collection listed above also includes two plays in David Cohen's translation intended for performance on the Oxford stage: *La Double Inconstance* ('Infidelities', first produced in 1723), which was Marivaux's own favourite; and *Le Jeu de l'Amour et du Hasard* ('The Game of Love and Chance', first produced in 1730), generally considered his most satisfactory play.

In the same rococo atmosphere of Marivaux, one can enjoy the paintings and drawings of Antoine Watteau (1684–1721), who crowded almost all of his major output into the five years 1715 to 1719. As well as *L'Opera Completa di Watteau* (Rizzoli, Milan, 1968) and Malcolm Cormack's *The Drawings of Watteau* (Hamlyn, 1970), read the classic *French Eighteenth-Century Painters* (Phaidon Press, 1981) translated by Robin Ironside from *L'Art au Dix-huitième Siècle* (1859–75) by Edmond and Jules de Goncourt.

LUIS VÉLEZ DE GUEVARA (1579–1644).
El diablo cojuelo. First published 1641. Edited in Clásicos Castellanos by Francisco Rodríguez Marín (Espasa-Calpe S.A., Madrid, 1960).

Seventeeth-century Spain produced a vast literature of disillusion, from stern sermons to witty caricatures; Quevedo's sombre allegory, *Sueños,* was followed by those of Rodrigo Fernández de Ribera, (*Los anteojos de mejor vista, c.* 1625) and Luis Vélez de Guevara.

While escaping from justice over the rooftops of Madrid, the student Don Cleofás takes refuge in an astrologer's laboratory, where he unwittingly releases the lame devil of the novel's title. As they fly together above Madrid and other cities, the devil points out the evils and hypocrisies which are hidden from ordinary view. One chapter holds up to contempt the *nouveaux riches* who love their gilded carriage so much that they prefer to live in it, never emerging from one year to the next. The comedy is less bitter than that of Quevedo: the language erudite and the metaphors playfully absurd. The novel was adapted, losing much of its satirical bite, by Lesage in his *Le diable boîteux* (1707).

This is the age of Velázquez (1599–1660), the painter of King Philip IV in Madrid, and Van Dyck (1599–1641), court painter of Charles I in London. Van Dyck had been the pupil of one of the greatest painters of any age, the Fleming Peter Paul Rubens (1577–1640). See Jacob Burckhardt's *Recollections of Rubens* (Phaidon Press, 1950), Michael Jaffé's *Rubens and Italy* (Cornell U.P., 1977), Frans Baudouln's *Rubens* (Abrams, 1977), and *Rubens: Drawings and Sketches* (Scribners, 1978).

MOSHE BEN MAIMON (MAIMONIDES) (1135–1204).

Moreh Nebukhim. First published in Rome 1473–5. First Latin translation from Hebrew published in Paris (1520) as *Dux seu Director Dubitantium aut Perplexorum.* Standard edition (3 vols., Paris, 1856–66) translated as *Guide for the Perplexed* by M. Friedlander in 1881–5 (reprinted by Dover, 1971). Also translated by Shlomo Pines (University of Chicago Press, 1963).

Originally written in Arabic as *Dalalat al-Ha'irin,* this is one of the most celebrated books of the Middle Ages, by the author of an Arabic commentary on the *Mishnah* (see the translation of the *Mishnah* by Herbert Danby, Oxford U.P., 1933) and the finest mediaeval exposition of Jewish Law: the *Mishnah Torah* of 1180.

Born in Cordova, Maimon and his family were forced to leave Spain in 1160 as a result of persecution by the Muslim Almohad rulers. Having learned what his father knew of mathematics and astronomy, Maimon became a leading scholar of his time in law and philosophy, and in all rabbinical studies.

The *Guide for the Perplexed* attempts to reconcile Judaic revelation with Aristotelian philosophy, and concludes that reason alone is insufficient to explain religious and scientific phenomena. Its influence on Spinoza was very marked, as it was on St Thomas Aquinas, who attempted to reconcile Aristotelianism with Christian revelation. This is an appropriate moment to survey the work of Averroes (like Maimon a native of Cordova), who essayed the harmonising of Islamic revelation with scientific knowledge as transmitted from Aristotle.

Averroism taught that the world is eternal, not created from nothing but moved by a creative force always at work – a concept not a million miles away from evolutionary theory. Its impact on Islamic thought was slight, but the medieval Christian and Jewish philosophers learnt what they knew of Aristotle through the intermediary of Averroes, or Muhammad ibn Ahmad ibn Rushd as he is known in Arabic. See George F. Hourani's translation of Ibn Rushd's *Kitab fasl al-maqal, On the Harmony of Religion and Philosophy* (Luzac, 1961).

HERMANN BROCH (1886–1951).
   Der Tod des Vergil. First published 1945. Translated as *The Death of Virgil* by Jean Starr Untermeyer (Grosset, 1946).

An Austrian Jew, Broch seemed happily settled in his father's textile business until in 1928 he suddenly decided to study philosophy, psychology and mathematics at Vienna University, and then turned to writing novels. When the Nazis invaded Austria, Broch was arrested, but some influential friends (including James Joyce) managed to contrive Broch's emigration to the United States in 1938.

It was in the U.S.A. that Broch composed his account of the last eighteen imagined hours in the life of Virgil, a prototype of Western man. Obsessed by death, Broch summons up the spirit of the dying Roman by interior monologue. Highly complex, mystical, many-sided and to be approached from many directions, *Der Tod des Vergil* is a literary masterpiece which may help readers to come to terms with the fact of their own death more easily.

Broch's first book was more ambitious in scope and length, if not in technique and wisdom. This is the trilogy *Die Schlafwandler* (1931–2; translated by Willa and Edwin Muir as *The Sleepwalkers,* Grosset, 1964), a work of profound disillusionment with the world as Broch saw it, tarnished with opportunism, convention, greed, and amorality. It is only by the redeeming qualities of timeless art, literature, and music, Broch concludes, that man can rise beyond the shallow norms of society.

See Ernestine S. Bradley's *Hermann Broch* (Twayne, 1978).

MILAREPA (1052–1135).
   Mila Grubum. Translated by Garma C. C. Chang as *The Hundred Thousand Songs of Milarepa* (2 vols., University Books, New York, 1962).

This compilation of Milarepa's teachings was compiled (as was the *Mila Khabum*) by Sans. rGyas. rGyul. mTshan ('The Insane Yogi from gTsan') and is considered one of the most precious books in Tibetan literature.

Milarepa led an extraordinary life, to go by traditional accounts. After the early death of his father, it is said that his relatives ruthlessly stripped the boy of his inheritance. To avenge himself, by sorcery he caused the death of many of these relatives and destroyed the harvest with hailstorms. Having realised the evil he had wrought for evil, the young singer and poet sought the Buddhist Dharma as a disciple of the guru Marpa. To purify him and prepare him for endurance on the path to enlightenment, Marpa set him extreme penances, and tasks such as building houses on a mountain single-handed and then tearing them down without reason. In a dream, Milarepa saw his mother lying dead in his ruined house and his sister as a wandering beggar. He left for home, and soon found that these visions had been true. Visited by a sense of the futility and evanescence of human life, he retreated to isolation on a mountain, eating only nettles for twelve years, until his body turned green and he reached enlightenment.

His life thereafter was devoted to teaching the Way through practice and song. Avoiding the temptation to set up his own order, temples, or discipleship, he travelled the hard tracks of Tibet to sing of the Way in poems suited to the receptivity of his hearers, but often couched in ecstatic mysticism reminiscent of the canticles of St John of the Cross.

See W. Y. Evans-Wentz's *Tibet's Great Yogi Milarepa* (Oxford U.P., 1951).

For the background, one might read R. A. Stein's *Tibetan Civilization* (Faber & Faber, 1972) or *Tibet: its History, Religion and People* (Penguin, 1972) by Thubten Jigme Norbu and Colin Turnbull.

APOLLONIUS RHODIUS (*fl.* 220 B.C.).

Argonautica. Text, with a facing prose translation by R. C. Seaton, in the Loeb Classical Library (Heinemann and Harvard U.P., 1912). Translated by E. V. Rieu (Penguin, 1959).

Few facts are known about Apollonius, who called himself *Rhodius* (of Rhodes) after his adopted home. He was certainly Librarian to the great Alexandrian library, for nine centuries the most influential in the Western world, on which see E. A. Parsons' *The Alexandrian Library* (Cleaver-Hume Press, 1966). Apollonius succeeded Callimachus, the lyric poet .who may have been responsible for the literary and subsequently personal quarrel which induced Apollonius to leave Alexandria for triumph in Rhodes, though he eventually returned to Alexandria, pride of Egypt and the Hellenistic world.

The quarrel was over the style of literature most appropriate to Alexandria and the heirs of Homer. Callimachus and his school believed that the essence of the new literature lay in brevity, polish, and subtlety. Apollonius believed fervently that the smart new belles-lettres was a diminishing of Greek writing, and undertook to prove the vitality – and the superiority – of the Homeric epic style by producing a new epic – on Jason's voyages in search of the Golden Fleece. Alexandrianism has been defined by Robinson Ellis as: 'Precision in form and metre, refinement in diction, a learning often degenerating into pedantry and obscurity, a resolute avoidance of everything commonplace in subject, sentiment or allusion'. And while the work of Callimachus can roughly be thus described, many features of Alexandrianism are present too in Apollonius, for only the greatest can rise above the characteristics of the age. The *Argonautica* is not an epic in unity, but only in length. It is as episodic as a novel, but for the episode concerning Jason's love for Medea one can forgive Apollonius his occasional *longueurs*.

One should contrast the poem with the poems of Callimachus of Cyrene (fl. 3rd century B.C.), with a text, facing prose translation and notes by C. A. Trypanis (Heinemann and Harvard U.P., 1958); and with the idylls of the Syracusan Theocritus (c. 316–260 B.C.), the latter in the Loeb Classical Library volume translated by J. M. Edmonds as *The Greek Bucolic Poets* (Heinemann and Harvard U.P., 1912) together with the surviving works of Bion, Moschus, and others.

The novelist E. M. Forster wrote a guide to Alexandria, but the city's main connection with modern English literature is the 'Alexandria Quartet' of novels by the poet Lawrence Durrell (b. 1912): *Justine* (1957), *Balthazar* (1958), *Mountolive* (1959), and *Clea* (1960) published by Faber & Faber and Dutton. See also Durrell's evocative travel books on Cyprus (*Bitter Lemons,* Dent & Dutton, 1959), on Rhodes (*Reflections on a Marine Venus,* Faber & Faber, 1953), and *The Greek Islands* (Faber & Faber and Viking, 1978).

Year 47

Anthology of Korean Poetry, from the earliest era to the present, compiled and
translated by Peter H. Lee (John Day, New York, 1964).

As in China and Japan, poetry in Korea is considered one of the three major arts,
with painting and calligraphy. The earliest Korean poetry, we may be certain, was
related to primitive religious incantation, including the cult of fertility and the
turning year. Peter Lee's selection begins with the Silla dynasty (57 B.C.–A.D.
935) and concludes with three poems by Cho Pyong-hwa (b. 1921).

One of the most popular of Korean verse genres is the *sijo,* a short, polished
stanza of three lines with fourteen to sixteen syllables in a line to a maximum of
forty-five in all. Richard Rutt has compiled and translated an anthology of *sijo:
The Bamboo Grove* (University of California Press, 1971).

This is a good time to listen to the exquisite traditional music of Korea, and to
enjoy the arts and crafts of the gifted Korean in books imported from Korea or J.
Barinka's *The Art of Ancient Korea* (Peter Nevill, 1962). For the nation's history,
see William E. Henthorn's *History of Korea* (Free Press of Glencoe, 1971).

ETTORE SCHMITZ ('ITALO SVEVO') (1861–1928).
> *La coscienza di Zeno.* First published 1923. Included in the U. Apollonio
> edition of Sve⅄o's *Opere* (4th ed., 1964). Translated by Beryl de Zoete as
> *Confessions of Zeno* (Penguin, 1964).

Not the least of James Joyce's virtues is that he encouraged the Triestine Jew
Schmitz to take up the practice of literature again after he had abandoned writing,
following the disastrous failure of his books – published at his own expense – to
obtain recognition in Italy.

Svevo's Triestine mannerisms appealed to few outside Trieste, and he had no
fellow-feeling with his Italian contemporaries Carducci and D'Annunzio. He is
closer to the Austrians Musil and Arthur Schnitzler, and was in fact an Austrian

citizen at the time when his first two books appeared.

Svevo's fiction, from the earliest *Una vita* (1892, not 1893 as the title-page states) and *Senilità* (1898; translated by Beryl de Zoete as *As a Man Grows Older*, Penguin, 1965) to the posthumous *Corto viaggio sentimentale* (1949), is a remarkably homogeneous *oeuvre*. He is always obsessed with giving up smoking, with fears of senility even when thirty, and with his ceaseless self-analysis. Svevo read and used the works of Freud critically, taking psychoanalysis to the analyst's as it were. *La coscienza di Zeno* purports to be an analyst's unethical exposure of his patient's weaknesses. Eugenio Montale, the major Italian poet who was a friend and admirer of Svevo, suggested that Svevo's characters are infected with a case of multiple *bovarysme;* that is, whereas Flaubert's Emma Bovary believes herself to be a great romantic heroine, Svevo's characters delude themselves into thinking they are several different personae, and oscillate between these identities. Like Emma, they are unfit to inhabit the real world.

See P. N. Furbank's *Italo Svevo: the Man and the Writer* (Secker & Warburg, 1966).

Ch'u Tz'u: the Songs of the South. An ancient Chinese anthology collected by Wang I in A.D. 125. Edited and translated by David Hawkes (Oxford U.P., 1959).

Literally 'Songs from the Kingdom of Ch'u', this anthology contains a nucleus of poems composed about 350 years after the later parts of the *Shih Ching* ('Book of Songs'), the other great classic anthology of poetry from ancient China.

The Kingdom of Ch'u extended, at its zenith, over the present provinces of Hupeh and Chekiang, with parts of Kiangsu, Anhwei, Hunan, Kiangsi, Szechwan, Shensi and Honan: a total area larger than England and Wales, and far to the south of the area from which the *Shih Ching* came.

Most of the *Ch'u Tz'u* poems are written in the song style, so-called because it was originally used only in songs; or in the Sao style, named after the famous poem *Li Sao* traditionally attributed to the earliest-named Chinese poet Ch'ü Yüan, a nobleman banished by King Huai of Ch'u. The story goes that Ch'ü Yüan was slandered by jealous courtiers after he had repeatedly warned the King about the possibility of invasions from Ch'in to the north. After the King had been treacherously killed while a prisoner in Ch'in hands, Ch'ü Yüan wandered in despair among the barbarous tribes of southern Ch'u, finally drowning himself. It is also legend that the annual Dragon Boat Festival held everywhere where Chinese have access to water, from Singapore to Hong Kong, commemorates the death of this wise and loyal courtier.

The *Li Sao* ('Encountering Trouble') is an uncharacteristically long lament traditionally concerned with these experiences of Ch'ü Yüan, and imbued with the shamanism which also permeates *The Nine Songs* (also translated by Arthur Waley in a separate volume, Allen & Unwin, 1955). Nobody interested in ancient China can afford to overlook this splendid book by David Hawkes.

Saint THOMAS MORE (1477–1535).
   Libellus. . . de Optimo Reipublicae Statu, deque Nova Insula Utopia. First published in Louvain, undated, in 1516. Definitive Latin edition, March 1518. Text, with a parallel English translation based on that of G. C. Richards, edited by Edward Surtz and J. H. Hexter (Yale U.P., 1965). Translated by Paul Turner (Penguin, 1965).

First translated into English in 1551, St. Thomas More's denunciation has long been a classic more talked about than read. An imaginary 'Utopia' (a Greek-style compound word conveying the meaning 'No Place') is contrasted with the actual state of unhappy England under King Henry VIII. More laments the plight of the poor and the growth of crime, the cynicism of clergy and lawyers alike, corruption in the administration, the decay of towns and villages, and the increase of sheep-farms and enclosures.

Like Bacon, More urged mass education and attention to the physical and spiritual health of the people. He attacked the avarice of the rich. The people of More's Utopia all work, the idle being banished. Clothing and homes are durable rather than showy. Meals are to be taken communally, so that all may benefit from a healthy diet, and the young mingle freely with their elders. Happiness consists in deferring immediate pleasure for long-term gain.

Just as Johnson's *Rasselas* may seem a riposte to Voltaire's *Candide,* so *Utopia* may be judged a retort against the pragmatism of Machiavelli's *Principe.* In style, *Utopia* is a satire anticipating Swift's *Gulliver's Travels.*

And while the book can be read as eagerly by those interested in social agitation against Henry VIII as by anyone keen on a witty satire ably told, so the Catholic will hold the book up as a weapon in the holy war against Protestantism (More was executed for high treason), and the Communist will claim it as a historic document in the struggle against capitalism and the landed gentry.

See Tommaso Campanella's *La Città del Sole* (1602; in Henry Morley's compilation *Ideal Commonwealths,* Routledge, 1885) for a theocratic Utopia on communistic lines which he actually planned to create in southern Italy.

FARID AD-DIN ATTAR (*c.* 1136– *c.* 1230).
> *Ilahinama* ('The Book of Divine Wisdom'). Translated by Fouad Ruhani as *Le Livre Divin* (Paris, 1961). And *Mantiq at-Tair* ('The Parliament of Birds'). Translated by C. S. Nott as *The Conference of the Birds* (Routledge & Kegan Paul, 1961).

Attar's name denotes 'pharmacist', a profession in Persia then encompassing medical treatment.

Having travelled in his vocation throughout many cities and towns of the Saljuq-dominated empire, Attar settled in the Sufi city of Nishapur, where he wrote some of the large number of mystical books attributed to him (twelve of the 114, according to Sa'id Nafisi's *Justju dar ahval u athar-i. . . Attar* (Tehran, 1942).

The principal two are the *Ilahinama* and the *Mantiq at-Tair*. The first concerns a king who asked each of his six sons in turn to reveal his dearest ambition. Their wishes are: to marry the daughter of the Fairy King; to possess all the secrets of magic; to own the world-revealing cup of Jamshid; to obtain the Water of Eternal Life; to obtain the Ring of Solomon; and to turn base metal into gold. The king's reply, offered with a wealth of appropriate anecdote, is that each of them seeks only the material and transient, whereas real happiness can only be sought by pursuing the spiritual and the eternal.

The Conference of the Birds is an epic poem cast in the same anecdotal style, in the *ramal musaddas* metre. Thirty birds seek their king and discover, after an exhausting journey, that the *Simurgh* in question is in fact themselves (*si murgh* = thirty birds). The allegory of the human's soul quest for annihilation in the Godhead is wonderfully elaborated from the legend as it occurs in Abu Hamid al-Ghazzali, and even now the book is cited as a model of Persian poetic style.

Attar's prose Sufi hagiography, *Tadhkirat al-Auliya,* has been abridged by A. J. Arberry in *Muslim Saints and Mystics* (Routledge & Kegan Paul, 1965; University of Chicago Press, 1966).

CHRISTOPHER MARLOWE (1564–1593).
> *Complete Plays.* Edited by J. B. Steane (Penguin, 1969).

This modern edition includes the insignificant *Dido, Queen of Carthage* (written with Nashe, 1594); *Tamburlaine the Great* (1590), innovative in its bold and brilliant handling of blank verse; *Doctor Faustus* (1604), a play taken to its protagonist's native Germany by English strolling players; *The Jew of Malta* (written after 1588 but not published until 1633), whose hero was the prototype of Shakespeare's Shylock; *Edward II* (1594), the play which inspired Shakespeare's *Richard II;* and the trivial *Massacre at Paris* (1600?).

Though *Edward II* is the first great historical play in English, it is for the three major tragedies that Marlowe is honoured today. All are still performed to great effect.

In *Marlowe's "Tamburlaine"* (Vanderbilt U.P., 1964), Roy Battenhouse has carefully shown that *Tamburlaine,* essentially a condemnation of the lust for power through conquest, represented a Protestant world view then held in England, though Marlowe himself is known to have been an atheist.

The Jew of Malta, less profound and wide-ranging than *The Merchant of Venice,* concentrates on the destructive nature of the lust for power through wealth.

The Tragical History of Doctor Faustus is the apotheosis of Marlowe's literary and dramatic powers, taking as its theme the lust for power through knowledge. Goethe's great verse tragedy is much longer and more complex, but in its own way the *Faustus* of Marlowe achieves perfection. Certainly, as a playgoer who has seen a recent *Faustus* in London and a *Faust* in Heidelberg, I suggest that Marlowe's stagecraft and brevity leads to a more striking overall effect.

See J. B. Steane's *Marlowe: a Critical Study* (Cambridge U.P., 1970), and for the wider literary context, Muriel Bradbrook's *Themes and Conventions of Elizabethan Tragedy* (2nd ed., Cambridge U.P., 1980).

FRANCOIS-RENE DE CHATEAUBRIAND (1768–1848).
   Mémoires d'Outre-tombe. First published 1849-50. Edited by M. Levaillant
   and G. Moulinier in Pléiade (2 vols., 1960). Selections translated by Robert
   Baldick (Penguin, 1965).

One could spend a lifetime examining the life and times of the Vicomte de Chateaubriand through the twelve-volume *Oeuvres Complètes* (1929–38) and the background literature.

The clear point of departure is his own autobiography divided into four sections: his military career, travels and exile (to 1800); his literary career (1800–14); his political life (1814–30); and the period of retirement (1830–40). A fascinating Casanova figure in love affairs and infidelities, he was married in 1792 to a supposed heiress whose fortune was lost in the French Revolution. He spent the years from 1793 to 1800 in England, translating, teaching French in Beccles, and writing the *Essai sur les Révolutions* (1797). Restored to Christianity from scepticism by the shock of his pious mother's death, he wrote the apologia *Le génie du Christianisme* (1802), which incorporated the previously-published episodes *Atala* (1801) and *René* (1802). The latter in particular created or helped to reflect a fashion for romantic melancholy under the burden of existence: the *mal du siècle* of the Romantic movement.

Appointed by Napoleon to the embassy in Rome, Chateaubriand resigned in 1804 on hearing of the execution of the Duc d'Enghien. His political opinions wavered in a compound of opportunism and principle which no commentator has been able to simplify, but the *Memoirs* remain a monument to the art of autobiography. Egotistic as his senior the Marquis de Sade, and as brilliant a stylist as his predecessor Rousseau, Chateaubriand is a key figure in French Romanticism and the revival of the Roman Catholic Church in France.

At Savigny-sur-Orge, home of his lover the Comtesse Pauline de Beaumont, Chateaubriand met the philosopher Joseph Joubert (1754–1824) and edited the latter's *Recueil de Pensées* (re-edited by Pierre de Raynal, 1842; translated by H. P. Collins, Routledge, 1928). See also J. Christopher Herold's *Mistress to an Age: Mme. de Staël* (Hamish Hamilton, 1959).

CARLOS FUENTES (b. 1928).
> *Terra nostra*. First published 1975. Translated by Margaret Sayers Peden (Farrar, Straus & Giroux, 1976; Penguin, 1978).

World renown came to the Mexican novelist Carlos Fuentes with the publication of *La Muerte de Artemio Cruz* (1962; translated by Sam Hileman as *The Death of Artemio Cruz,* Farrar, Straus, 1964).

All his output to date, however, is eclipsed by the extraordinary *Terra nostra,* a fantasy in which Fuentes has changed the course of Spanish history by marrying Philip II of Spain to Elizabeth I of England. The prose is brilliantly varied, from the experimental to the parodistically dull. Allegory, the grotesque visions of a Bosch (Philip II's favourite painter, seven of whose works are still in the Prado), and the technical resources of a sophisticated modern novelist all combine to make this work as self-sufficient in its way as *The Tale of Genji* or *Pather Panchali* are in theirs.

It is intriguing to read the historical background to the imaginings of Fuentes: from R. Trevor Davies' *The Golden Century of Spain, 1501–1621* (Macmillan, 1937) to Walter S. Gibson's *Hieronymus Bosch* in the World of Art Library (Thames & Hudson, 1973). The Spanish music of the Spanish Golden Age is dominated by the choral compositions of Tomás Luis de Victoria (c. 1548–1611), born in Ávila, the 'City of Saints'. Outstanding records of Victoria's religious music can be heard on Oiseau-Lyre SOL 283 and 270 (both conducted by McCarthy), Argo Eclipse ECS 747 (conducted by Malcolm) and on Argo ZRG 620 (conducted by Guest).

RALPH WALDO EMERSON (1803–1882).
> *The Portable Emerson*. Selected and arranged by Mark Van Doren (Viking Press, 1946; Penguin, 1977).

The first American essay, as an intellectual adventure in the line from Epictetus to Montaigne, was the *Nature* of Emerson first published in 1836. In 1837 came *The American Scholar,* which has justly been termed the American 'intellectual Declaration of Independence'.

What had gone before included the death of his beloved wife and his departure from the ministry, in 1832, and his first journey to England and Scotland in 1833. He talked with Coleridge in Highgate, with Wordsworth in the Lake District, and above all with Carlyle at Craigenputtock. Carlyle's *Heroes* was to be influential in the composition of Emerson's *Representative Men.*

In 1840 Emerson joined Thoreau and Margaret Fuller to edit the transcendentalist magazine *The Dial* (6 vols., Russell & Russell, 1961) to promote a mystical approach to man and nature, in which God was seen to be immanent. The New England transcendentalists of the mid-nineteenth century, in reaction against the Unitarians, can be read in Perry Miller's anthology *The American Transcendentalists* (Doubleday, 1957).

Emerson viewed himself primarily as a poet, but his verse is obviously written to explain himself to himself, being gnomic and metaphysical. We value him for his rejection of dogmatism in religion and the reliance on individual experience; for the pragmatic avoidance of a set philosophical system to which disciples were expected to relate, and the need for hope and optimism in both personal and historical terms.

Oliver Wendell Holmes' *Ralph Waldo Emerson* (1884) has been reprinted by Gale (1968), but the best modern biography is still that by R. L. Rusk, *The Life of Ralph Waldo Emerson* (Columbia U.P., 1949).

DAVID JONES (1895-1974).
    In Parenthesis (Faber & Faber, 1937; Viking Press, 1963). And *The Anathemata* (2nd ed., Faber & Faber, 1955; Viking Press, 1965).

The basis of *In Parenthesis* is the experience of a Welsh rifleman in the trenches during World War I. It has been argued that certain actions leading up to the Somme offensive correspond in Jones' poem to parts of the Mass that precede its Canon, and it is quite clear that, as a Catholic, David Jones felt life and death to be sacramental. Welsh history and mythology are exploited to point up similarities between the lives of ancient or legendary heroes and the mundane or crucial events of a typical battle-front, with its boredom and terror. David Jones never makes the mistake of romanticizing war, but uses the experimental techniques of writers he particularly admires (such as Eliot and Joyce) to stress the essentially disjointed nature of life at the front.

The Anathemata is a long meditation in prose and verse on the Western Christian tradition seen by a Welshman, whose visual and verbal imagination is as keen as that of any of his contemporaries (one recalls that Pound's other great interest was music, while those of David Jones were water-colour and monumental inscriptions).

Writings in prose by David Jones have been collected by Harman Grisewood in *Epoch and Artist* (Faber & Faber, 1959) and *The Dying Gaul* (Faber & Faber, 1978). *The Sleeping Lord* (Faber & Faber, 1973) is a collection of fragments in verse, uneven in quality, which emphasise the mystical side of the author's nature. 'The Sleeping Lord' here is Arthur, defined also as the land he occupies, like Blake's Albion and Joyce's Humphrey Chimpden Earwicker and Anna Livia Plurabelle.

Year 48

Sir WALTER SCOTT (1771–1832).
> *Waverley; or, 'Tis Sixty Years Since.* First published anonymously (3 vols., 1814). Many current editions, including that in Everyman's Library (Dent and Dutton, 1969).

After having edited the ballads collected in *Minstrelsy of the Scottish Border* (1802–3), Scott began to write a historical novel but mislaid his manuscript before finishing it.

A decade later, when Byron's *Childe Harold's Pilgrimage* eclipsed all other English poetry, Scott thought of resurrecting *Waverley,* and prepared it for press in three weeks. In 1813 Scott had modestly declined the poet laureateship, proposing Southey in his place, and his own judgement that he was a better novelist than poet has been vindicated by posterity. The book was instantly successful not only in Britain but also – less expected – in the United States. French and German translations appeared and the demand for the true historical novel (as opposed to the 'Gothick' novel such as Horace Walpole's pseudonymous *Castle of Otranto,* 1765) began the vogue which has never since ceased.

Scott's method was to create a fictional web around historical events already familiar to his readers, and to reverse the usual precedence of history books, elevating the ordinary person (such as Edward Waverley) to principal rôles, and demoting the famous to supporting rôles. This was Shakespeare's method in dealing with Falstaff in the *Henry* cycle, and it would form – at the other end of the literary scale – the prototype for the novels of Jean Plaidy and Georgette Heyer. Scott produced some forty 'Waverley' novels, beginning the flood of historical novels which have attained the heights of Wilhelm Hauff's *Liechtenstein* and James Fenimore Cooper's *Last of the Mohicans* (1826), Manzoni's *I Promessi Sposi* (1827), and Victor Hugo's *Notre Dame de Paris* (1831).

See J. G. Lockhart's classic *Life of Sir Walter Scott* (Dent and Dutton, 1957).

FRANCESCO GUICCIARDINI (1483–1540).
L'Historia d'Italia. First published 1561. Translated as *The History of Italy* by S. Alexander (Collier-Macmillan, 1969).

Born into a Florentine patrician family, Guicciardini was appointed Florentine ambassador to Ferdinand of Aragón from 1512 to 1514, and thereafter served the Medicean Popes Leo X and Clement VII, being commissioner-general for the Pope's army at the time of the Sack of Rome (1527).

When the Medici fell in Florence, Guicciardini retired to compose the *Ricordi politici e civili* and the *Considerazioni sui discorsi del Machiavelli,* his friend and neighbour being Machiavelli himself.

After spending the years 1534–7 in the service of Alessandro de' Medici, Guicciardini once again retired, now to write the history of Italy on which his fame rests.

As a historian, he belongs to the synchronistic school, choosing to see Italy as one nation among many, for while in Spain he had come across the affairs of France, England, the Indies, and Spanish American interests. He sees the corruption and vice of Italian life clearly, as a foreigner might, and he resists as far as he can two besetting sins of the early historian: partiality (which distorts Dante's *Divina Commedia* as well as Machiavelli), and the imposition of a predetermined system (which distorts the interpretations of Dante as well as Vico). Guicciardini is too sophisticated to see any patterns in history, and too realistic to believe that Italy's corruption is destined to end (Belli is a sardonic witness in the nineteenth century).

But although Guicciardini's synchronistic method made an enormous impact on later thinkers and historians, among them Montaigne and Jean Bodin (1530–96), his reputation sank on the publication of Leopold von Ranke's important *Zur Kritik neuerer Geschichtschreiber,* an essay appended to the *Geschichte der romanischen und germanischen Völker* (1824). Dealing with the period from 1494 to 1535, Ranke starts with Guicciardini's claim to be a primary source, showing conclusively that Guicciardini was dependent on more secondary sources than he cared to confess. Ranke also indicates to what extent the judgments of Guicciardini were – perhaps inevitably – coloured by his private life, party loyalties, and even his professional career. In other words, Ranke tries to divorce the facts which a historian chooses to include and discuss from the opinions which he holds. Guicciardini is perhaps unfairly criticised, for many of his contemporaries and successors suffered from failings worse than his, but Ranke's intelligent criticism led generally to a more cautious use of primary and secondary sources, and a more objective approach to problems affecting race, religion, and nationality.

See R. Ridolfi's *Life of Francesco Guicciardini* (2nd ed., Routledge, 1970) and Felix Gilbert's *Machiavelli and Guicciardini: Politics and History in 16th century*

Florence (Princeton U.P., 1965).

GERARD MANLEY HOPKINS (1844–1889).
> *Poems.* Edited by W. H. Gardner and N. H. MacKenzie (4th ed. Oxford U.P., 1970).

Hopkins was a brilliant Greek scholar at Oxford, named by Benjamin Jowett as 'the star of Balliol'. The turning-point in his life was conversion to the Roman Catholic Church in 1866. Influenced by the life and teachings of St Ignatius Loyola, Hopkins entered the Jesuit novitiate in 1868 and burnt all his early poems, resolving to write no more until commanded to do so by ecclesiastical authority. This opportunity arose when a superior suggested that a member of the community should write an elegy for five Franciscan nuns drowned in the wreck of the 'Deutschland'. Hopkins' poem on this theme has become recognized as a milestone in English poetry although, like the rest of his work, it remained unpublished in his lifetime. Indeed it was not until 1918 that Robert Bridges produced the first edition of Hopkins' poems. They are as original in their way as the richly-wrought Welsh poems of Dylan Thomas or the Scots poems of Hugh McDiarmid (C. M. Grieve).

The 'sprung rhythm' of Hopkins is an innovation with few disciples because of its remarkable difficulty, but his 'inscapes' have passed into common practice, with the stridency of Ted Hughes in England and the more muted poetry-without-metaphor of Philippe Jaccottet in France.

See John Pick's *Gerard Manley Hopkins: Priest and Poet* (2nd ed., Oxford U.P., 1966).

HENRY JAMES (1843–1916).
> *The American Novels and Stories.* Edited by F. O. Matthiessen (Knopf, 1947).
> And *The Portrait of a Lady.* First published 1881. Many current editions, including one in World's Classics (Oxford U.P., 1947).

James wrote all of his perceptive, measured and elegant novels as if he were a cultured and leisured character, usually on the fringe of the action, given to discriminating judgments on people and manners.

The American Novels and Stories volume includes the unfinished *The Ivory Tower*, and *The Europeans* (1878) which brings Europeans to a New England background; *Washington Square* (1881), the story of the heiress Catherine Sloper in New York; and *The Bostonians* (1886), a satire against New England reformers.

Henry James himself singled out *The Ambassadors* (1903) as his best work, but many critics prefer the complex, subtle *The Portrait of a Lady,* in which the penniless American girl Isabel Archer becomes an heiress and, like Cathy Sloper, has to deal with an adventurer. The psychological realism of Henry James requires patience and concentration, for the grotesques that relieve the long novels of Dickens are absent, but he is one of the most rewarding writers in English for the grace of the mandarin style. His characters belong to the wealthy or leisured classes, and what he lacks in awareness of the lower classes he makes up in his sure handling of the many women he portrays.

Leon Edel has written the definitive biography: *Henry James* (5 vols., Lippincott, 1953–72), and has edited the *Complete Plays* (1949) and the *Complete Tales* (12 vols., 1962–7).

LI HO (791–817).
    San-chia Li Ch'ang-chi ko-shih. Edited by Wang Ch'i (1959). Translated by
    J. D. Frodsham as *The Poems of Li Ho* (Oxford U.P., 1970).

In the T'ang dynasty, Han Yü and Huang-fu Shih heard that a seven-year-old descendant of Prince Cheng could write original poems, and they called at the boy's house to verify the tale. Li Ho, styled Ch'ang-chi, immediately dashed off 'The Tall Official Carriage Comes on a Visit' to the astonishment of the scholars. The name of Li Ho was made, and though he died at the age of 26 or so he left a corpus of 241 lyrics, acknowledged to be genuine, which rank among the finest in all T'ang literature.

This is particularly remarkable since he stands outside the Apollonian tradition of Chinese poetry: none of his poetry is to be found in the standard anthology of three hundred T'ang poems *T'ang shih san-pai shou* compiled in Ch'ing times. Indeed there is no comparable poet in Chinese except possibly the Manchu writer Singde (1655–85), whose background was shamanistic. To find a voice like that of Li Ho one must go to the Englishman Keats, the Austrian Georg Trakl, or the Frenchman Baudelaire, all writing more than a thousand years after the Chinese prodigy.

Li Ho can easily be translated, because his bright, colourful images express perceptions without needing to refer for every meaning to a scholarly footnote. The footnotes do help, of course, and the apparatus by Dr Frodsham forms an integral part of one's view of the sensuous, philandering genius.

AMOS TUTUOLA (b. 1920).
   *The Palm-Wine Drinkard, and his dead Palm-Wine Tapster in the Deads'
   Town* (Faber & Faber, 1952).

African literature has traditionally been one of oral emphasis: tell-telling around
the hearth instead of novels; songs and chants instead of books of poetry; and
rituals instead of plays. Performance normally involves everyone: the listeners or
dancers or singers participate in a way lost to the literate European, with his habit
of silent reading.

   The Nigerian teller of tales Tutuola has grasped the essence of the Yoruba
tradition on the one hand, and western continuity of poetic vision and technical
brilliance. His first novel, like the others which have followed from Faber &
Faber, deals with a human's journey to the world of ghosts, spirits, and 'Deads'
His helter-skelter assimilation of European ideas to the Yoruba vernacular is
exactly comparable to the assimilation of the Yoruba gods Shango, deity of
thunder and lightning, and Ogun, deity of iron and war, to the popular Yoruba
views of electricity and metal technology.

   Magic is an integral part of the Yoruba world-view, so it finds its rightful place
in Tutuola's concept of beauty triumphing over power. The boundaries between
the Living and the Dead are not only hazy – they are according to Tutuola quite
illusory.

   Similar evocations of Yoruba myth in the graphic arts can be found in the work
of Twins Seven-Seven, a Nigerian artist who has illustrated ideas from Tutuola.
See Ulli Beier's *Contemporary Art in Africa* (Pall Mall Press, 1968),
supplementing the same author's *Art in Nigeria 1960* (Cambridge U.P., 1960).

   The archaeological background is provided by Thurstan Shaw's *Nigeria: its
Archaeology and Early History* (Thames & Hudson, 1978).

VLADIMIR VLADIMIROVICH MAYAKOVSKY (1893–1930).
   Poems. Translated by Herbert Marshall (Hill & Wang, 1964; Dennis
   Dobson, 1965).

Mayakovsky's work has been judged harshly by Soviet socialist realist
ideologues, who believe it is too difficult for the proletariat; and by western
critics, who believe it panders too much to the official Stalinist line. Certainly,
Stalin approved of Mayakovsky's poems openly, and a statue of the flamboyant
exhibitionist dominates Moscow's Mayakovsky Square. Even his home town,
Bagdadi in Georgia, has been renamed after him.

   But the truth is that, having joined the illegal Bolshevik party at the age of
fourteen, and having been imprisoned three times between 1908 and 1909,
Mayakovsky always felt impelled to serve the cause of revolution, and suffered

only when revolutionary ardour had cooled in political life. He committed suicide in 1930, after having expressed anger at Esenin's suicide five years earlier.

Mayakovsky travelled to western Europe and America, engaged in furious polemics, edited the journel *L.E.F.* as well as its successor *Novy L.E.F.,* and wrote hundreds of party slogans and posters.

Technically, Mayakovsky was a master of every poetic device, including visual and concrete poetry, the palindrome and pun, metaphor and hyperbole. His style is Futurist, though a year after signing the Futurist Manifesto he proclaimed his own, asserting that the very people of the Soviet Union were futurists.

Like Evgeny Evtushenko (b. 1933), Mayakovsky allied a gift for the public and declamatory poem with a rich personal lyric gift which occasionally tinges with irony one's experience of the 'noisy' works.

His spiritual autobiography, *Vo ves' golos* ('At the Top of my Voice', 1930) has been wittily rendered into Scots by Edwin Morgan as the title poem in his volume *Wi the Haill Voice: 25 poems by Vladimir Mayakovsky* (Carcanet Press, 1972).

He is an important playwright, *Klop* ('The Bedbug', 1928–9) and *Banya* ('The Bathhouse', 1929–30) being satirical comedies mordant enough to cause official unease. *The Bedbug and Selected Poetry* is a bilingual volume translated by Max Hayward and George Reavey (Indiana U.P., 1975), while *The Bathhouse* is included in *Twentieth-Century Russian Drama* translated by Andrew MacAndrew.

I strongly recommend *Kak delat' stikhi?* ('How are Verses Made?', translated by G. M. Hyde, Cape, 1971), in which Mayakovsky analyses his purpose and method in writing a poem on Esenin's suicide.

Susan P. Compton's *The World Backwards* (British Library, 1978) is a study on Russian futurist books from 1912 to 1916 which has much on Mayakovsky, and Umbro Apollonio's *Futurist Manifestos* (Thames & Hudson, 1973) sheds a good deal of light on the artistic ferment of the time. The general background to the European movement is explained in *Futurism* (Thames & Hudson, 1978) by Caroline Tisdall and Angelo Bozzolla.

ILANGO ADIGAL (2nd century A.D.).
> *Shilappadikaram.* ('The Ankle Bracelet'). Translated by Alain Daniélou (Allen & Unwin, 1967).

The Tamil verse romance, written by a Jain prince who was brother to King Shenguttuvan, a ruler on the west coast of South India, is one of the five great poems in Tamil – the *Mahakavya.* All are dated to the period from the second to the seventh centuries A.D., but only two others have survived, and *The Anklet* is superior to both in its interpolated poetic anthologies, and the exalted tone of the author's diction. The Daniélou translation follows the Tamil edition of Swaminatha Aiyar. There is another version in English, by V. R. Ramachandra Dikshitar (Oxford U.P., 1939).

The verse epic tells of the handsome young merchant Kovalan, his wife Kannaki, and his mistress Madhavi, whose gift of music leans heavily on Prince Ilango's intimate knowledge of early Indian classical music.

A contemporary of Ilango's, the Tamil poet Cattanar, wrote a poem in thirty cantos, the *Manimekalai,* which has been considered a sequel to the *Shilappadikaram* by some scholars, though others believe it to be earlier. The heroine, Manimekalai, is the daughter of Kovalan and the courtesan Madhavi. She eventually renounces the world, after studying all the religious systems, and becomes a Buddhist ascetic.

Listen to Indian music on a record such as Yehudi Menuhin's 'Classical Indian Music' (Decca LXT 5600) and consult an elementary work on Indian music such as B. Chaitanya Deva's *An Introduction to Indian Music* (Ministry of Information, Government of India, 1973).

BERTRAND, *3rd Earl* RUSSELL (1872–1970).
   History of Western Philosophy. First published 1946. (2nd ed. Allen & Unwin, 1961).

Russell, who tells the story of human thought in 'connection with political and social circumstances from the earliest times to the present day', was an outstanding example of a thinker who had the courage of his convictions, founding a school to practise his educational theories, and spending countless hours in propaganda in the cause of peace against nuclear weapons.

He made classic contributions to mathematical logic in *The Principles of Mathematics* (1903; 2nd ed., Allen & Unwin, 1950) and *Principia Mathematica* (with Alfred North Whitehead, 1910–13), but his most original contributions to the mainstream of western philosophy are *The Analysis of Mind* (1921), *An Inquiry into Meaning and Truth* (1940) and *Human Knowledge* (1940).

His *History* is not only remarkably balanced and comprehensive, but excels in the cardinal virtue of clarity.

Russell's central position in Cambridge and British intellectual life is brought out in the long *Autobiography* (3 vols., Allen & Unwin, 1967–9). This should be read in conjunction with *My Philosophical Development* (Allen & Unwin, 1959).

SHIMAZAKI HARUKI ('SHIMAZAKI TOSON') (1872–1943).
> *Hakai.* First published 1906. Translated as *The Broken Commandment* by Kenneth Strong (University of Tokyo Press, 1974).

The son of the head of a mountain village community in the Shinshu province of Central Japan, Shimazaki studied literature in a missionary college in Tokyo, and taught English Literature, being especially impressed with the English Romantic poets.

After writing derivative Romantic verse, he turned to prose impressions in the manner of Ruskin, exemplified by the *Chikumagawa no suketchi* ('Chikuma River Vignettes', 1912), written in the town of Komoro. But his real vocation lay in the novel, and a few weeks after reading *Crime and Punishment* in 1904, he started work on *Hakai,* five of whose characters can definitely be identified with prototypes in Dostoevsky. The period of writing, when he was completely unknown and desperately poor, was a time of immense hardship: one daughter died of meningitis while the book was being written, and his two other daughters succumbed within the next three months of dyspepsia and tubercular meningitis. The novel, published at his own expense, was advertised in the press as 'the book that had cost its author the lives of all his children'. The theme is that of the outcasts or *eta,* subjected to humiliation and even brutal attacks because of their birth. In 1871 the Edict of Emancipation had abolished the *eta* caste, but it was a double-edged weapon, since they had formerly been free of taxation in partial recompense for social degradation. In fact, the *eta* were made scapegoats for social discontent, as in the case of the Mimasaka Riot of 1873.

In its humanism and compassionate realism, *Hakai* broke new ground in Japan. Shimazaki wrote numerous other works, such as the major historical novel *Yoake mae* ('Before the Dawn', 1929–35), and a great deal of semi-autobiographical fiction, but the influence and example of *Hakai* has never been surpassed.

See Edwin McClellan: *Two Japanese Novelists: Soseki and Toson* (University of Chicago Press, 1969).

Year 49

Saint THOMAS AQUINAS (1225–1274).
> *Selected Writings.* Selected and edited by M. C. D'Arcy. Everyman's
> Library (2nd ed., Dent and Dutton, 1964).

St Thomas was born at the castle of Roccasecca, near the small town of Aquino in southern Italy. He entered the Dominican Order while a student at the University of Naples, continuing his studies under Albert the Great, also a Dominican, at Paris and Cologne. He became a professor of theology in Paris for a few years before returning in 1259 to Italy, where he taught until 1269. A life of teaching and writing, therefore, in which the two cardinal books were systematic Latin treatises: the *Summa Theologiae,* for novices, which was never completed because of the mystical experiences that made 'all I have written seem to me like so much straw compared with what I have seen and what has been revealed to me'; and the *Summa contra Gentiles.*

The latter, written first, was composed at the request of S. Ramón de Peñafuerte, ostensibly to convert the Muslims of Spain. But the book grew into quite a different tool, aiming at nothing less than the reconciliation of reason with revelation. Each is dependent on the other, he argues, but faith must be greater than human reason, for it comes direct from God. After studying Plato and the other Greek philosophers, Aquinas came to the conclusion that Aristotle represented best the tradition of natural reason.

In his Encyclical of 1879, Pope Leo XIII declared the *Summa Theologiae* to be the undisputable basis of Roman Catholic theology, though it must be remembered that Aquinas is not the author of the concluding part.

One must appreciate St Thomas Aquinas and his reputation among medieval scholars when reading Dante. For him Aristotle may have been *il maestro di color che sanno* ('the master of all those who know'), but St Thomas was *la fiamma benedetta* ('the blessed flame'). For background reading, try F. C. Copleston's *Aquinas* (Penguin, 1955).

The Duecento and early Trecento are great periods in Italian poetry and painting. The leading figure in art, after the sculptor Nicola Pisano, was Giotto (*c.*

1266–1337), but in poetry the field is so rich that it would be invidious to select one or two names from a valuable anthology such as Piero Cudini's *Poesia italiana del Duecento* (Garzanti, Milan, 1978).

GEORGE BORROW (1803–1881).
   Lavengro. First published 1851. And *The Romany Rye.* First published 1857. Many current editions, including those in Everyman's Library (Dent and Dutton, both 1961).

Son of a Cornish army captain and of a mother descended from French Protestant fugitives, Borrow was born in East Dereham, Norfolk, but his constant peregrinations with the regiment early determined an inclination to travel. In Edinburgh he acquired a more 'thorough proficiency in the Scotch' than in the Latin taught at school, and this gift for languages was another vital strand in his development. The third was riding: not systematically, in a riding school, but characteristically taking a spirited horse for a gallop which left him bruised and shaken in body, though exultant in spirit: 'give me the flush, the triumph, and glorious sweat of a first ride, like mine on the mighty cob!'
   'Lavengro' ('word-master') was the name given him by the gipsy Jasper Petulengro, on account of his remarkable facility in picking up Romany. Borrow not only learnt twelve languages before he was eighteen, but never missed an opportunity to learn another. Many adventures in his two great autobiographical works have the stamp of Dickensian coincidence about them, but we do not know enough of the 'veiled period' from 1826 to 1833 to judge their accuracy. Instead, we enter with gusto into the world of a wanderer of insatiable curiosity, inclined to fist-fighting, and to distributing Spanish, Catalan & Basque Bibles. *The Bible in Spain* (1843; Everyman's Library, Dent & Dutton, 1961) is based on his letters to the Bible Society, though the same energetic style and delight in bizarre anecdote enlivens what might have been in other hands a laboured account of missionary activities. The description of his walking tour of 1854, *Wild Wales* (1862; Collins, 1955), remains one of the most evocative travel books about the Principality to this day.

Kuruntokai. (1st–3rd centuries A.D.). Selections translated by A. K. Ramanujan as *The Interior Landscape: Love Poems from a Classical Tamil Anthology* (Indiana U.P., 1967; Peter Owen, 1970).

The 'Eight Anthologies' or *Ettuttokai* which have survived from the ancient Tamil are collections of mainly secular poetry. *Akananuru,* for instance, consists of some four hundred courtly love lyrics. *Purananuru,* the first of the anthologies devoted to *puram,* or poems of war and courage, contains this superb lyric:

> *What a Hero's Mother Said*
> You stand against the pillar
> of my hut and ask me:
> "Where is your son?"
>
> I don't really know.
> My womb is only a lair
> for that tiger.
> You can see him now
> only on battlefields.

The *Kuruntokai* consists of poems in the genre of courtly love, called *akam.* They have seldom been surpassed, and even in translation create an indelible impression.

To explore Tamil literature further, obtain *Two Thousand Years of Tamil Literature: an Anthology with Studies and Translations* by J. M. Somasundaram Pillai (Madras, 1959).

WILLIAM MAKEPEACE THACKERAY (1811–1863).
　　Vanity Fair. First published serially 1847–8. Edited by J. I. M. Stewart (Penguin, 1969).

Rebecca Sharp, it may be thought, should be encountered as early in life as we encounter her at Miss Pinkerton's Academy, and that may be so. But Thackeray's powerful barbs against arrogant snobs and incompetent civil and military men alike can really only be appreciated by those with a long understanding of Georgian England, and of Thackeray's complex position in it. He loved the comfortable armchairs of his London club too much to risk ostracism by open attacks on the aristocracy. But his very exaltation of Becky Sharp, that shrewd, pert, unscrupulous daughter of a penniless artist and a French dancer, above all the countesses and major-generals who fill his pages – that makes the point as carefully in its way as hypocrisy is shown up in *Great Expectations.*

The History of Henry Esmond, Esquire (1852; Penguin, 1970) is perhaps a more perfectly crafted book than *Vanity Fair,* but colder, more calculated, and lacking that pulsating life which we find surrounding Becky and Amelia first at Miss Pinkerton's, then in Brussels, Paris, and London.

Like all great novelists, Thackeray the man remains an enigma, despite such admirable attempts as Gordon N. Ray's *Thackeray* (2 vols., 1955–8, reprinted by Octagon, 1972), and the same author's crucial *The Buried Life: a Study of the Relation between Thackeray's Fiction and his Personal History* (Royal Society of

Literature, 1952). Thackeray himself requested that no biography be written, possibly due in part to the insanity of his wife (from about 1840) and possibly due to the double life he led (again not unlike the Dickensian experience) as a family man and a philanderer.

Sirat 'Antar ('The Romance of 'Antar'). First composed anonymously from disparate sources between 1080 and 1400. Translated in part as *The Adventures of Antar* by H. T. Norris (Aris & Phillips, Teddington House, Warminster, Wilts. BA12 8PQ, 1980).

'Antar bin Shaddad was a sixth-century Arab poet who won equal renown for deeds of valour and is immortalized not only in the *Mu'allaqat* of pre-Islamic Arabia, but also in the traditional prose epic *Sirat 'Antar*, with episodes in verse and in that rhymed prose (or *saj'*) in which the *Qur'an* was revealed. There are two principal variants of the epic: the Hijazi, from Saudi Arabia; and the shorter Syrian, also known as the Iraqi.

The core of the book is the love story between the slave-born poet-warrior 'Antar and the fair 'Abla, but the full Hijazi recension runs to thirty-two volumes in a standard Cairo edition, and the work has known as many transformations and accretions as the *Arabian Nights* itself, for it too has been declaimed in coffee-houses from Baghdad to Marrakesh.

BENJAMIN JONSON (1572–1637).
   Plays. Everyman's Library (2 vols., Dent and Dutton, 1954).

Born and educated in Westminster, Jonson came to be the major English dramatist of the time after Shakespeare, who took part in the first performance of Jonson's *Every Man in his Humour* (1598). Indeed, just as Marlowe was one of the young Shakespeare's closest friends, so Jonson was his most intimate associate in the Bard of Avon's closing years.

Jonson's style is as inimitable as Shakespeare's, and his learning was reputed to be as high and varied. Arrogant and fiery in temperament, he sought quarrels high and low, including one with Dekker (whom he attacked in his satirical comedy *The Poetaster*, 1601, answered by *Satiromastix*, 1602).

His finest plays are *Volpone* (1606), *The Alchemist* (1610), and *Bartholomew Fair* (1614). *Volpone* is a universal comedy which pillories cunning and deceit, a hilarious sub-plot involving English innocents abroad in Venice, Sir Politick Would-be, an absurd inventor, and his Lady, an absurd pedant. *The Alchemist* is a brilliant comedy of London low life set during an outbreak of the plague. The servant left in charge of a household, Face, conspires with Subtle and Dol Common to delude the gullible into paying for the secrets of the philosopher's stone. *Bartholomew Fair* is a brilliant series of cameos, rather than a play, on English types such as the hypocritical Puritan Zeal-of-the-Land Busy, the simpleton Bartholomew Cokes, and a host of minor characters such as stall-keepers and cut-purses who converge on the priory churchyard of St Bartholomew, Smithfield, in the latter half of August.

The Complete English Poems of Jonson have been edited by George Parfitt (Penguin, 1976), who has also written *Ben Jonson: Public Poet and Private Man* (Barnes & Noble, 1977).

SALVADOR DALÍ (b. 1904).
  The Secret Life of Salvador Dalí (3rd English ed. Vision Press, 1968).

Just as the balanced reader will seek to offset the quietism of the Tao with Confucian pragmatism, so he will attempt to achieve equal appreciation of Raphael's tranquil classicism with the paranoiac-critical method of the Catalan painter Salvador Dalí. This method, in the words of Robert Melville, 'involved the calculated use of delusion and hallucination in order to turn the objects of the real world into an iconography of sexual fears and desires'. And if this sounds abstruse at first hearing, a quick perusal of any album of Dalí's exquisitely finished paintings will show how accurately the theory has been put into practice.

His reputation was founded in the early 1930s by such masterpieces of fantasy, expressed in the most conventional techniques, as 'The Persistence of Memory' (1931) now in New York's Museum of Modern Art, incorporating soft watches lolling in a mysterious landscape.

The Secret Life was succeeded by *Diary of a Genius* (Doubleday, 1965; Hutchinson, 1966) and the repetitive *Unspeakable Confessions* of 1976. It contains the scenarios for the important surrealist films which Dalí made with Luis Buñuel: *Un Chien Andalou* and *L'Âge d'Or*.

Dalí's major contribution to the novel is *Rostros Ocultos* (1952; translated by Haakon Chevalier, Morrow, 1974), in which the de Sade-like hero, Count Hervé de Grandsailles, enacts with his mistress Solange physical and spiritual adventures familiar from Dalí's comments on his own life with Gala: witchcraft, eroticism, nightmares and violence are compounded into a welter of grotesque visions.

MARCEL PROUST (1871–1922).
À la recherche du temps perdu. First definitively published 1913–27. Translated by C. K. Scott-Moncrieff and (for the last section) Stephen Hudson as Remembrance of Things Past (Chatto & Windus, 1922–31; 3 vols., 1981).

Proust's great work, which he had begun to draft as early as 1895, is closely autobiographical: not only is the hero Proust in oblique perspective, but all his family, friends and even acquaintances become figures in a novel teeming with two hundred characters. Proust has already found his literary style, subtle and evocative, by the end of the first volume, Du côté de chez Swann (Swann's Way). Innuendo abounds, and if one can tolerate extended meditations and explorations in the realms of male and female homosexuality, Proust will surpass one's expectations for the clinical analysis of emotion in both love and lust.

From the age of four his body was racked by acute asthma, he suffered recurrent hay fever, and endured extremes of nervous tension and hypersensitivity. Following the death of his mother in 1905, he became a recluse in his Paris home, Boulevard Haussmann 102. Proust grew up in a rigidly stratified society, and lived through a period when social barriers were being eroded, if not eliminated altogether. The decadent aristocracy was giving way without a struggle before the rising middle classes, and it is a cardinal strength of Proust's cycle of novels that he dissects one class as pitilessly as another under the microscope. But while Balzac had shown up pretensions in the countryside as well as in Paris, Proust concentrated all his powers on a survey of manners and passions in the metropolis. His theory is simply that each of us is the product of all past actions and feelings, and that to understand anyone a meticulous analysis of these interactions and emotions is necessary.

In an authentically Borgesian sense, Proust the man is not confined within a grave: his hoarse breathing can be heard in the body which is À la recherche du temps perdu.

The literary pointillisme of Proust is comparable with the techniques of the school of painting begun by Georges Seurat (1860–91). See Pierre Courthion's Seurat (Abrams, 1968; Thames & Hudson, 1969) and William I. Homer's Seurat and the Science of Painting (MIT Press, 1978).

GEORG WILHELM FRIEDRICH HEGEL (1770–1831).
Selections. Edited by J. Loewenberg (Scribner's, 1929). Or The Philosophy of Hegel: Hegel's Basic Writings. Edited by C. J. Friedrich (Modern Library, 1965).

Hegel is immortal today for his influence, direct or indirect, on the biographer of Jesus, David Friedrich Strauss (1808–74), the Biblical critic Ferdinand Christian

Baur (1792–1860), Kierkegaard, Marx, and Lenin, and consequently the entire Western radical tradition of the last hundred and fifty years.

His chief works are *Die Phaenomenologie des Geistes* (1807; translated by J. B. Baillie as *The Phenomenology of Mind,* 2nd ed., Allen & Unwin, 1931) *Wissenschaft der Logik* (1812–16; translated by A. Miller as *The Science of Logic,* Allen & Unwin, 1969); *Encyklopädie der philosophischen Wissenschaften im Grundrisse* (3rd ed., 1830; translated as *The Logic of Hegel* by William Wallace, 2nd ed., Oxford U.P., 1892; *Hegel's Philosophy of Nature* by A. V. Miller, Oxford U.P., 1970; and *Hegel's Philosophy of Mind* by Wallace and Miller, Oxford U.P., 1971); and finally the *Grundlinien der Philosophie des Rechts* (1820; translated by T. M. Knox as *The Philosophy of Right,* Oxford U.P., 1942).

Hegel defies summary. Certainly he has been misunderstood by that majority of readers (including Marx or Lenin) who have looked into his works to find justification for their preconceptions. He rejected revolutionary idealism, believing that order should prevail. He divides knowledge into three categories: that which may be apprehended subjectively (psychology); that which may be apprehended objectively (political and moral philosophy); and that which may be apprehended absolutely (the philosophy of logic, art, and religion). His ideas on politics have become particularly crucial because of their interpretation in socialist countries. Dominated by his view of the State as the perfection of man as a political animal, *The Philosophy of Right* decrees the subservience of individual liberties to the balance of forces within an ordered community. Hegel's perfectly ordered state is an ideal Prussia which could be construed in any way a politician might desire between the extremes of Hitler and Ulbricht.

HIRAOKA KIMITAKE (MISHIMA YUKIO) (1925–1970).

Hojo no umi ('The Sea of Fertility', 1969–71), a tetralogy consisting of *Haro no yuki* ('Spring Snow'), *Homba* ('The Runaway Horses'), *Akatsuki no tera* ('The Temple of the Dawn') and *Tennin gosui* ('Decay of the Angel'). Translations published by Knopf (1972–4).

Mishima's early life is best understood by means of the autobiographical novel *Kamen no kokuhaku* (1949; translated as *Confessions of a Mask* by Meredith Weatherby, New Directions, 1968).

He was born into an upper-middle class Tokyo family, reacting at school and university against the contempt of his contemporaries for classical Japanese literature. Having taken a law degree and passed into the government service, he gave up his career almost immediately to become a full-time writer. Perhaps the best novel in a busy life producing numerous plays, novellas, and full-length novels was *Kinkakuji* (1956; translated as *The Temple of the Golden Pavilion* by Ivan Morris, Knopf, 1959). In 1950 a neurotic young priest had set fire to the

Kinkakuji, a magnificent creation of religious architecture, and Mishima's purpose is to investigate the motives for his act.

The tetralogy *Hojo no umi* was intended as a summation of Mishima's art and credo. After delivering the final statement to his publishers in 1970, Mishima with his associates broke into the eastern headquarters of the Japanese Defence Force, harangued the soldiers on the corruption and materialism of modern Japan and the need to return to the values of the *samurai,* and committed ritual self-disembowelling to draw the attention of the world to his beliefs, which insisted on selfless patriotism centred on the Emperor. The reasons adduced can be found in the second part of *Akatsuki no tera,* volume 3 of the tetralogy, and more specifically in *Yukio Mishima on 'Hagakure': the samurai ethic and modern Japan* (Penguin, 1979). While Mishima's ideology is widely respected in Japan, he has found few disciples.

See Akira Kurosawa's film *The Seven Samurai.*

Year 50

LUDWIG WITTGENSTEIN (1889–1951).
Logisch-philosophisches Traktat. First published in *Annalen der Natur-philosophie,* 1921. First book publication in bilingual form, as *Tractatus Logico-Philosophicus* (Routledge & Kegan Paul, 1922).

As concise as Kant is long-winded, the Viennese-born Wittgenstein nevertheless stands in relation to early 20th-century philosophy as Kant stood in relation to mid-18th-century philosophy: both concentrated on dismissing established but outmoded concepts before offering alternative constructions.

Wittgenstein argues that the 'logical form' of language and reality can be 'shown', but not 'stated'. After language has performed the function of 'picturing' reality, it must be discarded as of no further use. In the final paragraph: 'Wovon man nicht sprechen kann, darüber muss man schweigen', officially rendered as 'Whereof one cannot speak, thereof one must be silent'.

Other books which express the Wittgensteinian view of language and reality are the lecture-material contained in *The Blue and Brown Books* (2nd ed., Blackwell, 1969), *Philosophical Investigations* (3rd ed., Blackwell, 1967), *Zettel* (Blackwell, 1967), and *On Certainty* (Blackwell, 1969).

The influence of Wittgenstein has been very marked, particularly on linguistic philosophers. See Max Black's *Companion to Wittgenstein's "Tractatus"* (Cambridge U.P., 1964).

GIOVANNI BOCCACCIO (1313–1375).
Il Decameron. Completed in 1353. Best edition by Vittore Branca (5th ed., 1965). Translated by Richard Aldington (Garden City Press, 1949) and by J. M. Rigg in Everyman's Library (Dent and Dutton, 1953).

Chaucer and Froissart were both men of action as well as letters: Chaucer a bureaucrat and Froissart also a politician. But their contemporary the illegitimate Boccaccio was simply a writer, supported financially by his father who openly acknowledged him. Boccaccio's equivalent of Beatrice and Laura was 'Fiammetta', in fact Maria, an illegitimate daughter of King Robert of Anjou.

In the *Teseida,* a verse romance modelled on Virgil's *Aeneid,* Boccaccio invented the *ottava rima,* the octave form so suitable for verse narrative that was to achieve apotheosis in the writings of Ariosto, Tasso, and Camões.

Boccaccio is remembered today for the *Decameron* (from the Greek words for 'ten' and 'day'), that marvellous sequence of a hundred tales told by an aristocrat of aristocrats to mirror the life of the times in all its joy, grief, deceit, and topsy-turvy fortune.

Boccaccio knew the Florentine plague of 1348, from which his seven ladies and three cavaliers escaped. In the poem we see the deserted streets or the heaped and rotting corpses, for between March and July more than a hundred thousand had died.

The sources of the stories in the two gardens of the *Decameron* have been sought by Landau (*Die Quellen des Dekameron,* Stuttgart, 1884) and by others in Arabic, Indian, Persian and French literature: a third of them can be found in French *contes* and *fabliaux.* But Boccaccio the master story-teller is a genius in construction, style, and the trick ending. More than Dante or Petrarch he shows us the real world, where rascals are not always punished, and abbots not always chaste. If Chaucer's pilgrims are more rounded as individuals than Boccaccio's ten lords and ladies, then the characters in the stories of Chaucer are less memorable than Calandrino and Tezza, or Monna Belcolore, or Fra Cipolla.

We owe Boccaccio's friend Petrarch the service of having saved *Il Decameron* from the flames when Boccaccio suddenly believed them impious. Thereafter, to our loss, he wrote only in Latin.

For the artistic background, see Millard Meiss's *Painting in Florence and Siena after the Black Death* (Princeton U.P., 1978).

NUR AD-DIN 'ABD AR-RAHMAN JAMI (1414–1492).
Baharistan. Translated by Edward Rehatsek (Benares, 1887).

Jami (born in that small – now Afghan – city celebrated in Freya Stark's fascinating travel book *The Minaret of Djam,* John Murray, 1970) was the last of the Golden Age prodigies of learning produced by Persian civilization. See Jeannine Auboyer's *The Art of Afghanistan* (Hamlyn, 1968).

Jami has been woefully under-translated, and so those unwilling to spend time on learning classical Persian, with Dante's Italian and literary Chinese one of the most beautiful languages of the world, will have to be content with faint echoes of the polymath's voice.

Jami was called 'Jami of Herat' because he spent most of his life at the Timurid court there, spending only a brief period in Baghdad, and making the Muslim's obligatory pilgrimage to Mecca.

As a poet and prose-writer he is regarded as having achieved stylistic refinement equal to that of Sa'di, on whose *Gulistan* Jami based his *Baharistan* ('Spring Orchard'). As a Naqshbandi mystic, he wrote *Tuhfat al-Ahrar* in honour of Shaikh 'Ubaidullah Ahrar, but he felt akin also to Ibn 'Arabi's monism, writing an important commentary on the latter's *Fusus al-Hikam*. As a hagiographer he deserved the fame he achieved for the elegant if secondary *Nafahat al-Uns* ('Breaths of Friendship').

The *Haft Awrang* ('Seven Thrones') are long poems based on the *Khamsa* ('Five') of Nizami. Only two of these have been translated: the *Salaman u Absal* of 1479–80, newly edited from *Fitzgerald's Salaman and Absal* by A. J. Arberry (Cambridge U.P., 1956); and the *Yusuf u Zulaykha* of 1483, once available in metrical versions by R. T. H. Griffith (1881) and A. Rogers (1892). 'It cannot be said', notes Arberry ruefully, 'that any of these translations (and he includes Auguste Bricteux's, in French prose) does justice to the brilliance and subtlety of Jami's original'.

Neither do we have a satisfactory modern study of this many-sided Persian genius.

PLOTINUS (*c.* 205–*c.* 262 A.D.).

> *Enneads*. Text with a facing translation by A. H. Armstrong in the Loeb Classical Library (6 vols., Heinemann and Harvard U.P., 1966 ff.). Or the Oxford Classical Texts *editio minor* by Henry and Schwyzer (3 vols., Oxford U.P., 1977) with the translation by Stephen MacKenna (4th ed., Faber & Faber, 1969).

Heirs of the great Greek philosophers, the Neo-Platonists disputed against Gnosticism and Christianity. The principal figure in Neo-Platonism is Plotinus, pupil of the school's founder, Ammonius Saccas, none of whose writings survives.

Plotinus taught in Rome from 244 to his death, acquiring a large circle of brilliant disciples, and the support of the Emperor Gallienus. His life was written by his eminent pupil, the polymath Porphyry (232–302), whose *Against the Christians* was burned in 448. Among later neo-Platonists one must count Iamblichus (*c.* 250–*c.* 325), a Syrian who wrote on Pythagoreanism, and the Constantinople-born Proclus (410–485). The schools of Athens, which propagated Neo-Platonism, were closed by the Emperor Justinian in 529.

A man of extreme mysticism and asceticism, Plotinus set as his aim the escape from our material world to soul, then to reason, then to God, which Plotinus saw as formless, matterless, pure existence.

A particularly useful adjunct to Plotinian studies is W. R. Inge's *The Philosophy of Plotinus* (2 vols., 3rd ed., Longmans, 1929). I also recommend *Select Passages Illustrating Neoplatonism* (2 vols., S.P.C.K., 1923–4) compiled by E. R. Dodds.

The influence of Neo-Platonism on later thinkers can be seen in St Augustine, St Thomas Aquinas and mainstream Catholic theology on the one hand, and in the Florentine humanists such as Poliziano and Marsilio Ficino on the other.

ABU BAKR MUHAMMAD BIN 'ABDULMALIK IBN TUFAIL (*c.* 1105–1185). *Hayy ibn Yaqzan* ('Alive, Son of Awake'). Translated by Simon Ockley (1708; and reprinted, 1929) and into Spanish by A. González Palencia (1934).

Born in the Spanish port of Cádiz, 'Abubacer' (as he is known to the scholastics) arrived in the West through Pocock's Latin translation (*Philosophus Autodidactus,* Oxford, 1671) though Pico della Mirandola had ordered a Latin translation to be made from a Hebrew version of the Arabic original in the second half of the 15th century.

Ibn Tufail, a friend of Averroes (Ibn Rushd), practised medicine, but is now remembered for this allegorical romance based on a work of the same title by Avicenna (Ibn Sina).

The story is an adventure of intellectual development. Hayy was born on a desert island and has never known heterodoxy, achieving religious and scientific knowledge through his own efforts. Absal, by contrast, has come to the desert island to purify his soul in isolation, knowing already that the masses can be swayed only by appealing to their emotions and by sensuous parables and fables. Hayy gives up his attempts to become a missionary in disillusionment, realising that only the select few are able to understand the higher wisdom: traditional religion must remain the fodder for the masses.

Ibn Tufail's work was important in the development of the Catalan missionary Ramon Llull (1235?–1316?), but was unknown to Baltasar Gracián (1601–58), whose *El Criticón* (1651–7) had the same common primary source: an Arabic tale known as 'The Idol, the King, and the King's Daughter'.

See L. Gauthier's *Ibn Thofail: sa vie, ses oeuvres* (1909) and his French translation of the text (1936).

JOSÉ ORTEGA Y GASSET (1883–1955).
   España Invertebrada. First published 1921. Translated by M. Adams as *Invertebrate Spain* (1937; reprinted by Howard Fertig, 1974). And *La Rebelión de las Masas.* First published 1929. Translated anonymously as *The Revolt of the Masses* (Allen & Unwin, 1932; Norton, 1964).

In Plato's *Symposium,* Socrates argues against the tragedian Agathon and the comedian Aristophanes that the true poet should unite tragedy with comedy. Ortega claims, in his *Meditaciones del Quijote* (1914; 2nd ed., 1921), that Cervantes achieves this unity with *Don Quixote.* But later Spanish writers have failed to take the precedent seriously, and Ortega propounds a literature that can rise by symbolic allusion to the meaning of life.
   In *España Invertebrada* he takes the position that a fragmented literature leads to a fragmented nation. Castile may take the credit as a centralized power which united Spain, but she must also take the blame for retaining the centralized power too long. Ortega is persuaded that the 'spinelessness' of Spain is due to the absence of an intellectual élite capable of guiding the masses in a common interest.
   La Rebelión de las Masas continues Ortega's analysis of the Spanish predicament. The *hombre-masa* ('mass-man') is a vulgar cog in the wheel who behaves and thinks for preference just 'like the rest'. The natural aristocrat takes his individuality seriously, and Ortega calls for the rise of a benevolent élite which will unite Spain internally, and also externally with the democratic countries of Europe. Ortega was a Germanophile, though he reacted against his early neo-Kantianism, elevating life above thought and proposing a *razón vital* to replace the pure of mathematical reason of his predecessors. He founded the highly-respected intellectual magazine *Revista de Occidente,* which enjoyed a reputation akin to that of *Encounter.* He is now judged less for an original philosopher than a brilliant catalyst of ideas: he and his school kept Spanish intellectual life alive during the dark days of Franco.

Sir RABINDRANATH THAKUR ('TAGORE') (1861–1941).
   Collected Poems and Plays (Macmillan, 1966).

Tagore is the leading Bengali poet, and also wrote novels, plays, short stories, essays, set over 2,000 songs to music, established schools and late in life began to paint. A lifelong friend of Gandhi, Tagore was an Asian philosopher who passionately believed that the ideal man conjoined the best qualities of East and West, neither of which is innately superior to the other.
   The school he founded at Santiniketan in Bengal has become the Visva-Bharati International University. His novel *Gharer Baire* (1916) started a literary

controversy in Bengali circles, which is still unresolved, on whether it is licit to introduced colloquial speech into works of literature. His mystical verses *Gitanjali* ('Song Offerings', 1910; translated in part by the author, 1912) attracted so much attention in the West – partly due to the enthusiasm of Yeats and Pound – that Tagore was awarded the Nobel Prize for Literature in 1913.

See Tagore's *Religion of Man* (Allen & Unwin, 1953), and Krishna Kripalani's *Rabindranath Tagore* (Grove Press and Oxford U.P., 1962).

YÜAN MEI (1716–1798).

> *Sui-yüan ch'üan chi.* This edition published in 64 fascicules (Shanghai, 1918). Selections in various anthologies, including H. A. Giles' *Gems of Chinese Literature* (2nd ed., reprinted by Dover, 1964).

Arthur Waley's absorbing biographical anthology *Yüan Mei: Eighteenth Century Chinese Poet* (Allen & Unwin and Stanford U.P., 1956) is the most accessible work in English on the poet, essayist and critic Yüan Mei.

Yüan Mei retired from the Civil Service at the early age of 32 to become a professional writer, settling in the celebrated home and garden known as Sui-yüan, in Nanking. A hedonist as regards wine, women, and song, he wrote a classic on cookery and made a number of ambitious journeys in China, even when elderly.

His thought is expressed with the utmost clarity, leading critics to accuse his books of shallowness. In fact he preached and practised unbridled individualism in literature as in life, insisting that natural genius ('hsing-ling') must be allowed its fullest expression.

A constant companion of Yüan Mei on his travels was Li Fang-ying (1695–1754), the eminent painter of plum-blossom. Of this enchanting artist it is said that, appointed Prefect in successive places, he sided with the people in each and was imprisoned for incessant arguments against the higher authorities. The local people used to come to the prison where he was held and throw over the wall so much money and food that 'the culvert inside the wall was full to the top'. The works of this remarkable man show, as one might expect, a complete disregard for academic rules on the depiction of plum-blossom and are painted from nature.

JOHN MILTON (1608–1674).
Areopagitica; a Speech for the Liberty of Unlicenc'd Printing. First published
1644. Included in *Prose Writings* in Everyman's Library (Dent and Dutton,
1955) and in *Prose* edited by M. W. Wallace in World's Classics (Oxford
U.P., 1925). And *Poetical Works* edited by Douglas Bush (Oxford
U.P., 1966).

The practice of licensing books constituted governmental censorship in 17th-
century England, just as it does in dozens of countries around the globe today.
Milton wrote the classic statement against licensing in *Areopagitica,* named after
the Hill of Ares in Athens. Here, west of the Acropolis, a court supervised the
magistrates and the application of laws, controlled education, and debated
censorship questions. The Athenian statesman Ephialtes (murdered in 461) was
responsible for depriving the ancient Court of Areopagus of its rights, thus
enhancing democracy and curtailing dictatorship in public questions such as
censorship. It was the latter question that Milton fought in his pamphlet. For
although the abolition in 1641 of the Court of Star Chamber had taken with it
governmental censorship, reimposition was threatened – after the pamphleteers
had taken full advantages of press freedom – by the Ordinance of June 1643.

It is well to remember that following his wife's desertion Milton had just
written the pamphlet *The Doctrine and Discipline of Divorce,* which shocked
clerical opinion of the day. And we must not forget Milton's naïveté in professing
that in an open encounter with Falsehood, Truth must necessarily prevail. The
importance of the pamphlet at the time, and ever since, is the cardinal principle
raising freedom of the press above all political and religious sects and parties.

Milton deliberately trained himself as a poet from 1632 to 1637, when he wrote
L'Allegro ('The Cheerful Man') and its companion-piece *Il Penseroso* ('The
Meditative Man'); the masque *Comus,* and the pastoral elegy *Lycidas. On His
Blindness* is only one of the supreme sonnets for which he is still best loved. He is
respected, more than loved, for the little-read epic *Paradise Lost* (1667): only the
first three books of the twelve sustain any poetic intensity, and the theme of the
Fall of Man, while sublime, is not made immediate to the reader by narrative
drive or beauty of imagery. *Paradise Regained* (1671) is a misguided sequel, even
more obviously lacking the qualities of the early *Paradise Lost* or the poignancy of
the sonnets.

Of more interest to modern readers is the tragedy *Samson Agonistes*. Milton
was blind for the last twenty-two years of his life and, having been deserted by his
first wife Mary Powell, compared himself to the Samson of the Book of Judges
(xvi), blind and a prisoner of the Philistines, having been abandoned by the
deceitful Delilah. The major operatic treatment of the theme is the *Samson et
Dalila* by Camille Saint-Saëns (3 discs, HMV SLS 905, conducted by Prêtre).
See *John Milton, Englishman* (Crown, 1949) and *The Milton Handbook* (New

ed., Bell, 1947) by James H. Hanford; *Studies in Milton* (Chatto & Windus, 1951) and *Milton* (Chatto & Windus, 1966) by E. M. W. Tillyard, and Dame Helen Gardner's *A Reading of 'Paradise Lost'* (Oxford U.P., 1967).

For the context, see Basil Willey's *The Seventeenth-Century Background* (Chatto & Windus, 1934; Doubleday, 1953).

IMMANUEL KANT (1724–1804).
> *Critik der reinen Vernunft.* First published in Riga, 1781. Definitive edition 1787. Translated by Norman K. Smith as *The Critique of Pure Reason* (Macmillan and St Martin's Press, 1969).

It has been said that George Meredith's later novels should be read first for the fourth time, and this paradox applies very much to the writings of Kant. Just as the listener has to rise to the last string quartets of Beethoven, quite sure that on a second or third hearing he has still not understood them, so Kant must be approached by the enquiring mind in the knowledge that much that is obscure will later be clear. The arguments are very densely expressed, and many of the terms have a multiple meaning (as in Hegel) which must be explored and thought out paragraph by paragraph and even sentence by sentence.

But it is important to find out why Kant felt impelled to discard first the metaphysical categorization of the Cartesian school, and later the monads of Leibnitz's metaphysics. Scientific thought is, for Kant, an anticipation of objective experience, coupled with the experiment and observation which check its validity by objective perception. He therefore saved the integrity of science without prejudice to the principles of conduct, concluding that metaphysical speculation about the nature of reality can lead only to contradiction, since it applies the principles of thought beyond the limit of experience.

If we cannot agree with Goethe that reading the *Critik* (or *Kritik*, in modern spelling) *der reinen Vernunft* is like stepping into a brightly-lit room (Kant was both verbose *and* repetitive, giving German philosophy the bad reputation for turgidity from which it has never recovered), then at least one can suggest that, with an excellent guide like J. Kemp (*The Philosophy of Kant*, Oxford U.P., 1968) or S. Körner (*Kant*, Penguin, 1955), the effort to understand at least the first half of the Kantian system is well worth making.

Other writings by Kant may be sampled in *The Essential Kant*, edited by Arnulf Zweig (New American Library, 1970). They include the *Critik der praktischen Vernunft* (1788; translated by Lewis W. Beck as *Critique of Practical Reason*, (Bobbs-Merrill, 1956), whose 'categorical imperative' is the foundation of modern ethics; and *Zum ewigen Frieden* (1795; translated by Lewis W. Beck as *Perpetual Peace*, Bobbs-Merrill, 1957), a philosophic essay foreshadowing the optimism which gave rise to the first League of Nations and the modern, somewhat tarnished but nonetheless necessary United Nations.

Epilogue

It will have become obvious by now that a lifetime's reading is no more than a means to an end, which will be expressed in various ways by different readers. It might be described as self-awareness coupled with altruism; the Way or *Tao*; the Right Mindfulness or *Satipatthana* which is deliverance from greed, hatred, and delusion; or perhaps wisdom humanised by compassion.

The learning of facts is a necessary discipline of youth. So is the learning of languages. So is the mastery of technical skills.

But we have by now learnt more than all this, if we have been reading closely, with attention undeterred from inner meanings, metaphor, allegory, and symbolism. There is the mastery of imagination as one accompanies Dante and Virgil into the *Inferno;* the ecstasy of self-forgetting demonstrated by the yogi Patañjali and the mystic John of the Cross; the enlightenment of the spirit in Japanese Zen, and of the scientific investigator in histories of science and invention.

We can accept the divergent ways of Communism and Catholicism, of atheism and Islam, because mankind is essentially plural not only in language and nationhood, but also in religion and politics. We can learn from tradition and the accumulated experience of society, as well as from new technologies and new ways of looking at ideas or systems. We can devote our lives to what is positive, such as nursing, agriculture, or librarianship, and reject what is negative.

It will have become apparent that no ideology or dogma is propounded as self-evidently true at any point in *A Lifetime's Reading*: quite a novelty. Everyone is wrong for a part of the time, just as everyone is right for a part of the time. Wide reading shows that most ways of life should be viewed with tolerance, in context, and that we can learn from the collective experience of those who have lived before if we read critically, sceptically, and sympathetically.

You will by now have formed your own criteria of literary excellence, and you will not agree with all the inclusions or omissions from this book. That too is good.

Fare well, reader. I loved you.

Index

A.B.C. of Reading, The, 293
À la recherche du temps perdu, 337
Aakjaer, J., 100
Abdul Hadi, W. M., 181
Abe Kimifusa (Kobo), 174
Abélard, P., 6
Abeokuta and the Camaroons Mountains, 116
Abla, 116
Absalom! Absalom! 169
Abubacer, 341
Acharnians, The, 26, 101
Achebe, C., 223
Ada or Ardor, 288
Adam Bede, 253
Adams, B. 132; H. B., 131–2; M., 344
Adi Granth, 186
Adigal, Ilango, 329–30
Adler, A., 88
Advancement of Learning, The, 196
Aeneid, 40, 65, 309
Aeschines, 252
Aeschylus, 11–12, 101, 105, 177
Aesop, 22
Afghan art, 341
Africa, 167
African art, 265, 328; history, 265; literature, 264–5, 328
African Child, The, 223
After Babel, 5
Aftonland, 235
Age of Reason, The, 302
Agony of Christianity, The, 274–5
Agricola, 4
Ahlwardt, 115
Ahmad, A., 144
Ahnaf, A. ibn al-, 207
'Ah-ness' of things, 204
Aïda, 287
Ainslie, D., 42
Aiyar, S., 330
Ajax, 104
Akatsuki no tera, 338–9
Akhmatova, A., 252
Akira Kurosawa, 339
Akiyama Terukazu, 8
Akurgal, E., 108
Akutagawa Ryunosuke, 281
Alain-Fournier, 309
Alaskan Sneeze, 234

Alavi, B., 111
Albert, M O., 223
Alberti, R., 174
Alcestis, 101
Alchemist, The, 335–6
Alcina, 283
Aldington, R., 293, 340
Alegría, C., 251
Aleph, El, 62
Aleskerzade, A. A., 108
Alexander, A., 277; S., 325
Alexander the Great, 18
Alexandria, 314–5
Alexiad, 270
Alf Layla wa Layla, 56, 116, 121, 335
Algar, H., 43
'Ali, M., 122
Alice's Adventures in Wonderland, 1
Aliger, M., 135
Alisjahbana, S. T., 180
All For the Best, 45
All Men Are Brothers, 81
Allegro, L', 346
All's Well That Ends Well, 9
Almayer's Folly, 27
Alonso, D., 58
Alpert, M., 203
Also sprach Zarathustra, 124–5
Aluko, T. M., 223
Alvarez, A., 21, 263, 280
Alwyn, W., 19
Amadigi, 308
Amadis de Gaula, 308
Amado, J., 302
Amazon, 301, 303
Ambassadors, The, 326
Ambrosian chant, 278
American architecture, 245–6; literature, Year 37, 321–2, 326–7; poetry, 177, 239; way of life, 239
Amerika, 85
Amichai, Y., 132
Amin, M., 116
Ammianus Saccas, 342
Amnesty International, 154
'Amr, 116
Amyot, J., 22
Anabasis (Arrian), 17–18; (Perse), 227; (Xenophon), 99, 100
Analects, 152–3, 296
Analysis of Mind, The, 330

Anathemata, The, 322–3
Anati, E., 23
Anaxagoras, 79
Anaximander, 79
Ancel, P., 78–9
Ancien Régime et la Révolution, L, 303
Andorra, 32
Andreyev, L. N., 153
Ankle Bracelet, The, 329–30
Anna Comnena, 270
Anna Karenin, 78, 247
Annals (Tacitus), 4, 63
Annotated Alice, The, 1; *Snark,* 1
'*Antar,* 116, 335
Anteojos de mejor vista, Los, 311
Anthology of African and Malagasy Poetry in French, An, 265; *Chinese Literature,* 149; *Islamic Literature,* 113; *Japanese Literature,* 140, 225; *Korean Poetry,* 316; *Modern Arabic Poetry,* 43; *Modern Arabic Verse,* 43; *Modern Hebrew Poetry,* 132; *Modern Indonesian Poetry,* 180; *Sinhalese Literature,* 192
Antigone, 104–5
Antiphon, 252
Anton, F., 292
Antonioni, M., 44
Antony and Cleopatra, 9, 126
Anwar, C., 181–3
Apelman, M., 74
Apin, R., 181
Apocolocyntosis, 63, 249
Apollinaire, G., 219
Apollon Musagète, 154
Apollonio, U., 316, 329
Apollonius Rhodius, 314–5
Apologia, (Plato) 1–2; (Xenophon), 99
Appian, 18
Apples of Immortality, 268
Apresyan, S., 153
Apuleius, L., 16–17
Aquinas, *Saint* Thomas, 312, 332, 343
Arabian Nights, 56, 116, 121, 335
Arabic literature, 113, 207, Years 19–21
Aran Islands, The, 288
Araujo, V. de, 302

Index

Index

Index

Index

Index

011.7
W262p   Ward, Philip

A lifetime's reading